Conversion and Initiation in Antiquity

EARLY CHRISTIANITY IN THE CONTEXT OF ANTIQUITY

Edited by David Brakke,
Anders-Christian Jacobsen,
Jörg Ulrich

Advisory board:
Hanns Christof Brennecke, Ferdinand R. Prostmeier
Einar Thomassen, Nicole Kelley
Jakob Engberg, Carmen Cvetkovic
Ellen Muehlberger, Tobias Georges

Volume 16

Zu Qualitätssicherung und Peer Review der vorliegenden Publikation

Die Qualität der in dieser Reihe erscheinenden Arbeiten wird vor der Publikation durch die Herausgeber der Reihe sowie durch Mitglieder des Wissenschaftlichen Beirates geprüft.

Notes on the quality assurance and peer review of this publication

Prior to publication, the quality of the work published in this series is reviewed by the editors of the series and by members of the academic advisory board.

Birgitte Secher Bøgh (ed.)

Conversion and Initiation in Antiquity

Shifting Identities – Creating Change

Bibliographic Information published by the Deutsche Nationalbibliothek
The Deutsche Nationalbibliothek lists this publication in the Deutsche Nationalbibliografie; detailed bibliographic data is available in the internet at http://dnb.d-nb.de.

Published with financial support from
Aarhus University Research Foundation.

ISSN 1862-197X
ISBN 978-3-631-65851-2 (Print)
E-ISBN 978-3-653-05082-0 (E-Book)
DOI 10.3726/978-3-653-05082-0

© Peter Lang GmbH
Internationaler Verlag der Wissenschaften
Frankfurt am Main 2014
All rights reserved.
Peter Lang Edition is an Imprint of Peter Lang GmbH.

Peter Lang – Frankfurt am Main · Bern · Bruxelles · New York ·
Oxford · Warszawa · Wien

This publication has been peer reviewed.

www.peterlang.com

Contents

Abbreviations

Abbreviations of journals are made according to S.M. Schwertner, *Internationales Abkürzungsverzeichnis für Theologie und Grenzgebiete/International Glossary for Theology and Related Subjects*, Berlin ²1992. Abbreviations of Greek and Roman authors and works follow H.G. Liddell / H.S Jones /R. Scott, A *Greek-English Lexicon*, Oxford ²1996. Abbreviations of Christian sources follow A. Blaise /H. Chirat, *Dictionnaire latin-français des auteurs chrétiens*, Turnhout ²1997. Other abbreviations:

AGRW	Ascough, R. / Ph. Harland / J. Kloppenborg (eds. and trans.), *Associations in the Greco-Roman World. A Sourcebook*, Berlin 2012
BGU	W. Schubart and E. Kühn (eds.), *Berliner griechische Urkunden egyptische Urkunden aus den Königlichen Museen zu Berlin*, Berlin 1922
CIMRM	M.J. Vermaseren, *Corpus Inscriptionum et Monumentorum Religionis Mithriacae*, 2 vols., The Hague 1956–1960
IGBulg	G. Mikhailov (ed.), *Inscriptiones Graecae in Bulgaria Repertae*, Sofia 1964
IKyzikos	E. Schwertheim (ed.), *Die Inschriften von Kyzikos und Umgebung*, Bonn 1980
ISmyrna	G. Petzl (ed.), *Die Inschriften von Smyrna*, Bonn 1982
TAM	P. Herrmann, *Tituli Asiae Minoris*, vol. 5.1 *(Tituli Lydiae, linguis Graeca et Latina conscripti)*, Vienna 1989

Introduction

The religious life of Graeco-Roman antiquity never ceases to attract attention. Scholars continually seek to gain a better understanding of the character and development of the religious landscape with its numerous cults and religions. Recent years in particular have witnessed a renewed interest in individual religious identity and religious experiences, and numerous studies have brought forth much knowledge and new opinions on these.[1] The articles in this volume contribute to this progress by focusing specifically on the experience of the individual transformation found in initiations and conversions, by applying new theories to ancient materials (archaeological, epigraphical, and textual), and by presenting new perspectives and correctives to established "truths" in relation to initiation and conversion and their definitions, content, and characteristics. Most importantly, the conference papers question Nock's influential concept of conversion (1933) by exploring different facets of this phenomenon through new lenses, by approaching Christianity as one among many diverse religions in antiquity, and by seeing each religion's idea of change or reorientation or initiation in its own context. In doing so, we gain a more nuanced and differentiated view on the religious life in antiquity. The papers were originally presented at a conference held in Ebeltoft, Denmark, December 1ˢᵗ – 4ᵗʰ 2012 as the conclusion of an interdisciplinary research project at Aarhus University (conducted

---

1 For example J. Lieu, *Christian Identity in the Jewish and Graeco-Roman world*, Oxford 2004; I. Sandwell, *Religious Identity in Late Antiquity*, Cambridge 2007; L.T. Johnson, *Among the Gentiles*, New Haven 2009; Ph. Harland, *Dynamics of Identity in the World of the Early Christians*, New York 2009; J. Rüpke / W. Spickermann (eds.), *Reflections on Religious Individuality*, Berlin 2012; cf. also the recent studies of personal religious experiences among cognitive scholars. The more specific subject of ancient conversion and initiation also continues to attract attention, see, e.g., A. Moreau (ed.), *L'initiation. Actes du colloque international de Montpellier, 11–14 avril 1991*, 2 vols., Montpellier 1992; T.M. Finn, *From Death to Rebirth. Ritual and Conversion in Antiquity*, New York 1997; J. Assmann / G. Stroumsa (eds.), *Transformations of the Inner Self in Ancient Religion*, Leiden 1999; J.T. Sanders, *Charisma, Converts, Competitors*, London 2000; S.J. Chester, *Conversion at Corinth*, London 2003; J.N. Bremmer et al. (eds.), *Cultures of Conversion*, Leuven 2006; J.B. Rives, *Religious Choice and Religious Change in Classical and Late Antiquity*, in: ARYS. Antigüedad, religiones y sociedades 9 (2011), 265–280.

by Anders-Christian Jacobsen, Jakob Engberg, Carmen Cvetković, Rubina Raja, and Birgitte Bøgh) which aimed at investigating the significance of conversion and initiation for the formation and transformation of religious identity among pagans and Christians from 100 – 500 CE.[2]

Initiations are known from all cultures in different forms and refer, in short, to a formalised, secluded, once-and-for-all ceremony during which an initiand undergoes a transformation from one (e.g., social and/or religious) status to another. The term conversion cannot be so easily recapped (for which reason this phenomenon receives the most attention in this book). A classic definition is that of Arthur D. Nock (1933) who understand conversion as "a re-orientation of the soul, a deliberate turning from indifference or from an earlier form of piety to another, a turning which implies a consciousness that a great change is involved, that the old was wrong and the new is right;" it is to "abandon the old spiritual home for a new one" and results in a sense of perceiving previously unknown truths, an "ecstasy of happiness," the removal of anxiety, and a new start, a new faith, a new life.[3] However, this understanding of conversion is not just widely cited, but also disputed and is in fact under critical review in the present volume.

In the history of research, there has been a tendency to prefer the terms *initiation* and *adhesion* in relation to the Graeco-Roman mystery cults, while the term *conversion* has been restricted to the change found in Christianity and Judaism. To a great extent, this is due to the influence of Nock's book on conversion in antiquity mentioned above. One of Nock's aims was to oppose the views of some earlier scholars, like Cumont and Reitzenstein, who saw little or no difference between Christianity and the mystery cults. Nock argued against these that the character and significance of the change that people experienced when turning to Christianity and Judaism was unique compared to other religious shifts in antiquity and therefore claimed that the term *conversion* should be reserved for a shift of religious affiliation to monotheistic religions and philosophy while other types of lesser and insignificant changes – among them those at offer in the mystery cults – resulted in *adhesion* (1933, 7–14). For Nock, exclusivity was a defining feature of conversion, but there were a number of other qualitative differences between conversion and adhesion as well, e.g., in psychological impact, emotional content, and seriousness.[4]

---

2 Perhaps needless to state: the term pagan is not used in any derogative sense.
3 A.D. Nock, *Conversion. The Old and the New in Religion from Alexander the Great to Augustine of Hippo*, London 1933, 7f.
4 Nock, 1933, 14. 137 *et passim*. Only in its final phase did pagan religious transformations attain a "seriousness" that brought them close to Christian conversions (1933, 15).

Nock also distinguished between Christian baptism and pagan initiation. Christian baptism was a ritual necessary for becoming a member of the Christian community, following and thus expressing a prior inner conversion (as such it was the formal rite of conversion), whereas pagan initiation was a supplementary, voluntary act and an efficient action in itself – a tool effecting, most importantly, *gnosis* and a happy afterlife (1933, 7–15. 58 *et passim*). Partly as a result of Nock's classic book, later scholars have most often discussed *initiates* and the implications of *initiation* when talking about the personal transformation we find in the mystery cults (note that the word adhesion does not come with natural connotations of *change*), while the terms *converts* and *conversion* have been used in connection with the change experienced when turning to Christianity.

The distinction between conversion and baptism on the one hand, and initiation and adhesion on the other implied for Nock a fundamental difference between Christianity and the mystery cults, and this view has been quite influential; for example, Walter Burkert (the author of one of the most cited works on the mysteries still today) wholeheartedly supported Nock's arguments, including the view that baptism is not comparable to initiation in the mystery cults.[5] But it is continually up for debate – and so it should be, because the subject is central for our understanding of the nature and dynamics of different religious experiences in antiquity, and a continued debate will eventually lead to more nuances of this understanding. This volume aims at providing such nuances, among other things, by problematising Nock's concepts of and distinction between adhesion and conversion.

Previous research into the relationship between Christianity and the mystery cults has often been haunted by apologetic and other subjective concerns.[6] Today, many scholars try to avoid biased approaches, but nevertheless still disagree on the subject of conversion and initiation. Many regard Christian baptism and mystery initiation as similar, though not necessarily identical, rites of passage,[7] but most scholars still, implicitly or explicitly, follow Nock's differentiation between conversion and adhesion. Sometimes, the distinction (still) reflects the view that converting to Christianity was qualitatively and essentially different from being initiated into and (simply) adhering to a mystery cult. At other times, it is merely a question of using different terms for the (otherwise comparable) change found in polytheistic

---

5   W. Burkert, *The Ancient Mystery Cults*, Cambridge 1987, 101 *et passim*.
6   Cf. J.Z. Smith, *Drudgery Divine. On the Comparison of Early Christianities and the Religions of Late Antiquity*, Chicago 1990.
7   Cf., e.g., E. Thomasson, *Becoming a Different Person. Baptism as an Initiation Ritual*, in: L.H. Martin / P. Pachis (eds.), *Theoretical Frameworks for the Study of Graeco-Roman Religion*, Thessaloniki 2003, 209–222.

and monotheistic religions, respectively. Still others have questioned Nock's conception of conversion as well as the validity and value of upholding the dichotomy between adhesion and conversion, and today we can hardly claim that any consensus exists on the subject.[8]

One reason why scholars disagree on how to approach and capture the phenomenon is that they disagree on fundamental questions related to this phenomenon: What does it mean to convert: Do we use it as an objective *terminus technicus* for any religious change, or do we invest it with a number of positive qualities that must be included? Is a "change of mind" (as expressed in the term *metanoia*) equal to a conversion, or does this have to include other changes as well?[9] Does conversion have to be a radical change, and if so how radical? For example, must a convert always repent and turn away from something, like his past, or burn the bridges to outsiders (as implied in *epistrophê* in its specific sense of turning away), or can it also signify a supplement, e.g., that a person experiences the feeling of a new life in some sense or another? And do we want the change to include future commitment and obligations? Which areas does conversion have (to have) an effect on (theological ideas, beliefs, behaviour, emotions, worldview, habits, values, social circles, missionary tendencies) if we insist that not all religious change is a conversion? What if a person's behaviour is changed, but not his way of thinking? Has a person necessarily converted if he or she is initiated (including baptism) and, *vice versa*, can a person convert without undergoing an initiation? Is conversion a moment in time or a long process? Is every religious change – monotheistic *and* polytheistic – a conversion? Or can a person only convert to monotheistic religions? If yes, what then of Christian converts who still acknowledged the pagan gods and continued to take part of polytheistic rituals and *collegia*? And how to detect and evaluate a "proper" conversion in the cases where no literary autobiographies have been preserved? Scholars working with conversion will find that there are no universally accepted answers to these

---

8   For references to these different points of view: See B. Bøgh, *Beyond Nock. From Adhesion to Conversion in the Mystery Cults*, in: *History of Religions* (forthcoming) which offers a critical review and discussion of earlier research history on ancient conversion (or not) outside of Christianity and Judaism. It also includes an introduction to new theories on conversion as well two case studies on conversion in the mysteries, the Isiac and Mithraic cults.

9   For example, W. Burkert concluded in his authoritative book on the mystery cults that mystery initiation (besides being a method of salvation comparable to other votive habits) effected a "change of mind." Yet, still it was not the consequence of or comparable to a conversion (1987, 11. 14f. 17–19. 23. 44–46. 101), despite the fact that *metanoia* is a well-known term for (Christian and philosophical) conversions.

and other questions even though numerous attempts to define conversion exist.

The aim of this volume is not to answer all these questions (although the contributions deal with many of them) or to reach consensus, but to create a platform for re-investigating and nuancing the characteristics of religious transformation found in initiations and conversions in the ancient world from new theoretical and empirical perspectives.

The contributors come from various academic fields, such as history of religions, archaeology, history, and theology, and their articles each focus on different and specific aspects of conversion and initiation, namely:

1. The choice: reasons, motivations, and results
2. Agency and agents: The context of the decision
3. The change: the nature and degree of reorientation
4. Education: instructing and guiding the converts

In the course of our research project, we came to see these themes as recurring elements in initiation and conversion processes, even if they are not found equally often in or expressed in the same way by different religious groups. The themes are of course interrelated and the papers thus supplement each other; for example, the motivations and results of the *choice* are intrinsically interwoven with the nature of the *change*, and these topics cannot be completely ignored when discussing *agency* or *education*. But the systematic division invites to reflection on specific nuances of (and thus a new and focused research on) questions related to the overall theme of religious transformation. The thematic approach allowed the invited authors to explore these elements in depth or to use each theme as an illustrative point of departure for discussing the overall topic of the conference. Below, a short introduction to the ideas behind each theme will illustrate the central problem around which the papers in the relevant theme revolve. Not all aspects mentioned in the introductions are treated in the papers. But since the articles reveal how new approaches to the subject in question can bring about a deeper understanding of the dynamics of individual religious change in antiquity, we hope that future studies will also be inspired by the questions and issues raised in the introductions.

1. The choice: reasons, motivations, and results

When deciding to devote one's loyalty, trust, or time to a religious group or movement, a more or less explicit, and more or less radical, personal choice is involved. Some groups would nurture certain ideals as to why people should join a group, such as redemption, knowledge, or "calling"; sometimes the personal choice would be presented as a choice made according to such collective ideals, at other times as a result of miracles, dreams, healing, etc. In earlier scholarship, there was a tendency to seek the motivation to become initiated into a mystery cult in the hope for eschatological or mundane salvation or social prestige, and to investigate Christian conversion from a purely theological or "Pauline" perspective. Later scholars have increasingly added alterations and nuances to this picture by stressing other reasons for and results of the choice (such as communal and emotional concerns), both in relation to antiquity and in studies of modern changes of religious affiliation. Nonetheless, the topic still needs further exploration, especially in a comparative framework, and there are further questions to be asked of the ancient materials in regard to the choice. What made people choose to convert to Christianity or be initiated into a mystery cult, and how is it represented in the sources? Was it family or peer pressure, a quest for status, social welfare, eschatological salvation, belonging, or knowledge? If a local group consists mainly of family members or friends, or if being initiated was "the thing to do," was joining a group ever a choice? What did the choice entail in terms of "visibility", i.e., did it have to be (and was it) advertised to others, or was it a purely private or "inner" matter? And should it be expressed in all aspects of the converts' lives? What was the connection between the choice and future commitment? And what are the (temporal) relations between choice, initiation and conversion? This theme thus investigates what factors may have been involved in the transformation process, and what characteristics defined the choice in different religious groups.

The first paper by **Birgitte Bøgh** is *In life and death: choice and conversion in the cult of Dionysos*. Its main goal is to question the assumption that the choice to be initiated into the Bacchic cult primarily originated in and was focused on eschatological concerns or was an excuse to get drunk, and to posit that Bacchic initiation need not be distinguished from the question of conversion. The article first explores how the choice to be initiated in this cult is represented from different insider and outsider perspectives. There are great differences, not least in regard to the portrayal of the seriousness surrounding the choice to be initiated, but there are also notable similarities, especially the importance of the choice in this life, and the weight put on ritual participation. The author finally addresses the question of conversion and concludes with a characterisation of Bacchic conversion as soft, revivalist and affectional – terms inspired by modern conversion theories.

In the next paper, *Becoming Christian in Carthage in the age of Tertullian*, Éric Rebillard focuses on the aftermath of choice and conversion. Thus, the author considers what the choice of becoming Christian entails in terms of visibility and commitment in second-century Carthage. In the first part of the paper, he reviews the Christian identity markers (such as the kiss or making the sign of the cross) and contexts in which Christians could express their religious choice. Next, the author analyses a second aspect of the choice, namely how much relevance Christians gave to their new religion. In contrast to what Tertullian wished and claimed, many Christians did not consider, e.g., occupation to be determined by religion, and they usually operated with a multiplicity of identities, not just one (namely "Christian"). Rebillard calls this the intermittency of Christianness, but emphasises that this should not be interpreted as a measure of the importance or significance of the choice.

Finally, in **Jan Bremmer's** *Conversion in the oldest Apocryphal acts*, the author challenges Nock's individual and psychological approach to the phenomenon of conversion in antiquity by investigating the conversions found in the often overlooked *Apocryphal acts*. In many ways, these differ from other ancient texts, e.g., in regard to their portrayal of the converts' gender and status. In the *Acts*, conversions are most often spurred by miracles and are mediated through other Christians, and the texts repeatedly stress the fact that the newly converted have yet to be further educated in the faith, i.e., that there was a long process of integration into a Christian community. Nock's definition thus neglects the social factor in conversion, which plays a role both before and after conversion. The conclusion sums up the results, situates and evaluates the sources in their broader context, and poses some final questions to be taken into consideration when studying conversion and converts in the ancient world.

2. Agency and agents: The context of decision

Related to the aspect of choice and religious change is the question of agency. Some research has already been conducted in regard to one obvious expression of agency, namely missionaries and other active agents of cults in antiquity. But there are more aspects to this topic, for example, the role of divine beings, the culture, the group's ideology, or the converts themselves in shaping the process. These aspects of agency have yet to gain in-depth investigations in relation to antiquity, albeit many scholars have more or less implicitly touched upon the role of the converts by viewing them as passive. Thus, some models of conversion – especially those built on the experiences of Paul and Augustine – see the (Christian) convert as being passively influenced or transformed by god or other superhuman agents. In earlier sociological studies on modern converts, he or she was also regarded as passive, but now in the sense that he or she had been brainwashed by a religious group. In contrast, starting in the 1970s, many later sociological and anthropological studies have focused on the active role played by the converts themselves,[10] by asserting that they not only play an active role in their own conversion, but also affect the religious community they are socialised into. Inspired by such tendencies, the second theme revolves around the question of agency involved in situations of religious change in antiquity. Who are the agents in conversion processes, in accounts of conversion, and in initiation rituals? How do the different agents relate to each other? Who is active and taking the initiative, and how is this presented in the sources? What inhibits and supports a person's decision to convert, to remain in a group, or disaffili- ate? How is the role of divine beings described in accounts of conversion? And why is it that converts are sometimes presented as passive objects in the sources rather than active decisions-makers?

First, **Jakob Engberg** discusses the roles assigned to divine and human agents in a number of Christian apologies in his paper, *Human and divine agency in conversion in apologetic writings of the second century*: To *"dance with angels."* His aim is to study the normative conversion ideals of the apologists through the aspect of agency, but also to demonstrate that they portray conversion as a process, and to argue that such ideals shaped the actual conversion experience of converts. The texts show that the apologists ascribed important agency in conversion to both human and divine agents, that the apologists perceived the agency of the convert to be important (thus confirming the view of converts as active agents found in modern schol- arship), and finally that they strived to become agents in the conversion processes of their readers as well. Thus, by focusing on agency, this article builds a bridge between modern and ancient conversion patterns and be- tween a normative and a descriptive approach to conversion, a dichotomy found both in patristic scholarship and in the study of modern conversion.

The next contribution similarly suggests a new way to conceive conver- sion based on an exploration of the role that different agents play in conver- sions, but from a pagan point of view. In *Ontological conversion: A descrip- tion and analysis of two case studies from Tertullian's* De baptismo *and Iamblichus'* De mysteriis, **Nicholas Marshall** suggests that the concept of "ontological conversion" provides a fruitful entry into the issue of agency in conversion because it defines the religious group and its ideology as central agents in the conversion process; thus it can help us understand why peo- ple convert even in those cases where we have no first-hand attests to the change. The author focuses his study on the theurgical work *De mysteriis* by Iamblichus and compares postulated features of conversion in Iamblichus' text to those drawn from Tertullian's *De baptismo*. After a textual analysis,

---

10 See an overview by S. Bruce, *Sociology of Conversion. The Last Twenty-five Years*, in: J.N. Bremmer *et al.* (eds.), *Paradigms, Poetics, and Politics of Conver- sion*, Leuven 2006, 1–12.

the conclusion detects aspects of coercion in circles operating with this type of conversion, in that the worldview created by such a community seems to leave the convert no choice but to convert.

The last paper in this theme, *Agents of apostasy, delegates of disaffiliation* by **Zeba Crook**, illuminates the importance of agency in another, related context, namely by analysing the problem of apostasy among Jews and Christians in antiquity. With the outset in a methodological focus on allocentric and idiocentric behaviour, the author first argues that agency will operate very differently in collectivistic and individualistic cultures, and that this fact has implications for our understanding of apostasy in the ancient and profoundly collectivistic world. Analysing the language of apostasy (or disaffiliation as a more precise term) he then shows that the charge of apostasy is a collectivistic act, because it is essentially about loyalty to the group and thus of social control; Apostates exercise agency by rejecting the collectivistic pressure to uphold tradition and express loyalty to the old community. The collectivism-individualism construct also nuances earlier scholarly assumptions that apostasy was relatively common in antiquity. More likely, disaffiliation was in fact rare because it is inconsistent with a collectivistic setting.

3. The change: the nature of reorientation

Implied in the terms conversion and initiation is that an individual undergoes and experiences a transformation, but the implications of the transformation, and the adjectives that we would use to describe it, would undoubtedly differ from one religion, type of source, or personal experience to another. Yet, some characterisations seem to be generally accepted. One is that *rites de passage* – best known from the classic work of van Gennep from 1909 – always result in a new, permanent status, as usually assumed when dealing with initiation in antiquity. But which rituals actually fall under this category? Other elements are often regarded as typically Christian, such as conversion as a radical, inner event, or that conversion often involves a complete break with the past, conflicts with relatives, and withdrawal from non-converts (including friends and family) – what we may call "bridge-burning". But to which degree are such elements parts of a conversion *topos*? And can the element of familial conflict in conversion narratives be understood in a different light? This phenomenon of bridge-burning is best known from Christianity and from literary sources, but to which degree can we trace it in other types of sources as well, like inscriptions or funerary settings, or among other distinct groups? Is bridge-burning at all possible in a polytheistic environment, or is it exclusive of religions with strong notions of sin or monotheistic religions? Did initiation in the mystery cults rather result in the opposite of bridge-burning, namely "bridge-building" – to others and to the surrounding social context? Turning to other established "truths" concerning the nature of the change, were Christian conversions actually the sudden and spiritual turn-around that many early scholars imagined them to be, or were they rather dominated by elements of continuity as well as by more worldly matters? Taking well-established models under serious scrutiny the papers in this theme deal with some of the features that characterise the change.

The aim of **Carmen Cvetković's** contribution, *Change and continuity: reading anew Augustine's conversion*, is to present a new understanding of the conversion of Augustine by taking his own view on this phenomenon into account and by drawing on both early and late texts. This famous example of conversion largely shaped Nock's understanding of conversion, namely as an ideal of great sinners redeemed from the errors of their past life in the flash of a moment which initiated a radically different life. However, when modern scholars have attempted to interpret Augustine's experience of change in light of Nock's theory, the result has been a serious misrepresentation of Augustine's own view on his transformation and a number of irreconcilable scholarly viewpoints. Cvetković's reinterpretation of Augustine's conversion as a long, gradual process with several significant moments suggest a solution to the previous problems and presents a more coherent understanding of his experience able to accommodate both Augustine's general theology and the early and late works preserved by this famous bishop.

In the next contribution, *'The devil is in the details.' Hellenistic mystery initiation rites: bridge-burning or bridge-building?*, **Luther H. Martin** uses theories from the cognitive study of religion to argue that previous views on the nature of the change – including the aspect of bridge-building – that took place in the initiation rites of the mystery cults have often rested on a misconceived conception of the character of these cults. Among other things, he reminds us that the question of the cults' exclusiveness or inclusiveness would have differed from one local cult group and period to another, a claim that is exemplified by a survey of the Eleusinian cult through time. Martin further argues that there were fundamental differences between Christianity and the various mystery cults, especially in the area of change. Thus, in the latter, the change occurred in the minds of the individual, it was social rather than (just) religious, and while the Christian religion emphasised bridge-burning, mystery initiation rituals were highly bridge-building which Martin argues with examples from the Eleusinian and the Mithraic mysteries.

The article by **Kate Cooper** and **James Corke-Webster** (*Conversion, conflict, and the drama of social reproduction: Narratives of filial resistance in early Christianity and modern Britain*) examines the element of family conflict in conversion experiences. In many stories of early Christian conversion, young females find themselves in conflict with their families. Intergenerational tension similarly occurs in disputes over arranged marriages. As a way to understand what is often at stake in these conflicts, the authors compare an early Christian martyr text, the *Acts of Paul and Thecla*, with a recent novel about the Pakistani community in modern Britain. Both narratives are examples of "literature of dislocation" and are related to the question of identity crises. Mother-daughter tension is at the core of both narratives, and in both cases it functions to explore the vulnerability of social reproduction in a marginal community. *The Acts of Paul and Thecla* thus present an identity model which encourages the reader to reject the requirement of social reproduction via marriage – but not where the rejection of the family is concerned, although this is the immediate image painted by the conversion narratives.

Finally, in his paper *There and back again: Temporary immortality in the Mithras Liturgy*, **Radcliffe G. Edmonds III** analyses the so-called Mithras Liturgy as a way to problematise the dominant van Gennepian model of personal change for explaining the nature of immortalisation in antiquity. If any transformation should involve a permanent change, becoming immortal would seem to do so, but the Mithras Liturgy provides instructions for multiple performances of the spell, up to once a month – the immortalisation is obviously temporary. Such an apparent paradox shows the need to re-examine assumptions about rites of passage. This is what Edmonds does in the present article. He argues that many rituals previously categorised as rites of initiation, because they fit the tripartite structure in Gennep's model, should be analysed in terms of another model, that of rites of purification or sanctification. In such rituals that bring close contact with the divine, the religious focus is upon the shifts in relationship with the god, rather than upon the change of status on earth or any change of lifestyle afterwards.

4. Education: instructing and guiding the converts

The phenomenon of "religious education" in connection with conversion is mostly associated with the so-called catechumenate in Christianity, an elaborate institution only existing in its full form from the 4th century, but with earlier roots. Here, education played an important role in conversion processes mainly as a way to educate and socialise new converts into the social and moral rules and the belief system of the new group, but which role did education play in processes of identity formation? And what role did teaching play in other contemporary cults? Polytheistic cults were non-dogmatic, and there is little to prove that prolonged teaching in the form of verbal, doctrinal education played a part in the process of religious change in general. However, other means could serve to attract, educate, and affirm member participation and to transmit the cult's values, such as highly emotional initiatory rituals, specific clothing, the claim of secrecy, regulations, and so on. Thus, instead of understanding "education" only in a narrow Christian sense, we can regard it more broadly as a notion implying that specific rules and values of the cults in question are transmitted to initiates and converts one way or the other. Hence, we may start reinvestigating the case from a wider comparative angle. What were the similarities and differences in the different religious groups in regard to their attitude towards education as part of conversion and initiation processes? Which Graeco-Roman sources are relevant to the question of education? If pagan cults taught their members anything, how did they accomplish that, and what was the aim? Similarly, a new understanding of Christian education can be gained by asking what role pagan philosophy played in Christian education. Finally, religious education in a broad sense is especially famed for playing a major role in Judaism, but to which degree is it actually found in connection with conversion itself?

The first contribution by **Anders-Christian Jacobsen,** *Identity formation through catechetical teaching in early Christianity,* focuses on the catechumenate institution in late antiquity. With an outset in identity theories, the author discusses whether and to which degree 4th century Christian catechetical teaching contributed to identity formation and transformation among persons who recently converted to Christianity. Drawing on the catechetical instructions found in the writings of Cyril of Jerusalem and Augustine, Jacobsen focuses on questions such as: Did early catechetical instruction attempt to form an individual or a collective identity – or both? Did the catechetical instruction aim to transform the candidates' way of life or their beliefs – or both? After detailed textual analyses, Jacobsen concludes that Christian catechesis aimed at transforming both the individual and collective identity of the newly converted in the strongest sense of the term "identity" even if this "ideal" degree of transformation was not always reached in the actual congregations.

The next two papers focus on religious education in pagan cults, which are usually disregarded in connection with this topic. **Per Bilde's** contribution is entitled *The role of religious education in six of the pagan religions of the Hellenistic-Roman period.* After a critical evaluation of the scholarly views that deny that any kind of education took place in the mysteries, Bilde continues with an examination of sources from Orphism, the mysteries in Eleusis, the cult of Bacchus, Cybele (and Atargatis), Isis, and Mithras which illustrate the existence of pagan education. Although nothing identical to the elaborated Christian catechumenate has been preserved in the remaining sources, Bilde demonstrates that religious education was not unique to Christianity. However, he also notes the differences between the Christian catechumenate and the pagan cults, in particular the length of the former – a fact which can undoubtedly be explained by different factors, such as the need for the Christian religion to distinguish itself from its Jewish and pagan competitors.

Roger Beck's paper, *Educating a Mithraist*, explores facets of education in a specific pagan context – the cult of Mithras – with an outset in cognitive theories of religion. As the author argues, initiation into the mysteries was itself the supreme educational experience obtained through emotionally loaded rituals; but the initiands of the Mithras cult must also have received some kind of formal instruction, since the mysteries were too complicated and too coherent to have been transmitted solely by rituals and Q&A sessions with a senior member. Beck explores how this might have been done, beginning with the "Mithraic Catechism from Egypt" and moving on to esoteric Mithraic words and sentences known to us partly from Christian literary sources, partly from graffiti and dipinti found in mithraea. Beck shows that the function of these was, at least partly, educational; they instructed both the initiand and the immediate Mithraic community, by reminding it of functions, relationships, and authority within the group. The method by which such education is transmitted was through a paradoxical and the counter-intuitive language which is crafted to convey dense, but memorable messages.

The fourth article puts a further comparative perspective on religious education in antiquity. Elisabetta Abate's contribution, *Observations on late antique rabbinic sources on instruction of would-be converts*, investigates which kind of education rabbinic Judaism envisioned in connection with conversion and illuminates a complementary phenomenon, namely a relative lack of concern about defining the process that would lead converts to become competent members in the new religion. According to late antique rabbinic views, some of the requirements for valid conversion to Judaism were acceptance of the Torah, proper intention, circumcision, immersion, and sacrifice. But only two passages are devoted to instruction of converts-in-the-making taking place *during* the formal procedure of conversion, and not as a preparation for it. The sources also imply that an on-going process of acculturation will continue to unfold after formal conversion, but they display no attempt at exerting control over the further stages in this process, e.g., by going into details with some of the representative pieces of information, or by appointing figures endowed with formal educational tasks.

The final contribution, *The role of philosophy and education in apologists' conversion to Christianity: The case of Justin and Tatian* by Tobias Georges, explores a specific aspect of Christian education. Christian converts had to learn the basic contents of the Christian faith and its rules which in the second century and onwards developed into so-called catechumenate. However, in the preserved accounts of a (probably small) Christian elite of "intellectuals", the catechumenate does not play a role. Instead, we find the connection between philosophy and conversion which is what Georges explores with a focus on the cases of Justin and Tatian. Philosophical education played an important role in the conversions of these two second-century writers – not coincidently, as Georges argues, since Tatian was most likely Justin's pupil. Besides illustrating this relationship and the role of philosophy in their Christian education, Georges investigates the two apologists' relation towards Greek philosophy after their conversion and compares the close connection between philosophy, education, and conversion in Justin's and Tatian's situation to other contemporary conversions.

As is clear from the above, each theme includes both monotheistic and polytheistic perspectives. This organisational choice reflects the view that personal religious transformation and its various elements in Christianity, Judaism and the pagan mystery cults are comparable and at least potentially similar (not all will agree to this view), but it does not reflect a wish to smooth out their differences. On the contrary, the comparative approach has been chosen because it provides a methodological framework for teasing out and investigating both similarities and differences between the various cults and religions in antiquity. The different elements in the process would undoubtedly differ greatly in significance and character from one group or individual to another, and also from one period and place to another. Moreover, the different nature and unequal preservation of sources from Christian and pagan religions prevent a full and fully documented investigation. Nevertheless, a deeper reflection on these matters will provide a more nuanced picture of the religious landscape in antiquity, and of its development from early to late antiquity. Many more studies should be conducted in order to be broadly comparative, but the limited number of papers presented in this volume nevertheless present illuminating insights both on their own and taken together. Thus, cross-thematically they all present, implicitly or explicitly, critical reflections on the old Nockian paradigm of conversion based on modern, and often theoretical, insights. Some authors present new definitions of conversion which are suitable for all cults and religions in antiquity; others criticise the very kernel of the Nockian "truth", or nuance specific aspects of the old definition which are either outdated or have been claimed to be so. Still others investigate relevant aspects of the mystery cults that have mostly been overlooked in previous research on religious change in antiquity due to the distinction between adhesion and conversion.

Much more can be explored and debated in connection with the subject of individual religious transformation in antiquity, but we are convinced that readers from many different scholarly positions and with different kinds of interest will find new and provocative opinions and insights in the papers collected in this volume. It remains, therefore, only to give our heartfelt thanks to the contributors for their participation in the conference, for presenting such interesting papers, and for willingly transforming these into written articles. We also want to thank the authors as well as the other participants for contributing to the many lively and fruitful discussions during the conference. Moreover, we are very grateful to the peer reviewer of this volume for contributing with numerous valuable comments and suggestions. Last, but not least, we thank Velux and the Faculty of Arts at Aarhus University for their generous financial support without which the conference and the publication of the present volume would not have been possible.

On behalf of the Velux group members,

Birgitte Bøgh

Birgitte Bøgh

In Life and Death: Choice and Conversion in the Cult of Dionysos

Abstract: The article explores how the choice to be initiated in the Bacchic cult is represented from different insider and outsider perspectives. Bøgh argues that Bacchic initiation was not simply a question of eschatology or drunkenness and posits that we on basis of modern conversion theories can characterise Bacchic conversion as soft, revivalist and affectional.

Introduction

The ultimate aim of Dionysism was "to become a Bacchos – that is to say to become identified with the god." These are the words of Turcan which are a relevant starting point for the question of choice in the cult of Dionysos.[1] Bacchoi / Bacchai are cultic titles used for initiates of Dionysos both by outsiders and by the initiates themselves. It is related to the epithet of Dionysos, Bacchos, and to the verb *bacchein* which can refer both to the feeling and to the performance of Bacchic rites that caused enthusiastic *mania*.[2] It is found everywhere in the Mediterranean region, from early to late antiquity, sometimes referring to a specific grade, sometimes as a generic term for all those who have been initiated to Dionysos. In the following, I want to expand on Turcan's statement and ask why an individual wanted to become a Bacchant, what the consequences were, and how important the choice was, according to outsiders and insiders.[3] This

---

1   R. Turcan, *The Cults of the Roman Empire*, Oxford 1996, 295.
2   J. San Cristóbal, *The Meaning of* βάκχος *and* βακχεύειν *in Orphism*, in: G. Casadio / P.A. Johnston (eds.), *Mystic Cults in Magna Graecia*, Austin 2009, 46–61. Bacchos is an epithet originally referring to wine (A. Henrichs, *Changing Dionysiac Identities*, in: B.F. Meyer (ed.), *Jewish and Christian Self-definition*, vol. 3, London 1982, 137–160 (139)).
3   Below, I retain the gender-specific designation Bacchos or Bacchê when relevant, but use the collective term, Bacchants, when speaking of both female and male followers of Dionysos for practical and ideological reasons: Many scholars have regarded Bacchism as an umbrella-term for more or less unrelated Bacchic sub-groups or "separate provinces" which never mingled: maenads who frenzy, males who drink wine, and esoteric believers in the afterlife (e.g., Henrichs, 1982). As A-F. Jaccottet has demonstrated, there never was such a division (*Choisir Dionysos*, vol. 1, Zürich 2003, 69–100). Moreover, in Euripides' drama *Bacchae* (which has been the main basis for this assumption) both men and women

will bring forth different aspects of becoming a Bacchant which allows us to discuss conversion in a Bacchic context.

I have chosen to focus on choice in the cult of Dionysos for two reasons. One is that we possess a large number of different types of sources which allows us to illuminate the subject from different angles; another, that it has often been assumed that Bacchic initiation was primarily about a happy afterlife, or a pretext for drinking.[4] It follows from such views that the choice itself was not important, and becoming a Bacchant was most certainly not a conversion. This squares badly with Livy's description of the Italian Bacchants (Liv. 39) who act like fanatic converts, and with the characterisation by Versnel of Euripides' drama *Bacchae* as the "first dim" of the conversion stories which are otherwise only attested much later.[5] Yet, these two famous literary sources are written by more or less hostile outsiders (and one is merely a drama), so to which degree can they actually say anything realistic of the choice to become a Bacchant? Is it not a fact that insider sources show that the afterlife was a reason to be initiated, and that Dionysos' cult centered on wine? The aims of this contribution is to enlighten the differences and similarities between outsider and insider perspectives in regard to choice, to argue that the choice cannot be reduced to either of those motivations, and finally that we can in fact speak about conversion in a Bacchic context.[6]

---

participate, females drink wine, and the cult's esoteric aspects are also referred to (179–185; 221; 472). Also, Maenad is a synonym for Bacchê derived from the verb μαίνεσθαι (to frenzy) which men do too, seen, e.g., in Herodotus (cf. below). In a sense, Orphics were Dionysiac "separatists" with distinct ideas, myths and traditions, and as such a "separate province". But they also shared traits with other Bacchants, and we can no longer uphold a sharp distinction between one strand and the other (W. Burkert, *Bacchic Teletai in the Hellenistic Age*, in: T. Carpenter / C. Faraone (eds.), *Masks of Dionysos*, Ithaca 1993, 259–275 (259)). As such there is no reason to abstain from using the collective term Bacchants for all Bacchic initiates.

4　From earlier to later researchers, e.g., M. Nilsson, *The Bacchic Mysteries of the Roman Age*, in: HThR 46 (1953), 175–202 (195); J. Holzhausen, *Poetry and Mysteries. Euripides'* Bacchae *and the Dionysiac Rites*, in: Electronic Antiquity 12/1 (2008), 41–72 (41).

5　H.S. Versnel, *Ter Unus. Isis, Dionysos, Hermes. Three Studies in Henotheism*, vol. 1, Leiden 1990, 172, cf. 194.

6　This investigation includes a variety of literary and epigraphic sources from different periods. It is not possible on basis of the preserved sources to detect profound differences between being a Bacchant in, say, the Classical and Roman periods, cf. A.-F. Jaccottet, *Un dieu plusieurs mystères?*, in: C. Bonnet et al. (eds.), *Religions orientales*, Stuttgart 2006, 219–230 (226) and R. Seaford, *Dionysos*, London 2006, 50. Even though we must assume that the cult developed, the sources

Aspects of the choice as represented by outsiders

Some of the best known outsider descriptions have been produced by Euripides, Herodotus, and Livy. In his *Histories* (4.78–80), Herodotus tells of the Scythian king Skyles who "formed a desire to be initiated to Dionysos" (ἐπεθύμησε Διονύσῳ Βακχείῳ τελεσθῆναι). The motivation for his wish is not explained, but the result is that he both "acts like a Bacchos and is maddened by the god" (βακχεύει τε καὶ ὑπὸ τοῦ θεοῦ μαίνεται). More important is that his choice is presented as very serious, even the gods try to prevent him from being initiated. Zeus warns him by burning down his house, but Skyles ignores this and completes his initiation – with grave consequences. When the Scythians see him roaming the streets while "bacchanting", "they regarded it as a *very* great misfortune (κάρτα συμφορὴν μεγάλην), and they went out and declared to the whole company what they had seen." The only solution, they decide, is to kill Skyles, but the king manages to escape to the neighbouring region of Thrace. Just before it comes to actual war between the Thracians and Scythians because of his initiation, Skyles is caught and his head is cut off. Rather than just witnessing the seriousness of initiation in the cult of Dionysos, Herodotus' portrayal also reflects a battle of cultures (cf. 4.76–78). But this is not the only explanation. According to the Scythians themselves, the reason for their aversion against Skyles' decision was that "it is wrong to seek out a god like this, one who impels men to frenzy" (4.79). Moreover, we find a similar image of the great significance of the choice in another contemporary source, the *Bacchae* by Euripides.

In this drama, Dionysos comes to Thebes in order to force the city to accept him. He compels the women to celebrate his orgies by making them mad, but a few men also join voluntarily (see, e.g., 170–191). The king, Pentheus, is disgusted by the rituals and argues that they are nothing but excuses for getting drunk and engaging in sexual escapades, so he resists. Some of the sensible men in the city try to convince Pentheus to surrender as does Dionysos in the guise of his own prophet, but in vain. The result is that Pentheus' own mother, Agave, kills her son and everything ends in ruin for everybody: to accept or reject the rituals of Dionysos is no easy matter in the drama. The instigator is the deity himself (20–26) or his missionaries (the choir of devoted Maenads), and their aim is that every individual should

---

suggest continuity rather than transformation in, e.g., rituals, self-designations, cult symbols, and hopes; very little in the Imperial cult is not evidenced in earlier periods as well, with the exception of the strongly hierarchical organisation of the groups (which starts already in the Hellenistic period). Evidence of mysteries is found abundantly in this cult already from the 6th or 5th century BCE and onwards (see references in Burkert, *Initiation*, in: *Thesaurus Cultus et Rituum Antiquorum*, vol. 2, 91–124, *passim*), cf. Bilde in this volume (232, n. 26).

accept the god and his rituals – a decision that will make those who do happy and blissful. Those who do not will be destroyed. As such, the choice is not presented as a free and voluntary decision, as in the story of Skyles, but it is presented as equally serious – a matter of life and death.

The importance of the choice is also clear in Livy's story of the Bacchanalian affair in Italy in 186 BCE (Liv. 39).[7] There are many points of overlap between the two texts, but for Livy, the seriousness of the choice is connected to accepting Dionysos' rituals, not to withstand them. People risked getting killed by the Bacchants if they refused to join the cult (39.13), but many people were also killed during the initiation rituals because of their violence (39.10). Thus, initiation itself was dangerous, but the main danger of accepting his rituals was the participation in the cult afterwards. Thus, when Hispala (the mistress of Aebutius) learns that her lover is going to be initiated, she exclaims "Heaven forbid. Better for us both to die than that you should do this," and then invokes "deadly curses on the heads of those who had advised him to take this course" (39.10). Nonetheless, a great number of people were attracted to the cult, either because they were stupid or naïve or because of its drunken and frenzied rituals which, according to Livy, "offered the opportunity to satisfy whatever lust a person were prone to" (39.8). But as in the *Bacchae*, the choice is not always a personal and voluntary matter. Thus, Aebutius is going to be initiated because his mother and step father had promised it in exchange for his recovery after a serious illness (he nevertheless voluntarily chooses to proceed with the initiation). But the cult also grew because people were forced to join it. Thus, Hispala herself was forced by her mistress to participate, "but had never gone near it after she was set free" (39.10).

Accordingly, all three authors present the choice as very serious, but not always as a result of a personal wish. In all sources, it has great consequences for the individuals to be initiated, but they are evaluated very differently. In Herodotus, we only learn that one result of Skyles' initiation was that he could now participate in the frenzied rituals. We cannot be certain that this ritual participation was the only reason for his choice, but it is certainly possible. In other literary sources we find explanations of the positive effect of the ritual frenzy. Plato writes on the μανία that "he who has part in the rites is made whole (ἐξάντη) in the present and in the future and has a release from the evil which is afflicting him."[8] A musicologist, A. Quintilianus, writes that the purpose of Bacchic initiation is "that the depressive anxiety (πτόησις) of ignorant people, produced by their state of life, or some

---

7   In the following, translated passages are taken from W.M. Roberts / C. Roberts, *Livy's History of Rome*, vol. 5, London 1905.

8   Pl., Phdr. 244d–e. A later section (265b) reveals that he speaks specifically of Bacchic madness.

misfortune, be cleared away through the melodies and dances of the ritual in a joyful and playful way."[9] But we find no better description of the positive impact of the rituals than the one presented by the missionary choir of Maenads in the *Bacchae*.[10]

According to the choir, the rituals fill you with all-consuming joy and happiness. The wine obviously plays a role, because it "gives pleasure and removes grief" (425), but it is the ecstatic rituals that gain prime attention.[11] By participating in Dionysos' rites, Bacchants are drawn into an entire second universe created wherever Dionysos is worshipped – on islands of love, in the mountains, or in meadows; it is a ritual place that overflows with gold, milk, wine, honey, and consist of banquets, dances and singing with Dionysos and other mythical beings, such as satyrs, the Graces, Muses, Peace, and Love.[12] The result of the *enthousiasmos* is not just the loss of self-control, but the loss of "self": Individualism is not merely ignored in the Bacchic rituals, but is virtually annihilated. Thus, the choir praises the man "whose spirit (ψυχὰν) merges with these Bacchic celebrations in the mountains" (75). The result is a spiritual union on several levels, between god and man, between the human and the divine *thiasos*, and between fellow Bacchants. The actual and spiritual communality is continuously stressed throughout the play in the words used for the Bacchants and in the numerous examples of verbs which include the prefix "συν". Dionysos "joins together" with the maenads (ξυνάψει), and he "partakes" in the dances of the Bacchai (συμμετασχήσει). Teiresias and Cadmus "take hold of and join hands" (ξύναπτε καὶ ξυνωρίζου χέρα) on their way to the celebrations. The Bacchai are sisters (ἀδελφάς) and fellow revelers (συγκώμοι), they all make noise together (πᾶσα ὁμοῦ βοή) and call upon their god with a "united voice" (ἀθρόῳ στόματι). The Bacchai are Dionysos' companions (παρέδρους), his fellow travelers (ξυνεμπόρους),

---

9 *De musica* 3.25, trans. by T.J. Mathiesen (ed.), *Aristides Quintilianus on Music in Three Books*, New Haven 1983.

10 Even though the most negative consequences in the drama – violence and death – are the result for those who resist the cult, and despite the numerous positive results that the author has put in the mouths of the Maenads, the drama is not a Euripidean advertisement of the cult. The rituals are essentially bad because they entail a complete loss of self-control and an undivided loyalty and obedience to Dionysos. This is dangerous for the *individual* (e.g., 1296) as well as for the *polis* because it no longer has control of its citizens, cf. the sectarian statement in 1037: "Dionysos, not Thebes, has power over me." Cf. Cooper and Corke-Webster and Crook in this volume for the dangers of individuals making choices contrary to those expected of them by society.

11 The following translations are taken or modified from I. Johnston (ed.), *Bacchae by Euripides*, Arlington 2008.

12 E.g., 133–145; 402–424; 556–576; 704–711.

fellow exiles (συμφυγάδας), co-workers (συνεργούς), fellow hunters (ξυγκύναγας), and accomplices (ξυνεργάτους). The Bacchai sit together (συγκαθημένας), while the outsider, Pentheus, just sits (καθήμενος).[13]

Moreover, the one who *knows* (εἰδώς) the rituals and lives a pious and pure life is hailed as blessed (μάκαρ), fortunate (εὐδαίμων), and prudent (σώφρων) (72–82; 329; 472). The idea of a special knowledge gained through initiation thus casts a shadow on your entire life, according to the choir – the cult is not just about the frenzy of the moment. The rituals and the values of joy and freedom that are invoked during their performance thus come to epitomise a way of life. The perfect life hailed by the choir is a peaceful one of wisdom and tranquility. But "being clever is not wisdom, and thinking deeply about things is not suitable for humans." Since life is brief, "it should not be spent in a chase for great things. That is what idiots do, men who have lost their wits." A life free of sorrows and complaints, appreciating the daily life and the little things, "that is how men ought to live," the choir exclaims. Dionysos even hates the man who does not care to live a daily life of carefree bliss (390–425). Similarly positive consequences of being a Bacchant (now with an Orphic taint) is represented in another tragedy by Euripides, the *Cretans* (fr. 471) in which it is stated that now that the initiate has become a Bacchos, he leads a pure life, he is made godly (σιωθεις), he wears all-white clothing, and avoids sex and meat. Thus, these dramas portray positive consequences of the choice, not just found in the bliss of the Bacchic rituals, but also representing a particular way of life – in one case a life of abstinence and purity, in the other a happy and carefree life.

In Livy's recounting of the Bacchanalian affair, the choice is a result of allurement, force, deceit, or pollution, and it does not lead to a holy or happy life, on the contrary. Hispala knew the cult to be "a sink of every form of corruption" (39.13) and joining the cult results in, she tells her lover, "the ruin of your modesty, your reputation, your hopes, and your life" (39.10). According to Livy, when the initiates had sworn the oath of loyalty towards the movement, they proceeded to commit all sorts of crimes and immoral acts, not just promiscuous intercourse, drinking, and stealing, but also giving false witness, forging testaments and committing murder. "To regard nothing as impious or criminal was the very sum of their religion."[14] Many other outsiders have expressed similar opinions on the immorality of the Bacchants, calling them impious, blood-sucking, or driven by lust, insanity and drunkenness – all reflecting badly on the result of the choice.[15] But

---

13 See 52–63; 198; 512; 725; 811–816; 1131–1146; 1172; 1382.
14 *Nihil nefas ducere, hanc summam inter eos religionem esse* (39.13).
15 Impious: Heraclit., fr. 115 Kahn; blood-sucking: Plaut., Bac. 3.1; lust, insanity, and drunkenness: Aug., civ. 6.9.

another serious negative effect of participation, according to Livy, was the undivided loyalty towards the cult and each other. Such exclusive commitment put the entire city of Rome in danger, because the initiates could not be good soldiers: "Romans, can you think youths initiated, under such oaths as theirs, are fit to be made soldiers?"[16] Livy was not alone in this view; in fact this was probably the main reason why the Roman authorities banned the cult in the first place.[17]

The above-mentioned sources are literary productions made by outsiders with widely different agendas who represent the choice and the cult from different, but similarly (often) extreme viewpoints. In reality, the decision was never that serious, and surely it would never have been a matter of life or death. There is a world of difference between the positive and negative effects of joining the cult as presented, e.g., by the missionary Maenads and Hispala, but they agree on one thing: Bacchic initiation was important *in this life* and for the way you lived it, not the next. This does not mean that eschatological aspects of the Bacchic cult should be disregarded, but they was not as important as the this-worldly aspects of initiation.

Aspects of choice represented by insiders

The sources left by the Bacchants themselves make no elaborate explanations of the reason for being initiated. The importance of the choice is also difficult to assess. The sources do not tell of conflicts with families, of considerations or worries that the initiates may have had before deciding to be join the cult, or of the level of positive impact that may have followed initiation. Nonetheless, there is no reason to doubt that it was important in some way for the individuals, and not just in regard to a happy afterlife. Surely, some – especially funerary – sources clearly focus on the eschatological benefits, but this cannot be taken as evidence that initiation was not important in this life, as I will argue below.

Some of the better known sources that attest to eschatological concerns are the Orphic-Dionysiac gold plates which through their burial context and content attest to this aspect of initiation. They have (rightly) gained the Orphics the reputation for being interested in eschatology and release from the world. But in fact, as Edmonds has argued, their content primarily focuses

---

16 *Hoc sacramento initiatos iuuenes milites faciendos censetis?* (39.15). This entire affair reveals bridge-burning tendencies, but see Martin in this volume that this was not generally the case in the mystery cults.

17 This mutual loyalty is also obvious in the senate's decree prohibiting (or restricting) the Bacchic cult (CIL I², 581, 13–15): "Nor hereafter shall anyone take common oath with them, shall make common vows, shall make stipulations or promises for each other, nor shall anyone place trust in each other."

on the personal identity of the deceased and the (moral) values that the deceased considers important in this life rather than on eschatological visions.[18] It is of course impossible to prove that all those buried with the tablets actually practiced an *orphikos bios*, but the message contained in them is that the idea of standing apart from the others *in life* (perhaps just resulting in an "Orphic attitude") was at least as important as concerns about the afterlife.[19] Other testimonies to eschatological concerns are relatively few and, not surprisingly, most are funerary epitaphs.[20] An exception is a letter from Plutarch to his wife written on the occasion of their daughter's death: "Furthermore, I know that you are kept from believing the statements of those who win many to their way of thinking when they say that nothing is in any way evil or painful to "what has undergone dissolution," by the teaching of our fathers and by the mystic symbols of Dionysiac rites (τὰ μυστικὰ σύμβολα), the knowledge of which we who are participants share with each other."[21] Thus, Plutarch's words are actually meant to prevent his wife from believing those who say that nothing bad awaits after death. Taking into account that their daughter has just died, this would be of limited comfort to his wife unless the point is that Bacchic initiation and the knowledge transmitted to those who participate prevents the evil and painful events of the afterlife that others must endure.[22]

In the funerary epitaphs, it is also clear that eschatological concerns were indeed a reason – or part of the reason – for being initiated. One says that the deceased was taken by Dionysos to be a companion (ἑταῖρον) and fellow initiate (συνμύστην) of his own dances, another that Bacchos had invited her to dance in his *thiasos* as leader of her own group in the afterlife.[23] The

---

18 R. Edmonds, *Who are you? Mythic Narrative and Identity in the 'Orphic' Gold Tablets*, in: Casadio / Johnston (eds.), 2009, 73–94. Cf. F. Graf / S.I. Johnston, *Ritual Texts for the Afterlife*, London 2007.

19 This-worldly concerns are also the main focus of the Orphic hymns (Seaford, 2006, 70). Even if Orphic sectarian *groups* did not exist, there is no reason to doubt that there were Orphic practitioners, i.e., individuals who incorporated Orphic principles into their life and world-view.

20 See S.G. Cole, *Voices from Beyond the Grave*, in: Carpenter / Faraone (eds.), 1993, 276–295 for an analysis of Bacchic funerary sources.

21 Plu., *Consolatio ad uxor* 611d. Translation slightly modified from P.H. De Lacy / B. Einarson (eds.), *Plutarch's Moralia*, vol. 7, London 1959.

22 Cf. Origen: "After this again Celsus thinks […] that 'we do not speak the truth about the punishments' which are necessary 'for those who have sinned.' For this reason he compares us to 'those in the Bacchic mysteries who introduce phantoms and terrors'." (Or., Cels. 4.10, transl. by H. Chadwick (ed.), *Origen. Contra Celsum*, Cambridge ²1980).

23 TAM 5.1, 477; Cole, 1993, 289.

most famous is probably that of the dead boy in Philippi whose parents comfort themselves that their son has now come refreshed to the Elysian fields: "Now either the tattooed initiates (*signatae mystidis*) of Bromios call you to them in the flowering meadow among the satyrs, or the basket-bearing Naiads in the same way, so that you can lead the festival procession under the lightning torches" (CIL 3, 686, 17–20).

But can we deduce from such testimonies that the afterlife was in fact the only or primary reason for initiation? The latter epitaph is a good starting point for this discussion. The word *signatae* is often translated as "tattooed" (e.g., Cole, 1993, 289), and it is possible that some were in fact physically branded with symbols of Dionysos, since this was indeed the case with the Seleucid king Ptolemy IV Philopator.[24] But it was hardly standard practice. It is more likely that we should understand it as a spiritual or mental branding similar to the idea that Christians had the cross imprinted on their forehead.[25] Thus, it is possible that the Bacchic initiates were claimed to be symbolically marked through initiation as belonging to Dionysos. There is little reason to assume that this belonging was only important in the afterlife. Expressions of purely eschatological hopes are few compared to the many that attest to the significance of the cult, especially ritual participation, in this life. Further, one of the (actually) tattooed Bacchants, Philopator, seems to have been very devoted to Dionysos during his life; it is nowhere revealed that the afterlife played any role for him.[26] Hence, the idea of "marked" initiates probably indicates that Bacchants belonged to and should be devoted to the cult of Dionysos when alive, and, probably, that the devotion was to be continued after death. Likewise, it is clear from a speech by Himerius, who grieves for his boy who has died, that initiation was thought to provide protection in this life: "In what ground lies now your holy hair that you after your first birth (πρώτην γένεσιν) let grow for Dionysos?" [...] "Oh Dionysos, how could you endure that the holy boy was snatched away from your holy precinct? What a sad Bacchic revelry (βακχείας)," he weeps; "How can I trust Dionysos when he has not preserved my holy boy?" (Him.,

---

24 Etymologia Magna, s.v. *gallos*; Plu., *De adulatore et amico* 56e; 3 Macc 2:2,7 (the king threatened Jews to be branded on their bodies with fire if they did not partake in Dionysiac mysteries).

25 E.g., Clem., protr. 5.12,92: "I am made holy by initiation. The Lord is the hierophant, and he places his seal on the initiated." Cf. Engberg in this volume. Cf. F.J. Dölger, *Zur Frage der religiösen Tätowierung im thrakischen Dionysoskult*, in: AuC 2 (1930), 107–116 for the interpretation of the Bacchic tattoos as signs of submission and dependence.

26 Cf. n. 24. His devotion to the cult is also seen in a decree (BGU 6.12,1) demanding that all Dionysiac initiators in Egypt come to Alexandria to justify their ritual genealogy and leave copies of their written scrolls.

Or. 8.7). Moreover, several funerary inscriptions reveal only the grief of the family or fellow *mystai* and express no hopes that the deceased lives on. At the same time, however, they (and many others) do mention the deceased's initiation, participation in and commitment to Dionysos' cult while alive. One epitaph (2nd century BCE) advertises the Bacchic rituals to whoever may pass, but mentions nothing of the afterlife; on the contrary, it states that "being an initiate is the whole story of one's whole life."[27] Some mention cultic participation together with other this-worldly matters (such as athletic achievements), while others paint the picture that celebrating the Bacchic rituals was the only occupation ever undertaken by the deceased.[28] According to such insider testimonies, initiation was not a ticket to heaven, but involved an active participation in the Bacchic cult, even your whole life. Hence, the Dionysiac insider sources hinting at or even testifying to the hope of a happy afterlife probably signal that such hopes were a natural consequence and extension of the importance of the cult in this life, just as we assume that this and after-worldly concerns were intermingled when people became Christians. This intermingling of concerns is indeed what is expressed in a funerary epitaph inscribed on a statue of Dionysos: "Dionysos – I, Dion, was dear to you when alive, dancing with my young fellow carousers holding Bromius' nectar. And now, I have set you beside my grave, beside me, for all to see, so that I, dead but not gone, may look upon you."[29]

If we next turn to the question of why and how initiation was important in this life, we are on somewhat shakier ground. The fact that it gave access to the group and its ritual activities was surely one reason, since ritual activities in a group context are conspicually often referred to in the sources. The cathartic effect in and the experience of the loss of "self" in Bacchic ecstasy should not be neglected as an explanation of the importance of participation in the rituals. But other aspects of the rituals were at least as important: their ability to inspire communality and to create a paradisiac world for those who participated. These aspects are clearly described in the *Bacchae*, but we also find hints of these effects in a number of other sources. Thus, the particularly communal aspect of the Bacchic cult has been stressed by Dionysiac experts for a century.[30] Dionysos' power to foster communality

---

27 SEG 28, 841, 2f. (trans. Ph. Harland: www.philipharland.com/greco-roman-associations/?p=10995 2013).
28 Contrast, e.g., nos. 328 and 93 in AGRW.
29 SEG 34, 1266 (trans. S.G. Cole, *Life and Death, a New Epigram for Dionysos*, in: Epigraphica Anatolica 4 (1984), 37–48). Cf. also IKyzikos 1, 540.
30 According to E.R. Dodds (*Bacchae*, Oxford 1969, xx), the Bacchic rituals were about "merging individual consciousness in a group consciousness." See especially Henrichs, 1982, and Seaford, 2006, for the congregational, non-individualistic

and a collective identity has been ascribed to his being the supreme Greek *deus praesentissimus* inspiring an unsurpassed intimacy with his *thiasos*, his connections with freedom, peace and harmony, the role of wine which shared the same fundamental ability as the deity to break down barriers[31] between people and cultivate the values of freedom, equality and harmony, and – especially – to the ecstatic rituals which were profoundly collective and communal in nature.

In the epigraphic sources, the collective aspects of Bacchism are expressed in the fact that dedicatory inscriptions made by groups far outnumber those made by individuals which is not the case in other mystery cults – "the cult did not attract loners" (Henrichs, 1982, 150f.). This confirms the impression gained in most descriptions of Bacchants, namely that they act in groups. Many literary testimonies of different kinds and periods thus most often refer to the collective actions of the Bacchic *thiasoi* performing their cultic activities.[32] Obviously, the funerary epitaphs are mainly centered on the individual, but even these often envisage the deceased as an eternal member of the Bacchic *thiasos* or are donated by the fellow *mystai* of the deceased.

The description in the *Bacchae* of the Bacchic paradise invoked during rituals – a world of joy, freedom, peace and harmony, in which there are no walls between human and divine – is also found in other types of sources, such as in the Bacchic cult language (e.g., ivy, erotes, and *kantharoi*), words used of their meeting places, such as *stibas* (literally a couch of branches and leaves hinting at a merry country life, cf. the cultic title *boukolos*, shepherd), Dionysos' alternative name Liber (and his epithet liberator, *Lyaios*), and in numerous inscriptions. One thus records a gift from Timokleides to Dionysos, namely "a temple under the open sky, surrounding an altar and covered with ivy" as well as a "handsome evergreen cave," and an *oikos* where "the initiates can cry out '*euoi*' while the nymphs blend the sweet nectar that suspends the worries of mortals" (Jaccottet, 2003, no. 31). Numerous iconographic sources (vases, sarcophagi, mosaics) represent Dionysiac scenes of bucolic paradises with flowering gardens, doves, tame lions, wine, dance, small erotes, muses, and other mythical beings, and a great amount of epigraphic evidence similarly shows how Bacchic initiates conceived of and

---

character of Dionysism, and for earlier studies stressing the communality in this cult.

31 E.g., the boundaries between male and female, young and old, and life and death (Henrichs, 1982, 233, nn. 193–199); see Seaford, 2006, 29. 39–48 for the god's promotion of peace and harmony.

32 Cf. Livy, Euripides, and Herodotus (above) and, e.g., D., *De corona* 18.259; D.S., *Library* 4.3,2–5, Paus. 10.4,39; Clem., paed. 2.73,1–2; and Aug., ep. 17.4, cf. civ. 7.21.

cast themselves in Dionysiac roles or held positions (like nymphs, satyrs or *boukoloi*) that in some way or another harked back to world of Dionysos.[33] Thus, participating in Bacchic rituals was attractive not just for personal, but also for communal reasons and for invoking an experience of utopian harmony in the company of (and as) a divine figure.

A number of sources reveal that children were initiated by their parents.[34] Many cult groups were thus – partly – a family affair into which at least some had been members since childhood. Usually, these groups also included many members who were not of the family, but a few inscriptions reveal that all members were of the same household.[35] This fact minimises the aspect of personal choice to be initiated, but it illuminates the parental commitment to the cult. It also suggests that an import benefit of being initiated was to be around people with whom you had close-knit bonds. The existence of affectional bonds to other members in Bacchic groups is thus obvious from the many inscriptions which emotionally refer to the other group members (including those who are not family) as fellow initiates or as (cultic) brothers, mothers or fathers.[36]

Life-long membership was probably typical for all members. Thus, one inscription (Jaccottet, 2003, no. 19) mentioning the names of the members (illustrating that they were not of the same family) mentions that a group of *mystai* who had dedicated an area with vineyards to the group must "swear by the god that they would share (or partake in) the produce for the rest of their lives." Membership until death is similarly confirmed by numerous inscriptions made by fellow Bacchants honouring the deceased members.[37]

Some testimonies present the benefits in unclear terms, such as on a grave stone dedicated by fellow Bacchai to a deceased priestess of Dionysos who "knew her share of blessings" (καλῶ(ν) μοῖραν ἐπισταμένη).[38] This is

---

33 See Henrichs, 1982, 149f.; Merkelbach, 1988, 60–72; Jaccottet, *Integrierte Andersartigkeit*, in: R. Schlesier (ed.), *A Different God? Dionysos and Ancient Polytheism*, Berlin 2011, 413–432.

34 This is documented in numerous sources mostly from the Roman period, but also before (e.g., D., *De falsa legatione* 199–200, from 343 BCE). See above, and W. Burkert, *Ancient Mystery Cults*, Cambridge 1987, 151, n. 115 for references to children's initiations in the Bacchic mysteries.

35 ISmyrna 766 is a dedication in the memory of Zôtion Artemidoros from οἱ συνβιωταὶ καὶ συνμύσται. The lack of article with the *symmystai* suggests that they are identical to the *symbiôtai*.

36 E.g., IGBulg 3², 1864; SEG 31, 983. Cf. Harland, *Familial Dimensions of Group Identity*, in: JBL 124/3 (2005), 491–513.

37 E.g., IG 2², 1326 and IG 10 (2.1), 260.

38 AGRW, no. 176. Cf. Henrichs, *Greek Maenadism from Olympias to Messalina*, in: HSCP 82 (1978), 121–160 (148).

reminiscent of the passage in the *Bacchae* where Bacchants are called fortunate and blessed, and of a passage in Demosthenes' *De corona* (18.259) which, although written by a hostile outsider, unwittingly reveals the positive outcome expected of initiation by insiders, namely refuge from evil. Thus, after their initiation they cry out "I have escaped evil; I have found the good." Demosthenes' passage does not reveal whether the benefits were this or after worldly, but it was probably both, as testified in Plato's Phdr. 244d–e, cited above. The play between good and evil is also mentioned or hinted at in other sources, such as in the flogging of the initiate seen in the Villa of Mysteries in Pompeii, and in literary sources. One author, Servius, tells us that men's souls are purified in the mysteries the same way that grain is purified in the winnow – a *vannus* or *liknon*, an agrarian instrument used in initiations.[39] Initiation thus made the initiates pure or exempt from evil, but it is doubtful that it entailed fundamental changes in moral behaviour, except perhaps towards your fellow initiates.[40] Initiation rather put Bacchants in some kind of permanent state of elevated purity and holiness. Thus, it is nowhere mentioned that the Bacchants must strive to remain free of evil, and the inscriptions virtually never make claims of general moral superiority (in sharp contrast to Isiac and Christian sources).

Other sources simply reveal that the initiates had changed in some way or another. This is seen in new titles or qualities (e.g., Bacchoi, *mystai, boukoloi*, or holy), or in new ritual behaviour, such as leading the reveling *komos*, or accepting new obligations. The lengthy inscription of the Athenian Iobacchoi provides an example of the latter. Only a person who had been approved by existing members could join the group, and only if he appeared "to be worthy and suitable for the Baccheion."[41] Each member should "speak and act and be zealous" for the group and "contribute to the fixed monthly dues for wine," in addition to participating in all their (frequent) assemblies (sick and other disabled persons excluded) and obeying a number of other regulations.[42]

---

39 Serv. A. 1.166. The *liknon* becomes a prominent Bacchic symbol only from the 1st century BCE, but it does not signal a fundamental change in the mysteries. Purification was a central characteristic of the Bacchic rites from an early period, and a *liknophoros* is mentioned already in D., *De corona* 18.259.

40 It is likely that demands of doing good deeds towards fellow initiates were widespread in all mysteries since two of the pagans' Jewish-Christian opponents each criticise "initiates" (in general) for not expanding their good deeds and moral invectives to all of humanity (Philo, *De specialibus legibus* 1.319f., Aug., civ. 2.26).

41 A *Baccheion* is the name for a Bacchic meeting place, a festival, and for the group at the same time.

42 IG 2², 1368, 45f.; 50f.; 63–145. The Iobacchoi convened once a month, as well as to funerals of group members, Bacchic festivals, holidays, and other "occasional feasts."

New cultic names are also an expression of change. In a Dionysiac context, these are mostly related to ritual aspects.[43] A funerary inscription reveals that the deceased was called Claudia Nebris (deer-skin, a Dionysiac
symbol),[44] another that the priestess' by-name was Euia (taken over from
their ritual cry).[45] A series of cultic names related to Dionysiac feasting is
known from different places in Asia Minor, e.g., "fine wheat," "honey-
cake," "white grape," and "wine pitcher."[46] According to Plautus, theonyms
could also be a result of the parents' initiation. Thus in *Bacchides* (prol.), a
couple initiated during a Bacchic festival afterwards called their twin girls
"Bacchis", two girls who later became "most determined" Bacchants (*Bacchae sunt acerrumae*). In other sources, the reasons for and consequences
of initiation are more specific. Apuleius, who in his defense speech states
that he has been initiated in many mysteries in his "search for truth," mentions the Dionysiac ones as an example (*Apologia* 55). This is not typically
a theme in the preserved sources although it is also hinted at by the author
of the Derveni papyrus (4th century BCE) who pities the Orphic-Dionysiac
initiates who *think* that they will gain some knowledge, but in reality do not
(col. xvi).

To sum up, certain aspects of the choice to become a Bacchant were
presented differently by outsiders and insiders, but not on all accounts.
Both types of sources attest that the choice resulted in a change and that
this change was valid in this life, not the next. The differences pertain in
particular to the seriousness of the choice and to the evaluation of the consequences. According to some of the outsider reports, the choice could be
a question of life and death, and the consequences were distinctly negative.
Insider sources generally do not reveal the importance of the choice, nor
(in many cases) the specific consequences, but those who do report or hint
at a positive outcome. Some call themselves holy, one expresses the relationship to Dionysos as one of great affection, another that initiation was a
search for knowledge, and many that it meant a deliverance from evil. But
most of them stress the initiates' active, sometimes life-long participation
in the group and rituals. This is a point of similarity with the numerous

---

43 In the Isiac cult, by contrast, new names are usually based on names and epithets
    of the deities (Bøgh, forthcoming, see n. 47 below).
44 See Merkelbach, 1988, 97 and pls. 12, 219.
45 Jaccottet, 2003, no. 22. Cf. the name of the Iobacchoi derived from the exclama-
    tion of the frenzied Maenads in the *Bacchae* (577), *Iô Bacchantes*, when going to
    the mountains (Jaccottet, 2003, vol. 1, 84).
46 See Merkelbach, 1988, 106 for the 7 inscriptions (with references). It is likely that
    the epithets had a further symbolic meaning related to their initiation, e.g., "hon-
    ey-cake". Thus, according to Harpocration (referring to D., *De corona* 18.259),
    happiness was presented to the initiates in the form of a cake (s.v. *neelata*).

outsider sources that (apart from immorality) almost exclusively focus on the frenzied rituals of the Bacchic revelers. Another point of similarity is that, as have been seen above, not all initiations were a result of a personal choice. But whereas this was a question of force or allurement to the outsiders, it was a result of the parents' devotion to Dionysos in the insider sources.

Conversion in the cult of Dionysos?

This brings us to the final part of the paper, namely to situate the previous discussion in the context of conversion. From a well-established perspective, talking about Bacchic conversion does not make sense. Many scholars have considered this phenomenon to be a Christian particularity and held that people only adhered to the mysteries.[47] To some degree it is a matter of definition. Some scholars regard monotheism as a prerequisite of conversion, others that it has to include "faith" or a rejection of the past, still others that it is a purely spiritual experience – all definitions based on Christian reports on conversion.[48] Often, however, the reasons for and consequences of the distinction between conversion and adhesion have been a great depreciation of the choice of becoming an initiate. This is obvious in Nock's classic book on conversion in antiquity in which he fashioned the distinction between "conversion" and "adhesion." To Nock, adhesion was a useful supplement, and initiation was primarily undertaken for the purpose of deliverance from fate, i.e., protection from illness and securing a happy afterlife; it was, roughly speaking, a one-time experience with no foregoing conversion, no substantial content and no consequences (1933, 7–15); until the final phase of paganism, it was "lacking in seriousness" (58). This devaluation of initiation is also echoed by many later scholars, especially those that deny the existence of conversion in the mysteries.[49]

---

47 This is the subject of a forthcoming article to appear in the *History of Religions* (B. Bøgh, *Beyond Nock. From Adhesion to Conversion in the Mystery Cults*).

48 See A.D. Nock, *Conversion*, London 1933, 7f. His definition of conversion in fact did not apply to most Christians either (cf. R. MacMullen, *Christianizing the Roman Empire*, New Haven 1984, 1 and *passim*). Other studies have shown that many Christians "on the ground" did not forsake their past or the surrounding society like the elite wanted them to, yet we still refer to them generally as converts.

49 E.g., W. Burkert and R. Stark who both follow Nock's views. To Stark, embracing new gods was a "relatively trivial action" (*Cities of God*, San Francisco 2006, 3). According to Burkert, initiation was a "useful supplement" essentially similar to Graeco-Roman votive habits, namely a quest for salvation (1987, 11. 14f. 17–19. 23. 44–46. 101).

There are, however, good reasons to apply the word "conversion" to the mystery cults in general (and many scholars after Nock have done so);[50] firstly, the distinction between adhesion and conversion often implies a fundamental difference between Christianity and the mystery cults; using the word conversion thus serves to break down the high wall built between them by Nock and other scholars.[51] Secondly, to reestablish the value and importance of initiation – not as an exciting experience or a short-cut to salvation, but as a choice which implies a change with future consequences, something which is always intuitively to be understood in the word conversion, whatever its definition. Finally, since there is a vast difference between a Mithraic pater, a Metroac eunuch, a frenzied Bacchant, a Christian "believer", and an Isiac devotee crying out her sins, a more nuanced picture of the ancient marketplace of religions can be gained by acknowledging different *types* of converts (with which modern conversion studies operate today) rather than using only two categories: Christian conversion and pagan adhesion.[52] In doing so, we can begin to understand better the differences between these cults, and the different reasons for joining them.

Obviously, we cannot use a very narrow or culture specific conception of conversion if we want to include the mystery cults. A broader definition is needed, not in order to dilute the concept, but to avoid Christianising terms (like "exclusivity" or "faith") and other culture-specific biases; i.e., the Christian particularities should be acknowledged without being considered a *sine qua non* for conversion. We can preliminarily define it as a change in religious identity, community, behaviour, and commitment, a definition which is neither too exclusive, nor too inclusive. All four aspects

---

50 E.g., N. Shumate, *Crisis and Conversion in Apuleius' Metamorphoses*, Ann Arbor 1996; T.M. Finn, *From Death to Rebirth*, New York 1997; J.T. Sanders, *Charisma, Converts, Competitors*, London 2000; S.J. Chester, *Conversion at Corinth*, London 2003; cf. Marshall and Bilde in this volume, but *contra* Bremmer's understanding (72). Moreover, since most scholars (including those who argue against conversion in mysteries) acknowledge that conversion took place in the philosophical groups, i.e., within a polytheistic framework, monotheism itself is not an argument. Many scholars also speak of modern conversions outside monotheistic religions, e.g., P. van der Veer, *Conversion and Coercion*, in: J.N. Bremmer *et al.* (eds.), *Cultures of Conversion*, Leuven 2006.

51 This wall was gradually formed after and because of the first decades of scholarship in which the mysteries were regarded as mere (prior and primitive) versions of Christianity.

52 Modern scholars work with many types of conversions (moral, intellectual, affectional, social, etc.), and these can be applied to antiquity as well (cf. Bøgh, forthcoming). Cf. Georges and Marshall in this volume for intellectual and ontological conversions.

signal that we must expect conversion to have consequences in this life, not just the next. Only few testaments from the initiates themselves will fulfill all requirements, but this is primarily due to the preservation and nature of the relevant materials which are often archaeological. But here, the literary outsider sources are valuable. They mention conflicts with families, they describe the importance of the decision, the values entailed in the choice, and the profound level of change, and they paint a picture of undivided loyalty to the cult, all of which (in its admittedly exaggerated form) we cannot expect to find in, say, inscriptional evidence from Bacchants themselves.

The literary sources analysed in the first part of the paper reveal that talking about conversion in the Bacchic cult should not present a problem in light of the definition mentioned above. Initiation led to a new religious identity as a Bacchant, strong commitment, and new ritual behaviour in the context of a new religious community. Versnel (1990, 170–74) has called Euripides' *Bacchae* the only pagan example of a "forerunner" of conversion before the Roman period.[53] The drama is loaded with the terminology of transformation, constant incitements to embrace Dionysos' rites, terms signaling complete loyalty to the god, and dichotomies of in – out, right – wrong, happiness – devastation. All of this comes close to patterns of later conversion stories. The drama also portrays a clear distinction between "insiders" and "outsiders" who oppose them,[54] just as in Livy. In the story of Skyles, his choice puts him in total opposition to his former community, and the picture painted by Livy of the Italian Bacchants is also a typical portrayal of single-mindedly devoted converts, interested in little other than their new cult, fanatically recruiting new victims, killing their opponents, and with no other loyalties than to the cult and each other. And as in modern times where new cults have often been accused of brainwashing new members or alluring them with false promises, we also find in the ancient texts outsider assumptions that initiates were either forced or tricked into joining the cult or allured by (false) promises of happiness and bliss. We thus find in these literary texts a number of themes recognisable from later conversion studies and stories. Hence, instead of denying the existence of conversion in the cult of Dionysos because we lack extensive evidence for it in the insider sources, or because we cannot take outsider sources at face value, it is more interesting to investigate, on basis of the points of agreement between insider and outsider testimonies what *type* of conversion we find in a Dionysiac context.

---

53 With reference to Nock, Versnel, 1990, 194 abstains from calling it a conversion story, because pagans were not monotheistic, but adds that polytheistic henotheism – so clearly conveyed in the *Bacchae* – could provide similar experiences.

54 E.g., in *Bacchae* (331), where Cadmus urges the resisting Pentheus: "come and live with us" (οἴκει μεθ᾽ ἡμῶν) – the dichotomy is clear.

A first point of similarity is, as mentioned, that both outsider and insider sources testify that Bacchic initiation was important for this life and not the next, and that initiates were thought to undergo some sort of transformation. However, in contrast to Euripides' representation in his dramas, we have no insider testimonies that participation in the cult had consequences for the way the initiates generally lived their life or for their general identity. To be a Bacchant was rather in tune with a specific way of and certain values in life, not a profound change in behaviour outside of the rituals.

There were obvious differences in regard to how the seriousness of the choice was presented. But even though it was never a question of life or death in real life, there is no reason to doubt that the choice was indeed important for most individuals. Both insiders and outsiders agree that initiation was not always a personal choice although the aspect of force and deceit is only found in outsider testimonies.[55] When children were initiated by their parents, as seen in the insider sources, we can hardly speak about conversion (even if they may reflect their parents'). Yet even in these cases, we cannot refute the possibility, indeed some sources testify, that initiation and subsequent participation in the rituals was important to the child and required future commitment.[56] Moreover, it is highly relevant to take affectional and social benefits of conversion into consideration when we speak of becoming part of a group whose members had known each other most of their life.[57] According to researchers of modern conversions, conversion is not primarily about embracing a new ideology or spiritual transformations, but about bringing one's religious behaviour in alignment with that of one's social circles.[58] Moreover, it is gradually being realised how conversion can be instrumental in achieving social approval or the feeling of being loved by others.[59] But this is not characteristic for all types of conversion. In fact, some modern theories have designed a specific terminology for the conversions which are

---

55 This was also the case in Christianity; often entire families (were) converted as the result of a paternal decision.

56 Many testimonies mention only the convert's participation in the Bacchic cult, not in other cults. All pagans were polytheists, but their actual commitment to one cult may have mattered more than any others, especially after initiation (cf. the concept of henotheistic conversions, see, e.g., Alvar, 2008, 161).

57 Actually, change in *belief* precedes participation in only 2 out of 6 conversion types in the Lofland /Skonovd model (J. Lofland / N. Skonovd, *Conversion Motifs*, in: JSSR 20/4 (1981), 373–385).

58 R. Stark / R. Finke, *Acts of Faith. Explaining the Human Side of Religion*, Berkeley 2000, 11.

59 D. Hak, *Conversion as Rational Choice*, in: J.N. Bremmer / W. van Bekkum / A. Molendijk (eds.), *Paradigms, Poetics, and Politics of Conversion*, Leuven 2006, 19–24.

primarily characterised by affectional relations to other group members.[60] Thus, even when we cannot properly speak of prior conversion, such as in cases of children's initiations,[61] initiation undoubtedly mattered to a much higher degree on the personal level than generally assumed, although neither for the benefit of a happy afterlife, nor (at first) because of ideological or "religious" concerns.

Also interesting for the topic of conversion are other points of overlap between outsiders and insiders. As we saw, the consequences of the choice were presented differently in the two types of sources. This is also recognisable from modern conversion stories and is thus not surprising in regard to the theme of morality, values, and virtues, but the differences may not be so great after all. Briefly put, converting to the Bacchic cult signalled an embracement of freedom, harmony, joy, and equality seen from the positive angle, death and moral corruption from the negative. Nonetheless, it is noticeable that the number of examples of outsider viewpoints that conversion was decidedly bad for your morality was *not* equalled by a similar amount of insider statements that initiates had superior moral virtues, except in the Orphic-Dionysiac sources. In many other insider testimonies we find the theme of good and evil, but not in the sense that people should act according to new, superior moral standards. Rather, the *topos* of good and evil reflects that initiation placed the convert once and for all in a new state of "good-ness", perhaps somewhat similar to Christian grace. This state was dependent on both the rituals and the secret knowledge transmitted during initiation, but it seemed to have an effect on how you basically conceived of your life, not on behaviour or your view on other people's behaviour.

Nor was the knowledge presented as an intellectual benefit – indeed, the seeking of wisdom was explicitly denounced in the *Bacchae*. Understanding or knowing the "truth" of life and death, and of good and evil was thus part of Bacchic conversion, but both types of sources seem to confirm that it was neither a moral, nor an intellectual type of conversion. An important point is the reports of undivided loyalty to the cult which both Livy and Euripides reported. The above-mentioned funerary epitaph of Dion also suggests a high

---

60 Lofland / Skonovd, 1981, call them "affectional", K. Pargament "religious group conversions" (*The Psychology of Religious Coping*, New York 1997), others "interactionist/horizontal" conversions (L. Berzano / E. Martoglio, *Conversion as a New Lifestyle*, in: G. Giordan (ed.), *Conversion in the Age of Pluralism*, Leiden 2009, 213–242.

61 However, L. Rambo, *Understanding Religious Conversion*, New Haven 1993, operates with a form of conversion called "intensification" which refers to a strengthening of "belief" within your already existing religion; some Bacchic children probably underwent this kind of conversion in later life, cf. the twins, Bacchides, mentioned above.

degree of emotional devotion to Dionysos. Such self-portraits of emotional converts are very rare in the Bacchic cult compared to some testimonies from other cults (especially the Isis cult), despite the fact that Dionysiac sources are the most widespread among cults in antiquity. Nonetheless, the image of more or less exclusive loyalty towards the cult is also found in other primary sources, e.g., in the many inscriptions that mention only the role of the Bacchic cult (and not other cults) in the deceased's life and in the testimonies that suggest mental or physical branding of initiates.

However, the most important point of agreement between the two types of sources is the weight put on the ritual participation. In some cases, the rituals may have simply been the natural extension of personal devotion to Dionysos, but in many insider and outsider sources alike, the rituals take the primary place and are the only thing mentioned. Moreover, it is significant that the initiates' new status, Bacchos or Bacchê, is not only identical with the epithet of the deity, but also with the verb and ritual, to *"bacchein"*. Hence, there is every reason to acknowledge the importance of the rituals if we want to understand the value and type of conversions which, probably in many cases, were characteristic of the Dionysiac cult. The personal effects of ecstatic rituals, of course, should not be underestimated.[62] But equally important is the fact that celebrating Bacchic rituals was always a communal (and utopian) experience. All cults included ritual praxis and collective action, but the profoundly communal aspects of Bacchism do in fact stand out among contemporary cults and have for this reason been stressed by numerous scholars (see n. 30). Thus, in the Bacchic cult, collectivity was actually a precondition for performing rituals, and communality was not only a sort of by-effect, but it was the main result of them. The aim of Bacchic rituals was to annihilate individualism by merging each soul into the united experience of the *thiasos* as well as annihilating personal identity by casting the participants as members of the mythical *thiasos*.[63] The rituals mattered because they were of great personal value (this is clear in the sources), but their value actually lay in being anti-personal and profoundly communal. This particularity of Bacchic rituals probably illuminates why both Livy and Euripides were struck by the overwhelming degree of close bonds between the Bacchants, a state of affairs confirmed by wording of the senatorial decree and the great amount of group dedications found in the Bacchic context;

---

62 As seen above, they make you happy, they clear away "depressive anxiety," make you whole again, etc.

63 Through initiation, humans became members of the mythical thiasos: "All the dancing of a Bacchic kind and cultivated by those who indulge in drunken imitations of Nymphs, Pans, Silens and Satyrs (as they call them), when performing certain rites of expiation and initiation" (Pl., *Laws*, 815c).

their feeling of close-knit communality thus derived, in part, from their communal and repeated ritual experience. Thus if, as I claim, access to and participation in the rituals because of the utopian and actual community (and the joy deriving from this context) was one of the most important reasons for, and indeed characteristic for, Bacchic conversions, we can characterise them as communalistic, or – with a modern terminology – *interactionist* or *revivalist* (Lofland / Skonovd, 1981). These are characterised as mild conversions which rely on crowd conformity and are characterised by feelings of intensive joy in group contexts. In addition, the Dionysiac type of conversion was clearly also social and affectional in character, since the converts either had or (because of the communal rituals and life-long participation) developed emotional ties to other participants in a group. Finally, since almost no sources reveal that their conversion had a profound impact on life and behaviour outside of the rituals and group meetings it is certainly a so-called "soft conversion".

Conclusion

Above, I have tried to illuminate different aspects of the choice to become a Bacchant as they were reported by outsiders and insiders. The importance and consequences of the choice were greatly exaggerated by the outsiders, but their perspective should not be overlooked as a source of information on why people chose to become Bacchants and how much it mattered to them because there were considerable and significant points of overlaps with the insider sources as well. This is important because the outsider descriptions come closer to conversion stories than do the mere glimpses of reality preserved by insider sources. The outsider testimonies do not prove that all Bacchants were converts, nor do they tell us what it was always like to be a Bacchic convert, but they tell us how it could be because conversion was a real possibility in Dionysism, although the experience, motivation and outcome were not identical with that of Isiac or Christian "hard" convert. Bacchic conversion did not imply a life devoid of interest in this-worldly affairs or a life filled with spiritual concerns, as was an ideal in Christianity.[64] There was no ideal in Dionysism to alter the total identity of the converts, as in Christianity, but there were other ideals and values, such as joy, freedom, and communality; even though the choice to be initiated as a part of the conversion process was not so serious in reality as it is presented in the literary sources, where it caused weeping, gnashing of teeth and destruction, this does not mean that it was insignificant or without consequences for

---

64 See Engberg and Rebillard in this book for examples of these ideals, and that they were not always lived out.

this life. It thus placed the individual in a new religious community, both an actual close-knit group and a spiritual one experienced during rituals, and it provided him or her with new religious – Bacchic – identity, a new perspective on life and death, new cultic behaviour, as well as a life-long loyalty and commitment.

Éric Rebillard

Becoming Christian in Carthage in the Age of Tertullian

Abstract: The author considers what the choice of becoming Christian entails in terms of visibility and commitment in second-century Carthage. He reviews Christian identity markers and analyses how much relevance Christians gave to their new religion. In contrast to what Tertullian wished and claimed, many Christians usually operated with a multiplicity of identities, not just one, namely "Christian".

In his magisterial study of Tertullian, Timothy Barnes notes: "It can surely be no accident that Tertullian's three earliest extant works are *De spectaculis*, *De idololatria* and what appears in modern editions as the second book of *De cultu feminarum*. All three address themselves to similar problems: how ought Christians to live out a life of faith in a pagan society?"[1] To present the conciliation of Christian faith and social life in Carthage at the end of the second century as a problem is to implicitly adopt Tertullian's own point of view. Indeed, most scholars have underestimated how crucial it was to Tertullian's rhetorical strategy to challenge Christians on this "problem". In this paper, I will consider what the choice of becoming Christian entails in terms of visibility and commitment in second-century Carthage without assuming that conciliation was an issue for all Christians. In order to do so, first, I will review identity markers and contexts in which Christians identify themselves to others and/or could be identified by others, and, second, I will examine when and how much Christianness is relevant in the everyday life of Christians.[2]

1. Identity markers

To become Christian, i.e., to acquire membership in one of the Christian "organisations" of Carthage at the time of Tertullian (I use organisation in order to avoid such terms as community or church), was in most cases an individual choice. Tertullian attests to the practice of baptising small children, a practice that he does not approve of, but does not present as novel.[3] However, it seems clear that most Christians were baptised in adulthood.

---

1 T.D. Barnes, *Tertullian. A Historical and Literary Study*, Oxford ²1985, 93.
2 "Christianness" simply means "the Christian quality"; I use it to designate the religious identity of the Christians. See É. Rebillard, *Christians and their Many Identities in Late Antiquity. North Africa, 200–450 CE*, Ithaca 2012.
3 Tert., bapt. 18.

Christian membership started before baptism with the admission to the ranks of the catechumens. Tertullian explicitly addresses the catechumens in some of his pastoral treatises. In *On the shows*, for instance, he says at the outset that both catechumens and baptised Christians must stay away from public shows.[4] Furthermore, he also explicitly envisages that catechumens be caught up in persecution, and he presents martyrdom as a baptism of blood.[5] Tertullian does not provide any information about the duration of the catechumenal stage, but his advice not to grant baptism too readily to unmarried people and even widows, unless they are firmly committed to continence,[6] suggests that some people stayed in this liminal position for quite some time. In *On the prescriptions of heretics*, Tertullian rants about "heretics" who do not adequately distinguish catechumens and baptised Christians and let the former take part in the Eucharist.[7] Though these attacks clearly imply a difference of status between catechumens and baptised Christians, the distinction does not seem to be relevant to Tertullian when he discusses pastoral issues. Therefore, I will not distinguish between catechumens and baptised Christians in the following discussion.

External markers

I will not discuss external markers at length. Just as Jews in the Diaspora are not distinctive because of their looks, clothing, speech, names, or occupations,[8] so Christians are not in Carthage. In *To Scapula*, Tertullian states that Christians "can be recognised only for the reformation of their former vices."[9] He is even more explicit in *On the shows* where he addresses an imaginary Christian going to the amphitheater to watch a gladiatorial game in the following terms:

> What will you do if you are caught in the heat of these impious applauses?
> It's not as if you could suffer anything from men (nobody recognises you as a
> Christian), but think about what will happen in heaven.[10]

There is of course much sarcasm in the rhetorical question. However, the general sense of the message depends on the truth of the assertion that a

---

4   Tert., spect. 1.1. Cf. also Jacobsen in this volume on instructions of Christian catechumens and for the creed used as an identity marker in later periods.

5   Tert., bapt. 16.1–2.

6   Tert., bapt. 18.6.

7   Tert., praescr. 41.2; 41.4.

8   S. Cohen, *The Beginnings of Jewishness. Boundaries, Varieties, Uncertainties*, Berkeley 1999, 25–68.

9   *Nec aliunde noscibiles quam de emendatione uitiorum pristinorum*, Tert., Scap. 2.10.

10 *Quid facies in illo suffragiorum impiorum aestuario reprehensus? Non quasi aliquid illic pati possis ab hominibus (nemo te cognoscit Christianum), sed recogita, quid de te fiat in caelo*, Tert., spect. 27.2.

Christian cannot be identified through external markers. Some physical signs and behaviour could however function as visible identity markers.

Tokens of membership recognition

Two physical gestures could reveal Christian membership to others. The first is the kiss as a greeting among Christians. Tertullian mentions it as a practice for which a non-Christian husband might fault his Christian wife.[11] Michael Philip Penn has shown that this greeting kiss functions as a sign of identification, "both to reaffirm membership in the community and as a tool of exclusion."[12] Though a public greeting kiss was quite common among non-Christians, it was restricted mostly to family and friends;[13] the extension of the practice to coreligionists would therefore have distinguished the Christians.

The second gesture is the making of the sign of the cross on the forehead.[14] In *To my wife*, Tertullian mentions this gesture among other signs through which a Christian wife might betray her religion to her non-Christian husband.[15] In *On the military crown*, he lists all sort of circumstances and contexts in which a Christian could cross himself:

> At every forward step and movement, at every going in and out, when we put on our clothes and shoes, when we bathe, when we sit at the table, when we light the lamps, on couch, on seat, in all the ordinary actions of daily life, we trace upon the forehead the sign [scil. of the cross].[16]

This gesture is not (or rather is not only) a token of membership recognition, but could also function as an identifier in the eyes of others when performed in public.

Identification by association

Christians could make their religious affiliation known simply by locating themselves among other Christians. This is what Shaye Cohen calls "identifying oneself by association."[17]

---

11 Tert., ux. 2.4,2.
12 M.P. Penn, *Kissing Christians. Ritual and Community in the Late Ancient Church*, Philadelphia 2005, 59.
13 Penn, 2005, 13.
14 F.J. Dölger, *Beitrage zur Geschichte des Kreuzzeichens I*, in: JAC 1 (1958), 5–13.
15 Tert., ux. 5.1.
16 *Ad omnem progressum atque promotum, ad omnem aditum et exitum, ad uestitum, ad calciatum, ad lauacra, ad mensas, ad lumina, ad cubilia, ad sedilia, quacumque nos conuersatio exercet, frontem signaculo terimus*, Tert., cor. 3.4.
17 Cohen, 1999, 53.

While most other groups, whether religious or not, would have met at most once a month or even less regularly, Christians in second-century Carthage had daily morning gatherings in addition to the weekly evening meeting.[18] These meetings, if we are to believe Tertullian, made the Christians quite conspicuous in Carthage. Indeed, Tertullian voices the concern that their meeting places were known to outsiders and that they could be harassed there: "Every day we stand siege; every day we are betrayed; above all in our gatherings and our assemblies we are surprised."[19] Christians, according to *On flight in time of persecution*, reluctantly go to meetings when they are under pressure: "Since we assemble without order, and assemble at the same time, and flock in large numbers to the church, the pagans make inquiries about us and we fear lest they become agitated about us."[20] What Tertullian reports as true under the conditions of persecution was very likely true also in ordinary times: to join the Christian gatherings was a clear way of expressing one's membership.

Beyond church-going, there were a number of other occasions for a Christian to associate with other Christians. In *To my wife*, Tertullian mentions two types of charitable expeditions: visiting martyrs in prison and visiting the poor.[21] Because of the conditions of imprisonment, it was very common for prisoners to rely on family and friends for their maintenance.[22] However, Christians who visited martyrs were quite likely identified as Christians by the guards and even other visitors because the prisoners they visited were known to be Christians awaiting their trial or execution.[23] Visits to the poor would also have made Christians conspicuous, especially when they were called into areas where they were not expected to be seen. This is clearly what Tertullian has in mind when he describes how uncomfortable a non-Christian husband would be with his wife making such visits: "For who

---

18 A. McGowan, *Rethinking Agape and Eucharist in Early North African Christianity*, in: StLi 34 (2004), 165–176; V.A. Alikin, *The Earliest History of the Christian Gathering. Origin, Development, and Content of the Christian Gathering in the First to Third Centuries*, Leiden 2010, 93f. 142f.

19 *Cottidie obsidemur, cottidie prodimur, in ipsis plurimum coetibus et congregationibus nostris opprimimur*, Tert., apol. 7.4; cf. nat. 1.7,19.

20 *Quoniam incondite convenimus et simul convenimus et complures concurrimus in ecclesiam, quaerimur a nationibus et timemus, ne turbentur nationes hae*, Tert., fug. 3.4.

21 Tert., ux. 2.4,2.

22 P. Pavón, *Régimen de vida y tratamiento del preso durante los tres primeros siglos del imperio*, in: C. Bertrand-Dagenbach (ed.), *Carcer. Prison et privation de liberté dans l'antiquité classique*, Paris 1999, 105–113.

23 See A. McGowan, *Discipline and Diet. Feeding the Martyrs in Roman Carthage*, in: HThR 96 (2003), 455–476.

would let his wife, for the sake of visiting the brethren, go round from street to street to others' houses, and especially all around the slums?"[24]

Identification by abstention

Christians could also make themselves conspicuous in a Roman city like Carthage by what they did *not* do and by associations they did *not* maintain. Two accusations seem to have been quite common and are reported by Tertullian in the *Apology*: Christians do not worship gods and do not offer sacrifices for the emperors.[25]

I will leave aside for now the question of their actual abstention and focus on how abstention would make Christians visible. James B. Rives concludes a review of the evidence with this statement:

> Conspicuous refusal to observe a civic festival would no doubt have drawn the unfavourable attention of neighbours and provoked suspicions of disloyalty and misanthropy; if the occasion concerned imperial cult, it might even have led to charges before a Roman official. But those who were simply uninterested could no doubt quietly absent themselves without anyone caring, and some people presumably did just that: such events were not to everyone's taste.[26]

The reactions in Carthage to the incident reported in *On the military crown* confirm that Christians might have opted for a quiet abstention if they absented themselves at all from civic festivals. In 212, in Rome,[27] during a *donativum* ceremony, a soldier refused to wear his crown and so disclosed himself as Christian. Carthaginian Christians disagreed about the propriety of the soldier's attitude: the pro-New Prophecy Christians, such as Tertullian, praised his behaviour while "mainstream" Christians did not.[28] However, even Tertullian does not recommend conspicuous abstention. In a city of the size of Carthage,[29] quiet abstention would most likely escape attention.

---

24 *Quis autem sinat coniugem suam uisitandorum fratrum gratia uicatim aliena et quidem pauperiora quaeque tuguria circuire*, Tert., ux. 2.4,2.

25 Tert., apol. 10.1.

26 J.B. Rives, *The Decree of Decius and the Religion of Empire*, in: JRS 89 (1999), 135–154 (147).

27 I follow the dating and location of Y. Le Bohec, *Tertullien, De Corona, 1. Carthage ou Lambèse?*, in: REAug 38 (1992), 6–18; see Y. Duval, *Lambèse chrétienne, la gloire et l'oubli. De la Numidie romaine à l'Ifrîqiya*, Paris 1995, 31f.

28 Tert., cor. 1.4; see J. Fontaine, *Tertullien, Sur la Couronne*, Paris 1966, 50, and now W. Tabbernee, *Fake Prophecy and Polluted Sacraments. Ecclesiastical and Imperial Reactions to Montanism*, Leiden 2007, 232–234.

29 The population of Carthage in the second century is now estimated to 70,000 inhabitants; see P. Gros, *Carthage romaine. Résurrection d'une capitale*, in: J.-C.

It is probably not an accident if neither Tertullian nor any North African martyr narrative record any denunciation brought before a governor as having originated in Carthage. It is as if denunciations by neighbours, family or friends were less likely to arise in a large city.

I also wonder whether accusations of not worshiping the gods were sustained more by early examples of martyrs and common knowledge about Christian beliefs than by any controversy generated by Christians' actual abstention from participation in public worship of the gods. Indeed, in the *Apology*, the only example brought forth by Tertullian is that of a Christian compelled to sacrifice who heroically (or stubbornly) holds to his refusal.[30] However, Tertullian does indicate that Christians were accused of not celebrating the holidays of the emperors along with the rest of the population.[31] A discussion in *On idolatry* about decorating doors with lamps and wreaths on the occasion of an imperial holiday also suggests that abstention from this ritual would have marked out the Christian houses quite clearly.[32] Thus, abstention from religious practices shared by other inhabitants of Carthage would have singled out Christians at least to some extent.

Conclusion

It seems that, whether through participation or abstention, Christians made themselves identifiable in their proximate social contexts. This impression is supported by a passage of the *Apology* in which Tertullian mentions those who gossip about the conversion of Christians:

> Well, then, what does it mean when most people shut their eyes and run so blindly into hatred of the Christian name, that, even if they bear favourable testimony to a man, they throw in some detestation of the name? 'A good man,' they say, 'this Caius Seius, except that he is a Christian.' Then another says: 'I am surprised that that wise man, Lucius Titius, has suddenly become a Christian.' [...] As sure as a man is reformed by the name, he gives offence. The advantage does not balance the hatred felt for Christians.[33]

Depaule / R. Ilbert / C. Nicolet (eds.), Mégapoles méditerranéennes. Géographie urbaine rétrospective, Rome 2000, 534–544.

30 Tert., apol. 27.1.
31 Tert., apol. 35.5.
32 Tert., idol. 15.
33 *Quid quod ita plerique clausis oculis in odium eius impingunt, ut bonum alicui testimonium ferentes admisceant nominis exprobrationem? Bonus vir Gaius Seius, tantum quod Christianus. Item alius: Ego miror Lucium Titium, sapientem virum, repente factum Christianum. [...] Ut quisque hoc nomine emendatur, offendit. Tanti non est bonum, quanti odium Christianorum,* Tert., apol. 3.1–4.

The names, Caius Seius and Lucius Titius, are not only fictive, but they actually come from law books where they are used as typical names in stories invented to illustrate a point of law.[34] Although Tertullian's point is apologetic – we have already seen his argument for the moral superiority of Christians – it is very likely that an individual's conversion to Christianity gave rise to gossip among his neighbours and acquaintances.

2. Christianness

So far, I have considered a number of possible contexts in which Christians identify themselves and could be identified by others. I now want to shift from a review of identity markers to an analysis of how much relevance Christians give to their Christianness. It is a way of asking about the nature of their commitment.

Situational selection

As mentioned already, Tertullian's goal in *On the shows* is to prove that the pleasures of public shows are contrary to Christian faith.[35] He refutes the following objection, attributed to pagans and thereby automatically disqualified:

> Pleasures of the eyes and the ears in things external do not hinder religion in the mind and conscience, and God is not offended by human enjoyment, of which it is no crime to partake, in its proper time and in its proper place, with all due fear and honour secured to God.[36]

What lies behind this justification is the affirmation of a principle of situational selection, according to which time and place define whether Christianness is relevant.

The same principle is opposed by Christian women who do not intend to change the way they dress and adorn themselves. According to Tertullian in *On the apparel of women*, most Christian women "so conduct themselves as if chastity consisted only in the integrity of the flesh and the avoidance of actual fornication."[37] He thus acknowledges that Christian women agree

---

34 S. Lancel, *Monsieur Dupont en Latin*, in: M. Renard / R. Schilling (eds.), *Hommages à Jean Bayet*, Brussels 1964, 357–364.

35 Tert., spect. 1.1.

36 *Nihil obstrepere religioni in animo et in conscientia tanta solacia extrinsecus oculorum vel aurium nec vero deum offendi oblectatione hominis, qua salvo erga deum metu et honore suo in tempore et suo in loco frui scelus non sit,* Tert., spect. 1.3.

37 *Ita ingrediuntur quasi pudicitia in sola carnis integritate et stupri auersione consistat,* Tert., cult. fem. 2.1,2.

that chastity is required by their faith. However, his contention is that these women have too narrow a conception of what chastity implies. In fact, his argument provides evidence that these women think that their religion is irrelevant to the way they dress and adorn themselves.

The treatise *On idolatry* works in much the same way. Tertullian acknowledges that Christians regard only a limited number of acts as idolatrous:

> Most people simply think that idolatry is only then to be assumed if somebody makes a burnt offering or brings a sacrifice or organises a sacrificial banquet or makes himself guilty of certain other sacred activities or priesthoods.[38]

However, he himself defends a much broader understanding of idolatry as the worship of demons, such that "every sin is called *idololatria*, because it is directed against God, and every thing directed against God is in fact a service to the demons."[39] Thus, one area of contention is that of occupation, which some Christians do not consider relevant to religion. Tertullian's discussion of idol makers and other artists involved in religious activities reveals that the extent of disagreement within the Christian organisations is quite impressive. He sets out to refute the objections raised by artists who seek to become Christian yet do not want to renounce their occupation.[40] The excuse that they are merely making a living is quickly dismissed, but Tertullian must also reject several scriptural texts presented in favour of the artists' admission to membership: 1 Cor 7:20 ("As everybody is found, so let him remain"), 1 Thess 4:11 ("Work with your hands, just as we told you"), and Numbers 21:8–9 where Moses makes a bronze serpent. The discussion is not just theoretical: "The hands of idol-makers are not content to receive from other hands what they defile, but they themselves even transmit to others what they have defiled: makers of idols are chosen into the ecclesiastical order."[41] There are idol-makers not only among the lay Christians, but even within the ranks of the clergy in Carthage. Other occupations are debated as well: astrologer, schoolmaster, trader. The range of issues associated with them makes clear that Christians do not consider the social arena of occupation to be determined by religion.

---

38 *Plerique idololatrian simpliciter existimant his solis modis interpretandam, si quis aut incendat aut immolet aut polluceat aut sacris aliquibus aut sacerdotiis obligetur*, Tert., idol. 2.2.
39 J.C.M. van Winden, *Idolum and Idololatria in Tertullian*, in: VigChr 36 (1982), 108–114 (113).
40 Tert., idol. 5.1.
41 *Parum sit, si ab aliis manibus accipiant quod* contaminent, *sed etiam ipsae tradunt aliis quod contaminauerunt: adleguntur in ordinem ecclesiasticum artifices idolorum*, Tert., idol. 7.2–3.

Multiple identities

In the case of schoolmasters, although he proposes clear-cut solutions, Tertullian reveals how complex it can be to negotiate different roles: Christian believer and schoolmaster, Christian believer and parent. He mentions a common objection: "If teaching literature is not permitted to God's servants, learning it will not be allowed either."[42] It seems that there were some schoolmasters who did not want to change occupation after their conversion, and also some parents who (lacking the option of an exclusively Christian educational institution) were hesitant to send their children to school. Tertullian's answer is unequivocal: Christian children must go to school as there is no other way to learn to read and write,[43] but learning and teaching are two different things. The school-master must inevitably catechise about idols, while the pupil can always reject some of what he learns at school.[44]

Tertullian's awareness that other identities can conflict with Christian-ness is clear also in *On the apparel of women*. Thus, he concedes that some women may be compelled to display their status in public, but he calls for restraint: "those of you who are compelled by consideration of wealth, birth, or past dignities to appear in public in such pompous apparel, do make use of moderation in this domain."[45] Again, he grants that behaviour might be dictated by considerations other than religion when he imagines that women might be concerned about what their social peers would say if they were to change their dressing habits: "Well, but it is urged by some: 'Let not the Name be blasphemed in us, if we make any derogatory change from our old style and dress'." The answer is again ironical: "This is a grand blasphemy if it is said: 'Ever since she became a Christian, she walks in poorer garb'."[46] In another passage, Tertullian accepts that interpersonal relations can also create obligations: "And if the requirements of friendships or duties towards pagans call you, why not go forth clad in your own armor?"[47] Tertullian's concessions on these

---

42 *Si docere litteras dei seruis non licet, etiam nec discere licebit,* Tert., idol. 10.4.
43 Tert., idol. 10.6.
44 Tert., idol. 10.5–6.
45 *Tum si quas uel diuitiarum suarum uel natalium uel retro dignitatum ratio com-pellit ita pompaticas progredi, ut sapientiam consecutae, temperare saltem ab huiusmodi curate,* Tert., cult. fem. 2.9,4.
46 *Sed enim a quibusdam dicitur: Ne blasphemetur nomen in nobis si quid de pris-tino habitu et cultu detrahamus* [...]. *Grandis blasphemia si qua dicatur: Ex quo facta est christiana, pauperius incedit!* Tert., cult. fem. 2.11,3.
47 *Ac si necessitas amicitiarum officiorumque gentilium uos uocat, cur non uestris armis indutae proceditis,* Tert., cult. fem. 2.11,2.

points refer to contexts and situations in which Christianness is not necessarily activated by Christian women.

The same notion of social duty is used by Tertullian himself in *On idolatry* in order to allow Christians to participate in private celebrations (such
as betrothals and weddings) organised by non-Christians. To the objection
"But sacrifices are attached to these solemnities," Tertullian replies: "Sup-
pose I am invited and the reason for my social duty is not a sacrifice, then
the performance of my service can take place at pleasure."[48] The objection
could have come from Christians who have reservations about participating
in private ceremonies during which a sacrifice is performed, or from those
who see a possible contradiction in the regular participation of Christians in
betrothals, weddings, and other non-Christian ceremonies. Tertullian's position on the topic needs to be emphasised as it departs from the exclusivism
that is traditionally attributed to him.[49]

Intermittency

Finally, the way Tertullian constantly challenges Christians to justify their
behaviour attests indirectly to the fundamental intermittency of Christianness. Indeed, we should always bear in mind that, whether or not we sup-
pose that the objections refuted by Tertullian were actually argued by some
Christians, they are presented in response to Tertullian's challenge and it
need not be assumed that they reflect ordinary cares and concerns. We need
to allow for the disjuncture between the thematisation of religion in the discourse of Tertullian and its enactment in everyday life.[50]

The final section of *On idolatry*, where Tertullian turns his attention to
idolatry in speech and deals with oaths in the names of pagan gods, provides
interesting examples. Tertullian reviews situations in which Christians may
be required to take an oath and in which Christianness was not necessarily
relevant in their eyes. The first scenario is that of a non-Christian confirming

---

48 *Sim uocatus nec ad sacrificium sit titulus officii, et operae meae expunctio quantum sibi licet,* Tert., idol. 16.3.
49 But see G.G. Stroumsa, *Tertullian on Idolatry and the Limits of Tolerance,* in:
G.N. Stanton / G.G. Stroumsa (eds.), *Tolerance and Intolerance in Early Judaism
and Christianity,* Cambridge 1998, 173–184.
50 I owe this insight to R. Brubaker *et al., Nationalist Politics and Everyday Ethnicity in a Transylvanian Town,* Princeton 2006; see 362f. for a similar "disjuncture"
related to ethnicity and nationhood. Cf. Martin in this volume for the ideal of
bridge-burning in Christianity, and Jacobsen's contribution for the acknowledge-
ment that the Christian elitist ideals on Christian identity did not always have a
full impact on the converts' everyday lives.

by oath that he will do what he had promised for a Christian.[51] The second is that of a Christian returning a malediction,[52] and here Tertullian presents himself as an eyewitness to such behaviour. The third scenario involves a non-Christian blessing a Christian in the name of the gods or in the name of the genius of Carthage.[53] Lastly, he addresses the case of a Christian who borrows money and is required to give a guarantee under oath.[54] Tertullian takes up an initial objection: "I have written, but I have not said anything; it is the tongue, not the letter which kills."[55] This is obviously a reference to some scriptural authority, but no one text matches the citation. It looks as if it is a conflation of incorrect reminiscences of 2 Cor 3:6 ("for the letter kills") and James 3:5–10 on the evil of the tongue. (Curiously, Tertullian does not note that the scriptural reference is incorrect.)

Another objection claims exculpation in the fact that the written document has been dictated by the lender.[56] And a final objection says that "the silent voice of the pen and the mute sound of the letters do not count."[57] Tertullian counters this objection with the example of Zacharias, the father of John the Baptist, who was punished by a temporary privation of speech because he did not believe the angel who announced the birth of his son, and regained his voice after he wrote on a tablet the name he chose for his son (Luke 1:20 and 1:62–64). What these exchanges reveal is that such situations were ordinary enough, and that Christians did not routinely activate Christianness within them. It is Tertullian who challenges them to do so and their justifications are after-the-fact. Challenged to interpret their behaviour as Christians, they come up with a reference to the Scriptures or some other argument. However, the justifications themselves clearly show that at the time of their action Christianness was not activated (though it was clearly available). This is what I call the intermittency of Christianness.

Conclusion

Thus, we need to resist Tertullian's selective focus on Christianness. When he evokes everyday situations, he consistently decontextualises them in order to force on them his own agenda about what Christianness should entail. However, the numerous objections he feels compelled to refute show that his point of view is not shared, or at least not shared by all Christians. On the

---

51 Tert., idol. 21.1–3.
52 Tert., idol. 21.4–5.
53 Tert., idol. 22.1–2.
54 Tert., idol. 23.1.
55 *Scripsi, inquit, sed nihil dixi: lingua, non littera occidit*, Tert., idol. 23.2.
56 Tert., idol. 23.3.
57 *Non ualet tacita uox in stilo et mutus in litteris sonus*, Tert., idol. 23.5.

other hand, the intermittency of Christianness must not be interpreted as a measure of its importance or even of its significance. Christians are aware of the issues associated with handling multiple identities, and their awareness is all the more acute that religion was new as a type of identity that could affect one's behaviour.[58] It is difficult to compare the way Christians handle their religious identity with the way members of other groups do, with the exception of Jews, who seem to have handle it in much the same way once Judaism can be considered as a religion.[59] What I emphasise in this paper is that we cannot assume that Christians give constant salience to their Christianness, but it does not mean that Christianness was irrelevant to their behaviour. Once this qualification is taken into account, it remains to compare Christians on a new basis with the members of other religious groups.

---

58 See J. North, *The Development of Religious Pluralism*, in: J. Lieu / J. North / T. Rajak (eds.), *The Jews among Pagans and Christian in the Roman Empire*, London 1992, 174–193; J. North, *Roman Religion*, Oxford 2000, 66–71.

59 S. Mason, *Jews, Judaeans, Judaizing, Judaism. Problems of Categorization in Ancient History*, in: JSJ 38 (2007), 457–512; D. Boyarin, *Rethinking Jewish Christianity. An Argument for Dismantling a Dubious Category (to Which is Appended a Correction of my Border Lines)*, in: JQR 99 (2009), 7–36; S. Schwartz, *Imperialism and Jewish Society, 200 B.C.E. to 640 C.E*, Princeton 2001, 162–176.

Jan N. Bremmer

Conversion in the oldest Apocryphal Acts

Abstract: Bremmer challenges Nock's individual and psychological approach to the phenomenon of conversion in antiquity by investigating the conversions found in the often overlooked *Apocryphal acts*. In the *Acts*, conversions are most often spurred by miracles and are mediated through other Christians. Nock's definition thus neglects the social factor in conversion, which plays a role both before and after conversion.

In that fateful year 1933, the Harvard Frothingham Professor of the History of Religions, Arthur Darby Nock (1902–1963) published his study *Conversion* with the subtitle *The Old and the New in Religion from Alexander the Great to Augustine of Hippo*.[1] The book is rightly considered a classic and, together with William James' *Varieties of Religious Experience* from 1902, it may be considered the only book from before the Second World War that people still read on the topic, certainly the only ancient history book. Yet, if we want to have a good idea of what conversion meant in antiquity, should we still turn to Nock? There are several ways of answering this question, and I will try to do so here by looking at conversion in the *Apocryphal acts*. Their illustration of the reasons and motivations for the choice to convert, namely mostly miracles and social aspects, will serve as a starting point to make some observations on the phenomenon of conversion in second-century Christianity.

In his book, Nock supplies us with a wide ranging survey of conversion in the ancient world, but the part about Christianity is hardly the strongest. Nock's heart was not really with Christianity in the later centuries, and his best work concentrated on the Jewish, Christian, and pagan inter-relationships at the turn of the Christian era.[2] That is perhaps why he did

---

1 A.D. Nock, *Conversion*, Oxford 1933. In the main text, I refer to the book just by page numbers; see also A.D. Nock, *Bekehrung*, in: RAC 2 (1954), 105–118.

2 For Nock and his work, see the obituaries by A.-J. Festugière, in: RAr 1 (1963), 203–205; M.P. Nilsson, in: Gnomon 15 (1963), 318f., and H. Chadwick / E.R. Dodds, in: JRS 53 (1963), 168f.; Z. Stewart *et al.*, *A Faculty Minute. Arthur Darby Nock*, in: HSCP 68 (1964), xi–xiv; note also W.M. Calder III, *Harvard Classics 1950–1956*, in: Eikasmos 4 (1993), 39–49 (41f.) and J.P. Harris / R.S. Smith (eds.), *Men in Their Books*, Hildesheim 1998, 233f.; G. Casadio, *Ancient Mystic Religion. the Emergence of a New Paradigm from A.D. Nock to Ugo Bianchi*, in: Mediterraneo antico 9 (2006), 485–534; rather ungenerous, S. Price, *The Conversion of A. D. Nock in the Context of His Life, Scholarship,*

not take a look at the *Apocryphal acts* for his work on conversion. It must be admitted, of course, that our present time is much more interested in apocryphal literature than the generation of Nock, but its absence from his work, just like a proper study of the martyrs' acts, suggests that Christianity comes a bit short in his still highly readable and inspiring book. Yet, the *Apocryphal acts* constitute an important window into Christian life in the second half of the second century, and it will be the aim of this article to explore its contents in order to gain a better view of early Christian conversion.

Now, the usage of the *Apocryphal acts* as a historical source is of course not without pitfalls. But before we will turn to the methodological questions that their usage raises, I will first turn to the *Acts* themselves. Recent research has made it probable that we should read them in the chronological order *Acts of John*,[3] *Peter*, *Paul*,[4] *Andrew*, which all date from the period ca. 160–200 CE, and *Thomas*, the latter clearly being somewhat later than the other four. The earlier four seem to derive from the same area, Anatolia (the first two perhaps from South West Asia Minor and the next two perhaps from Bithynia), and clearly precede the *Acts of Thomas*.[5] However, from these early *Acts*, the manuscript tradition of the *Acts of Andrew* is particularly poor. The only primitive textual witness is the Codex Vaticanus graecus 808, which does not contain any conversion scenes.[6] I will therefore limit myself to the *Acts of John*, *Peter*, and *Paul*.

---

and Religious View, in: HSCP 105 (2010), 317–339. Note also Mario Mazza's valuable introductory essay to the Italian translation of *Conversion*, *La conversion. Società e religione nel mondo antico*, Rome 1974, i–xlvi.

3   Probably, our present version is a second, revised edition, written in Alexandria at the beginning of the third century, cf. I. Czachesz, *Eroticism and Epistemology in the Apocryphal Acts of John*, in: Nederlands Theologisch Tijdschrift 60 (2006), 59–72. For a possible case of intertextuality of this revised version with the *Acts of Peter*, see K. Sier, *Zum Text der Martyrien von Petrus und Paulus*, in: ZPE 173 (2010), 35–44 (39).

4   Regarding the chronological order of the *Acts of Peter* and *Paul*, I am now convinced of the priority of *Peter* by the discussion of O. Zwierlein, *Petrus in Rom*, Berlin ²2010, 37–39. 82–85. 116; similarly, with a different argument, J. Spittler, *Animals in the Apocryphal Acts of the Apostles. The Wild Kingdom of Early Christian Literature*, Tübingen 2008, 147.

5   Cf. Bremmer, *The Apocryphal Acts. Authors, Place, Time and Readership*, in: J.N. Bremmer (ed.), *The Apocryphal Acts of Thomas*, Leuven 2001, 149–170.

6   This has been overlooked by K.C. Wagener, *Repentant Eve, Perfected Adam. Conversion in the Acts of Andrew*, in: SBL (1991), 348–356; cf. L. Roig Lanzillotta, *Acta Andreae Apocrypha. A New Perspective on the Nature, Intention and Significance of the Primitive Text*, Geneva 2007, 36.

1. The *Acts of John*

In the *Acts of John*, the apostle John arrives in Ephesus, the first place of his wanderings. Here, he is approached by Lycomedes, a member of the executive council of the city. He tells John that he is wondering what to do about his wife Cleopatra who has been paralysed for seven days. But while lamenting his wife's fate, somebody whose identity remains unrevealed, but who, as we learn only shortly later (21) looks like God himself, tells him in a vision that God has sent a man from Miletus who will lift up his wife. Interestingly, Lycomedes approaches John at the moment that he enters the city, as he is at the gate when this conversation takes place. In other words, from the moment of entry into Ephesus the apostle has to do God's work (19).

When they arrive at Cleopatra's bed, Lycomedes bursts out into a moving lament that betrays his already alluded to, but not elaborated, idea of committing suicide before he sees Cleopatra dying. Moreover, he ascribes the bad condition of his wife to the influence of magic: the evil eye of his enemies had hit him because of their envy,[7] an interesting glimpse into the role of magic in everyday life of even the elite (20).[8] The apostle, however, reproaches him for his lamentations and tells him to call upon the Lord and to entreat him for her life and health. Yet, Lycomedes does not do so, but continues to lament in such a manner that he finally gives up the ghost.

The scene seems to be a moment of skillful retardation of the plot as the apostle now starts to reproach God for having sent him, but not having given him the glory that a voice from heaven promised him on his way to Ephesus. It is characteristic of the intellectual level of the *Acts of John* that we do not hear of God manifesting himself in person. In fact, even Homer is rather sparing in his description of a divinity during his or her epiphany.[9] In the enlightened world of Greek and Roman intellectuals, an anthropomorphic epiphany would probably have been too much. We should remember

---

7   For this omnipresent belief in late antiquity, see M.W. Dickie, *Plutarch and Heliodorus on the Evil eye*, in: CP 86 (1991), 17–29; J.D.M. Derrett, *The Evil Eye in the New Testament*, in: Ph. Esler (ed.), *Modelling Early Christianity*, London 1995, 65–72; R. Kalmin, *The Evil Eye in Rabbinic Literature of Late Antiquity*, in: B. Isaac / Y. Shahar (eds.), *Judaea-Palaestina, Babylon and Rome. Jews in Antiquity*, Tübingen 2012, 111–138.

8   Cf. J.N. Bremmer, *Magic in the Apocryphal Acts of the Apostles*, in: J.N. Bremmer / J.R. Veenstra (eds.), *The Metamorphosis of Magic from Late Antiquity to the Early Modern Period*, Leuven 2003, 51–70.

9   *Iliad* 2.182; 10.512; 20.380, cf. the perceptive comments of P. Pucci, *The Song of the Sirens*, Lanham 1998, 81–96.

that in the ancient novel, it is always the less educated or socially inferior who believe in a real epiphany.[10]

As he was complaining, a huge crowd has assembled in front of Lycomedes' house, and John uses this crowd as an argument for Christ to intervene at this moment. Having touched the face of Cleopatra, he tells her to get up. And this she does while crying out with a loud voice: "I arise, Lord, save your Cleopatra" (23). When Cleopatra asks for her husband, John guides her to the other bedroom where she sees him lying. But she controls herself and John orders her to address her husband and to tell him to rise. So she does, and Lycomedes duly returns from the dead. But instead of thanking God, he falls to the ground and kisses John's feet, who of course declines this honour. After being entreated by Cleopatra and Lycomedes, John decides to stay with them instead of going to Kleobios, as he intended to do before (25).

We next read about a miracle performed on behalf of old women. In other words, we go from the pinnacle of society to the very bottom, as old women were in very low standing in antiquity.[11] John dismisses the crowd that had assembled at Lycomedes' house and asks them to reconvene in the theatre the next day in order to witness the power of God, as he will heal the sick and paralytic among those old women.[12] The explicit intent of this healing is the conversion of some of those present in the theatre. Another *stratêgos*, Andronicus, also hears of this promise and is curious to see how the apostle will work "the impossible and incredible." But he also requests John to appear naked without holding anything in his hands and not to mention "the magical name" of Jesus (31), another interesting indication of the place of magic in contemporary society.[13]

---

10 T. Hägg, *Parthenope. Studies in Ancient Greek Fiction*, Copenhagen 2004, 141–155 (146).

11 For an excellent recent bibliography, see J. Masseglia, *"Reasons to be cheerful." Conflicting emotions in the Drunken Old Women of Munich and Rome*, in: A. Chaniotis (ed.), *Unveiling Emotions*, Stuttgart 2012, 413–430; add J.N. Bremmer, *The Old Women of Ancient Greece*, in: J. Blok / P. Mason (eds.), *Sexual Asymmetry. Studies in Ancient Society*, Amsterdam 1987, 191–215.

12 For the central place of the theatre in public life in later antiquity, see A. Chaniotis, *Theatricality beyond the Theater. Staging Public Life in the Hellenistic World*, in: Pallas 47 (1997), 219–259, and id., *Theatre Rituals*, in: P. Wilson (ed.), *The Greek Theatre and Festivals*, Oxford 2007, 48–86; D. Elm, *Mimes into Martyrs. Conversion on Stage*, in: I. Henderson / G. Oegema (eds.), *The Changing Face of Judaism, Christianity, and Other Greco-Roman Religions in Antiquity*, Gütersloh 2006, 87–100.

13 For the name of Jesus in magic, see M. Smith, *Jesus the Magician*, London 1978, 114; B. Kollmann, *Jesus und die Christen als Wundertäter*, Göttingen 1996, 350f.

In the theatre, John tells the crowd that Christ will convert them from their unbelief and shameful desires through a miracle, namely by letting him heal the old women who are exhibited in the theatre, thus convincing even the *stratêgos*. But before he proceeds to the healing, he gives a speech in which he censors all kinds of wrong desires and practices, such as greed, envy, adultery, cruelty, sorcery, swindling, etc. – all of them leading to the final judgement of being condemned to eternal fire. The threat was apparently such stock-in-trade of early Christian preaching that even Celsus notes that Christians "threaten others with these punishments" (Or., Cels. 8.48).[14] In other words, John's method of conversion consists of both the carrot and the stick: healing and resurrecting from the dead, but also threats of eternal doom (36).

Unfortunately, the text with the episode about the healing of the old women and its consequences has been lost, so we proceed with John's preaching of the gospel to a group of men as well as Drusiana, the wife of Andronicus. John focuses on the polymorphy of Christ (88–93) and the mystery of Christ's passion (94–102), which need not concern us here. But it is interesting to note that they "in some ways were not yet established in the faith" (87). Conversion is clearly seen as a process and not only as a sudden event or decision. This fits better modern views of conversion, and we will have to come back to it.

Having listened to John's oration, we next move to the episode of the destruction of the Temple of Artemis (37–47). The apostle ascends a high platform and tells the "men of Ephesus" that they have remained unchanged in their hearts regarding "the true religion" despite the miracles they had seen. He even threatens them that God might kill them and then prays to God to show mercy and to convert them. In response, the altar of Artemis splits into pieces and half the temple falls down, killing the priest of Artemis in the process.[15] This is enough to convince the Ephesians who cry out "unique is the god of John, unique is the god who has mercy upon us; for thou alone art God! We are converted, now that we have seen thy marvellous works!" (42). And after John has berated those Ephesians that have fallen to the ground or tried to flee, and has scolded Artemis, the Ephesians once again call out: "The god of John [is the] only [God] we know; from now on we worship him, since he has had mercy upon us" (44). And when they request John to stay, he tells them that he will stay until, as he says, "I have weaned

---

14 Note also *Passio Perpetuae* 18.8.
15 For the Ephesian priests of Artemis, see J.N. Bremmer, *Priestly Personnel of the Ephesian Artemision. Anatolian, Persian, Greek, and Roman Aspects*, in: B. Dignas / K. Trampedach (eds.), *Practitioners of the Divine in Ancient Greece*, Cambridge 2008, 37–53.

you like children from the milk of the nurse, and have set you upon a solid rock of faith."

Here, it is clearly a single moment in time that converts the Ephesians. And it is the marvellous work of God that makes them proclaim these acclamations,[16] which we of course also know from other, Christian and pagan, sources. It is important to note that a significant part of this description, *mutatis mutandis*, could have been found in a pagan work as well, as it is typical of ancient religiosity that the great works of a mortal can lead to his deification or at least to him being called a god; this we can even see in our *Acts* where Lycomedes says to John, when the latter questions him about having commissioned a portrait of him: "But if besides this God, we may call our earthly benefactors gods, etc." (27).[17] Important, too, is the stress on seeing: they have *seen* the marvellous works. It is typical of ancient culture that seeing was rated above hearing.[18] Moreover, we notice that conversion, as described in the *Acts*, is not an intellectual process of gradually realising the truth, but a sudden change of heart caused by being impressed by "marvellous works." Yet, the apostle realises that this is only the beginning. From a modern point of view, then, one must credit the apostle with a realistic look of his new converts.

After the conversion of the Ephesian crowd, the *Acts* proceed with a perhaps even more impressive conversion. A kinsman deposits the body of the priest of Artemis before the door of Andronicus' house, where John is staying, and then joins the people inside the house. Naturally, this does not escape the apostle who charges him to resurrect the priest. When the latter is raised, the apostle exhorts him to believe so that he could live for all eternity. "And," as the *Acts* tell us, "there and then he believed in the Lord Jesus and from that time kept company with John" (46–47). In this case, too, it is the "marvellous work" of the resurrection that makes the priest believe in God. One would think that the author of the *Acts* would have exploited this particular conversion in more detail, but perhaps he himself realised that this conversion was rather exceptional and perhaps hard to accept as true and therefore remained somewhat reticent about it.

---

16 For interesting observations on these acclamations, see H.S. Versnel, *Coping with the Gods*, Leiden 2011, 239–307.

17 J. Strubbe, *Cultic Honors for Benefactions in the Cities of Asia Minor*, in: L. de Ligt *et al.* (eds.), *Roman Rule and Civic Life. Local and Regional Perspectives*, Amsterdam 2004, 315–330; Ph. Gauthier, *Études d'histoire et d'institutions grecques*, Geneva 2011, 577–591 (the article originally published in 2003), both overlooked by Versnel, 2011, 487, n. 145 (with further bibliography).

18 See P.J. Finglass on *Sophocles' Electra*, Cambridge 2007 (on vv. 761–63).

The next case concerns a parricide – the murder of one's father being one of the worst crimes imaginable in ancient Greece.[19] As can be expected at this point, John raises the murdered father who naturally starts to believe (52). The murdering son repents so much that he castrates himself and throws his testicles before the woman for whose sake he had murdered his father.[20] But when he has told John about this, the apostle does not heal him, but stresses that he should control his thoughts rather than cut off the members that reveal the thoughts. Once again, we notice the stress in John's preaching on self-control; this is clearly important for the author of the *Acts*, although not to the same degree as in the *Acts of Andrew*.[21] The young man regrets his sins and stays with John. Here, it is not the demonstration of supernatural qualities, as with the priest of Artemis, but the message of self-control that seems to be the most important part of the episode (54).

Our final case concerns an even more sensational conversion as it relates to *necrophilia*. This is not a common theme in Greek literature although not wholly unknown.[22] Apparently, John has returned to Ephesus where, as we are told, a certain Callimachus falls in love with Drusiana who after her conversion no longer has intercourse with her husband (63). But as he does not succeed in winning her favours, Callimachus lapses into a state of melancholy. This distresses Drusiana to such an extent that she becomes ill and, rather improbably, dies "because of the bruising of the soul of that man" (64). Andronicus also grieves excessively, if not to the same degree as Lycomedes. Thus, he regularly bursts into tears in the company of others so that John repeatedly has to silence him (65) – one more sign of the importance attached to self-control in these *Acts*.

After her burial, Drusiana is not yet free from her suitor. On the contrary, together with Fortunatus, the corrupt steward of Andronicus, Callimachus, breaks into her tomb in order to commit *necrophilia* (70). They are on the point of succeeding with their perverse plan and have already started removing Drusiana's last garment, the rather expensive *dikrossion*,[23] when suddenly a huge snake appears, fatally bites the steward, and remains on

---

19 J. Lightfoot, *Parthenius of Nicaea*, Oxford 1999, 398f.
20 M. Kuefler, *The Manly Eunuch*, Chicago 2001, 262, unpersuasively connects this self-castration to that of the followers of Cybele and Attis, the *galli*.
21 Roig Lanzillotta, 2007, 238–243 and *passim*.
22 See the evidence collected by Lightfoot, 1999, 535, where our case has to be added.
23 The discussion by P.J. Lalleman, *The Acts of John. A Two-stage Initiation into Johannine Gnosticism*, Leuven 1998, 258f., now has to be corrected in the light of the very full collection of references to this type of garment in F.R. Adrados (ed.), *Diccionario Griego-Español*, vol. 5, Madrid 1997, s.v. *dikrossion* and *dikrossos*.

Callimachus after he falls to the ground (71).[24] The next day, Andronicus, John, and some other brothers go to the tomb. They have forgotten the keys, but the apostle opens the doors by a simple order (72), a motif which derives from pagan literature,[25] as does another detail in this scene. When they enter the tomb, they see an attractive, smiling young man (73). The same smiling figure is also encountered in the *Acts of Paul* where a smiling youth of great beauty loosens Paul's bonds (7), and in the *Acts of Peter* where Jesus appears smiling to Peter in his prison (16). The motif is well known from pagan epiphanies where the god traditionally smiles to reassure anxious mortals.[26] Andronicus considers Fortunatus unworthy of being saved, but asks John to resurrect Callimachus in order that he should confess exactly what had happened (74), not – we may observe – so that he should convert. After John has also raised Drusiana (79–80), she generously asks the apostle to resurrect Fortunatus as well, but Callimachus opposes her request. When John points out that God prefers repentance above retribution, he charges Drusiana to do so (81), and she performs the resurrection with enthusiasm (82–83). Fortunatus, however, does not convert but runs away and dies shortly after (83; 86). Apparently, he is the model for what happens when people do not convert, thus, presumably, reflecting the reality of the frequent rejection of conversion. With this negative result we have come to the end of the *Acts of John* and turn to the *Acts of Peter*.

2. The *Acts of Peter*

The oldest part of these *Acts*, the so-called *Actus Vercellenses*, immediately starts with a conversion. Claudia, the wife of the prison officer of Paul, becomes a convert by the words of Paul, and in turn converts her husband (1) – the conversion of prison officers being a kind of *topos* in early Christian literature since the *Acts of the apostles* (16:26–34). After this so-to-speak happy conversion, the scene shifts to Paul and the distribution of the Eucharist. When a woman called Rufina also wants to participate, Paul refuses her because she lives with an adulterer. She falls down fully paralysed on

---

24 For the snake, see Spittler, 2008, 110–116.
25 The classic study is O. Weinreich, *Religionsgeschichtliche Studien*, Darmstadt 1968, 45–290 (first printed in 1929). For more passages and the most recent bibliography, see J.J. Smoolenaars, *Statius Thebaid VII. A Commentary*, Leiden 1994, 40f.
26 Many parallels: O. Weinreich, *Antike Heilungswunder*, Giessen 1909, 3, n. 2; J. Nollé, *Kleinasiatische Losorakel*, Munich 2007, 144. 272; A. Chaniotis, *The Ithyphallic Hymn for Demetrios Poliorcetes and Hellenistic Religious Mentality*, in P.P. Iossif *et al.* (eds.), *More than Men, Less than Gods. Studies in Royal Cult and Imperial Worship*, Leuven 2011, 157–195 (178).

one side of her body. Interestingly, this sight frightens the newly converted who now remember their own sins (2). Afterwards, Paul leaves Rome and embarks on a ship to Spain (3; 6). The religious vacuum created by Paul's departure is filled by Simon Magus, who impresses people by seemingly being able to fly; this means that he is on the verge of being accepted as a new god instead of the Christian God (4). It is only now that Peter arrives from Jerusalem via a boat trip, during which he has converted the captain Theon by telling him of "the wondrous works of God," his being chosen as an apostle, and his reason for sailing to Italy. Thus, when the sea was calm and the rest of the crew lay in drunken stupor, the captain was baptised and given the Eucharist (5). We may note here that it is the most important member of the crew that converts, just as it is usually the chief of the prison.

After his arrival in Rome, and rather different from the *Acts of John* and *Paul*, Peter now concerns himself with those who have become apostates because of Simon Magus – their most prominent representative being a senator, Marcellus. Peter goes up to the latter's house and charges a dog to speak to Simon Magus (who is inside), and it indeed tells Simon that Peter is standing at the door. When Simon is lost for words because of the speaking dog, Marcellus repents and asks for forgiveness which he duly receives.[27] But when a possessed youth kicks a statue of the emperor to pieces, he almost falls back in his unbelief. Fortunately, Peter manages to make him see the error of his ways, and Marcellus sprinkles water over the statue that is restored to its former glory. It is this miracle, the text stresses, that makes him believe (11). As he grows in faith, Marcellus eventually acquires the strength to throw Simon Magus out of his house (14).

Although the dog, by his speaking, persuades some of those present to become Christians, others request another sign as Simon Magus had also performed miracles. In answer to their requests, Peter lets a dried fish come to life again and even eat bread. This is enough to persuade "a great number" to follow him and to believe in the Lord (13).[28] Afterwards, Marcellus tells Peter that he has purified his house and invited the widows and aged people to come to his house in order to give them a piece of gold (19). Among them is a blind widow whom Peter heals by laying his right hand on her (20). When he is on the brink of leaving, other blind widows, who say that they believe in Christ too, naturally also request to be healed. And indeed, Christ appears in a polymorphous manner and heals them by, according to some,

---

27 For a fine discussion of the scene with the dog, see Spittler, 2008, 130–148; for dogs in antiquity, see also J.R. Harrison, *Every Dog has its Day*, in S.R. Llewelyn / J.R. Harrison (eds.), *New Documents Illustrating Early Christianity*, vol. 10, Grand Rapids 2012, 126–135.

28 For the miracle, see Spittler, 2008, 148–154.

touching their eyes. Here, belief seems to precede the healing instead of, as is normally the case, following it. Peter then sees to the "virgins of the Lord" (22), once again, presumably, poor young women that found support in the Christian community, surely a not negligible side of Christian conversions.

When Peter and Simon Magus have come together on the Forum, the prefect requests Simon to kill a man and Peter to raise him. Simon kills one of the prefect's slaves by whispering some words into his ear – whispering being characteristic of magic in antiquity.[29] Immediately afterwards, virtually at the same time, one of the widows of Marcellus' house cries out that her son, of course her only son and life's support in this kind of dramatising literature, has died. So Peter sends out 30 young men, who are also prepared to believe, to fetch the corpse of the youth (25). In the meantime, the prefect urges him to raise the youth killed by Simon Magus, which Peter does, as he does also with the son of the widow (26–27). These resurrections (which give rise to acclamations of God's uniqueness, but do not seem to lead to conversions) induce the mother of a senator to ask for the resurrection of her son who presumably has just died. Peter agrees to do so, and the mother lets her slaves, whom she has freed for the occasion, bring the body as if it was prepared for a proper funeral.

When the funeral procession has arrived at the Forum,[30] Peter challenges Simon to resurrect the body. He accepts the challenge on the condition that if he succeeds in doing so, the crowd will chase Peter out of Rome. Although he manages to make the boy move, he cannot in fact revive him – in contrast to Peter who properly resurrects him. Not surprisingly, the senator now believes, but it is not mentioned that the crowd starts to believe, nor do we hear anything further about Simon (28). On the contrary. The crowd now starts to venerate Peter as a god, just as they had already done with Simon after witnessing the latter's tricks (4). These passages are highly interesting testimonies to ancient ruler cult and deserve more attention than they have

---

29 L. Soverini, *Hermes, Afrodite e il susurro nella Grecia antica*, in: S. Alessandri (ed.), *Historie. Studi Giuseppe Nenci*, Galabina 1994, 183–210; L. Moscadi, *"Murmur" nella terminologia magica*, in: SIFC 48 (1976), 254–262; E. Valette-Cagnac, *La lecture à Rome* (PhD diss.), École pratique des hautes étude 1997, 42–47; P.W. van der Horst, *Hellenism-Judaism-Christianity*, Leuven ²1998, 300–302; D.K. van Mal-Maeder, *Apuleius Madaurensis, Metamorphoses. Livre II*, Groningen 2001, 60; M. Andreassi, *Implicazioni magiche in Meleagro AP 5.152*, in: ZPE 176 (2011), 69–81 (74f.).

30 Although situated in Rome, these funerals are clearly modelled on Greek customs, cf. C.P. Jones, *Interrupted Funerals*, in: PAPS 143 (1999), 588–600 and A. Chaniotis, *Rituals between Norms and Emotions. Rituals as Shared Experience and Memory*, in: E. Stavrianopoulou (ed.), *Rituals and Communication in the Graeco-Roman World*, Liège 2006, 211–238.

received so far. Naturally, after these impressive feats others also bring sick people to Peter, and those are healed who believe in Jesus Christ, "and very many were added every day to the grace of the Lord." Here, once again, believing precedes healing, but can hardly be separated from it (29).[31] The confrontation with Simon is eventually concluded to Peter's advantage when he shoots, so to speak, Simon out of the air while flying over Rome. This even convinces one of Simon's greatest supporters, Gemellus, that he is not a god, and he desires "to be one of those that believe in Christ" (32).

3. The *Acts of Paul*

The protagonist of the *Acts of Paul* is of course the apostle Paul. In this text, we are told of his wanderings which probably began in Damascus (the text has come to us only incompletely) where he himself converted.[32] But we get a glimpse of Paul's activities in his subsequent stay in Syrian Antioch. Here, he raises the son of Phila and Anchares from the dead. Just as John was considered to be meddling in magic (see above, § 1), Paul too is considered to be a magician by (Pseudo-) Philo.[33] This suspicion must be a reflection of reality as the accusation of magic is also the underlying theme in the *Acts of Peter* where Peter defeats Simon Magus (see above, § 2). But Anchares testifies to his belief, surely because of the resurrection of his son. However, the rest of the population is not convinced, and Paul is chased out of the city (Ant. 3).

If this passage is fairly traditional, we see a most interesting new aspect of Christianity's mission in the passage about Paul's stay in Iconium. Here, Paul's sermons in the house of Onesiphorus are overheard by a young girl Thecla sitting at a near-by window, and Paul's words are enough for her to become a believer.[34] This is a rather unique case in the *Apocryphal acts* since in virtually all other cases people are converted through "marvellous works", not by persuasive discourses. Interestingly, the text notes that many women and virgins went into Onesiphorus' house.[35] The passage suggests that Christianity appealed to rather young people, and in fact, on the basis of modern evidence, the late Keith Hopkins (1934–2004) has indeed postulated

---

31 For a discussion of these resurrections, see Bremmer, 2003, 64–68.
32 For the narration of Paul's conversion, see J.N. Bremmer, *Greek Religion and Culture, the Bible and the Ancient Near East*, Leiden 2008, 224–232.
33 Ant. 1; note also APTh 15; 20; Ephesus 24.
34 Cf. the contribution by Cooper and Corke-Webster in the present volume.
35 APTh 7, see also 9; 12; and Myra 3. For Myra, I follow the chapter order of Willy Rordorf in F. Bovon / P. Geoltrain (eds.), *Écrits apocryphes chrétiens*, 2 vols, Paris 1997–2005, vol. 1, 1142–1146.

a higher incidence of youngsters as possible targets of Christian recruitment.[36] And indeed, around the 160s (?), that is, the probable time of our *Acts*, both Tatian (Or. 32.1; 33.1) and Celsus (Or., Cels. 3.44) mention the presence of young boys and girls among the Christians. We may also mention the fifteen-year old Ponticus in Mart. Lugd. 53, the young Perpetua and Felicitas in the *Passio Perpetuae*, and the 21-year old Pamoun in the more recently published POxy. 70.4759.[37] In this connection, we also note that Thecla brings young men and women along when looking for Paul in Myra (40).

In Pisidian Antioch, Thecla manages to convert the noble lady Tryphaena whose deceased daughter Falconilla she replaces to some extent. When seals have failed to kill her due to the intervention of Jesus (34), and the Roman governor has released Thecla (38), Tryphaena starts to believe and takes Thecla into her house. She instructs not only Tryphaena in the word of God, but also the majority of her maidservants (39). The passage is fairly unique, but must reflect one of the ways Christianity took hold: when a rich lady converted, her slaves surely would convert often too.

Thecla now disappears from sight, and we follow Paul to Myra. Here, he is approached by a certain Hermocrates, probably a local name like Hermippos below,[38] who suffers from dropsy. Unfortunately, the papyrus with the scene is rather fragmentary, but it is clear that Paul heals Hermocrates who surely converts since he is subsequently baptised with his wife. His two sons, however, display different reactions. The older one, Hermippos, had wanted his father to die in order to get hold of the inheritance whereas the younger one, Dion, "heard Paul gladly" (2). It is clear that the author tries to vary his "novel" a bit and employs the motif of feuding brothers that was well known to him both from the Greek and the biblical tradition.[39] From our text, it is unclear how it happened exactly, but Dion dies because of a fall. Naturally, the apostle raises him (4) even if we do not know how because a leaf of the papyrus is missing. The next day, Hermippos, accompanied by a group of young men armed with cudgels, tries to kill Paul, but instead he is blinded, presumably by the apostle. Hermocrates now sells his goods and gives the proceeds to the widows, an important category in the early Christian church.[40] Moreover, it

---

36 K. Hopkins, *Christian Number and Its Implications*, in: Journal of Early Christian Studies 6 (1998), 185–226 (205).

37 For more, somewhat later examples, see J.N. Bremmer, *The Social and Religious Capital of the Early Christians*, in: Hephaistos 24 (2006), 269–278 (274).

38 For names in Lycia with the element ERM-, see S. Colvin, *Names in Hellenistic and Roman Lycia*, in: YCS 31 (2004), 44–84 (61f.).

39 See Bremmer, *Greek Religion and Culture*, 2008, 57–72.

40 R. Bruno Siola, *Viduae e coetus viduarum nella Chiesa primitiva e nella normazione dei primi imperatori cristiani*, in: *Atti dell' Accademia Romanistica Constantiniani, VIII convegno internazionale*, Naples 1990, 367–426; J.N. Bremmer,

seems that Hermippos also converts, although the papyrus is too fragmentary to say exactly how.

Our narrative becomes more accessible when we are back in Ephesus, partially because of the more recent publication of the Coptic Bodmer papyrus with this part of the text.[41] Here *en route* Paul meets a speaking lion whom he manages to convert and to baptise.[42] The conversion of the lion is so complete that it immediately renounces sexual intercourse with a lioness it encounters.[43] Understandably, hearing this report the crowd is amazed and immediately "was added to the faith" (11). Among them, it seems, is a rich lady, Procla, who is also baptised together with all of her household – one more testimony of the influence the conversion of wealthy citizens must have exerted on their slaves.

However, also Artemilla (perhaps also inspired by a native Lycian name),[44] the wife of the Roman governor Jerome, becomes interested in Paul and after having been berated by him because of her clothes and her jewellery, she requests, together with Euboula, the wife of Jerome's freedman Diophantos, to be baptised. Paul is actually chained and in prison, but at the appearance of an extremely attractive child his chains loosen themselves. Subsequently, the gates of the prison open spontaneously (cf. § 1) and the apostle, with his female followers, goes out to the sea lead by a young man whose radiance makes a torch superfluous. Here, he baptises Artemilla. On his return into the prison, Paul presents her with the Eucharist and then sends her home (19–21).

The next morning, he is led into the arena where a fierce lion awaits him, of course the one he has previously baptised. An enormous hail storm kills

---

Pauper or Patroness. The Widow in the Early Christian Church, in: J.N. Bremmer / L.P. van den Bosch (eds.), *Between Poverty and the Pyre. Moments in the History of Widowhood*, London 1995, 31–57; J.R. Harrison, *Benefaction Ideology and Christian Responsibility for Widows*, in S.R. Llewelyn (ed.), *New Documents Illustrating Early Christianity*, vol. 8, Grand Rapids 1997, 106–116.

41 R. Kasser / P. Luisier, *Le Papyrus Bodmer XLI en édition princeps. L'épisode d'Ephèse des Acta Pauli en Copte et en traduction*, in: Le Muséon 117 (2004), 281–384.

42 Note that lions were present in southern Anatolia until the nineteenth century and may well have been familiar to the readers of the *Acts of Paul*, cf. Nollé, 2007, 171.

43 C.R. Matthews, *Articulate Animals. A Multivalent Motif in the Apocryphal Acts of the Apostles*, in: F. Bovon et al. (eds.), *The Apocryphal Acts of Apostles. Harvard Divinity School Studies*, Cambridge 1999, 205–232; Spittler, 2008, 182–187.

44 For the complicated question of names with Artemis in Lycia, see Colvin, 2004, 60f.

all the other animals and even tears off the ear of Jerome. The people present flee, and the lion returns to the mountains and no longer speaks with a
human voice. Jerome, apparently, prays for the healing of his ear and presumably converts just like his wife. But Paul has already left for Macedonia
where we meet him again in Philippi. No more clear conversions are now
told of in the surviving *Acts* until we arrive in Rome where Paul will be
martyred. Here, he preaches in a barn outside Rome where he once again
gains many followers and converts, in particular from the Imperial household (14.1). A wine pourer of Nero with the name of Patroclus, once again
a young man, listens to him, but falls from the window from where he was
listening. After he has been resuscitated by the apostle and has converted,
Patroclus is arrested by Nero together with some other prominent members
of his household. It is with these important conversions that we have to take
leave of the *Acts of Paul* and move on to the conclusions.

Conclusions and general observations

1. Nock has rightly argued that conversion is not part of the polytheistic
world of antiquity, but belongs to the rise of Judaism and Christianity, the
only contemporary monotheistic religions;[45] yet, he was still under the influence of William James' mainly psychological approach which has to be seen
against the background of contemporary American revivalism.[46] This means
that Nock's famous definition of conversion, "the reorientation of the soul
of an individual, his deliberate turning from indifference or from an earlier
form of piety to another, a turning which implies a consciousness that a
great change is involved, that the old was wrong and the new was right" (7),
neglects the social factor in conversion,[47] and his emphasis on the personal
experience obscures the fact that only the new Christians had become members of an exclusive, totalising community.[48] Instead of following Nock, we

---

45 But see Bøgh, Marshall, and Bilde in this volume for another point of view.
46 For an excellent contextualisation of modern conversion studies, see H. Zock,
    *Paradigms in Psychological Conversion Research. Between Social Science and
    Literary Analysis*, in: J.N. Bremmer / W.J. van Bekkum / A.L Molendijk (eds.),
    Paradigms, Poetics, and Politics of Conversion, Leuven 2006, 41–58.
47 N.H. Taylor, *The Social Nature of Conversion in the Early Christian World*,
    in Esler (ed.), 1995, 128–136; Z. Crook, *Reconceptualising Conversion*, Berlin
    2004, although his insistence on loyalty as an important factor in conversion is
    less persuasive.
48 This is well argued by J. Rives, *Religious Choice and Religious Change in Clas-
    sical and Late Antiquity. Models and Questions*, in: ARYS 9 (2011), 265–280
    (written in connection with the first international conference held by the Velux
    group in 2010); see also H. Leppin, *Christianisierungen im Römischen Reich.*

will look at our fictional sources and ask who is the object of conversion, how do they portray the reasons for conversion, and what was the measure of success of a conversion.

2. Let us first, though, reflect on our sources and the value we can attach to them when mining them for historical data. The relationship between fiction and history is of course not an easy one to analyse. Fiction can represent reality as closely as possible, as for example, in a realistic novel, but it can also subvert reality or portray a utopian world. In other words, there is no direct road from fiction to facts, and we always have to correlate the world of fiction to other data available. No historical reality can be reconstructed from fiction alone.

3. Jakob Engberg has written a fine article on conversion as used and described by the apologists in which he also touches on the insoluble question of the intended readership of the apologies.[49] In his discussion, he neatly distinguishes between offensive and defensive uses of the accounts of conversion, that is, accounts to counter false allegations and accounts to influence other potential converts; from his discussion it is clear that the apologies are aimed at an intellectual readership. It should be noticed that in the *Apocryphal acts*, we find a rather different approach to conversion. These *Acts*, as I noted some years ago in a mostly neglected article, were aimed at women of the higher classes.[50] Although they do contain many discursive passages, as we can see from my survey, the scenes with conversion are nearly all in a narrative mode. In other words, we have to be attentive to the genre of the conversion accounts.

4. Regarding the *reasons* for conversion, looking at our *Apocryphal acts* we notice that they in general follow what I would call the sudden, Pauline model of conversion. Yet, in (almost) all cases, the reasons for conversion are a demonstration of divine power and miracles, something which differs from other reasons for conversion.[51] Yet, the conversions are usually mediated by other Christians – the social aspect. This important aspect was completely ignored by Nock.[52] Moreover, conversion is depicted as a sudden event as

Überlegungen zum Begriff und zur Phasenbildung, in: Zeitschrift für Antikes Christentum 16 (2012), 247–278 (265–276).

49 J. Engberg, *"From among You are We. Made, not Born are Christians."* Apologists' Accounts of Conversion before 310 AD, in: J. Ulrich / A-C. Jacobsen / M. Kahlos (eds.), *Continuity and Discontinuity in Early Christian Apologetics*, Frankfurt 2009, 49–79.

50 Bremmer, 2001.

51 See, for example, Georges in this volume for intellectual conversions found in a higher social class.

52 This social aspect is also crucial to acknowledge in other cults, such as the mysteries: see, e.g., Beck and Martin in this volume for the Mithraic cults, and Bøgh for the Bacchic cult.

was the case with Paul on the road to Damascus. This presents us with a problem. Engberg has persuasively argued that the apologists' accounts can be considered as normative sources when we study conversion in antiquity. In addition, he has argued that they (as normative) reveal that conversion was a process rather than an event.[53] But how does this compare with the accounts of the *Apocryphal acts*? Are they not normative? The trouble of course is that most of the healings or resurrections cannot have happened in reality. Yet, the persistent occurrence of sudden conversions in these *Acts* makes me wonder if, in antiquity, things did not go differently than in modern times. In this respect, I would once again like to point to the passages in which the people call Peter a god after a spectacular miracle. This kind of reaction was not abnormal in antiquity. Given the fact that people could start worshipping mortals as gods after impressive feats, it does not seem impossible that people also converted suddenly after some impressive event. It is perhaps a sign of our own reflexive time that we prefer to think of conversion as a long lasting process. This we can certainly observe too in antiquity – Constantine and Augustine are obvious cases[54] – but we should perhaps keep an open mind regarding the actual process.

5. Who were the converts? Nock looked at the ancient world very much from the point of view of an intellectual and focused his interest more on the upper-class than the "man in the street", whom he clearly dismissed as credulous (90. 224. 226). This means that he hardly had an eye for a more varied study of the nature of the newly converted. It is therefore perhaps understandable – also given his time of writing – that he had little interest in the conversions of women, although perhaps there also is a personal aspect to this as Nock was not at ease with women.[55] But we should note that also among the apologists studied by Engberg there is not a single woman. Thus the *Acts* present us with a different view of early Christian conversion by focusing on the women of whom we know that they constituted an important part of the early church. Moreover, the *Acts* show us different types of women: rich upper class ladies, virgins, as well as old crones and widows. As such, the *Acts* do give us a more differentiated view of the early Christian converts. Rather striking, too, is the attention to the young. When we take

---

53 See Engberg's and Cvetković's contributions in the present volume who both argue for the often processual nature of conversion.

54 See especially P. Brown, *Conversion and Christianization in Late Antiquity. The Case of Augustine*, in: C. Straw / R. Lim (eds.), *The Past Before Us. The Challenge of Historiographies of Late Antiquity,* Turnhout 2004, 103–117; J.N. Bremmer, *The Vision of Constantine*, in: A. Lardinois / M. van der Poel / V. Hunink (eds.), *Land of Dreams*, Leiden 2006, 57–79.

55 Price, 2010, 330.

into account Rodney Stark's rational choice theory, we may perhaps conclude that the costs for women and the young were less than for the upper
class males: whereas we know plenty of female and young converts,[56] there
are no Christian senators known and few knights before Constantine.[57]

6. How successful were the conversions? This question is hard to answer,
not least because neither the miracles themselves (such as a resurrection)
nor their effects, such as conversions of whole towns, are very probable, to
say the least.[58] Evidently, we have to do with a kind of missionary discourse
that should not be confused with reality, although their popularity suggests
that there was a large market for such stories. This is obviously not surprising in a world that hardly knew proper medical care. Hence surely, just like
today, miracles must have often been seen as the only possibility in desper-
ate situations. Reports of miracles may well have produced converts, but
our evidence for that result is extremely slim. Yet, the reactions of a pagan
author like Lucian show that such miracle stories were extremely popular in
his time.[59] The Christians had realised this niche in the religious market and
exploited it as no other contemporary religious cult. Moreover, it is interesting that our texts repeatedly stress the fact that the newly converted still had
to be further educated in the faith. This process will have been an obvious
fact for many of the fresh Christian converts as the Christians had instituted
the catechumenate to instruct in the faith those who wanted to join them.
In other words, even if we are witness to an instant conversion, there would
still be the social process of integration into the Christian community. The

---

56 R.L. Fox, *Pagans and Christians*, Harmondsworth 1986, 308–311; J.N. Bremmer, *The Rise of Christianity through the Eyes of Gibbon, Harnack and Rodney
Stark*, Groningen 2010, 56.

57 W. Eck, *Christen im höheren Reichsdienst im 2. und 3. Jahrhundert? Zu zwei
Thesen Th. Klausers*, in: Chiron 9 (1979), 449–464; id., *Religion und Religiosität
in der soziopolitischen Führungsschicht der Hohen Kaiserzeit*, in: W. Eck (ed.),
*Religion und Gesellschaft in der römischen Kaiserzeit. Kolloquium zu Ehren von
Friedrich Vittinghoff*, Cologne 1989, 15–51; T.D. Barnes, *Statistics and the Con-
version of the Roman Aristocracy*, in: JRS 85 (1995), 135–147; M. Salzman, *The
Making of a Christian Aristocracy. Social and Religious Change in the Western
Roman Empire*, Cambridge 2002.

58 M. Frenschkowski, *Religion auf dem Markt*, in: M. Hutter et al. (eds.), *Hairesis.
Festschrift für Karl Hoheisel*, Münster 2002, 140–158. It would transcend the
limits of my contribution to discuss here the problem of miracles, which has
been an important subject since Hume, but see Bremmer, 2010, 13f. 35. 71; for
Hume, add C. Ginzburg, *Une conversation sur les miracles (Hume au Collège de
la Flèche, entre 1735 et 1737)*, in: Asdiwal (Geneva) 7 (2012), 55–69.

59 Cf. J.N. Bremmer, *Richard Reitzenstein's Hellenistische Wundererzählungen*, in
T. Nicklas / J. Spittler (eds.), *Credible, Incredible. The Miraculous in the Ancient
Mediterranean*, Tübingen 2013, 1–19.

occasional attention of the authors of the *Apocryphal acts* to this fact speaks for their intermittent realism. In his book, Nock did not focus on unsuccessful conversions or apostates. This is a neglected category altogether, but should not be overlooked in a study of conversion.[60] Except for Julian the Apostate, we hardly know anything about such retro-conversions as they perhaps could be called, although the problem of the *lapsi* would become more urgent after Decius' persecution.[61] Let it here suffice to call attention to the problem as our *Acts* do not give us any help in understanding this process.

7. Finally, the focus on the apostles in these *Acts* leaves us largely in the dark as to who the "brokers" of the new religion were: male missionaries, women, adolescents, merchants, administrators, soldiers? The *Acts* suggest that the conversion of upper class women could lead to the conversion of whole households which does make sense. But what about the reading of the *Acts*? Did that promote early Christianity? Even posing the question shows how little we still know, and how much we are still groping in the dark when we try to understand the rise of Christianity and the phenomenon of early Christian conversion.[62]

---

60 Cf. Crook in the present volume for a theoretical view on apostates in a given culture.

61 Cf. W. Ameling, *The Christian* lapsi *in Smyrna, 250 A.D. (Martyrium Pionii 12–14)*, in: VigChr 62 (2008), 133–160.

62 For information, I am grateful to Patrick Finglass. Ton Hilhorst, as always, saved me from various mistakes and improved my argument.

Jakob Engberg

Human and Divine Agency in Conversion in Apologetic Writings of the Second Century: To "Dance with Angels"

Abstract: The author discusses the roles assigned to divine and human agents in a number of Christian apologies. His aim is to study the normative conversion ideals of the apologists through the aspect of agency, but also to demonstrate that they portray conversion as a process, and to argue that such ideals shaped the actual conversion experience of converts.

> O truly sacred mysteries! O pure light! My road is lighted by torches, and I have a vision of the heavens and God. I am made holy by initiation. The Lord is the hierophant and he places his seal on the initiated, gives him light to guide his road, and presents him who believes to the Father's care where he is guarded for the coming ages. Such are the celebrations of my mysteries. If you wish, you should also be initiated, and then you shall dance with angels around the un-begotten, imperishable, and only true God, the Logos of God, and you shall join with us in the hymn of praise.[1]

In this text, Clement both alludes to his own conversion and exhorts his reader to convert like him. The vast majority of the authors whom we conventionally label early Christian apologists also make references to their own conversion in one or more of their apologetic writings, and all of them exhorted their readers to conversion.[2] In this article, I will discuss the roles assigned to divine and human agents in a number of these references and exhortations to conversion – who is presented as taking the initiative: Is it God calling the convert? Is it a Christian advocate exerting an influence on the convert? Or is it the convert being presented as searching for the truth, turning from error, etc.? The quoted passage may serve as an example. The divine agency is evident: Christ is presented as the guide placing his mark on the convert and bringing the convert to the Father; the Father in turn cares for and guards the convert. The convert on the other hand is not passive – there is a road to walk, belief and wish are required, and we learn that the convert will end up dancing with angels and singing hymns of praise. It

---

1 Clem., protr. 5.12,92; this and the following translations are my own unless otherwise stated.

2 J. Engberg, "*From among You are We. Made, not Born are Christians,*" in: J. Ulrich / A.-C. Jacobsen / M. Kahlos (eds.), *Continuity and Discontinuity in Early Christian Apologetics*, Frankfurt 2009, 49–79 (52f.).

takes two to tango, but in this case, there is not only the agency of the divine
and of the convert; Clement issues an invitation, and the convert is invited
to "join with us," indicating that Clement sees himself and other Christians
as agents in the conversion of the convert/reader. In this text, we are dealing with an ideology of conversion. It is the main purpose of the article to
study such ideals of conversion – the conversion theologies of the apologists.
Secondarily, I will also discuss more tentatively how such ideologies may
have shaped the conversion experience of converts to Christianity in 2nd – 3rd
centuries, and how our study of ideals may help us understand such conversions.

Approach, terminology, and previous scholarship on accounts of conversion

In the study of conversion to modern religious movements, it is standard to
distinguish between a normative and a descriptive approach to conversion:
The normative approach deals with the ideological or theological ideas and
ideals for a conversion found within a given tradition whereas the "descriptive approach observes the nature of the process. [...] What actually happens in conversion processes? What behaviours are changed? What beliefs
are changed? What sorts of experiences are elicited in the process?"[3] When
studying "what actually happens" scholars who study modern religious conversion will most often observe participants, interview converts and advocates, make quantitative studies, etc. None of these options are accessible
when studying conversion in the ancient world. Does this mean that we are
barred from learning anything about "what actually happened"? Is there
no possibility for us to move beyond a study of what Christians thought
ought to happen in conversion and move to a study of the actual conversion
experience?

In 1978, James Beckford published a seminal study of modern Jehovah's
Witnesses' conversion narratives.[4] Beckford demonstrated that converts produced narratives about their own conversion that followed the normative
ideas of conversion promoted in the *Watchtower*. Beckford's results have
since been confirmed by other studies examining converts to other religious
groups. Thus, studies of conversion to contemporary religious groups have
demonstrated that the ideal of conversion in a religious group influences the
perception and consequently the conversion experience of the convert, but
also that the ideologies of conversion are by no means immune from the

---

3 L. Rambo, *Understanding Religious Conversion*, New Haven 1993, 6f.
4 J.A. Beckford, *Accounting for Conversion*, in: British Journal of Sociology 29
   (1978), 249–262.

influence exerted by experiences related by converts.[5] In the history of research, these results prompted scholars, including Beckford, to conclude that conversion narratives and the answers given by converts when interviewed could neither reveal the real circumstances related to the conversion, nor the real motives of the convert. Unknown, presumably, to both Beckford and the scholars following in his footsteps, similar conclusions had already been reached in studies on Justin and Tertullian in the late 1960s and the early 1970s.[6] Along these lines, it would be standard to claim that the ideology of conversion discussed in this article would have had little or no bearing on the actual conversion experience of converts, that, in Jonathan Smith's parable, "map is not territory."[7]

It is however time to move beyond such a traditional approach to the reading of normative texts both in patristic scholarship and in the study of modern conversion. That accounts of conversion are stereotypes, and that norms of conversion shape the experience of converts are distinct advantages when trying to approach "real" conversion experiences – especially if we rid ourselves of the fascination of studying individuals and focus rather on the historically more significant problem of patterns in conversions. If we stick to Smith's parable, we should acknowledge that a map (accurate or inaccurate) will often guide travel, that the travel of many will shape the territory in accordance with the map, and that maps in turn may be redrawn by new generations of travellers. Thus, this study of the human and divine agency in the conversion ideals communicated by the apologists has ramifications for our understanding of the actual conversion processes of converts to Christianity in the 2nd to 3rd centuries.[8] Experiences are always culturally mediated so by studying the conversion ideals of the apologists we study the cultural codes available for converts when they laboured to make

---

5 This and the following: Rambo, 1993, 7–12; J.T. Richardson, *The Active vs. Passive Convert. Paradigm Conflict in Conversion/Recruitment Research*, in: JSSR 24 (1985), 163–179 (165–179); C.G. Griffin, *The Rhetoric of Form in Conversion Narratives*, in: Quarterly Journal of Speech 76 (1990), 152–163; P. Stromberg, *Language and Self-transformation*, Cambridge 1993, 3–13; H. Gooren, *Towards a New Model of Conversion Careers*, in: Exchange 34 (2005), 149–166 (153. 159); D.A. Snow / R. Machalek, *The Sociology of Conversion*, in: Annual Review of Sociology 10 (1984), 167–190 (172f.). Cf. also R. Stark, *The Rise of Christianity*, Princeton 1996, 19f.

6 N. Hyldahl, *Philosophie und Christentum*, Copenhagen 1966; J.M. van Winden, *An Early Christian Philosopher*, Leiden 1971; T.D. Barnes, *Tertullian*, Oxford 1971.

7 J.Z. Smith, *Map is not Territory*, Leiden 1978.

8 See Rebillard and Jacobsen in this book for the point that converts that did not live fully up to such ideals.

sense of their conversions. This labouring should not in itself be perceived as detached from the conversion; rather it should be seen as an integral part of a conversion process. Hence, in the following, the apologists' exhortations to conversion and the references to (their own) conversions will be analysed as normative rather than descriptive – thus giving us access to studying the conversion ideals that influenced contemporary converts (including the apologists themselves) during their conversion processes.

But first, I will present my understanding of conversion. I have already revealed that I prefer to see conversion as a process rather than an event. This is in tune with the dominating paradigm in the study of conversion to modern religious groups in the last generation of scholarship. In a much used textbook on conversion, Lewis Rambo defined conversion as "basically a process of religious change."[9] Rambo developed his definition partly in opposition to an earlier understanding of conversion as a sudden event. He further sees conversion as a broader phenomenon ("religious change") rather than just change of religion, and he argues that (most) conversions involve more than just a change of faith, namely also changes in behaviour and in affiliation.[10] The primary focus of this article is to study agency in conversion, but at a secondary level I will also discuss whether conversion was perceived by the apologists as a process or an event, as gradual or sudden, and as entailing changes in more than just faith. These secondary questions are related to the primary since it has bearing on the understanding of agency also: what is being changed by whom, and is this done momentarily or over time? But first we need some preliminary definitions of conversion. There is no consensus on the meaning of the term conversion in either everyday English or in scholarship.[11] For some, it means a change of religion, for others, a change of denomination; for yet others an intensification of already existing belief. Preliminary, I define conversion as: a) A religious change, rather than narrowly only a change of religion; b) A change comprehensively involving multiple aspects of life rather than only a change of faith. I will label this as a change in "belief, belonging, and behaviour."[12] And c) A process rather than only an event.

---

9   Rambo, 1993, 5, also for this and the following, id., 1–7.
10 As was typical for his time, Nock saw conversion as a sudden and psychologically motivated event (A.D. Nock, *Conversion*, Oxford 1933, 7–10).
11 See, e.g., the nine articles found in RGG under "Bekehrung/Konversion"; Nock, 1933, 5–10; L. Ahlin / C. Dahlgreen, *The Religious Market and the Problem of Conversion*, in: U. Görmann (ed.), *Towards a New Understanding of Conversion*, Lund 1999, 155–167; H. Gooren, *The Religious Market Model and Conversion*, in: Exchange 35 (2006), 39–60 (52f.); R. MacMullen, *Christianizing the Roman Empire (AD 100–400)*, New Haven 1984, 2–6.
12 In conversion studies, such a comprehensive understanding has a long history, see, e.g., Gooren, 2005, 154. 157. The formulation, a change in "belief, belonging

The three points in this definition partly follow from each other. When studying conversion in antiquity, a narrow understanding of conversion as just "change of religion" will be both anachronistic and distorting. The idea of "a religion" as being an entity that may be distinguished and compared to other "religions" or entities, and the idea that a convert could leave behind one religion for the sake of another, was only under development even in late antiquity. With no such conceptual framework, with no concept of one religion as distinct from another, Christian apologists used other designations to distinguish between their own group and other groups. For instance, Aristides, one of the first Christian apologists,[13] described Christians as a new people comparable with and in the same category as other people: barbarians, Egyptians, Greeks, and Jews.[14] Others, both apologists and outsiders, viewed and described Christianity as a philosophical school.[15] Seeing that the apologists were immersed in the culture of their time, it is more fruitful to analyse their understanding of conversion up against a broader understanding of conversion that includes not only a change from, e.g., being pagan to becoming Christian, but includes a change from, e.g., being a non-Christ-worshipping Jew to becoming a Christ-worshipping Jew, and even an intensification within Christianity.[16] However, with a broad understanding of conversion as not just a

---

and behaviour," was first coined by A. Kreider, *The Change of Conversion and the Origin of Christendom*, Harrisburg 1999. Kreider studies conversion in patristic literature. This phrasing has since found its way into studies of modern conversion (or has been developed independently), even to the degree that it is now possible to talk of the "3B's of conversion," cf. A.R. Lewis, *Belonging Without Belonging*, in: JSSR 49 (2010), 112–126 (112). I thank Søren S. Jensen for this reference.

13 For a discussion of Aristides as an apologist and a dating and analysis of his *Apology*, see N.A. Pedersen, *Aristides*, in: Engberg / Jacobsen / Ulrich (eds.), 2014, 35–49.

14 For Christianity prompting the development of the idea of "religions," see also Nock, 1933, 10–14 and M. Beard / J. North / S.R.F. Price, *Religions of Rome*, vol. 1, Cambridge 1998, 312. 364f. 375.

15 Galen, *De pulsum* 2.4 and 3.3 and a fragment of Galen's commentary on Plato's *Republic* preserved in Arabic translation, cf. R. Walzer, *Galen on Jews and Christians*, Oxford 1949, n. 6.

16 As such, I avoid giving primacy to belief/faith as the central component in religious identity. Cf., e.g., D. Frankfurter, *Beyond "Jewish Christianity,"* in: A.H. Becker / A.Y. Reed (eds.), *The ways that Never Parted*, Tübingen 2003, 131–144 (140) and A.Y. Reed, *"Jewish Christianity" after the "Parting of the Ways,"* in: Becker / Reed (eds.), 2003, 189–232 (190. 192. 194. 200). Whereas belief in Christ was certainly important to the first Christians, behavioural aspect or the aspect of belonging were surely equally important.

change of religion, but as a *religious change* we run the risk of broadening
the understanding so much that it loses its meaning. But a comprehensive
understanding of conversion as change in belief, belonging, and behaviour
helps us to avoid this, and it removes us from a characteristically Lutheran
understanding which gives primacy to faith over other dimensions in religious life.[17] From the comprehensive understanding of conversion, it follows that it is difficult to accept an understanding of conversion as merely a
sudden event. Even if we do allow for sudden conversions, would these be
able to have lasting effects on belief, belonging, and behaviour of converts
if they are not followed by processes, where such converts are integrated
in new religious communities learning how to cope with, comprehend, and
account for[18] their changes? How is a person to be transformed or transform herself/himself overnight in all three aspects of life? Thus, whereas
traditionally scholars perceived conversion to be a psychologically motivated event, conversion is now more often perceived to be a process of socialisation with the convert as an active agent.[19] Narratives and ideological
understandings of conversion – including those of the apologists – might
nevertheless emphasise the suddenness of conversion and describe as irrelevant or pass by everything leading up to or following such moments;
or they might (if we are to believe the now dominant strand of modern
scholarship), in closer correspondence to most convert's conversion experiences, emphasise how even dramatic moments fit into processes of ongoing
conversion.[20] This remains to be explored in the case of the apologists and
in this article with a focus on agency in conversion.

Conversion is therefore preliminarily seen as a process (rather than an
event) of religious change (and not only change of religion) which is comprehensively involving (not only change of faith but), typically, a change in
belief, belonging, and behaviour.[21] When we take the passage from Clement
(quoted above) as an example and apply our definition of conversion to it,
we notice that this understanding fits Clement's passage rather well. For
Clement, there was a change of a) *Belonging*: the Lord's seal is placed on
the initiated, the convert is placed in the Father's care, the convert is here

---

17 For a warning against deluding the term and for employing it only in cases of
   comprehensive change, see Rambo 1993, 16f. 164–170; Gooren, 2006, 53.
18 Stromberg, 1993, xi and 5.
19 Richardson, 1985, and Stromberg, 1993, 3. 11–13.
20 Cf. Cvetković in this volume.
21 We risk finding that the apologists understand conversion as similar to this preliminary definition of conversion because this definition has made me focus on
   passages confirming that view. Such circularity is however unavoidable; we are
   here in the hermeneutical circle.

guarded, and the convert "joins with us"; b) *Belief*: it happens to "him who believes;" and c) *Behaviour*: the convert is "made holy" and guided on a road.

The convert as an active agent in his/her conversion

In traditional scholarship on conversion, the convert was often seen as a rather passive object being enticed, prompted, ensnared or even manipulated by the advocates of the religious group he or she was being drawn to. Modern scholarship has demonstrated that most converts are active agents in re-interpreting not only their own lives, but also in making sense of the religious group they are joining.[22] Let us now examine whether the apologists depicted themselves and other converts as active subjects ore merely passive objects in their conversion processes.

In the first of the preserved *Apologies*, dated to the 120s or 130s and addressed either to the emperor Hadrian or Antoninus Pius,[23] Aristides writes that the Christians "have found the truth by going about and seeking it." But equally important, they do good deeds without telling everybody so, and "they labour to become righteous as those that expect to see their Messiah and receive from Him the promises made to them with great glory."[24] Aristides communicates the idea that conversion both in regard to belief and behaviour is a process rather than an event. Conversion requires an effort of the converts: They have found the truth by *seeking it* and *they labour to become righteous*. This is also clear when Aristides in describing those who have not attached themselves to the Christian people repeatedly claim that they are unwilling to know the truth, being deceivers and deceived, staggering around, tumbling and drawing others with them in their fall. Rhetorically, Aristides addressed the emperor, and he did so by depicting and speaking to the addressee as a potential convert even being directly exhorted to read the Christian writings.[25] It is not the place here to discuss whether Aristides ever intended the emperor to read his petition, or whether this addressing was a literary trope.[26] It is for our purpose sufficient to note that the reader

---

22 Richardson, 1985. See further Gooren, 2006, 42f. 49, for a critique of some even recent scholarship that inadvertently describe converts as passive.

23 Pedersen, 2014, 43–47.

24 Arist., apol. 16. These and the following translations from Aristides are from J.R. Harris, *The Apology of Aristides on Behalf of the Christians*, Cambridge 1893.

25 Arist., apol. 1; 16; cf. Pedersen, 2014, 43.

26 Kinzig and Millar have argued that the apologies addressed to emperors or magistrates were written for (among others) these addressees, see W. Kinzig, *Der "Sitz im Leben" der Apologie in der Alte Kirche*, in: ZKG 100 (1998), 291–317, and F. Millar, *The Emperor in the Roman World*, New York ²1992, 556–560. For

is encouraged to convert, and that argumentation and rhetorical strategy is well-designed to address and impress a (potential) convert: Those who accept the message, the converts, are presented as seeking and finding the truth and as striving for righteousness whereas those who reject it are described as groping, drunken, staggering, and falling – all being active agents. Further, in contrast to other apologies,[27] Aristides shows very little concern for the persecution of Christians, forms of prosecution, reasons for animosity, etc. It is mentioned in passing that some Christians are "imprisoned or oppressed for the name of their Messiah," and (at the end of the text) that the Greeks turn "the ridicule of their foulness upon the Christians" and accuse the Christians of incest (apol. 15; 17). But even his point about these false allegations is meant to relate to the reader the "information" that some of those who falsely accuse the Christians realise their own error and turn Christian themselves. Thus, the main concern is the conversion of the reader.

The same focus on the conversion of the reader and the same focus on the reader and potential convert as an active seeker are found two generations later in Clement of Alexandria's apologetic text *Protreptikos*, in which he writes that conversion entails a change of *behaviour* from an old wicked way full of passions, a change of *belief* where the course is turned after truth, and a change of *belonging* where the convert moves from a life without God to a search of him "who is our real Father" (protr. 10.73p). The idea that (some) converts seek after God, find God, believe in God, and serve God is also brought forward by Tertullian who similarly contrasts such seekers with those who do not want to seek God and listen (apol. 18.1; 40.11).

As a final example, Tatian too is explicit about conversion as a comprehensive reform involving change of belief, behaviour, and belonging, he is explicit about the role of the convert as an active agent in this reform, and he addresses his reader as a potential convert – even addressing the reader in imperative:

---

further proponents of this view and specific authors, see J. Engberg, *Truth Begs no Favours,* in: A.C. Jacobsen/ J. Ulrich / D. Brakke (eds.), *Critique and Apologetics,* Frankfurt 2009, 177–208 (177–179); Pedersen, 2014, 42f.; A.-C. Jacobsen, *Athenagoras,* in: Engberg / Jacobsen / Ulrich (eds.), 2014, 81–100 (83–86. 99f.); N. Willert, *Tertullian,* in: ibid. (ed.), 2014, 159–198 (162). For the view that this address was just a literary convention, see, e.g., G. Clark, *Christianity and Roman Society,* Cambridge 2004, 17f.; F. Young, *Greek Apologists of the Second Century,* in: Edwards *et al.* (eds.), 1999, 81–104 (82–84); L.P. Buck, *Athenagoras' Embassy,* in: HThR 89 (1996), 209–226.

27 I distinguish between apologies and the broader category of apologetic texts: apologies are addressed to emperors or magistrates; apologetic texts are addressed to non-officials or are without an addressee. That legal issues are (comparably) absent from Arist., apol., is observed by Pedersen, 2014, 42f. For comparison, see, e.g., Just., 1 apol. 1–12; 68 and 2 apol. 14–15; Tert., apol. 1–6.

"Die to the world by rejecting its madness, live to God by comprehending him and rejecting the old birth. We were not born to die, but die through our own fault. [...] God has done nothing bad, it was we who exhibited wickedness; but we who exhibited it are still capable of rejecting it."[28] After ordering the reader to die to the world and live to God, Tatian changes to first person plural so that the pre-conversion state is one shared by Tatian, and so that he invites the reader to join him in rejecting wickedness. Elsewhere, Tatian describes to the reader his conversion and what prompted him to convert, he mentions what the reader must do to follow him in conversion, and he states that "my purpose is to set in order the disorderly matter in you."[29]

In tune with recent scholarship on conversion in the modern world, we thus find the apologists describing themselves and other converts as active agents in conversion. Some of these descriptions show stereotype traits of the convert/apologist familiarising himself with different schools, ways of life, and doctrines before embracing Christianity.[30] Such descriptions emulate similar descriptions in contemporary philosophical (auto)biographies.[31] The stereotype character cannot, however, be used to argue that this was not how the apologists experienced and conceived of their own conversion. Converts are prone to reinterpret earlier stages in their lives and formulate them into a coherent whole.[32] Further, some evidence suggests that some of the apologists were indeed very active agents in their own conversion: Thus, many circumstances suggest that at least Tertullian, Cyprian, Arnobius, and Lactantius composed some of their apologetic works containing references to their own conversion at early stages in their own conversion processes, thus playing a very active role in interpreting and ascribing meaning and importance to their own conversion.[33]

---

28 Tatian, *Oratio* 11.2; this and the following translations of Tatian are from M. Whittaker, *Tatian. "Oratio ad Graecos" and Fragments. Edited and Translated*, Oxford 1982. Cf. Martin in this volume on Christian "bridge-burning" vs. the "bridge-building" found in the mystery cults.

29 For the quotation: Tat., orat. 5.2; for the other passages see 1; 30; 35.

30 Just., dial. 1–8, Arist., apol. 1 and Tat., orat. 29 and 35.

31 Josephus, *Vita* 2.9–12; Lucian, *Menippus* 4–5; (Ps.)Clem., hom. 1.1–5.9; cf. Hyldahl, 1966, 148–159 and H. Remus, *Pagan-Christian Conflict over Miracle in the Second Century*, Cambridge 1983, 147.

32 M. Warburg, *Fra Konversionsberetninger til Konversionsanalyser. Kildeproblemer og Fortolkningsstrategier*, in: Mogensen / Damsager (eds.), 2007, 31–42 (33–35).

33 J. Engberg, *From among you*, 2009, 65–68 and id., *The Education and (Self-) Affirmation of (recent or potential) Converts. The Case of Cyprian and the Ad Donatum*, in: Zeitschrift für Antikes Christentum 16 (2012), 129–144 (142f.).

The apologists (seeing themselves) as agents in the conversion of readers

The role of the apologist in inviting the reader to conversion has already been seen in some of the passages discussed above. Clement was also explicit that this was his purpose. In *Protreptikos* (12.95p), both the divine agency and the agency of Clement as a Christian advocate are highlighted as Clement presents his own purpose, namely inviting men to salvation and passing on what he has received from God. Justin similarly claims that he has attempted to move his reader, both employing rational argumentation and a symbolic interpretation of the cross of Christ, having done so, he says, so that he will be without guilt if the reader fails to heed his message.[34]

Immediately prior to these passages, both Justin and Clement had argued for the truthfulness and appeal of the Christian message, trying to convince and exhort their readers. Fourteen out of the sixteen Christian apologists, whose writings have been preserved, tried to convince their readers of the truthfulness of the Christian message or the venerability or innocence of Christians by referring to their own conversion.[35] Such references could be intended to further the possibility of identification between the reader as potential convert and the apologist as an advocate for Christianity who had himself undergone the change that he now exhorts the reader to experience. As the (to us) anonymous author of the *Discourse to the Greeks* (referred to as Pseudo-Justin) wrote in the middle of a lengthy reference to his/her own conversion: "Therefore come and be taught. Become as I am for once I was as you. This has convinced me: The divinity of the doctrine and the power of the Word." Notice, how this invitation to follow the author's example also points in the direction of an important divine agency in conversion. This is followed up upon when the author goes on to describe how the Word, as an expert snake handler, drives out passion and lust from the secret hiding places of our soul, how the Word subsequently gives back peace and serenity to the soul, and how the soul thus liberated from the evils, in which it was immersed, returns to its Maker ([anon.], *Oratio ad Graecos* 5). Again, we see conversion as change in belief, behaviour, and belonging. In other cases, an apologist's purpose in making references to his own conversion could be to strengthen his argumentation. Such a purpose is stated explicitly

---

34 Just., 1 apol. 55.8. For similar statements of purpose, see 1 apol. 10.1–2; 14.2–3; Just., 2 apol. 2.1; 12.8–13.1 (arguing from his own example as convert) and [anon.], *Oratio ad Graecos* 5. See also Fiedrowicz, 2000, 182–185.

35 Engberg, *From Among You*, 2009; on Justin's use of his conversion narrative for converting his readers, cf. also R. Grant, *Greek Apologists of the Second Century*, Westminster 1988, 51.

by Tatian when he writes that "I do not try, as is the habit of most men, to strengthen my case with other men's opinions. [...] I want to compose an account of everything that I personally came to know." Thus, he spent time travelling and studying the Greeks' and Romans' "incoherent doctrines" before embracing Christianity (orat. 35.1). Thus, Tatian also presents himself as a seeker in quest for knowledge.

In two apologetic dialogues, Justin's *Dialogue with Trypho* and Minucius Felix' *Octavius*, it is also part of the setup that a Christian dialogue partner is described as narrating about or referring to his own conversion in order to impress the non-Christian dialogue-partners and entice them to conversion. The author Justin depicts how the dialogue partner Justin in order to influence Trypho and his friends narrates about his own quest through different philosophical schools and his encounter with an old man, an encounter which leads to his conversion to Christianity.[36] Similarly, but less elaborately, in Minucius Felix' apologetic dialogue *Octavius*, the author depicts how the Christian Octavius at one point in the dialogue tries to impress his pagan dialogue partner, Caecilius, by referring to his own conversion and pre-conversion condition – a condition described by Octavius as similar to the one Caecilius finds himself in (thus, Caecilius' identification with Octavius is promoted).[37] Similarly, recent studies of conversion demonstrate that modern conversion narratives are used by converts to influence potential or more recent converts.[38]

Christians (described as) setting examples for converts in charity, morality and by courage

The apologists, however, also claim that Christians exert an influence on potential converts in less verbal ways, firstly through their ethical conduct and philanthropy, secondly through the testimony provided by martyrdom. In Justin's *First apology* 16.2–4 (a context where Justin is presenting obedience to Christ as another motivation for Christians when they exhort potential converts), we learn that conversion entails a behavioural change because the converts are to be guided away "from shame and the love of evil." It is

---

36 Just., dial. 1–8. See also dial. 23.3.
37 Minuc., *Octavius* 28.1–4. In his speech, Octavius is presented as describing himself as a former enemy of Christians who was prompted to conversion by observing the courage of persecuted Christians. Octavius is presented as encouraging Caecilius to identify with him.
38 R. Stark / R. Finke, *Acts of Faith. Explaining the Human Side of Religion*, Berkeley 2000, 107–112. See also Aug., conf. 8.5,10 where Simplicianus narrates about the conversion of Victorinus to Augustine. Augustine explicitly claims that Simplicianus did so in order to prompt him to conversion.

further claimed that many have already converted "from their violent and tyrannical disposition," and that they were prompted to conversion by observing the ethically superior behaviour of Christian relations (neighbours, travel-companions and business-partners). Their conversions have further entailed a change in belief. With his argument from morality, Justin also presumes that his readers will be impressed by reading about the moral reform of converts.[39] In both cases, Justin employs forms of argumentation – the proof from morality and the proof from conversion – commonly found in other early Christian apologetic texts.[40] In congruence with Justin's idea that some are lead to conversion by Christian friends or relations, we find Aristides claiming that Christian heads of households "out of love" persuade non-Christian children and slaves to become Christians (apol. 15). The idea that Christians prompt friends and family members to convert, some we might presume by less gentle means, finds further backing in the setup of some of the apologetic texts.[41] That such setups do not only follow literary patterns, but *also* reflect a reality where Christian friends and relatives played crucial roles in conversion, is confirmed by other ancient evidence matching Celsus' polemic depiction of Christian mission as well as by the repetition of the trope in more (auto)biographic Christian texts.[42]

Modern studies of conversion strongly suggest that crucial roles in conversion are played by "significant others: spouses, relatives, or friends" acting as advocates.[43] The depictions of the roles of friends share stereotype traits so surely we are dealing with a trope, but that fact should not lead us to assume that social networks were unimportant for conversion in antiquity. Thus, our sources also give evidence that the conversion of one or more members of a formerly pagan household or of a group of pagan friends could lead to strife and persecution.[44] Such conversions could, in modern terms, lead to loss of social capital which for pagans meant two ways of redressing the situation: Following the convert in conversion or exerting pressure on the convert to make him or her re-convert – hence a powerful need for the convert to affirm the meaning and value of the conversion through, e.g., the formulation of conversion narratives conforming to the ideals of conversion prevalent in the Christian group joined. This indicates that in

---

39 Cf. Arist., apol. 15–16 and Just., 2 apol. 2.
40 Engberg, *From Among You*, 2009, 52–77, and id., 2012, 132f. See, e.g., Just., 1 apol. 15.7; 2 apol. 2; Tert., Scap. 2.10.
41 See Theophilus' *Ad Autolycum*, the *Letter to Diognetus*, Minucius Felix' *Octavius*, and Cyprian's *Ad Donatum*.
42 Celsus on Christian mission in Or., Cels. 3.51–53.
43 Gooren, 2005, 158.
44 E.g., Tert., Scap. 3.4 and Tert., nat. 1 and 4.

conversion accounts there is no clear dichotomy between the normative and the descriptive level, between description and experience of conversion, between literature and reality. The apologists describe friends and other "significant others" following each other in conversion, and they do so in a way which indicates that we are dealing with literary *topoi*. But such *topoi* likely reflect and give expression to an actual experience and a historical reality. The *topoi* of one friend following another in conversion, and of Christians exerting influence on non-Christian friends and family members correspond to one of the most central observations in studies of modern conversions: friends do follow each other in conversion, and family members and other relations do exert influence in conversions![45]

With the apologists we are dealing with the literary and educated segment of the population in the ancient world, and this also applies largely to the addresses of their works.[46] The author of the *Letter to Diognetus* thus presumes that the distinguished Diognetus, to whom he is addressing himself, observes that the Christians are charitable towards those in need. He presumes that this observation is not a matter of indifference to Diognetus, rather that it has contributed to his curiosity about the Christians, that it will make Diognetus realise that the Christians here on earth are imitating God in Heaven, that it will make him love and admire the Christian martyrs, condemn the deceits of this world, and recognise the true heavenly life.[47] There is, however, no reason to presume that the importance of influence through behaviour and exerted by friends, family members, and other relations should be limited to the educated segments of society. It is to both Justin and Tertullian especially noteworthy that uneducated Christians, too, are able to, in Tertullian's words, "find God and show him, and all that is asked for concerning God, that is confirmed by the craftsman in deeds."[48]

Some evidence suggests that some pagans were indeed impressed by Christian charity and by the morality of Christians. Galen, for example (guided by the ancient prejudice about females being more morally corruptible than educated men from the high orders), was impressed that some Christian women were leading lives not inferior in temperance from that lived by true philosophers.[49] This is not contradicted by the evidence that (others)

---

45 Stark, 1996, 15–21; cf. also R. Fox, *Pagans and Christians*, London 1986, 316f., arguing that friendship conversion was most likely crucial to the growth of Christianity in antiquity.

46 See Georges in this volume on the philosophical interests of Justin and Tatian.

47 *Ad Diognetum* 1.1 and 10.

48 Tert., apol. 46.9–14; Just., 2 apol. 10; Just., dial. 29.

49 The passage from Galen's commentary on Plato's Republic is preserved in Arabic translation. For the Arabic text and an English translation, see Walzer, 1949,

perceived the Christians to be morally depraved practicing incest and eating human flesh.[50] In two chapters of his *Second apology*, Justin refers to his own conversion to counteract such allegations of Christian debauchery (2 apol. 12–13). He claims that he, as a Platonic philosopher, heard the rumour that Christians were cannibals, but that he himself observed their courage when faced with persecution, torture, and even death, and that this proved to him that the allegations could not be true, and finally that this lead him to strive to become known as a Christian himself. In the middle of the passage, he invites the reader to also change ways and come to good sense.

References to the courage of martyrs and references to conversion could thus be used with the defensive purpose of countering allegations. But the chapters also communicate the message that the observation of Christian courage when faced with persecution could lead to conversion, i.e., that persecuted Christians could be agents in the conversion of spectators. This idea was already presented by Justin once in his *Second apology* and twice in his *First apology*, but also in later sources.[51] The argument is especially frequently repeated in the small apologetic *Letter to Diognetus* where it appears to have been one of the author's favourite arguments (7.7–9). In this text, the persecuted Christians "thrown to the wild beasts to make them deny the Lord" are depicted as leading to more conversions, but this human agency has its ultimate source in God's power and presence: "These things do not appear as human accomplishments. They are due to the power of

---

n. 6. For a recent English translation, see J. Engberg / P. Fritz / R. Hansen / J. Larsen, *Translation of Second Century pagan Authors on Christians and Christianity*, in: Engberg / Jacobsen / Ulrich (eds.), 2014, 229–236 (235). See also Engberg, *Condemnation, Criticism and Consternation*, in: Engberg / Jacobsen / Ulrich (eds.), 2014, 201–228 (222–224) and Engberg, 2011, 105f. For the significance of Christian ethics in attracting converts, see Stark, 1996, 209–215 and I. Issermann, *Did Christian Ethics have any Influence on the Conversion to Christianity?*, in: Zeitschrift für Antikes Christentum 16 (2012), 99–112. For the significance of Christian charity for conversions, see Fox, 1986, 324–326. 590–592, and Stark, 1996, 72–94.

50 E.g., Engberg, *Impulsore Chresto. Opposition to Christianity in the Roman Empire c. 50–250 AD*, Frankfurt 2007; A. McGowan, *Eating People. Accusations of Cannibalism against Christians in the Second Century*, in: Journal of Early Christian Studies 2 (1994), 413–442; A.N. Sherwin-White, *Why were the Early Christians Persecuted? An Amendment*, in: Past and Present 27 (1964), 23–27; J.J. Walsh, *On Christian Atheism*, in: VigChr 45 (1993), 255–277; Jacobsen, 2014, 97–99; Engberg, *Truth*, 2009, 197–202; Arist., apol. 17; Just., 1 apol. 26–27; 29.2; 2 apol. 12.2; dial. 10; Tat., orat. 25.3–28.1; 33.1–2; Tert., apol. 4; 7–9; nat. 16; Athenag., leg. 3.1; 31–36; Theo., Autol. 1.9–11; 3.4; 3.14.

51 Just., 2 apol. 10; 1 apol. 21; 25; dial. 110; *Ad Diognetum* 1.1; 5.11–17; 6.9–10; 7.7–8; 10.7–8; Tert., apol. 50.12–15 and Scap. 5.4.

God – they are proofs of his presence." In scholarship, it is hotly debated whether such apologetic claims reflect a real situation of people being impressed by the courage of persecuted Christians and turning to Christianity, or whether it represents an argumentative strategy designed either to convince non-Christian readers (especially magistrates and emperors) that it was futile or even counterproductive to persecute and prosecute Christians or to impress Christian readers giving them courage and attaching meaning and value to the sufferings they were occasionally facing.[52] The dichotomy is false: The claims served argumentative purposes (the two mentioned above and a further one, as discussed below), and they reflected a reality of non-Christians truly being astounded by the behaviour of confessing Christians.

Most of the pagan authors who wrote about the Christians noticed the courage of Christians when faced with persecution; they all (except Galen) tried to attribute this admirable courage to bad motives like habit, obstinacy, or foolishness, but their need to do so shows that some of them worried that at least some of the readers would be favourably impressed by the Christians. The apologists' use of the references to martyrdom as an argument in contexts where they tried to exhort their readers to conversion demonstrates – if we presume that their texts were intended for readers who were recent or potential converts – that the apologists suspected such arguments (and the behaviour of martyrs) to indeed impress (some) recent or potential converts. In a number of instances, we see Christian apologists directly comparing the courage of such Christians with the suffering and death of Socrates or other suffering figures whom they presumed their pagan readers to admire, or we see them alluding to exhortations to courage made by Cicero, Seneca, Diogenes, and other admired authors.[53] This demonstrates that their arguments could find resonance in the fact that courage and endurance were admired character-traits. Finally, let us remember that most of the apologists were themselves converts; hence, their arguments may be viewed as arguments that also served purposes of self-legitimisation – a crucial process for any convert. Reading the apologists is thus not only reading arguments that they presumed would impress potential or recent converts; it is reading arguments that made sense to the authors as converts in whatever stage of a

52 E.g., Fox, 1986, 315; Engberg, *Martyrdom and Persecution*, in: J. Engberg / U.H. Eriksen / A.K. Petersen (eds.), *Contextualising Early Christian Martyrdom*, Frankfurt 2011, 93–117; D. Boyarin, *Dying for God*, Stanford 1999, 94f.; G.W. Bowersock, *Martyrdom and Rome*, Cambridge 1995, 66, and W.H.C. Frend, *Martyrdom and Persecution in the Early Church*, Cambridge 1965, 257f.

53 Athenag., leg. 31.2; Tert., apol. 50. See also Jacobsen, 2014, 88; Engberg, *Truth*, 2009, 204–206 and id., 2011, 104f.; Bowersock, 1995, 9; Fiedrowicz, 2000, 189f.

conversion process they might be. The claim that some non-Christians were impressed by the courage of Christian martyrs is again not contradicted by the evidence revealing that other, non-Cristian observers saw the behaviour of the martyrs as evidence of madness or obstinacy.

Human and divine agency in conversion (conceived as) prompted by prayer and miracles

Two final aspects of human agency or rather human-divine co-agency in conversion should be discussed: some apologists stress that Christians prompted others to conversion through prayer for potential converts or through healings and exorcisms. Aristides, for example, claims in chapter 17 of his *Apology* that the Greeks (because they are themselves immoral) blame the Christians for being immoral, but that the Christians pity and pray for those who wrongly deride them.[54] Some then convert and are ashamed of their former lives, their former ignorance and false accusations leading those converts to confess to God and obtain forgiveness. Again, conversion involves in this passage a change of behaviour (from foulness to cleanness of heart) and of belief (from a state where the Greeks are "destitute of knowledge" to a state where they embrace the "true knowledge of the Christians"). Regarding agency, we see both the convert and God being active. What is of most interest in this part of our investigation is that the prayers of Christians are also described as important in bringing conversion to potential converts – the efficacy of prayer in itself entailing a divine agency. Thus, in the opening of his *Cohortatio ad Graecos*, Pseudo-Justin prays to God that he may be given (by God) what he needs to say to his readers that they may give up their former bias and the errors of their forefathers and choose what is rewarding. Similar openings are found in the (to us) anonymous *Ad Diognetum* 1.2 and in Theophilus' *Ad Autolycum* 3.23. As part of the narrative of the *Dialogue with Trypho*, Justin ends with praying for his Jewish dialogue partners (by then depicted not as full converts, but as favourably impressed by Justin's exposition of Scripture and willing to study the matter further) that they may fully believe that Jesus is the Christ of God, and that the Christian way (of life) brings wisdom to every man (Just., dial. 142.3).

The final issue to discuss in this section on the role of Christian advocates in the conversion of outsiders is that of different miracles. In Cyprian's *Ad Donatum*, we see Cyprian referring to spiritual gifts in the forms of healing, prophetic foreknowledge, and exorcism not in order to convince an as yet unconvinced addressee. These gifts are instead referred to as gifts which he

---

54 In Scap. 1.3, Tertullian writes that Christians pray for their persecutors, like Scapula. They do so out of love and in the hope of bringing them to conversion.

himself and his addressees as recent converts (or as converts in a conversion process) have begun to receive in conversion. Such spiritual gifts will, according to Cyprian, flow in ever increasing abundance. Thus, if, as Cyprian writes to Donatus, "depending on God with all your strength and your whole heart you continue to be what you have begun to be, much power is given to you." Concretely, both Donatus and Cyprian are described as having and expecting in greater measure "modest chastity," "sound mind," to be empowered "to console the grieving," restore health, bring peace, give rest to the violent, gentleness to the afflicted, and to force "those unclean and wandering spirits to confess" (ad Don. 4–5). Cyprian writes to Donatus that "our power is from God, I say, it is all from God." Cyprian's *Ad Donatum* is especially interesting because there are many indications that it was written at a time when Cyprian was himself a recent convert (a convert at a stage in his conversion process), and that the same applied to the addressee. Hence here, we are dealing not only with arguments which Cyprian presumed would be convincing to recent or potential converts among the readers, but with arguments that made sense to Cyprian himself in this stage of his conversion process.

In comparison, Tertullians *Ad Scapulam* is directly addressed to an outsider who is even persecuting the Christians. But he, too, is presented with proof from miracles. This shows that the apologists regarded miracles (or references to miracles) as potentially convincing evidence for a spectrum of recent or potential converts – ranging from a persecutor through a neutral outside observer to a catechumen or newly baptised. In the short and focused apology *Ad Scapulam* addressed, as the title indicates, to the proconsul of Africa in 212, Scapula, Tertullian pursues the dual purpose of bringing persecution to an end and of converting the persecutor Scapula (1.3–4 and 3.5). Tertullian provides in one section a proof from miracle. In this, he claims that it is possible for Scapula himself to ascertain how a barrister's clerk, another barrister's relative, and a third barrister's son were all set free from afflictions by Christians. He further claims that many people of all classes have been delivered from daemons and cured by Christians; that the Christian Proculus Torpacion, the steward of Euhodias, had anointed and cured the late emperor Severus, that the prayer of Christian soldiers had delivered the army of Marcus Aurelius from thirst, and that droughts are routinely repelled by "our kneelings and fastings" (Tert., Scap. 4.4–6).

In both Cyprian's and Tertullian's view there is important agency in the Christians bringing these benefits/gifts to the potential converts. There is, however, also a clear emphasis that the power is God's. The agency is therefore human-divine. In this, Justin totally agrees as seen in a passage where he, too, provides proof from healing and exorcism.[55] A more surprising combination of human-divine-demonic co-agency is found in Tertullian's *Apologeticum* where he speaks of daemons and exorcisms (and the witness to Christ's power that the daemons involuntarily bear when exorcised): "This kind of witness, then, offered by your gods regularly makes Christians. The more we believe them, the more we believe in Christ as Lord. They kindle our faith in our sacred books; they build up our assurance in our hope" (23.15–18). Tertullian goes on to claim that the governor worships the daemons by killing Christians, but that the daemons might fear that he (the governor) will one day turn Christians and exorcise daemons.

Divine agency in conversion

So far in our discussion of agency in conversion in early Christian apologetic texts, I have given examples of the agency of humans: a) The convert as an active agent in his own conversion; b) Christian advocates, be it the apologists in relation to readers or as dialogue partners in an apologetic dialogue, or be it others described as preaching and exhorting to conversion; c) Christians influencing through actions, i.e., integrity, ethical or charitable behaviour, or courage when faced with adversity or even persecution and execution; and d) Christians influencing converts through prayers or through the administering of or reference to gifts of the Spirit seen in the healing of the sick or the exorcism of daemons. It is, however, noticeable that all the examples given above (as all the apologists in general) included in their references and exhortations a strong element of divine agency.[56] Surely, this indicates that divine agency was crucial according to the theology of conversion of the apologists. In this final section of the article, I will focus on passages permeated with such divine agency, passages, however, that will also often ascribe importance to human in collaboration with divine agency.[57]

In Justin's *Dialogue with Trypho*, he describes what conversion entails, and it is obvious that the primary agent is God and Christ. Thus according to the "will of the Father," grace is "conferred upon us by our Jesus"; "The Angel of God" protects Justin and other converts, and Jesus "snatches us" from dangers. Jesus will reward with garments and an eternal kingdom; it is through Jesus that "we" believe in God. "His calling" has set Justin and the other converts "on fire," and they are "now of the true priestly family of

---

55 Just., 2 apol. 6.5–6. See also Tert., apol. 18.5.
56 See also Arist., apol. 16–17; Theophilus, *Ad Autolycym* 3.11–12; Clem., protr. 5.12,92.
57 Even passages that come close to focusing on human agency end with pointing to the agency of God: Tat., orat. 29.

God." There is some agency on the part of the converts since they ("through the name of Jesus") "have taken off [their] dirty clothes," and since the converts are expected to "obey his commands." We see again that conversion entails a change of belief, behaviour, and belonging (to "the true priestly family of God"), and that conversion is more a process than an event.[58]

Justin, like Tatian, ascribed much importance to the study of Scripture in his own conversion and in his dialogue in his attempt to convert Trypho and the followers of Trypho. Much of the conversation between Justin and Trypho is depicted as focusing on Jewish Scripture. But Justin also alludes to a passage from Matthew which seems to have been of particular significance to him in apologetic contexts because he also alludes to it in his *First apology*.[59] In the *Dialogue* 100.1–2, Justin quotes the words of Christ according to Matt 11:27 and says: "He thus revealed to us all that we have learned from the Scriptures by His grace, so that we know Him as the First-begotten of God before all creatures." The change of belief is thus not the result of an intellectual human study of Scripture, it is Christ who through the Scriptures reveals the Father and himself to Justin and other converts. That Christ himself is ultimately the chief agent in the conversion of converts, and that conversion entails the establishment of direct contact with Christ (change of belonging) is often mentioned by Justin.[60] The author of the *Letter to Diognetus* equally describes how it is impossible for humans to reach life and salvation through their own means, and how God has revealed that this is obtainable only in the Saviour. The author then goes on to admonish that "we" should believe in God and his Son as our provider, father, teacher, councillor, physician, healer, mind, light, honour, glory, strength, and life (*Ad Diognetum* 9.6).

Such language of intimacy in the relation between the divine and the convert is again mirrored in Clement. The whole setup and the titles of the *Protreptikos* and *Paedagogos* presume that Jesus is acting and is to act as the encourager and educator. Many passages display a high level of intimacy in this relationship, but let us take one lengthy passage as an example here and notice the role and relationship ascribed to God, the Holy Spirit, divine Scripture, and Christ: The Lord out of love encourages all men to come "to a full knowledge of the truth" and therefore sends the Comforter. God himself is the teacher, and he alone has the power "to conform man to his likeness." Scripture may play a role in this since "the letters which make us sacred and divine are indeed themselves sacred." And concerning Christ,

---

58 Just., dial. 116. All translations of Justin's *Dialogue with Trypho* are from T.B. Falls, *Saint Justin Martyr*, Washington 1948.

59 Just., 1 apol. 63.3; 13.

60 E.g., Just., 1 apol. 12 (Christ as our teacher); 2 apol. 2.1 and 10.6–8.

Clement continues by stating that man's salvation is his only work: "He cries out, urging men on to salvation: 'the kingdom of heaven is at hand'." Moreover, "let us, who are many, hasten to be gathered together into one love corresponding to the union of the One Being. Similarly, let us follow after unity by the practise of good works." There is no doubt in all of this of the centrality of divine agency, but the last sentence confirms that there is a human response to be given to the divine calling.[61]

The permeating attribution of importance to divine agency in the apologists' references and exhortations to conversion and their descriptions of the possibility of obtaining an intimate relationship and belonging to an all-powerful and benevolent God would have been important in the ancient world where divine protection was considered essential and the gods often considered erratic and vengeful.[62] Equally, the idea that such divine relationship and benevolence would have required a human response and commitment would be logical in a world where the relationship to those in power and authority (be it divinities or human authorities, like emperors, governors, magistrates, patrons and fathers) was often thought to rest on the exchange of benevolence and protection and honour and cult.[63] Thus, Arnobius as a recent convert and apologist explains to his readers that it is reasonable to accord divine honours to Christ because Arnobius has received liberation from superstition from him and because he is expecting even greater gifts in the future.[64]

Conclusion: Agency and from ideology to experience

The examples discussed above show that the apologists ascribed important agency in conversion to both human and divine agents. The apologists perceived the agency of the convert to be of importance as converts were described as seeking the truth, responding to Christ's calling, casting of an old life, laying aside prejudice, reading scripture, observing the behaviour of Christians, interacting with them, etc. The apologists saw themselves as playing a part in the conversion (processes) of their readers by exhorting,

---

61 Clem., protr. 9.71–72p. See also 12.91–94p, underlining the interaction of the divine and the convert in conversion.

62 E.g., Fox, 1986, 34–38. 69–72. 90–101. 219–237. 326. 575, for the need for divine protection and fear of divine retribution and the perceived erratic character of deities; and E.R. Dodds, *Pagan and Christian in an Age of Anxiety*, Cambridge ²1991, 133, for the temptation of embracing Christianity to rid yourself of such fears. See also, e.g., Tacitus, *Historiae* 1.3 and Plutarch, *De superstitione* 3; 7; 9; 11f.; 14.

63 E.g., Fox, 1986, 12–14. 52–61. 79f.

64 Arn., nat. 1.39. See also Engberg, *From Among You*, 2009, 49–51.

arguing, and by setting an example through references to their own conversion. The apologists argued with reference to Christian morality, charity, and courage when faced with persecution, simultaneously claiming that such examples exerted influence on converts and showing us both that they believed such arguments would carry weight with their readers (including potential or recent converts), and that they made sense to themselves as converts. The apologists prayed for and made references to prayer for (potential) converts (including the readers), and they argued with reference to miracles and to claims that such miracles prompted conversion, demonstrating that such references mattered to themselves and were believed to carry weight with others. But above all else, the divine agency was described as crucial with Christ, God or the Spirit calling, guiding, saving, guarding, enlightening, and making holy.

Throughout, many examples have been analysed of conversion being seen as entailing change of belief, of behaviour, and of belonging – all three aspects are quite often found even in single passages. In line with such a comprehensive understanding of conversion it is unsurprising that the dominant perception of conversion seems to be that it is a process rather than an event.[65] But the trend can be less pronounced, and we do find examples of apologists emphasising the suddenness of divine intervention in conversion, so that we are prompted to cautiously conclude that the apologists' ideal of conversion allowed for both sudden and gradual conversions.[66] The tendency to give priority to gradual rather than climactic conversions in exactly apologetic texts is not surprising. Most of the apologists attempted to present Christianity as a philosophy.[67] In especially the Platonic, philosophical tradition there was a comparable understanding that wisdom and virtue could not be taught, comprehended, or attained in a moment or even a short time, but that it rather required labour, exercise, and lengthy studies.[68]

It is not possible to discern neither any chronological development nor any marked difference in emphasis between individual authors in their perception of conversion and agency in conversion. From Aristides in the early 2nd century to Cyprian and Pseudo-Justin in the mid-3rd century, apologists rather consistently ascribe importance to both human and divine agency in

---

65 See further Arist., apol. 1; 15–16; Just., dial. 2; 142; Cypr., ad Don. 14; Tatian, *Oratio ad Graecos* 1.

66 Just., dial. 8 and Cypr., ad Don. 2–4. Cf. Bremmer in the present volume on stories of sudden conversions.

67 Fiedrowicz, 2000, 148–155. 215. 243. 291–300.

68 Plato, *Sophista* 234a, and Plotinus, *Ennead* 1.6,9. See also Josephus, *Vita* 7–12 and Just., dial. 1.4. See further A.F. Segal, *Paul the Convert*, New Haven 1990, 80. 84. 98. 113.

conversion and maintain the perception that conversion entailed a change in behaviour, belief, and belonging.

In the apologists' theology of conversion we have seen both diversity and consistency in emphasis and purpose. It is possible to argue that the apologists through such diversity and consistency provided their (intended) readers with multiple, but not mutually exclusive, conversion ideals; such ideals would likely reflect the kind of conversion ideals that the converts (including the apologist) would have encountered during their own conversion processes. When the apologists wrote about their conversion and described the divine and human agency in these processes, they provided their readers with examples to emulate or maybe rather with a framework, a theology of conversion, for understanding the conversion processes of the readers. We thus find the apologists striving to become agents in the conversion processes of their readers.

As we noticed above, some of the apologetic texts with their references to conversion were written during the conversion process of some of the apologists. In these cases, the writing of the apologies and the inclusion herein of references to divine and human agency in the conversion of the author himself and of other Christians would have contributed to the rationalisation and (self) legitimisation of the conversion process of the apologist – such (self) legitimisation is an important part in any conversion process. An autobiographical conversion narrative is a means through which justification and affirmation may be achieved and therefore provides us with a source to two stages in the convert's conversion process. Firstly, it allows for a traditional examination of the reference as a source to the time described. The text is studied as an account, and the scholars face the difficulty that the author may have forgotten or deliberately distorted events. Secondly, it allows for the study of the experience and self-perception of the convert at the later stage in this convert's conversion process where the narrative is composed – and this is the kind of study championed in this article. The reference to conversion is studied as a relic, and we take into account that it plays a role in providing self-affirmation, and that it therefore needs to make sense to the apologist as a convert at this later stage in the conversion process.[69] Studied in this way, the reference does offer an excellent opportunity to study the convert's experience of conversion at this stage in his process. Historically, the late stage is the more important:[70] if the apologists had not remained Christians (and found meaning in and reasons for remaining Christians) after their initial attraction, we would likely never have heard about them, and

---

69 Stromberg, 1993, 3: "the conversion narrative itself is a central element of the conversion," cf. 15 and xiii. See also Warburg, 2007, 35–37.
70 Compare Fox, 1986, 317.

they would not have taken part in the further spread of Christianity in the ancient world.

We thus find the apologists as active agents in their own conversion, in their own "dance with angels" (thus confirming the view on converts as active agents found in modern scholarship on contemporary conversion), and we find them aiming to be agents in the conversion of some of their readers, encouraging them to dance with angels, too, and showing them how to do so.

Nicholas Marshall

Ontological Conversion: a Description and Analysis of Two Case Studies from Tertullian's *De Baptismo* and Iamblichus' *De Mysteriis*

Abstract: Marshall proposes a new way to conceive conversion even in the cases where we have no first-hand attests. He suggests that the concept of "ontological conversion" provides a fruitful entry into the issue of agency in conversion because it defines the religious group and its ideology as central agents in the conversion process.

This essay[1] considers the possibility of conversion in Iamblichus' *De mysteriis* and compares posited features of conversion to those drawn from Tertullian's *De baptismo*.[2]

Many previous models of conversion have addressed the issue of passivity or activity in the individual's conversion. From an earlier dominant scholarly point of view, a group acted upon the passive converts by brainwashing them, taking their individuality away and making them unable to choose any other option than to join the cult. Today, however, most scholars have abandoned the view on the converts as passive objects and regard them instead as active seekers.[3]

Still the question of why people undergo conversion, why they change their minds in such, often, radical ways, remains pressing. While issues of agency are impossible to determine from only written evidence, one may in fact point to certain strategies of at least coercion in texts aimed at converts to a religion or philosophical group.

---

1   I would like to thank Dylan Burns for reading previous drafts of this essay and providing valuable support and criticism. All errors of transcription, translation, and interpretation remain my own.
2   All references to *De mysteriis* follow E.C. Clarke / J.M. Dillon / J.P. Hershbell (eds. and trans.), *Iamblichus. De Mysteriis*, Atlanta 2003; text based on E. Des Places (ed.), *Jamblique. Les mystères d'Egypte*, Paris 1966. I have chosen to rely on this translation as it is the most readable. All citations from Tertullian's *De baptismo* follow R.P. Refoulé (ed. and trans.), *Tertullian. Traité du Baptême*, Paris ²2002. I have made use of this edition in my own translation.
3   Cf., e.g., J.T. Richardson, *The Active vs. Passive Convert. Paradigm Conflict in Conversion/Recruitment Research*, in: JSSR 24/2 (1985), 119–136; H. Gooren, *Reassessing Conventional Approaches to the Study of Conversion*, in: JSSR 46/3 (2007), 337–353; L. Rambo, *Understanding Religious Conversion*, New Haven 1993, 44–46. 56–65.

In this paper, I will argue that the concept of "ontological conversion" offers an interesting way to address the issue of agency in conversion. In an ontological conversion, the worldview created by the community seems to leave the convert no choice but to convert, because the convert is asked to become who he or she really is, i.e., a divine being. This defines the religious group as a central agent in the conversion process.

Previous research in the field of ancient conversion has concentrated on the individual stories of converters, whether autographic or written by third parties. Although the texts examined in this study are non-narrative, they can still offer us compelling data about the phenomenon of conversion in late antiquity. Tertullian's *De baptismo* is, I wager, more familiar to the readers of this volume and so the analysis will revolve around Iamblichus' text. *De mysteriis* is a pivotal fourth-century work that offers us a glimpse into the ritual culture of theurgy which we can preliminarily define as the deployment of rites to attain Platonic goals of union with the divine. Previous research on theurgy has made the strong claim that theurgy is a religious system complete with a ritual of initiation meant to mark one's admittance into the group by means of a central, "magical" rite, built upon the model of an archaic Greek funeral.[4] Yet, the evidence for this rite is piecemeal and leaves open the fundamental question of whether or not the theurgists actually constituted a social group and whether they had a ritual of conversion. This essay argues that a particular ideological strategy of conversion, which I define as "ontological conversion", is present in the protreptic form of the *De mysteriis*. To test this claim, I will interpret features of ontological conversion in the two abovementioned texts. This paper is divided into four subsections. Part 1 offers a brief recap of existing theories and methods of analysing conversion and explains the gap that ontological conversion is meant to fill. Part 2 introduces and defines ontological conversion with brief references to features of ontological conversion in several examples. Part 3 fleshes out the theory by examining the texts of Tertullian and Iamblichus and highlighting within them references to ontological conversion. Part 4 offers some conclusions.

It will be noted that my approach differs somewhat from that of other researchers who have set out to contradict the Jamesian and Nockian model of sudden conversion by drawing on contemporary anthropological studies and new models of conversion which suggest a more processual and gradual shift in worldview.[5] I do not dispute such models, and I agree on the basis

---

4   H. Lewy, *Chaldaean Oracles and Theurgy. Mysticism, Magic, and Platonism in the Later Roman Empire*, Paris 1978, 184f.
5   Bremmer, Engberg, and Cvetković in this volume discuss processual conversions. Cf. also Bøgh's contribution which proposes new ways to understand conversion in a pagan context.

of evidence and intuition that conversion happens slowly and is re-imagined and written down as sudden, teleological and final. My approach, however, is to investigate the agency of the figures and texts offering the conversion (i.e., the missionaries) and inquire into their strategies.

1. The Study of religious and philosophical conversion from psychology to sociology

The topic of conversion has enjoyed a stimulating intellectual history, inextricable from the definitional and methodological trends of the study of religion. The early forages of William James (1902) focused almost exclusively on narratives of Christian conversion, influenced especially by prevailing theological attitudes and biblical stories such as the famous description of Saul of Tarsus' conversion on the road to Damascus (Acts 9:3–9). Conversion, according to James, was a single, intense, revelatory experience which caused a complete transformation of the moral and psychological being of the individual, healing a perceived existential lack. These early studies had a profound influence on the historical researches of Arthur Darby Nock who similarly focused on the individual and employed the "Pauline" model of a sudden, powerful, conversion. Nock theorised that only the "prophetic religions", Judaism and Christianity (curiously Islam is absent), impose sufficient psychological pressure on their followers to abandon the old way of life and pursue a new one, thereby coercing a real conversion out of the converted.

Nock also noted that the terminology of conversion had already been used in classical philosophy to denote a shift in allegiance from an ordinary to a philosophical way of life. However, after noting that the schools of Epicurus and Plato also had their prophets who looked at the world around them and demanded change, he refused to make a strong connection between philosophical conversion and Christian conversion, stating that the former was only "something like" a conversion.[6]

Since James and Nock, scholars have examined conversion with a number of different approaches. Some have attempted to argue that James' original theories of sudden and intense psychological transformation are based on more or less fictive constructions of post-converts meant to exaggerate the difference between the negatively-valued pre-conversion state and the hyper-valued post-conversion state.[7] Such scholars tend to favour methods that

---

6   Nock uses this phrase explicitly in the case of the Cynics (A.D. Nock, *Conversion*, London 1933, 169) and then again, more generally, in the case of second-century philosophies *in toto* (173).

7   Eshleman notes that "conversion narratives" are "ideologically constructed [...] which tell[s] us less about the process of conversion itself than about the convert's

focus on deconstructing binaries in the converter's narrative of conversion, as well as comparative insights drawn from modern sociological theories of conversion. Others have focused on philosophical conversion, noting that from a purely sociological perspective, joining a philosophical group is the same as a joining a religious group.[8]

This shift of emphasis towards the social factors has produced many valuable insights and theories, such as the notion that conversion is not reducible to a one-time intense moment in one's adolescence, but is rather the outcome of many different contributing elements, all of which play an important role in the conversion narrative. The concentration on social factors of conversion has also resulted in an overall de-emphasis on the value of strict theological (i.e., Christian) notions of conversion. Expanded definitions of conversion applicable to extra-Christian religious traditions and systems are employable. However, while conversion is perhaps primarily a matter of social networking,[9] it remains a complex phenomenon whose reduction to one factor is simply not feasible. Moreover, the practicality of applying modern social conversion theories to ancient texts is questionable in light of the vast cultural differences between converters ancient and modern. So then, how can we study social conversion in ancient texts?

There may be a solution in a different approach. Many previous studies of conversion have concentrated on data from first-person accounts of converters, whether those narratives are from ancient sources or modern surveys. Certainly, these are interesting sources of data, but they cannot tell the whole story. In the task of understanding why people convert to a particular paradigm of thinking, there is great value to looking at conversion from the perspective of the recruiter, exploring how the recruiting group frames their particular ideology in the manner it does. Such a point of view not only provides us with insight into the persuasive structural frames that the recruiting group's ideology uses to convince an audience of the rightfulness or truthfulness of their dogma/philosophy, but also helps us determine the underlying frameworks of conversion as a general phenomenon.

---

current understanding, the ideology and self-conception of the group as a whole or the interests of the third party [...] who tells the convert's story" (K. Eshleman, *Affection and Affiliation. Social Networks and Conversion to Philosophy*, in: CJ 103/2 (2007–2008), 129–140 (130)).

8 Ibid., 130.
9 Ibid., 131.

2. Ontological conversion: Definition and minor examples

> There is no religion that is not a cosmology as well as a speculation on the divine.
>
> – Émile Durkheim[10]

In his book *Understanding Religious Conversion*, Lewis Rambo identifies five attractive draws of conversion: "(1) a system of meaning (cognitive); (2) emotional gratification; (3) techniques for living; (4) charisma; and (5) power."[11] Rambo's notion of power provides a useful starting point for thinking about ontological conversion. As Rambo notes, "a theme that emerges in many [scil. conversion narratives] is that the convert feels filled with power, has access to power, or is somehow connected with either an external source of power (God) or an internal sense of power that may be perceived as spiritual or divine."[12] Belonging to a group is in some way seen as providing people with a feeling of connection to divine powers or an awareness of their own status as a supernatural being.

But how is such a status acquired? There may be several avenues to a metaphysical upgrade, but what I choose to concentrate on here is the substantial transformation – so substantial, one could call it "ontological", taking place at a deep, essential stratum – that is promised to converts in didactic writings of the recruiting group. These writings also seem to offer a symbolic discourse of the change in identity or status at the social level. Such promises offer the possibility of an individual transforming into something superior to mere humanity; alternatively, in the case of more pessimistic cults, the re-apprehension of an original powerful state from which one has fallen as part of a cosmological fall myth.[13] This ontological transformation is variously represented discursively through binary metaphors or language of completion/perfection. The value of the term "ontological conversion" lies especially in the fact that it captures not only some features of conversion once labeled "theological" or "religious" (rather unprecise and problematic terms), but it also incorporates features of other religious discourses (for example, certain branches of philosophy) that have circumvented in other respects various definitions of religion.

---

10 *Elementary Forms of Religious Life* (C. Cosman, trans.), Oxford 2001, 10 (originally published in French in 1915).
11 Rambo, 1993, 81–86.
12 Ibid., 64. 85f.
13 Two examples of this latter conversion are the Christian attainment of a pre-fall state through baptism, as well as the Christian Gnostic understanding of a reception of divine *gnosis* which allows human beings to recall their divine origins, prior to their enslavement in matter.

The term "ontology" requires some clarification as it is a term used in different ways in different contexts. For the purposes of this essay, ontology is probably best captured by the vague notion of "the science of what exists." In Platonic thought the entirety of the universe was hierarchically organised into levels of increasingly real "things". This hierarchy was accompanied by a cognate hierarchy of modes of epistemological understanding. Thus, certain forms of higher reality were thought to be inaccessible to ordinary modes of data-acquisition, e.g., sensory perception. The systems that describe ontological levels range from the very simple (those that posit only one or two levels to reality), to the relatively complex (systems that describe five levels of reality, subdivide the highest into three, etc.). The existence of these alternative levels of reality, closed to ordinary human understanding but open to sage minds, intuitive perceptions, or noetic understandings was variously defended on the basis of dialectical argument, quasi-religious authority, or some other form of a priori judgment. In familiar religious discourses, the higher levels of reality were peopled with various powerful spirits, such as gods, angels, or daemons, who had the responsibility for the maintenance of the lower levels which were occupied by human beings of ordinary consciousness and animals.

Such ontological divisions are common to many religious and philosophical traditions. In fact, it may be that the posited existence of supernatural realms is one of the most important defining characteristics of religion, though I recognise that this is still a problematic and debatable issue.[14] In any case, we may say religion is constituted by binary oppositions such as the distinction between human and divine, profane and sacred, multiplicity and unity, living and dead, current terrible existence and idealised state of harmony, and various other normative distinctions, which rituals and discourses create and reinforce.

Ontological transformation, the textual description of transformation of human beings into higher states, especially those of angels or gods, has been explored by Fletcher-Louis (though only in the domain of second temple Judaism). He concludes that ontological divisions (human vs. divine/angel) reflect locative (e.g., profane space vs. temple) and institutional (laity vs. priesthood) distinctions. In other words, the narratives of ontological transformation heighten the prominence and the perceived value of the religious leaders as well as the value of the sacred space where those leaders work.[15]

---

14 See the thesis of Spiro, cited in J.Z. Smith, *Religion, Religions, Religious*, in: M. Taylor (ed.), *Critical Terms for Religious Studies*, Chicago 1998, 269–284 (281).
15 C.H.T. Fletcher-Louis, *All the Glory of Adam*, Leiden 2002. Ontological transformation: 6–9 (terminology introduced, but left undefined), 214 (human undergoing ontological transformation thought to become larger). Temple: 61

My point of departure is to add that this heightening of status – when it is applied not only to the elite leaders of a community, but also to the general membership – may serve as a point of attraction for outsiders. I call the use of ontological transformation as a recruitment and conversion strategy "ontological conversion".

Ontological conversion is related to conversion at the levels of the ethical and social. It was a common belief in early Judeo-Christian thought that various holy men were capable of becoming angels.[16] This view later found its way into ascetic practice. Perpetuated by urban intellectual writers, it was a commonplace that Christian monks lived an angelic way of life, transforming themselves into angelic beings who, according to Christian doctrines, were superior ontologically to mere mortals.[17] Humans thus desired to become supra-human through their practice of the monastic way of life which is tied to their belonging to the monastic community and their acceptance of monastic doctrines. The interrelated domains of behaviour and belonging are expressed metaphorically through the image of monks becoming angels.[18] Another example which readily comes to mind is the ontological concerns surrounding the practice of circumcision in the Zohar, the 13th century Jewish mystical text par excellence. According to the Zohar, circumcision is, apart from being merely a signifier, also an effective, ontologically-transformative rite which transforms the circumcised Jew's essence from "closed" to "open" thereby permitting the circumcised to "see God." Cohen, in his comments on this feature of mystical Judaism, draws on Boyarin and Wolfson and compares this kind of spiritual circumcision

---

(description of layout of temple with "concentric rings of increasing purity"). Priestly Status: 5. 41 (Noah's angelic form is tied to his legitimate priestly status), 59 (priests and angels wear the same clothing), 194f. (priests ate angelic food).

16 J.H. Charlesworth, *The Portrayal of the Righteous as an Angel*, in: G.W.E. Nickelsburg / J.J. Collins (eds.), *Ideal Figures in Ancient Judaism. Profiles and Paradigms*, Chicago 1980, 135–151; C.A. Gieschen, *Angelomorphic Christology. Antecedents and Early Evidence*, Leiden 1998.

17 This "angelic way of life" has been thought to be merely a metaphoric expression for celibacy under the presumption that angels were sexless beings. However, other features of the monastic way of life suggest that this metaphor was also (later?) tied to the ability to exercise superhuman abilities, including the ability to go for long periods of time without eating and transforming oneself into fire (cf. [anon.], Apophth. Patr. (alphabetical version), in J.P. Migne (ed.), *Patrologia Graecae* 65,72–440 (229).

18 E. Muehlberger, *Angels in Late Ancient Christianity*, Oxford 2013, 148–175, repeats the evidence for "angelic way of life" as sexless, but also makes mention of a few of the more miraculous abilities reserved for those adept in ascesis. She also makes mention on p. 17 of the blurred lines between moral and ontological transformation in the Christian imagination.

to Christian sacramental theology, concluding that "circumcision in Zoharic mysticism is entirely analogous to Christian baptism: a physical operation with metaphysical results, performed once only, an imprinting of a special character on the soul."[19] We will address further examples of ontological conversion in the main comparanda of this paper, Tertullian's *De baptismo* and Iamblichus' *De mysteriis*, but for now the pattern should be clear enough; ontological conversion is the promise of transformation into a higher being, such as an angelic figure or a god, through admittance into the group, typically through a rite of initiation.

Ontological conversion, it should be noted, is not a *sine qua non* of "true" conversion. An observable transformation of behaviour and a subsequent rebranding of the self as belonging to this or that community, having this or that new goal in mind, and undergoing a complete reordering of an internal hierarchy of values may constitute perfectly legitimate conversion according to standing psychological or social definitions. However, ontological conversion as a theoretical tool may progress us a bit further in research by providing a way to approach conversion by using sources which emanate from the group offering conversion. A major problem for researchers studying conversion in ancient sources is that the only available objects of study are the texts which lack detailed or reliable accounts of conversion. Since James, there has been an intense focus on autobiographical statements about conversion. Classical sources commonly used to understand conversion in the ancient world, most notably Augustine's *Confessions* and Apuleius' *Metamorphoses,* are both valued as starting places for understanding conversion from a first-person perspective, but eventually the criticism is usually made that these texts are in one way or another unreliable. Augustine's account of his conversion is coloured by his post-conversion Christian perspective which overshadows the whole of his account, and the usefulness of Lucius' conversion to the Isis cult is predicated by a risky association of author (Apuleius) and character (Lucius).[20] Ontological conversion as a theoretical tool can potentially provide an alternative avenue into understanding conversion by isolating predisposing conditions of conversion (especially ancient conversion only accessible through texts). Therefore, while it may not be a totally necessary feature, it can nonetheless be a potentially important one, allowing us to identify as conversion various forms of behaviour (like theurgy) that have not yet been analysed in this light.

---

19 S. Cohen, *Why Aren't Jewish Women Circumcised?*, Berkeley 2005, 43–45.
20 See a summary of the arguments for, against, and for a more complex notion of the relationship between author and narrative figure in K. Bradley, *Contending with Conversion. Reflections on the Reformation of Lucius the Ass*, in: Phoe. 52 (1998), 315–334 (316f.).

Ontological conversion, or some variant of it, has already been used as a tool of analysis for exploring a particular example of conversion in a religious organisation about which we know very little. Anne McGuire has pointed to features of conversion in the *Gospel of Truth*. This text, written supposedly by the second-century Gnostic Christian Valentinus, is an exegesis of the meaning of the gospels for Valentinian Gnostics. The *Gospel* describes two, simultaneously-active levels of reality. One, a mythic level, tells the story of the divine Aeon's fall into ignorance and the subsequent generation of a being called Error. This being is rectified and cosmological balance restored when the saviour, Jesus Christ, delivers to humanity the truth about their divine nature. The status of returning to the father is represented as "perfection", a quality retained by the father (and therefore accessible only through him) and encompassed by Jesus (along with salvation bringing *gnosis*). McGuire notes that the "individual's reception of Gnosis" is linked "to a radical reorientation of emotional attitude toward existence, of theological conception, and of life in the world." The radical reorientation of the Entirety in the *Gospel of Truth*'s mythic dimension is directly linked to the individual's conversion. This becomes all the more clear because the Father withholds the outpouring of *gnosis* both of the cosmic order of things and of himself, allowing one only to reach it through conversion (*apokatastasis*). This, the text tells us, is not an act of jealousy or envy, but is for the sake of the Entirety. By withholding absolute Gnosis, the Father "permits" in some way the Entirety to come to a greater awareness (perhaps even appreciation?) of the Father's majesty.

The logic of the text is clear enough. By establishing a binary dichotomy between the actions of the current convert and the state of perfective knowing attained only through the Father's knowledge (which presumably is mediated through the group who communicates this story in the first place), the group emphasises the necessity of the individual conversion by applying pressure from the ontological system. McGuire uses these insights to build a case for reevaluating Nock's impoverished and overly specific definition of conversion. As she puts it, the reorientation posited in the *Gospel of Truth* may not be Nockian conversion, but it nonetheless constitutes "a reorientation of a different sort, [...] from ignorance to Gnosis, and from anxiety and rootlessness to repose. Moreover, it brings profound reorientation of thought, as it conceptualises the return of the Entirety to its source, and brings about a new form of practice [scil. by calling] its readers to act in conformity with the pattern established by the Son."[21] For present purposes, McGuire offers a useful example of a purely textual analysis of an expanded (post-Nockian) understanding of conversion. Moreover, some of the

---

21 A. McGuire, *Conversion and Gnosis in the 'Gospel of Truth'*, in: NT 28/4 (1986), 338–355 (354).

features of the conversion she notes, the change "from ignorance to Gnosis" and from "anxiety [...] to repose" are, I would argue, ontological states of being. The possession of knowledge confers equality with the aeons and the state of rest is commonly stated to be the natural state of God.

How does ontological conversion relate to other models of conversion? It may properly be classified under the larger category of intellectual conversion, because it seeks to convince the would-be convert by language and rational argument to make a personal and conscious decision to convert. It establishes a religious worldview by superimposing a filter on the preexistent worldview of the converter, making the religious reality of the group paramount. However, ontological conversion isolates a more specific kind of rationality. Whereas some figures may be convinced by rational argument that they should change their lifestyle in order to live a more sane or healthy way of life, ontological conversion demands that people change their lifestyle for the purposes of eschatological or even present gains at the ontological level.

From the above considerations, I conclude that ontological conversion is a strategy of discursive conversion (conversion through reason and argument as opposed to emotional or affective strategies). In order for an exemplum to properly be called an ontological conversion, it must possess three features: 1) It must posit an ontological worldview including a hierarchy of levels of reality; 2) the level of reality associated with the state desired by the recruiting group must be highly valued; and 3) admittance into the group in question must be accompanied by a transformation of the ontology of the converter.

3a. Tertullian's *De baptismo*

Tertullian's *De baptismo* was written in response to the "most poisonous teaching" (*venenatissima doctrina*) of a "woman of the Cainanite heresy" who had been teaching that baptism was not necessary. The treatise seems to have been presented in a catechetical setting, shoring up some weak points which had been exploited by this unnamed woman. Tertullian addresses his audience saying that "this particular treatise will not be useless, if it instructs those who are at this very moment being formed, and likewise those who, satisfied with faith, do not question the reasons of tradition."[22] The main goal of the treatise, therefore, is to enhance through emotionally-charged language and philosophical argument the importance of the upcoming baptismal ritual. Tertullian's argument focuses on the necessity and

---

22 *Non erit otiosum digestum istud instruens tam eos qui cum maxime formantur quam et illos qui similiter, credisse contenti, non exploratis rationibus traditionum temptabilem* (Tertullian, bapt. 1.1, translation mine).

righteousness of baptism, claiming that although the rite may seem simplistic in comparison with gaudy pagan processions, it nonetheless has its own miraculous features. In fact, it is especially wonderful because it is simple – in the same way the true God is simple.[23] Nonetheless, the specific foci of his argument elevate to prominence the individual, allegedly simple, foolish, and powerless features of the baptismal rite, such as water, which he extolls using scriptural citations: water has existed since the beginning of time; it was the resting place of divinity (Gen 1:2); the division of the waters was one of the principle acts of creation (Gen 1:6–7); water is the first source of living beings (Gen 1:20); human beings were formed from water since the mud from which Adam was formed is a mixture of earth and water (Gen 2:7).[24] All of these references presuppose that the water of ritual baptism is similar to and therefore shares characteristics with mythical waters that have existed *in illo tempore*[25] or by their common relation under the category of water; the idea being all waters are capable of performing this transformation (when properly activated by ritual attention).[26]

Tertullian's treatise consistently alludes to the notion of a strong division between an everyday world (earthly life) and a spiritual realm (heavenly realm). He notes (again in connection with the preceding discussion about the dignity of water) that "the material substance [scil. water], which governs earthly life, administrates in the heavenly [scil. realm]."[27] Likewise, post-baptismal anointing of oil "runs in a material sense, but it helps spiritually." Furthermore, the baptismal act, although it is a "material act,"

---

23 *Nihil adeo est quod obduret mentes quam simplicitas divinorum operum quae in actu videtur et magnificentia quae in effectu reprommitur* (2.1); *Mentior si non idolorum sollemnia vel arcana de suggest et apparatus deque sumptu fidem et auctoritatem sibi extruunt. O misera incredulitas, quae denegas deo proprietates suas, simplicitatem et potestatem!* (2.2). The argument is repeated at 3.2.

24 Waters has existed since the beginning of time: bapt. 3.2; was the resting place of the spirit of God (*divini spiritus sedes*): 3.2; division of waters was principle act of creation: 3.2; water was first source of living beings: 3.2; God formed Adam from mud (i.e., water and earth): 3.5.

25 With this phrase, borrowed from Eliade, I mean to signal how the scriptural waters to which Tertullian refers are thought to be original and transcendent, yet always accessible through ritual practice. See M. Eliade, *The Sacred and the Profane*, San Diego 1987, 94.

26 Ritual attention: bapt. 4.4: *Igitur omnes aquae de pristina originis praerogativa sacramentum antificationis consecunter invocato deo.*

27 3.6: *Licet eo plenius docerem non esse dubitandum si materiam quam in omnibus rebus et operibus suis deus disposuit, etiam in sacramentis propriis parere fecit, si quae vitam terrenam gubernat etiam caelestia procura.*

"becomes spiritual, in that we are freed from our sins."[28] This is made all the more clear when we consider an earlier passage where Tertullian relates that the physical act of baptism does nothing physically while nonetheless an "incredible consequence in Eternity" has apparently occurred.[29] We therefore have the clear identification of two separate worlds in which earthly activity has radically different ramifications.

It is likely that Tertullian's impetus for making this distinction between the spiritual and the physical has something to do with the original criticism made by the "Cainite" woman against whose views he writes *De baptismo*. According to Tertullian, this "temptress" had led many people astray by offering persuasive arguments for the inefficacy of baptism (1.2). His response is to counterattack on several points by noting both the prominent role of water both as a physical substance and as a powerful symbol in scripture, as well as by pushing the efficacy of baptism into a spiritual domain. The rite of baptism has consequences on the spiritual, invisible nature of man, and consequences of that nature cannot be questioned.

Tertullian further writes that baptism confers on the baptised a restoration to a prelapsarian state when one was made in the likeness of God. Thus,

> Man, who had in the past been made "in the image of God," will be restored to his likeness with God: "The image" is considered to be in physical appearance, "the likeness" in eternity. For he receives again the spirit of God, which he had at that time received when breathed upon by Him, but had afterwards lost through sin.[30]

This statement makes clear the ontological factors of the conversion. Baptism, the central and necessary rite for admission to the Christian community, confers divinity. Moreover, this divinity is thought in some way to be the proper state of humanity. Baptism is a restoration to what human beings are meant to be.

In light of the *Forschungsgeschichte* provided at the beginning of this essay, it is interesting that Tertullian makes no mention in this work for the social factors thought to be so important nowadays to conversion. Admittedly, the text is polemical in its scope as it seeks to defend the reality of the effect created by a theologically motivated rite; however, when we consider

---

28 Bapt. 7.2: *Sic et in nobis carnaliter currit unctio sed spiritaliter proficit, quomodo et ipsius baptismi carnalis actus quod in aqua mergimur, spiritalis effectus quod delictis liberamur.*

29 Bapt. 2.1: *Homo in aqua demissus et inter pauca verba tinctus non multo vel nihilo mundior resurgit, eo incredibilis existimatur consecutio aeternitatis.*

30 Bapt. 5.7: *Ita restituitur homo deo ad similitudinem eius qui retro ad imaginem dei fuerat: imago in effigie, similitudo in aeternitatecensetur: recipit enim illum dei spiritum quem tunc de adflatu eius acceperat sed post amiserat per delictum.*

its context, and the audience to whom it was probably addressed (catechu-mens), it seems reasonable to speculate that these metaphysical explanatory notes, especially those that speak of the elevation of the human soul to a higher state of being, probably fostered the importance of conversion by providing a vocabulary of ontological division. We can further speculate that an individual having received these teachings would have felt an intense pressure to stay a member of the group and not betray the awesome status which they obtain through their membership.

3b. Iamblichus' *De mysteriis*

Iamblichus' understanding of ritual and its relationship to conversion strongly resembles the understanding of conversion as an ontological trans-formation in Tertullian's text. The excerpts interpreted here are in the first and last books of *De mysteriis*. It is in these sections that we see the clearest presentation of theurgic doctrine to outsiders, and it is here that we find the most protreptic tone.

As we saw before, one of the obvious prerequisites for an ontological conversion model is the existence of a universe of multiple ontological lev-els. Tertullian's understanding of this relationship was somewhat implicit and had to be drawn from hints in the text of an underlying cosmology. Iamblichus much more explicitly describes such a universe in the opening chapter of *De mysteriis* where he discusses precisely how gods, demons, he-roes, and human souls are ordered, concatenated, and how we as beings at the lowest level of this hierarchy can possibly be aware of and come to know superhuman beings (Myst. 1.3–21). We do not have to go into too much detail about this argument. It suffices to say that Iamblichus builds upon the standard Platonist theory that there are two levels of reality, a higher level of abstract concepts and a lower, material level. The higher level of concepts is, in Plato, only accessible through reason.[31] Nearly 700 years of develop-ment in Platonic philosophy did not modify this doctrine much, and so the first proposition Iamblichus addresses in *De mysteriis*, the knowledge of the existence of the gods, is explained as being a kind of "innate knowledge" (ἔμφυτος γνῶσις), "coexistent with our nature" (συνυπάρχει γὰρ ἡμῶν αὐτῇ τῇ οὐσίᾳ), not subject to lower epistemological levels (Myst. 1.3). One cannot argue about the existence of the gods; this is simply not up for discus-sion, because such knowledge is indubitable.

Having concluded that such knowledge is innate, Iamblichus has to explain how there is disagreement over the nature of the gods. The argument follows lines familiar to those of Plotinus who claims that there is something in our

---

31 Cf. Pl., Phd. 65c–66a.

nature that tends to draw us away from this realisation, perverting our understanding of the truth of reality. In both Plotinus and Iamblichus these perverting factors correspond to epistemological modes and essential characteristics of humanity. The human condition is subject to "instability and indeterminacy" (1.3) which, according to Iamblichus, are related to the dialectical mode of thinking. Later, Iamblichus will imply that the embodied human, experiencing generative aspects of presumably sexual pleasure, will be drawn to "a return to the natural state" (τῆς ἐν αὐτῇ εἰς φύσιν ἀποκαταστάσεως, 1.10). By contrast, the pre-embodied soul, untouched by sexuality, experiences a way of life that is in complete conformity with the higher realities, and since the conjoint human (soul plus material body) retains a feature of this soul, there is nonetheless an "essential" strive of the soul to the Good (1.3). This argument, linking ontology with epistemology, is concluded on a protreptic note:

> So [...] let the human soul join itself to them [scil. the gods and other divine beings] in knowledge on the same terms, not employing conjecture or opinion or some form of syllogistic reasoning, all of which take their start from the plane of temporal reality, to pursue that essence which is beyond all things, but rather connecting itself to the gods with pure and blameless reasonings which it has received from all eternity from those same gods.[32]

In one sentence, Iamblichus conveniently summarises the ontological distinction and its epistemological component.

Iamblichus' setting out of the ontological levels contains sufficiently ebullient language to indicate his appreciation of these high levels of reality. But what about the other requirement for ontological conversion – evidence of ontological transformation simultaneous to the change of identity experienced by the convert undergoing social change in identity? Does becoming a theurgist equal becoming a god, and vice versa? It is easy enough to point to evidence of ontological transformation in *De mysteriis*. One example in particular stands out:

> It is plain, indeed, from the rites themselves that what we are speaking of just now is a method of salvation for the soul; for in the contemplation of the "blessed visions" the soul **exchanges one life for another** and exerts a different activity, and **considers itself then to be no longer human** – and quite rightly so: for often, having abandoned its own life, it has gained in exchange the most blessed activity of the gods (emphasis mine).[33]

---

32 Myst. 1.3: Οὕτω καὶ ἡ ἀνθρωπίνη ψυχὴ κατὰ τὰ αὐτὰ τῇ γνώσει πρὸς αὐτοὺς συναπτέσθω, εἰκασίᾳ μὲν ἢ δόξῃ ἢ συλλογισμῷ τινι, ἀρχομένοις ποτὲ ἀπὸ χρόνου, μηδαμῶς τὴν ὑπὲρ ταῦτα πάντα οὐσίαν μεταδιώκουσα, ταῖς δὲ καθαραῖς καὶ ἀμέμπτοις νοήσεσιν αἷς εἴληφεν ἐξ ἀιδίου παρὰ τῶν θεῶν, ταύταις αὐτοῖς συνηρτημένη.

33 Myst. 1.12: Δῆλον δὲ καὶ ἀπ' αὐτῶν τῶν ἔργων ὃ νυνί φαμεν εἶναι τῆς ψυχῆς σωτήριον· ἐν γὰρ τῷ θεωρεῖν τὰ μακάρια θεάματα ἡ ψυχὴ **ἄλλην**

The theurgist who experiences the mystical experience described here, "the contemplation of the 'blessed visions'" undergoes a complete change of ontology as signified by the phrases "exchanges one life for another," "considers itself to be no longer human," and "exerts a different activity." The term "activity" in the last phrase is a *technicus terminus* and refers to the Aristotelian concept of activity which indicates the proper function of an organism.[34] In this sense then, the exchange of activity indicates the complete transformation of the entity. The soul takes up a new activity, one wholly inappropriate its status as a soul; adoption of a divine activity necessitates the transformation of the essence to divinity.[35]

Here, we see that the soul is indeed transformed. It regards itself, correctly we are told, to have shed its human state. It takes up a new activity, the activity of the gods (i.e., theurgy). Elsewhere, Iamblichus confirms this view adding that this transformation of the human can be likened to the re-attainment of an original divinised state that has been lost, a godlike state that has been replaced with a human soul:

> I say, then, that the man who is conceived of as "divinised" (θεωτός) who once was united to the contemplation of the gods, afterwards came into possession of another soul adopted to the human form, and through this was born into the bond of necessity and fate.[36]

Later Neoplatonists attest to this view as well, noting that the whole goal of theurgy is divinisation:

> 'If, as you maintain, Hegias,' Isidore was telling him, 'the practice of theurgy is divine, I too admit it. But those who are destined to be gods must first become human [...] but it has come to pass that nowadays philosophy stands not on a razor's edge, but truly on the brink of extreme old age.'[37]

ζωὴν ἀλλάττεται καὶ ἑτέραν ἐνέργειαν ἐνεργεῖ καὶ **οὐδ᾽ ἄνθρωπος εἶναι ἡγεῖται** τότε, ὀρθῶς ἡγουμένη· πολλάκις δὲ καὶ τὴν ἑαυτῆς ἀφεῖσα ζωὴν τὴν μακαριωτάτην τῶν θεῶν ἐνέργειαν ἀντηλλάξατο. Trans. by Clarke / Dillon / Hershbell (eds. and trans.), 2003.

34 Cf. Arist., EN 1098b.

35 This is seemingly accomplished despite the standard Platonic trope that essences generate activities (Myst. 1.4). Iamblichus offers no clear way to reconcile this problem.

36 Myst. 10.5: Λέγω τοίνυν ὡς ὁ **θεωτὸς** νοούμενος ἄνθρωπος, ἡνωμένος τὸ πρόσθεν τῇ θέᾳ τῶν θεῶν, ἐπεις–ῆλθεν ἑτέρᾳ ψυχῇ τῇ περὶ τὸ ἀνθρώπινον μορφῆς εἶδος συνηρμοσμένη, καὶ διὰ τοῦτο ἐν τῷ τῆς ἀνάγκης καὶ εἱμαρμένης ἐγένετο δεσμῷ.

37 Dam. Isid., fr. 150 (trans. P. Athanassiadi, *The Philosophical History. Life of Isidore*, Apamea 1999). This brief fragment seems critical of the divinisation doctrines of theurgy.

Apart from believing the main purpose of their rituals to be divinisation, the theurgists recognised that theurgic rituals set themselves off from others. This notion seems to be first attested in the *Chaldean oracles* where it is said, enigmatically, "the theurgists do not fall into the herd which is subject to Destiny."[38] The importance of this passage is that the theurgists, as a class, (much like the class of Christians who return to their prelapserian state) are understood to all possess the same ontological status, superior to the vulgar throng, which must experience the negative consequences of fate. Only the individual who has become a theurgist, i.e., joined the theurgic school and obtained access to the information of theurgy which only the theurgists know (μόνοι δὲ οἱ θεουργοὶ ταῦτα [...] γιγνώσκουσι), is given the opportunity to become a god.[39]

4. Conclusion

> For to explain is to connect things to one another, to re-establish relations between them that make them appear to us as functions of one another, as vibrating sympathetically in accord with an internal law grounded in their nature. [...] I begin to *understand* only if it is possible to conceive of B from a perspective that links it in some way to A, joined to A by some relation of kinship.
>
> – Emile Durkheim[40]

Previous models of conversion have addressed the issue of passivity or activity in the individual's conversion. Whether through accident or intentional selection, it seems that many modern studies of conversion have focused on groups that occasionally are labeled under the derogatory name of cult, including the Divine Light Mission, the Moonies, Scientologists, etc. As such it seems that one of the reasons typically proposed for why people convert is that they are brainwashed, their individuality is taken away from them, and they are volitionally unable to choose any other option than to join the cult. Such sensationalistic theories, while prominent in journalistic media, have never been empirically proven.[41]

Barring the possibility of malevolent hypnotism, why do people even begin to change their minds and identities, and, having done so, what keeps them from changing their minds again? The method I have proposed in this essay has tried to answer this question in a situation where research lacks

---

38 [Anon.], *Oracula Chaldaica* 153: Οὐ γὰρ ὑφ εἱμαρτὴν ἀγέλην πίπτουσι Θεουργοί (trans. R. Majercik, *The Chaldean Oracles*, Leiden 1989, 107).
39 *Myst.* 5.20.
40 2001 (1915), 180f.
41 J.T. Richardson, 1985, 166 (cited in H. Gooren, 2007, 346).

first hand accounts of conversion. I have tried to show that metaphysics itself can serve as a form of coercion, especially when it is presented in a rationalistic or hyper-rationalistic manner, substituting for proofs unquestionable reasonings which transfer the "logic" of argument into discursively constructed realities.

Ontological conversion offers an interesting way to address the issue of agency in conversion. In an ontological conversion, or at least the examples explored in this essay, the worldview created by the community seems to leave the convert no choice but to convert, by making the consequences of conversion the growth of the individual into a truer form of the individual. In other words, to paraphrase Nietzsche, the convert is asked to become who he or she really is,[42] i.e., a divine being. There is an inherent tension in this understanding, because on the one hand, the group needs to explain how they offer something that is unavailable in other groups and or practices, and must therefore exaggerate the difference between the converter and the divine status promised to him or her. On the other hand, in order to make the conversion attractive, the group must offer to the converter some kind of permeable barrier between these two poles of absolute alterity. One way to do this is to claim that the convert is not really making a change, but is in fact, simply becoming who they already are, discovering their true nature, removing the masks that their previous life has forced them to wear. The rituals of theurgy realign the convert to a proper appreciation of the divine, an appreciation that has been "denied" to the individual human soul as a "result of their birth."

---

42 Was sagt dein Gewissen? – "Du sollst werden, der du bist" (F. Nietzsche, *Die fröhliche Wissenschaft*, Leipzig 1887, 194).

Zeba Crook

Agents of Apostasy, Delegates of Disaffiliation

Abstract: This article analyses the problem of apostasy among Jews and Christians in antiquity. With the outset in a methodological focus on allocentric and idiocentric behaviour, the author argues that agency will operate very differently in collectivistic and individualistic cultures, and that this fact has implications for our understanding of apostasy in the ancient and profoundly collectivistic world.

Introduction

In July of 2012, Gaza city saw a rare occurrence: a protest by a group of outraged Christians. The issue? Conversion, or perhaps apostasy. Christians in the Palestinian territory comprise a very tiny, and probably even shrinking, minority. When news of the conversion of a Christian man and a woman with her three children spread, the response of the Christian community was swift and certain: clearly these people had been kidnapped, forcibly converted to Islam and were being held against their will.[1]

In December of 2004, Coptic Christians in Cairo clashed with police over the disappearance of the wife of a priest from a Nile delta village. No one knew where she was, or under what circumstances she had disappeared, but the Christian protestors were certain that she had been abducted and forcibly converted to Islam.[2] She was later found at a friend's home, having left her husband freely, but angrily, after an argument with him.

However, in April 2011, Salafi Muslims turned the tables and began protesting in Cairo that this same woman had in fact freely converted to Islam, but that the Coptic Church had kidnapped her because of it. The Salafi protestors claimed that her Christian captors would not let her appear in public, and they claimed only to want to hear her say in her own words that she had *not* converted to Islam. They called on the military to free her.[3]

These three stories offer a complex constellation of social, religious, and cultural issues, all of which are thoroughly interrelated. First, no community

---

1 http://www.haaretz.com/news/middle-east/gaza-christians-protest-forcible-con versions-1.451544. Last accessed February 16, 2014.
2 http://news.bbc.co.uk/2/hi/middle_east/4080777.stm. Last accessed February 16, 2014.
3 http://www.egyptindependent.com/news/salafis-protest-release-alleged-convert-islam. Last accessed February 16, 2014.

can seem to imagine that anyone would willingly choose apostasy. Since no one would ever do such a thing voluntarily, the only conceivable explanation must be forced conversion. Clearly, community identity is highly charged, valued, and protected. By extension, and secondly, the departure of the individual is construed as a threat to the whole community; the individual rejects the group and its values. It is possible therefore the understand the reaction of the community as a ritual of sorts. Perhaps, the Gaza Christians knew full well that a forced conversion was unlikely – they are after all forbidden in Islam, and therefore quite rare. Perhaps, the Christian protest, though directed at the Muslim majority, was in fact something of an ostracisation ritual directed at the apostates themselves. The direction of the anger at the Muslim Palestinians protects the integrity of the rejected community, providing a safe outlet for the hurt caused by the acts of apostasy. Thirdly, conversion and apostasy in an environment so fraught with political tension become rhetorical ciphers: the protests over forced or reversed conversions actually have little to do with conversion. They have, rather, to do with fragile senses of community, identity, and concern over porous boundaries. Christians are out-numbered in the Middle East and naturally feel under siege. Muslims world-wide often feel underseige because of the "War on Terror." Both sides feel pressured and persecuted, and this will naturally be expressed when faced with disaffiliation. And finally, though their debates are cloaked in theological language (e.g., that certain behaviour displeases God, that such a person has turned their back on God), theology is not really the issue for these people. Rather, the issue is community, identity, and challenges to the collective. Of course, it is rather arbitrary to separate theology from community, identity, and challenges to the collective. Perhaps, it is more accurate to say that these threats to community, identity, and the collective are socio-theological.

What is abundandly clear from these modern examples is that apostasy in certain cultures is a highly charged and threatening event. It might not always be as fraught as the above examples suggest; clearly, that feature is a symptom of the politically tense relationships among religious communities in the Middle East. There is, nevertheless, considerable common ground with conversion, apostasy, or disaffiliation in ancient Mediterranean settings as well. The common ground here is provided by a shared cultural construction known as collectivism.

In what follows, I shall illustrate how individidual and group identity are formed in collectivistic cultures. In collectivistic cultures, individuals are more accountable to the group, so one should expect that self-centred acts will be interpreted differently than they are in individualistic cultures. But it would be a mistake to think that invididuals in collectivistic cultures lack all agency. The evidence we have from ancient sources shows that agency is exercised in collectivistic cultures, but that it is responded to differently by the group. As with the modern examples, it seems that the stakes are higher: individiuals that displease or threaten the group are suceptible to accusations of deviance. Labeling a person deviant becomes a way of correcting (ideally) or punishing (if necessary) behaviour that threatens the group. Of course, what qualifies as conversion/apostasy on the one hand and deviance on the other depends entirely on perspective. When rhetorical power is at stake, it is not always entirely clear that accusations are founded in actual deviance and not merely the perception of it. Regardless, however, labelling is a deeply collectivistic activity, and it tells us more about the labellers than the labelees.

Collectivism and allocentricity

The ancient Mediterranean was collectivistic. This is not a contentious statement, but it does require a few comments. The term "collectivism" and its counterpart "individualism" are best reserved for describing the *tendency* of groups, nations, or cultures.[4] Collectivism emerges as a cultural syndrome when the majority of individuals within a collective act allocentrically. This is because culture "emerges in interaction. As people interact, some of their ways of thinking, feeling, and behaving are transmitted to each other and become automatic ways of reacting to specific situations. The shared beliefs, attitudes, norms, roles, and behaviours are aspects of culture."[5] To say that collectivism is a cultural tendency is to say that there will always be exceptions. This is because there is no such thing as a purely collectivistic (or purely individualistic) culture. Yet, these cultural tendencies are real, they are powerful, and they are tenacious. The emergence, therefore, of collectivism happens when the default response of most individuals to situations involving human interaction is allocentric.

Allocentric – or other-centred – behaviour obtains when a person places the interests, expectations, and norms of the collective over her or his individual needs, desires, or aspirations.[6] Allocentrists and idiocentrists tend to place different values on the in-group. Allocentrists usually place great emphasis on loyalty to the group, and they expect it of others as well; they tend to "want their ingroups to be monolithic and homogenous – with

---

4   H.C. Triandis / K. Leung / M. Villareal / F.L. Clack, *Allocentric versus Idiocentric Tendencies. Convergent and Discriminant Validation*, in: Journal of Research in Personality 19 (1985), 395–415 (396).

5   Harry C. Triandis, *Individualism & Collectivism*, Boulder 1995, 4.

6   Cf. Cooper and James Corke-Webster in this volume for examples of the implications of such choices in Christian sources (and in modern society).

everyone thinking, feeling, and acting in the same way; they think that in such groups there will be harmony."[7] This relates to another feature of allocentrism: it exhibits a stronger "emphasis on relationships, even when they are disadvantageous."[8] The bonds of relationships and loyalty tend to be stronger in collectivistic settings, and the breaking of those bonds is taken quite seriously. Likewise, the past tends to hold a greater prominence in allocentric settings because allocentrists (and by extension, collectivistic cultures) "see themselves as links in a long chain that consists of ancestors and descendants."[9] Thus, one tends to find kinship as the central social institution and ancestor worship (or care) in collectivistic settings, but not in individualistic settings.

Distinguishing characteristics of individual behaviour (allocentrism and idiocentrism) from broader cultural patterns (collectivism and individualism) is important and useful. Doing so recognises that one can find examples of idiocentric behaviour in a collectivistic setting without denying the reality of the broader cultural pattern. In other words, calling a culture "collectivistic" does not imply a total absence of self-centered acts. It means that idiocentric actions are less common in collectivistic settings than they are in individualistic settings.

This process will not always be conscious, for when acculturation works (and it usually does), the will of the collective will usually be indistinguishable from the will of the individual. Thus, the allocentric individual tends to be happiest when in conformity with the wishes, expectations, and values of the collective. Of course, it is also the case that some individuals in collectivistic settings do not conform. Such people would be described as acting idiocentrically by placing their own wishes and aspirations above those of the group. The point is, when individuals in a collectivistic culture act idiocentrically, they are acting against the broad cultural patterns of the collective; they are acting counter-culturally. The category of counter-cultural behaviour obtains in cultures of any size and form: from "the Mediterranean" as a predominantly collectivistic culture block to subcultures such as an Italian family living in predominantly individualistic North America, but with a strong sense of its "Mediterranean" collectivistic culture.

Many surveys and studies reveal that in collectivistic cultures, individual behaviour tends to be regulated by the ingroup, people tend toward interdependence, to subordinate personal goals to the goals of the group, value harmony, to see their fate as shared with the group, and to see the group

---

7   Ibid., 8.
8   Ibid., 44.
9   Ibid., 10.

as an extension of themselves. Conversely, in individualistic cultures people strive for independence, self-sufficiency, to have personal goals, they tend to be comfortable with conflict with the group, and to see themselves as distinct from the group.[10]

Collectivism and Individualism are etic constructs that scholars use to explain and differentiate certain human behaviours.[11] They are etic because most actors are unaware of their conformity to culture (which includes idiocentrists in individualist settings as well). Collectivism and Individualism are constructs because they pertain to tendencies, not to social laws. Culture is not monolithic or static; yet, cultures arise from patterns of behaviour, or tendencies that are consistent, and thereby become *somewhat* predictable. People in collectivistic settings *tend* to follow certain patterns of behaviour, as do people in individualistic settings. Since Collectivism and Individualism are constructs and not social laws, they do not make any behaviour certain, because people can be unpredictable. Simply the fact that conversion and apostasy could happen in as collectivistic a setting as the ancient Mediterranean illustrates this.

Collectivism and agency

Related to a culture's collectivism or individualism is the issue of agency: to what degree do enculturated humans act independently, and to what degree do they act in conformity with the cultural structure around them? Which anticipates an individual's behaviour more: the structure of culture, which offers actors a limited set of options in any given scenario, or agency, which gives actors total freedom? Is individual behaviour constrained by culture, or is "culture" (and especially structure) only an illusion generated by individuals volunteering to act a certain way?

Cultural anthropology has seen a shift away from a near exclusive focus on structure (evident in the work of Durkheim, Weber, and Lévi-Strauss),

---

10 Triandis *et al.*, 1985, 397f.

11 To say they are constructs is also to say that they are not psychological states. Ratner and Hui rightly point out that "a relationship between psychology and [scil. individualism-collectivism] is spurious," since individualism-collectivism "correlates with many attributes such as wealth, educational level, and political system" (C. Ratner / L. Hui, *Theoretical and Methodological Problems in Cross-Cultural Psychology*, in: Journal for the Theory of Social Behaviour 33 (2003), 67–94 (71)). Thus, they also point out that "collectivism explains virtually nothing about peoples' psychology" (73). This is why the focus here is on collectivistic or individualistic *settings* and *behavior*, not on mental states or emotions, though Ratner and Hui are too negative on the heuristic utility of the collectivism-individualism constructs.

but it has not been replaced by a perspective that champions agency wholly.[12] Rather, the older paradigm has been replaced with a more nuanced recognition that culture (broadly speaking) is a combination of structure and agency, that human behaviour is in part determined and in part voluntaristic. For instance, Pierre Bourdieu argues that people are neither wholly constrained by cultural structure nor wholly free. Rather, they exercise agency within a range of options provided by a structure.[13] Anthony Giddens called this "structuration," echoing Bourdieu: individuals are free within limits imposed by culture.[14] More recently, Sherry Ortner argues "for the importance of a robust anthropology of subjectivity, both as states of mind of real actors embedded in the social world, and as cultural formations that [...] express, shape, and constitute those states of mind."[15]

It is impossible to know precisely in what ratio structure and agency pertain, for surely any putative ratio would differ from culture to culture, from subculture to subculture, and possibly from person to person. The latter (person to person) is relevant because how one responds to structure, or how readily one might exercise individuality at the expense of the group, is in part a symptom of individual personality. One thing is clear, however: Whether a cultural setting tends more toward collectivism or individualism will have an impact on the extent to which agency is exercised by individuals.[16] Louise Lawrence has thoughtfully questioned whether structure and agency can be practically separated.[17] For instance, if in fact all we have is "structurally reproductive agency" and "structurally transformative agency" (phrases she borrows from Hays[18]), then the two are too closely intertwined to be extricated from one another. Undoubtedly, Lawrence (and Hays) are correct, but I aver that at a level that is abstract

---

12 *Pace* L.J. Lawrence, *An Ethnography of the Gospel of Matthew*, Tübingen 2003, 51–56. Rasmussen puts it best when she observes that the debate remains unresolved, though the pendulum swings from one extreme to the other. See S.J. Rasmussen, *Cultural Anthropology*, in: J. Valsiner (ed.), *The Oxford Handbook of Culture and Psychology*, New York 2012, 96–115 (101). In a later work, Lawrence situates her position in way more clearly consistent with Rasmussen (L.J. Lawrence, *Structure, Agency and Ideology. A Response to Zeba Crook*, in: Journal for the Study of the New Testament 29 (2007), 277–286 (278f.)).

13 P. Bourdieu, *Outline of a Theory of Practice*, Cambridge 1977.

14 A. Giddens, *The Constitution of Society. Outline of the Theory of Structuration*, Berkeley 1984.

15 S.B. Ortner, *Subjectivity and Cultural Critique*, in: Anthropological Theory 5 (2005), 31–52 (46).

16 F.S. Niles, *Individualism-Collectivism Revisited*, in: Cross-Cultural Research 32 (1998), 315–341.

17 Lawrence, 2007, 283.

18 S. Hays, *Structure and Agency and the Sticky Problem of Culture*, in: Sociological Theory 12 (1994), 57–72.

and that allows for cross-cultural comparison, it is both possible and heuristically valuable to treat agency and structure as related but separate entities. The ancient Mediterranean world was culturally collectivistic. This is seen in a number of ways, the first of which is cultural analogy. Social scientists and cultural anthropologists are unanimous that cultures surrounding the current Mediterranean are predominantly collectivistic. Hofstede, for instance, charts over forty nations (and, in a few instances, groups of nations) on a collectivism-individualism continuum and finds that most nations surrounding the Mediterranean are collectivistic: Greece, Turkey, Lebanon, Egypt, Libya, Portugal, and Spain. Modern France and Italy have moved towards individualism in modernity. What is more, nations with a cultural heritage deriving from these Mediterranean cultures are also collectivistic: Argentina, Ecuador, Venezuela, Colombia, Uruguay, Brazil, Chile, and Mexico.[19] These cultures are not *newly* collectivistic, but are traditionally collectivistic. By analogy, the ancient Mediterranean was similarly collectivistic.

Secondly, we deduce that the ancient Mediterranean was collectivistic by the abundant evidence of ancient behaviour consistent with collectivism, such as stereotyping. To stereotype is to assume that a person's character, nature, or identity is determined by their ethnicity or nationality. In individualistic settings, people are taught not to stereotype; this is because individualists are taught that all people are unique, and thus one cannot know someone just because one knows where they are from. But in the collectivistic setting of the ancient Mediterranean, they held the opposite position. Aristotle's description of the nations around him illustrates this:

> Let us now speak of what ought to be the citizens' natural character [...].
> The nations inhabiting the cold places and those of Europe are full of spirit but somewhat deficient in intelligence and skill, so that they continue comparatively free, but lacking in political organisation and capacity to rule their neighbours. The peoples of Asia on the other hand are intelligent and skillful in temperament, but lack spirit, so that they are in continuous subjection and slavery. But the Greek race participates in both characters, just as it occupies the middle position geographically, for it is both spirited and intelligent; hence it continues to be free and to have very good political institutions, and to be capable of ruling all mankind if it attains constitutional unity.[20]

---

19 G.H. Hofstede, *Culture's Consequences*, London 1991, 129.
20 [Π]ερὶ δὲ τοῦ πολιτικοῦ πλήθους [...] τὴν φύσιν εἶναι δεῖ, νῦν λέγωμεν [...]. τὰ μὲν γὰρ ἐν τοῖς ψυχροῖς τόποις ἔθνη καὶ τὰ περὶ τὴν Εὐρώπην θυμοῦ μέν ἐστι πλήρη, διανοίας δὲ ἐνδεέστερα καὶ τέχνης, διόπερ ἐλεύθερα μὲν διατελεῖ μᾶλλον, ἀπολίτευτα δὲ καὶ τῶν πλησίον ἄρχειν οὐ δυνάμενα· τὰ δὲ περὶ τὴν Ἀσίαν διανοητικὰ μὲν καὶ τεχνικὰ τὴν ψυχήν, ἄθυμα δέ, διόπερ ἀρχόμενα καὶ δουλεύοντα διατελεῖ· τὸ δὲ τῶν Ἑλλήνων γένος, ὥσπερ μεσεύει κατὰ τοὺς τόπους, οὕτως ἀμφοῖν μετέχει. καὶ γὰρ ἔνθυμον καὶ διανοητικόν ἐστιν·

In collectivistic cultures, individuals are known less by their individual personality traits and more by their relationships with others, whether with other individuals around them or the nation from which they derive. So, for instance, in individualistic cultures, people are described as discrete entities: he is selfish, she is generous, she is hostile, he is friendly. These qualities are of course relational. This obtains because people in individualistic settings interact with others no less than people in collectivistic settings interact with others. The point is that the definitions above assume these individuals to be unique, bounded, and discrete entities. Conversely, people in collectivistic settings tend to be described in allocentric ways: he swears at his grandfather, she brings cakes to my family.[21] Consider how the author of the Gospel of Mark narrates the response of Jesus' fellow Nazarenes when he returns home and teaches in the synagogue (Mark 6:1–6). He teaches with wisdom and authority and even does miracles, but they are not fooled for this is the "son of Mary and brother of James and Judah and Simon" and they know his sisters, too. They know Jesus because they know his family.

Mark 6:1–6 not only illustrates the sociocentric way in which people are known, but also the place that family plays in the construction of collectivistic identity. Jesus is known by others according to his family, and according to Mark it was impossible for Jesus to transcend that identity (6:5). The Nazarenes knew Jesus because they knew his family; Jesus was not free, in their estimation, to forge his own identity. The importance of family is echoed in Jesus' radical rejection of family. For instance, Luke 14:26 claims that Jesus said, "The one who does not hate father and mother is not able to be my disciple, and the one who does not hate son and daughter is not able to be my disciple" (ὅς οὐ μισεῖ τὸν πατέρα καὶ τὴν μητέρα οὐ δύναται εἶναί μου μαθητής, καὶ ὅς οὐ μισεῖ τὸν υἱὸν καὶ τὴν θυγατέρα οὐ δύναται εἶναί μου μαθητής).[22] We have here evidence that early followers of Jesus (quite likely including Jesus himself) expected members of the movement to sever ties with their families. Such a sentiment is embarrassing and is multiply attested (Mark 3:32–35; Mark 13:12; Luke 6:59–62). Rejection of family when family thwarts individual aspirations is a feature of individualistic cultures; in a collectivistic setting, however, rejection of family would be deeply troubling.[23]

διόπερ ἐλεύθερόν τε διατελεῖ καὶ βέλτιστα πολιτευόμενον καὶ δυνάμενον ἄρχειν πάντων, μιᾶς τυγχάνον πολιτείας, Arist., Pol. 7.1327b.

21 R.A. Shweder, *Thinking Through Cultures. Expeditions in Cultural Psychology*, Cambridge 1991, 113–55.

22 See also Cooper and Corke-Webster in this volume for the element of family conflicts in relation to conversion.

23 B.J. Malina, *'Let Him Deny Himself' (Mark 8:34 & Par). A Social Psychological Model of Self-Denial*, in: Biblical Theology Bulletin 24 (1994), 106–119 (109).

There is no formula for anticipating what the ratio will be between structure and agency, regardless of the setting. This is because every setting, whether it is a micro-setting, like a sports team, or a macro-setting, like a nation or a culture block, will be unique. One even needs to account for individual personality; some people are less prone to exercise agency even when it is culturally expected of them. Despite these challenges, it is useful to bear in mind that such a ratio will exist, and that it cannot be *assumed* uncritically to be the same ratio as obtains in the scholar's own setting. The ancient Mediterranean was collectivistic as a culture block because people tended very strongly toward allocentricity. Yet, one must recall that collectivism does not imply an absence of idiocentric behaviour (or the exercise of agency). In a collectivistic setting, idiocentric behaviour will be less common, and likely to be considered deviant, but it will not be absent from the culture.[24] Assessment of deviance is a key and applies as well to individualistic cultures as to collectivistic ones.

In strongly individualistic North America, we see allocentric behaviour when people follow fashion fads slavishly, or rely on others exclusively to tell them what to think. Yet, how our culture responds to this, is what defines it as individualistic despite containing allocentric elements: we tend not to respect people who succumb too easily to peer-pressure. We teach children to form their identities and their thoughts independently; we teach them to disregard what others say about them, especially if it is negative. Likewise, Mediterranean antiquity reveals examples of idiocentric behaviour, as seen above, but the negative reaction to idiocentric behaviour is part of what marks ancient Mediterranean culture as collectivistic. Conversion and apostasy are two examples of idiocentric behaviour.

The rhetoric of apostasy

Conversion and apostasy are complex, fluid, and infinitely adaptable phenomena.[25] As Martin Goodman and Shaye Cohen have shown, "conversion" cannot be limited to the wholesale adoption of a new religion.[26] There

---

24 See, for instance, deSilva's astute observations about the "dangers" associated with apostasy (D.A. deSilva, *Exchanging Favor for Wrath. Apostasy in Hebrews and Patron-Client Relationships*, in: JBL 115 (1996), 91–116). See also B.J. Malina / J.H. Neyrey, *Calling Jesus Names*, Sonoma 1988.

25 In the interest of brevity, the discussion and examples of apostasy, both rhetorical and actual, will focus on Second Temple Judean sources and stories. For many other examples and a rich discussion, see S.G. Wilson, *Leaving the Fold. Apostates and Defectors in Antiquity*, Minneapolis 2004.

26 M. Goodman, *Mission and Conversion. Proselytizing in the Religious History of the Roman Empire*, Oxford 1994; S.J.D. Cohen, *Crossing the Boundary and Becoming a Jew*, in: HThR 82 (1989), 13–33.

is a range of behaviour that falls into an amorphous category of "conversion". According to Cohen, these include behaviours as diverse as

> admiring some aspect of Judaism; acknowledging the power of the god of the Jews or incorporating him into the pagan pantheon; benefiting the Jews or being conspicuously friendly to Jews; practicing some or many of the rituals of the Jews; venerating the god of the Jews and denying or ignoring the pagan gods; joining the Jewish community; converting to Judaism and becoming a Jew.[27]

Conversion admits to a range of interactions with or – in the language of A.D. Nock – a range of *adherences* to a group.[28]

It is no different with apostasy. For example, when he writes about Israelites in the Egypt of Joseph's day (*De Josepho*), Philo of Alexandria is likely thinking about Judeans in Egypt in his own day.[29] At stake is the ability of Joseph (or any Judean) to be able to maintain his loyalty to tradition when surrounded by a foreign culture. It is natural, Philo writes, for the young and impressionable, away from home and hungry for wealth and glory, to take on foreign practices (*De Josepho* 254). Philo himself labels this as apostasy, but it is not at all clear that he is imagining people who have actually converted away from Judaism. Rather, these are people who likely retain their Judean identity, but are attracted to some Gentile practices that happen all around them. That Philo considers this apostasy shows he is doing nothing more than identifying and proscribing behaviour he finds objectionable, and therefore applying a deviance label.

Fourth Maccabees contains another obvious example of labeling potentially deviant behaviour in order either to discourage such behaviour or to correct it. The story is about resisting the pressure to assimilate to Gentile culture. The Judeans in the story are offered apostasy or death by Antiochus IV, who, in a bid to break their resolve, claims they would surely be forgiven by God if they gave in just a little and under such compulsion. But the brave characters, exemplars in the narrative, refuse even to give up even a little. The issue here is not then wholesale apostasy, but simply any degree, no matter how minor, of assimilation to a foreign culture. Such behaviour is labeled pejoratively in order to discourage it and to encourage loyalty to Jewish tradition in every feature.

This language can be applied not only to Judeans who assimilate to non-Judean traditions, but also to those who practice their religion "incorrectly".

---

27 Cohen, 1989, 14f. See Abate in this volume for conversion to Judaism, the related sources, and the collective aspects of Jewish culture.

28 A.D. Nock, *Conversion,* London 1933.

29 J.M.G. Barclay, *Who Was Considered an Apostate in the Jewish Diaspora?*, in: G.N. Stanton / G.G. Stroumsa (eds.), *Tolerance and Intolerance*, Cambridge 1998, 80–98 (85).

Consider writings from Qumran that refer to other Judeans as "the congregations of traitors" who "sought easy interpretations, chose illusions, scrutinised loopholes, [...] violated the covenant broke the precept, colluded together against the life of the just man, [scil. and] their soul abominated all those who walk in perfection" (CD–A 1:12–21).[30]

Paul of Tarsus is another example of one who likely faced the charge of apostasy as a label of social control. We cannot say with certainty what others said about Paul, but Paul's letters and the *Acts of the Apostles* present data that fit together in this regard. Acts 21:21 relates second-hand (at best) that Paul had been accused of encouraging apostasy among Hellenistic Jews, marked by his attempts to persuade them away from circumcision. Paul relates that he was punished by Judean authorities for the positions he held and voiced: 2 Cor 11:24 refers to Judean punishment of thirty-nine lashes he had received on five separate occasions; 2 Cor 11:26 refers vaguely to "danger" from his countrymen, presumably resistance to his teachings; Gal 5:11 refers to persecution Paul experienced due to his position on circumcision.

While these passages tell us that Paul's positions on circumcision and food purity were unpopular, and that some may well have charged him with apostasy, they also tell us that Paul had not "left" Judaism. Surely, Jewish authorities did not punish people who were no longer part of their community. That Paul is resisted and punished suggests he remained within the religion, though also that he brought in unpopular innovations. It also suggests that even his opponents considered him still to be Judean, even if a wayward member. This is confirmed by Paul's own statements concerning his Judean identity (1 Cor 11:22; Rom 11:1), and by Acts' portrayal of Paul returning time and again to the synagogues to preach (Acts 14:1–6; 17:1–15; 18:4–7). If, as seems reasonable, charges of apostasy were part of the punishments Paul received, then it is clear that the charge would have functioned to identify and correct the deviant behaviour of an insider – Paul.

Charges of apostasy could be applied to mundane actions, but also of course to much more serious behaviours. Dositheos, son of Drimylos, was a Hellenistic Jew in Alexandria. Third Maccabees 1:3 refers obliquely to this figure who was apparently Judean by birth yet changed his mind about the law (μεταβαλὼν τὰ νόμινα) and became estranged from the traditions of his fathers (τῶν πατρίων δογμάτων ἀπηλλοτριωμένος). The writer of 3 Macc makes this assessment because Dositheos worked in the service of Ptolemy IV Philopator (221–205 BCE). In fact, he appears to have had a sufficiently high station in the court of Philopator that he could save his king from an assassination

---

30 Translation by F.G. Martínez, *The Dead Sea Scrolls Translated*, Grand Rapids 1996, 49.

attempt on the eve of a key battle against the Seleucids in 217 BCE. This act was objectionable to the Maccabbean writer not only because Philopator was a Gentile, which for the Maccabees was objection enough, but because Philopator persecuted the Jews in Alexandria and Egypt. After his victory against the Seleucids, which occurred at Raphia (present day Gaza), Philopator wished to offer sacrifice at the Jerusalem Temple.[31] He was, of course, denied entry as a Gentile and so retaliated, allegedly, by imposing Greek citizenship on Egyptian Jews and absurdly rounding them up to be stampeded by a herd of five hundred drunk elephants (3 Macc 2:24; 5:2). But the more serious conduct, as far as the Maccabbean writer is concerned, is not Dositheos' high-ranking station in the court of Philopator, but that he was apparently an eponymous priest of Alexander and the deified Ptolemies (P. Tebt. 815), a very high honour conferred by royal favour.[32] The charge, whether real or fictitious, is serious for surely being a priest in a rival religion qualifies as apostasy.

Likewise, Josephus refers to a more serious charge of apostasy: Antiochus in Antioch (*War* 7.3,3). A governor of the Jewish people in Antioch, and greatly respected because of his father, Antiochus suddenly turned against his people. He accused the Jews of Antioch, including his own father, of plotting to burn down the city. The Gentiles were very angry about this, and Antiochus only exacerbated their rage when he sought to prove his apostasy by "sacrificing in the manner of the Greeks." Antiochus, in addition, oversaw the forced conversion or execution of Jews in the city and the outlaw of Sabbath observance.

Contextualising Apostasy as Disaffiliation

We may draw several lessons from these illustrations. With John Barclay, we can see easily on the one hand that apostasy is not an "objectively definable

---

31 S. Gambetti, *Ptolemies*, in: J.J. Collins / D.C. Harlow (eds.), *The Eerdmans Dictionary of Early Judaism*, Grand Rapids 2010, 1117–1121 (1120). Polybius (5.86) confirms that after his victory, Philopator offered sacrifice in the cities near his victory, which would include Jerusalem, but Polybius does not mention Jerusalem in particular.

32 A. Fuks, *Dositheos Son of Drimylos. A Prosopographical Note*, in: Journal of Papyrology 7–8 (1953–54), 205–209 (207). There are some difficult questions about whether Dositheos was a real person or whether he was strictly a fictional character created to serve the rhetorical and theological needs of the Maccabean narrative (see S.R. Johnson, *Historical Fictions and Hellenistic Jewish Identity. Third Maccabees in Its Cultural Context*, Berkeley 2004, 127). To my mind, Fuks' prosopographical note resolves this issue: he gathers five papyri and a demotic ostracon that all refer to this figure. He concludes that "it would seem very likely that all the papyri refer to the same person" (Fuks, 1953–54, 205).

entity" that merely needs to be spotted in ancient sources, and on the other hand that charges of apostasy cannot be taken at face value.[33] The assumption that apostasy describes a self-evident type of behaviour is problematic for two reasons. First, there is in fact a broad range of actions that constitute degrees of apostasy as it related to Judean antiquity.[34] This behaviour might manifest as *assimilation* (some participation in Greek culture vs. the abandonment of specific Jewish practices), *acculturation* (some familiarity with Greek culture vs. full facility), or *accommodation* (the willingness to fit some Greek ideas into a Judean way of thinking vs. the full adoption of Greek ideas to the exclusion of distinctly Judean ideas).[35]

Ancient sources reveal that each of these types of behaviour could be met with the charge of apostasy, or none of them at all, depending on the mood or perspective of the observer.[36] Wilson shows that primary sources reflect the same debate about what constitutes apostasy. Some rabbis argued that apostasy applied only to serious actions, such as desecrating the Sabbath and rejecting *kashrut*, but others counted wearing a garment of mixed wool and linen as apostasy as well (t. Hor. 1.5).[37]

Secondly, apostasy is not an objectively definable entity because too often the issue is not really about what people are doing; it is rather about *how* what they are doing is perceived by others around them, and the mood and motivations of the people doing the perceiving (and assessing).[38] Barclay's introduction of the sociology of deviance and labeling theory into the scholarly discussion of apostasy has been extremely insightful. Labeling some behaviour as deviant is what collectives do in order to stigmatise forms of behaviour they disapprove of. In other words, "what makes an act socially significant as deviant is not so much that it is *performed,* as that it is *reacted to* as deviant and the actor accordingly labeled."[39]

In addition, we learn that the charge of apostasy is a collectivistic act; like all deviance labeling, it is an exercise in social control in which the collective

---

33 J.M.G. Barclay, *Deviance and Apostasy. Some Applications of Deviance Theory to First-Century Judaism and Christianity*, in: P.F. Esler (ed.), *Modelling Early Christianity. Social Scientific Studies of the New Testament in Its Context*, London 1995, 114–127 (118).

34 J.M.G. Barclay, *The Jews in the Mediterranean. Diaspora from Alexander to Trajan*, Edinburgh 1996, 93–97.

35 See also P. Borgen, *'Yes,' 'No,' 'How Far'? The Participation of Jews and Christians in Pagan Cults*, in: T. Engberg-Pedersen (ed.), *Paul in His Hellenistic Context*, Minneapolis 1995, 30–59.

36 Barclay, 1998, 81.

37 Wilson, 2004, 17.

38 Ibid., 7.

39 Barclay, 1995, 116 (emphasis original).

(or more accurately some representative of the collective, whether official or self-appointed) seeks to limit the agency of individuals within its boundaries. Whatever one finds objectionable in the behaviour of others might be labeled apostasy. The labels can be applied to anyone at all. Thus, different people in different locations will respond to similar behaviours differently, sometimes labeling that behaviour negatively, and sometimes not.[40] This was certainly the case among Judeans in the ancient Mediterranean: the different sects of Second Temple Judaism and discrete communities within each sect had differently established community boundaries.[41] Therefore, behaviour that elicits the charge of apostasy will rarely be uniform across groups, geographical locations, or over time.[42]

There is, however, one more key point to be gleaned from these examples, and it is a point both Barclay and Wilson seem to miss. The examples above reveal that "apostasy" is not in fact the best term to use in ancient contexts. Though ancient sources do use the term *apostasia*, the term does not carry the same meaning now as it did then. The ancient term *apostasia* related first and foremost to disloyalty to king, group, or *ethnos*; the modern term apostasy relates to conversion away from a religion. Of course, religion was often part of what construed ethnic identity in antiquity, in which case disaffiliation from a group usually also entailed disaffiliation from that group's god or gods as well. But the modern meaning of "apostasy" is exclusively religious and generally the opposite of devotion. Ancient *apostasia* is more akin to treason today than it is to apostasy, though I submit that disaffiliation is a less charged and therefore more appropriate term than treason.

This is seen throughout the ancient uses of the term, a few examples of which suffice to illustrate. Josephus uses the term *apostasia* twenty-five times throughout his body of writing, and in each instance it refers to actions resembling political rebellion. The LXX occurrences of the term, though few, are also illuminating in this regard. Joshua 22:22, for instance, contains an oath of loyalty which the Eastern Tribes made towards the God of Israel. In this oath, the LXX uses *apostasia* to refer to the abdication of loyalty which is of course treason where a covenant is concerned. Likewise, when Ahaz is described as sacrificing to another god (2 Chr 28:22), the term *apostasia* is used (2 Chr 29:19) which again, in the context of a treaty, is treason.

As with the examples at the opening of this paper, drawn from the modern Middle East, ancient charges of apostasy were merely clothed in theological

---

40 Ibid., 118f. Thus, for instance, the writer of 1 Macc considered those who took on any degree of Hellenisation, from the banal to the extreme, to be apostates (1:11–15; 41–53).

41 Borgen, 1995, 36–39.

42 Barclay, 1998, 80.

language. Indeed, apostasy is a theological charge exclusively; it is the charge that someone's behaviour angers God, is displeasing to God, or abandons God. But what we see in these examples is that apostasy is a communal event, a challenge to, and sometimes a rejection of the collective. It is about disloyalty to the group. The better term, therefore, is disaffiliation, and the closer analogy for understanding it, and for understanding how people responded to it, is treason, not religious apostasy. Charges of apostasy were in fact charges of disaffiliation, and this explains why collectives would respond to it as they did.

It also explains another feature of ancient writings from these communities, namely the rarity of references to disaffiliative acts. While ancient depictions and discussions of disaffiliation are relatively rare, Stephen Wilson argues that it would be premature to conclude from this that disaffiliation itself was rare (he uses the term "apostasy").[43] He points out that groups who were left behind would be unlikely to advertise that fact. Tales of conversion might be publicised by the group that was joined because such stories reflect well on that group; tales of defection, conversely, would reflect poorly on the abandoned group. In addition, Wilson suggests that those who left may not have wanted to be overly public about their act because of a lingering sense of guilt.

These are all reasonable observations, but there is another possible interpretation of the rarity of ancient discussions of disaffiliation: that it really was uncommon. Indeed, it would be consistent with a collectivistic setting for acts of disaffiliation to be uncommon. Recall, that Triandis defines collectivism in the following manner:

> a social pattern consisting of closely linked individuals who see themselves as parts of one or more collectives (family, co-workers, tribe, nation); are primarily motivated by the norms of, and duties imposed by, those collectives; are willing to give priority to the goals of these collectives over their own goals; and emphasise their connectedness to members of these collectives.[44]

On the other hand, some of Wilson's observations are also congruent with a collectivistic interpretation of the evidence: in a collectivistic culture, groups would not wish to draw negative attention to themselves, and the individuals in question could well be uncomfortable in retrospect with their idiocentric acts of disloyalty (e.g., disaffiliation). Privileging the collectivism-individualism construct does not necessarily contradict Wilson's observations, but it does perhaps add some cultural nuance.

---

43 Wilson, 2004, 8–10.
44 Triandis, 1995, 2.

Conclusion

When attempting to understand apostasy or disaffiliation in a collectivistic culture, there are two things we are invited to think about: first, making a charge of apostasy is a thoroughly allocentric act, in that it seeks to defend the collective and to defend the boundaries that define the community. Barclay shows that often the charge of apostasy was a mechanism invoked to identify threats to community boundaries, identity, and loyalty. On the other hand, regardless of whether one accepts or rejects a charge of apostasy, and regardless of whether the behaviour that invited the charge was merely objectionable assimilation or the wholesale abandonment of one community for another, apostasy also illustrates idiocentric behaviour. Those who left one community for another rejected tradition, traditional identity, and the collective. That they were exchanging loyalty to one collective for loyalty to another does not mitigate the idiocentric nature of the move.

Both forms of apostasy have agents. In the first instance, those who make charges of apostasy are themselves the agents of apostasy. It is the charge that creates the apostate since the offending person often remains within the community, ideally in a more pleasing state. Perhaps, the recipients of these accusations were forgetful or careless about the law, or perhaps they were attracted to features of other cultures, but had no intention of leaving their traditional group. The charge of apostasy is the collective way of letting an individual know that his or her behaviour is a threat or at the very least is unacceptable to those who decide such things. It is a line in the sand, a line that, as Barclay shows, is drawn in different places by different communities. The accusation either forces a correction in conduct, as the offending person returns to adherence to the traditional collective, or it forces the offending person out of the community, in essence creating an apostate. And of course those who do, in the end, leave a community are also agents of apostasy. They exercise agency – or idiocentric behaviour – by rejecting the collectivistic pressure to uphold tradition and express loyalty to a traditional community. An understanding of both forms of agency helps us better to understand apostasy in a collectivistic setting.

Carmen Cvetković

Change and Continuity: Reading Anew Augustine's Conversion

Abstract: Augustine's conversion shaped Nock's definition of conversion, but when scholars have attempted to interpret Augustine's experience in light of Nock's theory, the result has been a misrepresentation of Augustine's own views. Cvetković's reinterpretation of Augustine's conversion presents a more coherent understanding of his experience able to accommodate both Augustine's general theology and his early and late works.

Arthur Darby Nock's classic study *Conversion. The Old and the New in Religion from Alexander the Great to Augustine of Hippo* published in 1933 famously distinguishes "adhesion" from "conversion". In Nock's view, adhesion refers to a non-exclusive form of religious allegiance specific to the mystery religions and deity cults of Hellenism which does not involve a drastic change in the life of an individual. In contrast, conversion is seen as a phenomenon characteristic of what he labels "prophetic religions", i.e., Judaism, Christianity, and to some extent the philosophical schools and is memorably defined as:

> The reorientation of the soul of an individual, his deliberate turning from indifference or from an earlier form of piety to another, a turning which implies a consciousness that a great change is involved, that the old was wrong and the new is right.[1]

It is usually claimed that Nock's understanding of conversion as a dramatic and radical turning point from *a* to *b* resulting in the creation of a new person changed at the core is largely indebted to two classic Christian narratives: that of Luke in the *Acts of the Apostles* describing Paul's abrupt conversion on the road to Damascus and, more importantly, of Augustine's retrospective account of his sudden decision to change his life from the *Confessions*, Book 8. While this indebtedness may be said to be partially correct, there has been a tendency in modern scholarship to reduce Augustine's views on conversion to the influential model proposed by Nock and to scrutinise not only *Confessions* 8 but other conversion narratives presented especially in the *Confessions* and in his early *Dialogues* in accordance with Nock's

---

1   A.D. Nock, *Conversion*, Oxford 1933, 7. Cf. Rebillard in this volume on the intermittency of Christianness, a facet of Christian reality that Nock did not take into account.

view of the subject. This narrow reading of Augustine's conversion accounts contributed to maintaining and, indeed, to deepening a number of already extant problems with regard to Augustine's conversion discussed by previous scholarship.

When Augustine mentions his conversion in his works, it is clear that he refers exclusively to his decision to commit to Catholic Christianity in the summer of 386 in Milan.[2] However, usually armed with Nock's emphasis on the decisive moment of dramatic change, modern scholars identify not one, but several conversions narrated in the *Confessions*.[3] They refer to his reading of Cicero's exhortation to philosophy, *Hortensius*, as Augustine's "first" conversion (373). This is rapidly followed by Augustine's conversion to Manichaeism (373).[4] Augustine's discovery and reading of some books of the Platonists (*quosdam Platonicorum libri*)[5] has been considered by some to be, in fact, his conversion to Neoplatonism.[6] Augustine's acceptance of the Christian doctrine, facilitated by his encounter with the books of the Platonists, has been referred to as Augustine's intellectual conversion. Augustine's sudden decision taken in the Milanese garden to submit his will to the divine will in the summer of 386 is usually known as Augustine's conversion of the heart or of the will. Finally, taking to extreme some suggestions made by Peter Brown in his seminal biographical study of Augustine, where he considers that Augustine's thought underwent a revolution in the 390'ies due to his rediscovery of Paul's letters and of his new understanding of the notion of grace,[7] some scholars claim that this dramatic turning point in Augustine's thought amounts to a final conversion which contributed to establishing the features of his mature theology.[8] Apart from failing to notice the existing links between these

2 Conf. 9.3,6; trin. 15.12,21; Jul. 6.12,39; ench. 6.20.
3 J.M. Le Blond, *Les conversions de Saint Augustin*, Paris 1950; L.C. Ferrari, *The Conversions of Saint Augustine*, Villanova 1984; F. Masai, *Les conversions de Saint Augustin et les débuts du spiritualisme en Occident*, in: Le Moyen Âge 67 (1961), 1–40.
4 On Augustine's journey as a Manichean, see the excellent study of J. BeDuhn, *Augustine's Manichean Dilemma. Conversion and Apostasy, 373–388 C.E*, Philadelphia 2010.
5 Conf. 7.9,13.
6 P. Alfaric claims that "moralement comme intellectuellement, c'est au néoplatonisme qu'[Augustin] s'est converti plutôt qu'à l'Évangile" (*L'évolution intellectuelle de Saint Augustin*, vol. 1 (*Du Manichéisme au néoplatonisme*), Paris 1918, 399).
7 P. Brown, *Augustine of Hippo. A Biography*, London 1990 (originally published in 1967), the chapter *The Lost Future*. For a compelling critique of this chapter, see C. Harrison, *Rethinking Augustine's Early Theology. An Argument for Continuity*, Oxford 2005.
8 Probably the most recent and radical view supporting this position is B. Dobbell

isolated episodes in the life of Augustine,[9] modern scholars were faced with an additional problem. Among so many conversions of which at least three can be said to be to Catholic Christianity, the question that legitimately arises is: which of these numerous conversions ought to be considered the real one, i.e., which of these conversions may be said to be irrevocable involving the consciousness that the old was wrong and the new is right?

A further problem is that interpreting Augustine relying on Nock's model of conversion failed to result in a coherent picture of the former's conversion able to accommodate the main sources that document this episode of Augustine's life, primarily the *Confessions* and Augustine's earliest extant works, the philosophical dialogues written in the wake of his conversion at Cassiciacum.[10] Thus, adopting Nock's claims that Christianity makes all-demanding claims on its adherents, modern scholars find it difficult to justify why Augustine as a new convert in Cassiciacum is inclined to pay more attention to philosophical rather than religious matters. Rather than doubting the adequacy of the Nockian model of conversion as a heuristic tool for Augustine's texts, the historicity of the conversion narrative from *Confessions* 8 has been called into question while the early *Dialogues* have been considered as a more "trustworthy" source for documenting Augustine's conversion because of their proximity to the event.

In addition to this, Nock's paradigmatic model of a sudden and irrevocable conversion is of no avail in dealing with the frequent passages scattered throughout Augustine's works which stress or hint at the gradual nature of conversion.[11] It has been observed that when reading Augustine's early works

a sense of purpose and continuity is the most striking feature of Augustine's conversion. Seen in his works at Cassiciacum, this conversion seems to have

---

who claims that Augustine can be said to have intellectually converted to Nicene Christianity only in 395 (*Augustine's Intellectual Conversion. The Journey from Platonism to Christianity*, Cambridge 2009).

9 G. Madec, *Conversio*, in: C. Mayer (ed.), *Augustinus-Lexikon*, vol. 1, Basel 1986, 1282–1294 (1290).

10 See G. Boissier, *La conversion de Saint Augustin*, in: Revue de deux Mondes 85 (1888), 41–69, and A. von Harnack, *Augustins Konfessionen. Ein Vortrag*, Giessen 1888. They were the first to point out that there are marked discrepancies, even divergences, between Augustine's retrospective self-portrayal in the *Confessions* and the picture of the newly converted that emerges in his early *Dialogues* written at Cassiciacum before his baptism. Their remarks have sparked a long scholarly debate known as the "two Augustines" controversy.

11 An increasing number of recent studies acknowledge the gradual nature of Augustine's conversion. See K.F. Morrison, *Conversion and Text. The Cases of Augustine of Hippo, Hermah-Judah, and Constantine Tsatsos*, Charlottesville 1992, and BeDuhn, 2010, 1.

been an astonishingly tranquil process. Augustine's life in Philosophy was shot through with Paul; but it could still be communicated in classical terms.[12]

Other scholars noticed the same sense of continuity transpiring in the *Confessions* and described Augustine's conversion as an "evolution"[13] to or "reconciliation"[14] with Catholic Christianity. They also stressed the fact that far from being a turn from one religion to another, Augustine's conversion happened entirely on Christian ground.[15] Moreover, nor can it be understood as a turn from indifference to Christianity if we are to accept Augustine's testimony in the *Confessions* that whatever versions of truth he encountered in his youth, he judged them all against the standard of Christianity and that even during his years as a Manichean, his conviction was that he was an authentic Christian.[16] In the attempt to account for the blatantly contradictory features of Augustine's conversion, a sophisticated solution has been suggested by Paula Fredriksen who claims that while Augustine's conversion is in fact the result of a process, in the *Confessions* he has deliberately constructed an ideal of "great sinners redeemed from the error of their lives by a single, dramatic moment of conversion."[17] In doing this, she argues, Augustine modeled his narrative in the garden of Milan on the pattern of Paul's conversion as related by Luke in the *Acts of the Apostles*. The Lucan Paul in contrast with Paul of the epistles stressed the dramatic turning point on the road to Damascus.

Fredriksen's conclusion is that Augustine's conversion narrative from *Confessions* book 8 modeled on the Lucan Paul far from being grounded in reality is nothing else than a literary fabrication. Finally, she identifies Augustine as the initiator of a Christian paradigm of conversion based on a fragmentary and hence distorted reading of Paul's conversion. The connection of Augustine's conversion with that of Paul is, however, not supported by *Confessions* 8. The model he openly admits to following at the moment of his conversion is Antony, the hermit monk from Egypt. It has been accurately pointed out that Fredriksen attributes to Augustine some of Nock's assumptions on the nature of conversion, who relies solely on Acts when referring to Paul's conversion.[18]

---

12 Brown, 1990, 113.
13 G. Madec, *La patrie et la voie. Le Christ dans la vie et la pensée de Saint Augustin*, Paris 1990, 23.
14 Harrison, 2005, 23.
15 Madec, 1990, 24: "La conversion d'Augustin se passe entièrement dans le champ du christianisme."
16 Harrison, 2005, 23.
17 P. Fredriksen, *Paul and Augustine. Conversion Narratives, Orthodox Tradition, and the Retrospective Self*, in: JThS 37 (1986), 3–34 (33).
18 E.A. Matter, *Conversion(s) in the Confessiones*, in: J.C. Schnaubelt / F. van Fleteren (eds.), *Augustine. 'Second Founder of the Faith'*, New York 1990, 21–28 (23).

The inadequacy of Nock's views on conversion in deciphering the meaning of Augustine's texts is further reinforced by the fact that, as Peter Brown has recently demonstrated,[19] Nock's concept of conversion is based much more on his own *Sitz im Leben* than on the actual Christian sources. Brown indicates Max Weber and William James as Nock's major sources in the fashioning of this notion. The former lurks behind Nock's emphasis on the distinctive nature of the "prophetic" religions, defined primarily by the "sense of irrevocable commitment and of the obligation placed upon adherents to adjust their lives and their beliefs to a universal and intelligible order."[20] From William James, Nock derived a "high density" notion of conversion that involves "a passion of willingness and acquiescence, [...] a sense of clean and beautiful newness within and without."[21] He is also indebted to James for understanding conversion as "the experience *par excellence* of personal discontinuity."[22] Reading Augustine's texts on conversion relying on Nock's heuristic grid largely derived from modern sources leads inevitably to a partial and erroneous representation of the former's understanding of conversion.

My aim in this article is to argue that a more accurate understanding of Augustine's conversion cannot be achieved without taking Augustine's own views on this subject into consideration. More specifically, I argue that the episode depicted by Augustine in *Confessions* 8 may be better understood when reading it in the wider context, both of the *Confessions* as a whole and against the background of Augustine's theoretical views on conversion. Therefore it is important to ask: What does Augustine mean by conversion? Is conversion for him the result of a process or a sudden turning point in one's life? Is Augustine's description of his own conversion in any way at odds with his theoretical views of this notion? How does Augustine view change in relation with conversion? Does conversion involve the consciousness of a great change in the life of an individual? What was the essential change that conversion brought about in Augustine's life? Is it possible to claim that because Augustine's early works continue to pay great attention to issues of classical culture, his conversion to Christianity was not an authentic one? It is the contention of this article that these questions cannot be properly answered without taking into account the theological discourse in which Augustine's views about conversion as well as his own experience of

---

19 P. Brown, *Conversion and Christianization in Late Antiquity. The Case of Augustine*, in: C. Straw / R. Lim (eds.), *The Past before Us. The Challenge of Historiographies of Late Antiquity*, Turnhout 2005, 103–117.

20 Brown, 2005, 104.

21 Nock, 1933, 7f.

22 Brown, 2005, 104.

conversion are embedded. Having said that, I am totally aware that as historians we have access solely to the textual evidence, and that my conclusions should not be used as claims about Augustine's experience of conversion *per se* which remains, alas, inaccessible to us.[23]

Let us begin by looking at the way in which Augustine uses the terms *conversio* and *convertere*. These terminological remarks should not be regarded as totally superfluous because those who study Augustine know well that some of his most profound theological insights have as a starting point, or are even shaped by his deep involvement with the Latin language.[24] In classical Latin, the terms *conversio* and *convertere* have the basic meaning of turning toward an object, a person, a specific goal, etc. For Augustine, *conversio* also denotes in general the act of turning toward something or someone, and it can be applied both to God and the human being. It has been observed that in the *Confessions* Augustine rarely employs these terms,[25] however, when he does use them, it is primarily in this basic sense of general orientation. Thus, God is the one who turns toward the human being: "perhaps you too will smile at me, but turning (*conversus*) you will have pity on me."[26] Reflecting on his youthful sin of his theft of the pear tree Augustine praises the mercy of God towards those who turn to him (*conversis ad te*).[27]

Conversio and *convertere* also indicate the act of turning around, in the sense of revolving, and they were used, among others, to refer to the circular movement of the seasons or of the planets. From this derived a new meaning, *conversio* as return. In the Neoplatonic ontological framework, so

---

23 Under the impact of the so-called "linguistic turn" on historical studies which revised and refined our understanding of the relationship between language and reality, scholars became increasingly aware of the enormous difference between the experience of conversion and the conversion narrated in the texts (cf. Engberg in this volume). The experience as such escapes scholarly investigation which can never determine "what really happened"; the only evidence scholars can call upon comes largely in the form of written records, meaning that they have access solely to a *mediated, interpreted,* or *constructed* experience. For a theoretical view on this issue, see S.T. Katz, *Language, Epistemology, and Mysticism*, in: S.T. Katz (ed.), *Mysticism and Philosophical Analysis*, London 1978, 22–74, and W. Proudfoot, *Religious Experience*, Berkeley, 1985, 43: "there is no uninterpreted experience." For the way in which these theoretical insights have been taken into consideration when discussing Augustine's conversion, see E.V. Gallagher, *Expectation and Experience. Explaining Religious Conversion*, Atlanta 1990, and Morrison, 1992.
24 His teaching on *imago* and *similitudo* is a case in point. See R.A. Markus, *'Imago' and 'Similitudo' in Augustine*, in: REAug 10 (1964), 125–143.
25 Morrison, 1992, x.
26 Conf. 1.6,7.
27 Conf. 2.7,5.

influential among learned intellectuals in Augustine's time, *conversio* (*epistrophê*) designates the return of the inferior levels of reality to the One, the source and unity of all being. Augustine adapts this ontological model to the Christian doctrine of *creatio ex nihilo* and distinguishes two stages in the creation: *formatio*, the creation of the formless matter through the activity of the divine Word which still finds itself in a state of dissimilarity with God,[28] and *conversio*, the orientation of the *materia informis* from this state of dissimilarity to God through the combined activities of the divine Word and of the Holy Spirit in order to give it form.[29] Made, by God, ontologically oriented towards him, the entire created world presents an inherent tendency of returning (converting) to the source from where it originates. This principle, eloquently formulated in the opening lines of the *Confessions*: "You made us towards yourself and our life is restless until it rests in you,"[30] provides the key to understanding Augustine's conversion as "the individual's experience in microcosm of what is true, on the grand scale, of the whole creation."[31]

Augustine's understanding of conversion as return based on this principle is usually regarded with suspicion as tributary to his late theological agenda as a bishop. Thus, his vivid depiction of his conversion in the first nine books of the *Confessions* as the return to the religion which he drunk in with his mother's milk[32] has been dismissed as rhetorical flourishing and defiantly anachronistic.[33] And yet, his earliest extant text, the *Contra academicos*, contains evidence that already as a new convert Augustine viewed his conversion exactly in the same way as he presented it more than a decade later in the *Confessions*, namely as a return to the religion of his childhood:

---

28 Conf. 13.2,3.
29 Conf. 13.2,3; 13.4,13; 13.5,6. On the indistinguishable activities of the divine Logos and of the Holy Spirit in converting the world from its formlessness toward God, see J.J. O'Donnell, *Augustine. Confessions*, vol. 3, Oxford 1992, 347f.
30 Conf. 1.1,1: *Fecisti nos ad te et inquietum est cor nostrum donec requiescat in te.*
31 H. Chadwick, *Introduction*, in: H. Chadwick (trans.), *Saint Augustine. Confessions*, Oxford 1991, xxiv. See also R. McMahon, *Understanding the Medieval Meditative Ascent. Augustine, Anselm, Boethius, and Dante*, Washington 2006, 64–104, and id., *Book Thirteen. The Creation of the Church as the Paradigm for the Confessions*, in: K. Paffenroth / R.P. Kennedy (eds.), *A Reader's Companion to Augustine's Confessions*, Louisville 2003, 207–225. He shows how the allegory of Genesis 1 in *Confessions* Book 13 describes the Christian-Platonist paradigm of "return to Origin" and argues persuasively that this pattern provides the large-scale structure for the *Confessions* as a whole.
32 Conf. 3.4,8.
33 BeDuhn, 2010, 23.

"Now I confess that I looked back on the religion implanted in us as boys, binding us from the marrow, as though from a long journey's end. Yet, it was actually drawing me to itself without my realising it."[34]

In another early work, the De vita beata, conversion is described as the gradual return to the safe harbor of philosophy after a journey (peregrinatio) away from the fatherland (patria) across the dangerous sea of manifold worldly temptations.[35] The stages of his journey correspond exactly to those he presents in the Confessions: his reading of Cicero, the Manicheans, the Academics, the impact that Ambrose's sermons had on his understanding of God's incorporeality, his discovery of a few books belonging to Plotinus,[36] and their immediate comparison with the Christian scriptures.[37]

Augustine's understanding of conversion as return to one's fatherland (patria) also rests on a solid scriptural foundation. Among the various parables of the New Testament, it is especially the parable of the prodigal son that Augustine applies to his own spiritual condition when narrating his life story in the Confessions.[38] However, it is worth mentioning that Augustine also

---

34 Acad. 2.2,5: Respexi tamen, confiteor, quasi de itinere in illam religionem, quae pueris nobis insita est, et medullitus implicata: verum autem ipsa ad se nescientem rapiebat. Translation by P. King, Augustine. Against the Academicians and The Teacher, Indianapolis 1995, 30. For a series of significant similarities between the language of Augustine's conversion narratives in the Confessions and the language of his conversion accounts from the early dialogues, see J.J. O'Meara, Arripui, Aperui et Legi, in: Augustinus magister. Congrès international Augustinien, Paris 21–4 Septembre 1954, communications, Paris 1955, 59–65.

35 Beat. 2–4. For Augustine's meaning of peregrinatio, see G. Clark, Pilgrims and Foreigners. Augustine on Travelling Home, in: L. Ellis / F.L. Kidner (eds.), Travel, Communication and Geography in Late Antiquity. Sacred and Prophane, Ashgate 2004, 149–159.

36 This passage clearly indicates that "some books of the Platonists" vaguely mentioned by Augustine in conf. 7.9,13 included Plotinus. In addition to Plotinus, who is mentioned three times by name in the early Dialogues (acad. 3.18,41; solil. 1.4,9; beat. 1.4), modern scholars agree that Augustine also read some Porphyry although there is no general consensus regarding the amount of reading from this author. For a useful survey of the scholarly debate concerning Augustine's reading of the Platonist books before his conversion, see O'Donnell, 1992, vol. 2, 421–424.

37 The comparison of the Platonic books with the Scriptures mentioned in this passage confirms the impression given by conf. 7.9,13–15 and supported also by acad. 2.2,5 that Augustine's encounter with the books of the Platonists immediately led to a period of comparison with and scrutiny against the standard of Scriptures. See Harrison, 2005, 26.

38 D. Johnson, Story and Design in Book Eight of Augustine's Confessions, in: Biography 14/1 (1991), 39–60 (43–45). See also L.C. Ferrari, The Theme of the Prodigal Son in Augustine's Confessions, in: RechAug 17 (1977), 105–118.

made use of the parable of the prodigal son in his early works, and he already uses it as a model for his own circular life-journey in the *De ordine* (1.20; 2.14) and the *Soliloquies* (1.5; 15). The *Confessions* contain numerous allusions or explicit references to this parable, but one famous passage from Book 1, where Augustine combines elements of this parable with Plotinian and classical reminiscences of the theme of returning to fatherland, perfectly seizes all the influences at work in fashioning Augustine's understanding of conversion as return:

> One does not go far away from you or return to you by walking or by any movement through space. The younger son in your Gospel did not look for horses or carriages or ships; he did not fly on nay visible wing, nor did he travel along the way by moving his legs when he went in a far country and prodigally dissipated what you, his gentle father, had given him on setting you, showing himself even gentler on his return as a bankrupt.[39]

In the account of Marius Victorinus' conversion from Book 8 of the *Confessions*, Augustine amasses in a single paragraph three biblical parables which all stress the idea of return, or as Wilder remarked,[40] which are all based on the narrative pattern of the "lost and found": the parable of the lost sheep (Luke 15:12), of the lost coin (Luke 15:5–9), and of the prodigal son (Luke 15:24).

Conversion understood as return of the soul to God presupposes a previous turning away from the same God: "we have separated ourselves from you and if you do not turn us around, we will not be converted."[41] The wandering away from God followed by the return back to him is not true only of Augustine's personal situation, but it is also the story of the whole humankind, and indeed, as the last "theological" books of the *Confessions* make explicit, of the entire created order.[42] Augustine found his story of wandering away from God especially symbolised in Luke's account of the parable of the prodigal son: "I travelled away from you into a far country to dissipate my substance on meretricious lusts,"[43] and in the parable of the

---

39 Conf. 1.18,28: *Non enim pedibus aut a spatiis locorum itur abs te aut reditur ad te, aut vero filius ille tuus minor equos vel currus vel naves quaesivit, aut avolavit pinna visibili, aut moto poplite iter egit, ut in longinqua regione vivens prodige dissiparet quod dederas proficiscenti, dulcis pater quia dederas, et egeno redeunti dulcior.* Translation by H. Chadwick, 1991, 20.

40 A.N. Wilder, *Early Christian Rhetoric. The Language of the Gospel*, London 1964.

41 Psal. 79.8: *Converte nos. Aversi enim sumus a te, et nisi tu convertas, non convertemur.*

42 Chadwick, 1991, xxiv; Morrison, 1992, 25.

43 Conf. 4.16,30: *Sed profectus sum abs te in longinquam regionem, ut eam dissiparem in meretrices cupiditates.*

lost sheep: "I have gone astray like a sheep that is lost. Yet, upon the shoulders of my shepherd, your builder of the house, I hope to be bourne back to you."[44] The wandering away from God (*aversio*) leads inevitably to a period of sin (*perversio*): "Our good is life with you forever, and because we turned away from that, we became twisted. Let us now return to you that we may not be overturned."[45] The turning away from God makes human beings the prisoners of sins and hopeless wanderers in what he calls the "region of destitution",[46] or "the region of death"[47] or, using a Plotinian expression, the "region of unlikeness".[48] But even in this region of death where he totally turned away and was twisted from God, Augustine discovers that he cannot escape God. This inner presence of God in the most intimate depths of the human being makes conversion possible.[49]

Finally, apart from denoting a general orientation toward or the return (*epistrophê*) to the divine, for Augustine the terms *conversio* and *convertere* also convey a sense of change in one's life, beliefs, or behaviour, corresponding to the Greek term *metanoia*.[50] Thus, he explains *convertere* as a "changing of the old life"[51] which needs divine assistance in order to be perfected. The same meaning of change is manifest when Augustine mentions the case of Polemus who has suddenly converted to other customs.[52] It has been observed that the numerous conversion accounts narrated in the *Confessions* also involve a sense of *metanoia*: for example, that the change that took place in Augustine's life as a consequence of his conversion was a resolution to lead a celibate life and a rejection of all worldly temptations.[53] Since these narratives also describe conversion as an instantaneous event, the change that they involve has been perceived not only as sudden, but also as conclusive resulting in an essential and irrevocable transformation of the convert. Because of the emphasis on the immediacy of the event, they also seem to propose a new model of conversion which totally contradicts

---

44 Conf. 12.15,21: *Erravi sicut ovis perdita, sed in umeris pastoris mei, structoris tui, spero me reportari tibi.*
45 Conf. 4.16,31: *vivit apud te semper bonum nostrum, et quia aversi sumus, perversi sumus, revertamur iam Domine ut non evertamur.*
46 Conf. 2.10,18: *regio egestatis.*
47 Conf. 4.12,18: *regio mortis.*
48 Conf. 7.10,16: *regio dissimilitudinis.*
49 Conf. 3.6,11: *Tu autem eras interior intimo meo et superior summo meo.*
50 Madec, 1986, 1287.
51 Psal. 6.5.
52 Ep. 144.2: *Ad mores alios repente convertit.* Another reference to Polemus' conversion is to be found in Jul. 1.12,36.
53 F. van Fleteren, *St. Augustine's Theory of Conversion,* in: Schnaubelt / Fleteren (eds.), 1990, 65–80 (70f.).

the understanding of conversion as a gradual turning toward or progressive return to God. It has usually been claimed that this model of conversion patterned on the Pauline episode on the road to Damascus and on the numerous hagiographical accounts, which present conversion as a sudden event, is a late development in Augustine's understanding of conversion presented only in the *Confessions*. Due to these obvious literary influences, Augustine's description of his own conversion experience based on this model has been considered to be nothing more than a literary artifact.[54]

And yet, Augustine's *Dialogues* written as a new convert provide conclusive evidence that already at this early stage in his career Augustine views conversion as a sudden event and even speaks of his own conversion in terms which evoke immediacy. During his time at Cassiciacum, Augustine seems to have been preoccupied by the phenomenon of immediate conversion and its being met with distrust by others.[55] In the *De ordine* 2.8 speaking to Alypius about the difficulty of forming a correct judgement of another's inner state Augustine observes that: "some and not few convert themselves suddenly (*subito*) to a good and even admirable life, but so long as that fact does not manifest itself by means of notable acts, everybody believes that they are still the way they were." In the *Contra academicos*, Augustine's encounter with the books of the Platonists stirred up such a great fire that he swiftly (*cursim*) returned to himself and remembering the religion of his childhood, he seized the writings of the Apostle Paul reading through all of them with the greatest attention and care. The way in which Augustine describes his reading of the Apostle Paul in this early work conveys the same sense of urgency and immediacy present in the controversial narrative of his conversion experience from the *Confessions* 8. Moreover, the vocabulary of both accounts, being highly similar, supports the idea that these narratives written at a distance of more than a decade, reflect, in fact, the same historical event which Augustine without any doubt lived with great intensity.[56]

These examples should constitute sufficient evidence to temper the enthusiasm of anyone tempted to point out artificial divergences between Augustine's early works and the *Confessions* based on the usually vehiculated claims that in the early works Augustine understood conversion as a process while in the *Confessions* he depicted conversion as a sudden event. No matter how confusing the co-existence of these two models of conversion may

---

54 This claim has been first advanced in the seminal study of P. Courcelle, *Recherches sur les Confessions de Saint Augustin,* Paris 1950, and it has been enthusiastically embraced by numerous scholars.

55 R.J. O'Connell, *Images of Conversion in St. Augustine's Confessions,* New York 1996, 268.

56 O'Meara, 1954, 63.

be for the modern reader, it is clear that Augustine senses no friction between them; his usage of these models demonstrates that he does not only opt for one of them depending on the point he wants to make, but that he even fuses them into one. Thus, Augustine's first account of conversion from the *Contra academicos* describes this episode in his life both as a journey and as a sudden event.[57]

The fact that conversion is repeatedly presented in the *Confessions* in terms of immediacy may be due to the nature of the work itself. Augustine confesses that his aim in writing this work was not merely to inform his audience about his past, but to excite his own love for God and to inspire his readers to turn to the life in Christ.[58] The stories of sudden conversion which Augustine presents frequently in this work constitute, then, a more efficient rhetorical weapon – allowing him to achieve this goal more successfully – than does the model of conversion as a process.

Augustine refers to his experience in the garden of Milan using both the verb *convertere* and the noun *conversio*. Summing up his entire conversion episode and addressing God, he says: "Therefore you turned me toward yourself."[59] In Book 9 of the *Confessions*, he informs his readers that his friend Nebridius became baptised as a Catholic believer "soon after my conversion and regeneration by your baptism."[60] In other works, he refers to the period spent at Cassiciacum as "the first time of his conversion"[61] or as "the beginning" of his conversion.[62]

After establishing what Augustine understood by conversion, let us in the following briefly consider the theological underpinnings of this notion in an attempt to better understand how Augustine was able to perceive conversion both as a process and an instantaneous event.

There is a huge emphasis throughout Augustine's sheer corpus that the return to God from the region of unlikeness where the human being has turned away from God cannot be achieved through human efforts. Conversion is effected only through the mediation of Christ the Logos, the one who has first turned the world from its formlessness to its Creator and archetype[63] and through the work of his divine grace.

---

57 Acad. 2.2,5.
58 Conf. 11.1,1; retr. 2.6,1. For a convincing argument regarding the protreptic nature of the *Confessions*, see A.M. Kotzé, *Augustine's Confessions. Communicative Purpose and Audience*, Leiden 2004.
59 Conf. 8.12,30: *Convertisti me enim ad te.*
60 Conf. 9.3,6: *Quem non multo post conversionem nostram et regenerationem nostram per baptismum tuum.*
61 Trin. 15.12,21: *Primo nostrae conversionis tempore.*
62 Jul. 6.12,39; ench. 6.20.
63 Conf. 13.2,3.

In regard to the claims that Augustine's insistence on the necessity of grace is the result of his rediscovery of Paul's letters and, particularly, of the apostle's *Epistle to the Romans* in the 390s (and consequently absent from his early works), it is important to quote a short line from the *Soliloquies* written in the spring of 387, only a few months after Augustine's conversion in the garden of Milan and before his baptism. In the long, intimate prayer that Augustine offers to God in the opening pages of this work, which is reminiscent in style of the *Confessions*, Augustine identifies God as the author of conversion when he addresses him as "God who converts us."[64] The same idea occurs only a few lines later when he begs the divine mercy that "you convert me entirely to you."[65] Although the technical term *gratia* is absent in this text, it is nevertheless clear that already at this early stage of his career, Augustine does not attribute the ability to convert to the human being, but to God.

In the retrospective account of his life in the *Confessions*, Augustine presents God as the author of his turning around: "you turn us around to you in miraculous ways."[66] He also quotes Psalm 79: "Turn us, O God of hosts, and show us your face, and we shall be saved"[67] as undeniable biblical confirmation of this important idea. His conversion in the garden of Milan in *Confessions* book 8 is seen as the result of God's acting: "you converted me to yourself."[68]

In Augustine's view, conversion is God's gift granted to human beings regardless of their merits:

> What have you done, O man, that you should be converted to God and deserve his mercy? [...] What could you have done to be converted if you were not called by God? [...] Do not become, therefore, proud about your conversion because if he had not called you when you fled from him, you would not have been able to convert.[69]

Therefore, in order to effect conversion, God is the first to turn toward the human being. Augustine consistently taught not only in the *Confessions*, but throughout his works that God's conversion (i.e., turning) toward the soul was a precondition of the soul's conversion toward him. God called

---

64 Solil. 1.3: *Deus qui convertis nos.*
65 Solil. 1.5: *Ut me penitus ad te convertas.*
66 Conf. 4.6,7: *Convertis nos ad te in miris modis.*
67 Conf. 4.10,15.
68 Conf. 8.12,30: *Convertisti enim me ad te.*
69 Psal. 84.8: *Quid ergo? Hoc tibi tu praestitisti, o homo, ut quia conversus es ad Deum, merereris misericordiam ipsius; [...] Quid autem, ut convertereris, posses, nisi vocareris? [...] Noli tibi ergo arrogare nec ipsam conversionem; quia nisi te ille vocaret fugientem, non posses converti.*

Augustine to turn toward him long before he was able to hear that child's voice in the garden of Milan chanting the refrain *tolle lege* and to interpret it as a divine admonition.

Augustine displays meticulous care in the *Confessions* to identify God's direct action in his life long before the Milan episode. The action, in which God acted and he received, unfolds over many years, and scrutinising his past life Augustine cannot but wonder at how late he responded to God's constant call:

> Late have I loved you, beauty so old and so new: late have I loved you. And see, you were within and I was in the external world and sought you there, and in my unlovely state I plunged into those lovely created things which you made. You were with me, and I was not with you. The lovely things kept me far from you, though if they did not have their existence in you, they had no existence at all. You called and cried out loud and shattered my deafness. You were radiant and resplendent, you put to flight my blindness. You were fragrant and I drew in my breath and now pant after you. I tasted you, and I feel but hunger and thirst for you. You touched me, and I am set on fire to attain the peace which is yours.[70]

The sudden decision taken by Augustine in Milan after a long and painful interior struggle is the culminant aspect of a sequence of action and response, but in my view it neither begins nor does it end what Augustine understands to be conversion. As an act of grace, conversion begins long before the moment of recognition of God's direct acting in one's life and is far from being finalised in this life. It will be fully achieved only in the life to come. Thus, I totally agree with Karl F. Morrison who argued that, for Augustine, conversion is the "unfolding of a supernatural process, initiated and sustained by God, which empowered the soul to climb out of the valley of lamentations singing a song of degrees, and, after death to find rest and full enlightenment in God."[71] Although Augustine sporadically refers to his experience in the Milanese garden as his "conversion", the fact that he feels the need to speak rather of the "beginning" or the "first time" of his conversion coupled with his prayers to God to convert him "entirely" support the idea that what happened in Milan is a point along the course of a long conversion process.

---

70 Conf. 10.27,38: *Sero te amavi, pulchritudo tam antiqua et tam nova, sero te amavi! Et ecce intus eras et ego foris et ibi te quaerebam et in ista formosa, quae fecisti, deformis irruebam. Mecum eras, et tecum non eram. Ea me tenebant longe a te, quae si in te non essent, non essent. Vocasti et clamasti et rupisti surdidatem meam, coruscasti, splenduisti et fugasti caecitatem meam; fragrasti, et duxi spiritum et anhelo tibi, gustavi, et esurio et sitio, tetigisti me, et exarsi in pacem tuam.* Translation by H. Chadwick, 1991, 201.

71 Morrison, 1992, ix–x.

Without any doubt this is the culminant moment of the process of turning back to God, but the episode narrated in *Confessions* 8 does not tell the whole story of Augustine's conversion.

Despite taking a sudden decision to commit voluntarily to Catholic Christianity, Augustine makes it clear to his somewhat disconcerted contemporary readers in the *Confessions* that this does not bring about instantaneous and dramatic change in his life. In Book 10, Augustine confesses that he continues to struggle with sin even after his baptism. Peter Brown has observed that this is "not the affirmation of a cured man: it is the self-portrait of a convalescent."[72] Read in the light of *Confessions* 10, Augustine's Milanese conversion narrative appears as an atypical story of conversion, "for what the conventional Christian wanted, was the story of a successful conversion."[73] Pelagius, who took part in Rome in a public reading of the *Confessions*, was apparently terribly annoyed by the tone of this book.

And yet, such denouement does not come totally as a surprise, as it is already hinted at in the theological insights presented in Book 8. It is here that Augustine's inner turmoil experienced immediately before his conversion is expressed theologically as the opposition between two conflicting wills (*duae voluntates*): "one old, the other new, one carnal, the other spiritual."[74] This inner struggle makes Augustine acutely aware of the redoubtable force of habit (*consuetudo*) in his life manifest in his difficulty to conquer his old will by translating his willing into congruous action. Augustine's need for sexual satisfaction held him captive in the chain of habit. This chain of habit was broken in Milan when God set Augustine's will free. However, despite this divine act of grace, which Augustine himself termed as his conversion, the change that it produces in his life is neither total nor irreversible. It is not a total change because during this earthly existence the "bad will", although it can be diminished and overcome through divine assistance, cannot, however, be completely eradicated. The conversion is not irreversible because it does not prevent one from relapsing into the old habits. This explains why Augustine portrays himself even after his conversion as having remained still largely dependent on habit: "But I fall back into my usual ways under my miserable burdens. I am reabsorbed by my habitual practices. I am held in their grip. I weep profusely, but I am still held. Such is the strength of the burden of habit."[75]

---

72 Brown, 1990, 177.
73 Ibid., 177.
74 Conf. 8.5,10.
75 Conf. 10.40,65: *Sed recido in haec aerumnosis ponderibus et resorbeor solitis et teneor et multum fleo, sed multum teneor. tantum consuetudinis sarcina digna est.* Translation by H. Chadwick, 1991, 218.

What the sudden conversion in the Milanese garden taught Augustine is that no dramatic experience is sufficient to make someone get rid completely of his past self. If the immediate consequence of conversion is not the total eradication of habit, this may well explain why in the first years as a Christian, Augustine maintained his interest for pagan and philosophical culture.[76] He acknowledges the existence of continuities with his classical past in the wake of his conversion,[77] and, at the same time, he speaks about the gradual progress in the new faith in the years that followed immediately the same event.[78] All this indicates that the change that conversion brought about in Augustine's life was progressive despite the abrupt way in which this event has been experienced.

If we are to take into account the polemical context in which Augustine composed the *Confessions*, his reluctance to depict a perfect conversion story becomes even clearer.[79] Augustine's African enemies doubted the authenticity of his conversion from Manichaeism to Catholic Christianity and the validity of his baptism which had occurred all too conveniently in Milan far from trustworthy witnesses. Even as he was writing the *Confessions*, Augustine became the target of serious accusations concerning his orthodoxy. Two prominent Donatists, the bishop Petilianus and the grammarian Cresconius, claimed that despite Augustine's alleged conversion he continued to be a Manichean and that he used dialectic and eloquence in a deceptive way unsuited for a Christian.[80] As the Donatists perceived themselves to be the only authentic Christians on grounds of moral perfection and ritual purity, it is highly likely that Augustine's emphasis on the gradual course of the conversion which will reach completion only in the life to come, was meant to counter his enemies' claims of leading a morally perfect life as a result of an absolute conversion.[81] Thus, perhaps addressing primarily his Donatist critics, Augustine insists based on biblical evidence that all life is one temptation (Job 7:1),[82] and he goes on to

---

76 It is in terms of "habit" that the mature Augustine describes his preoccupation with classical culture at Cassiciacum in Retr. prol. 3.
77 Conf. 9.4,7.
78 Retr. Prol. 3; retr. 1.1,1–1.4,4.
79 Morrison, 1992, 7–12.
80 Petil. 3.10,11; Cresc. 1.1,2–1.3,5. In his life time Augustine was accused several times of being a Manichean. Megalius of Calama, the primate of Numidia made such objections refusing at first to ordain Augustine as an auxiliary bishop of Hippo Regius, see Petil. 3.16,19 and Cresc. 3.80,92. During the Pelagian controversy, Augustine was accused of being a Manichean by Julian of Eclanum, see Brown, 1967, 370. 386. 393.
81 Morrison, 1992, 11f., singles out Augustine's conflict with the Donatists as the backdrop against which the model of progressive conversion needs to be understood.
82 Conf. 10.32,48.

illustrate this scriptural dictum by offering in Book 10 a thorough account of his tormented inner self at the time of writing the *Confessions*.

The fact that the change brought about by conversion occurs only gradually is documented by a passage from the *De trinitate* where the larger context is that of the renewal of the image of God:

> Certainly, this renewal does not take place in the moment of conversion itself, as that renewal in baptism takes place in a single moment by the remission of all sins; for not one, be it ever so small, remains unremitted [...], so the first cure is to remove the cause of infirmity, and this occurs through the forgiving of all sins; but the second cure is to heal the infirmity itself, and this takes place gradually by making progress in the renewal of that image [...]. And the apostle has spoken of this most expressly, saying, 'And if our outer man perishes, yet the inner man is renewed day by day.' [...] He, then, who is day by day renewed by making progress in the knowledge of God and, in righteousness and true holiness, transfers his love from things temporal to things eternal, from things visible to things intelligible, from things carnal to things spiritual; and diligently perseveres in bridling and lessening his desire for the former, and in binding himself by love to the latter. And he does this in proportion as he is helped by God. For it is the sentence of God Himself, 'Without me you can do nothing.' And when the last day of life shall have found any one holding fast faith in the Mediator in such progress and growth as this, he will be welcomed by the holy angels, to be led to God, whom he has worshipped, and to be made perfect by Him; and so will receive in the end of the world an incorruptible body, not for punishment, but for glory.[83]

This passage makes clear that the sudden moment in which conversion may be said to begin, does not involve an immediate essential change of

---

83 Trin. 14.17,23: *Sane ista renovatio non momento uno fit ipsius conversionis, sicut momento uno fit illa in Baptismo renovatio remissione omnium peccatorum: neque enim vel unum quantulumcumque remanet quod non remittatur* [...] *ita prima curatio est causam removere languoris, quod per omnium fit indulgentiam peccatorum; secunda ipsum sanare languorem, quod fit paulatim proficiendo in renovatione huius imagines* [...] *De qua re Apostolus apertissime locutus est, dicens: Et si exterior homo noster corrumpitur, sed interior renovatur de die in diem.* [...] *In agnitione igitur Dei, iustitiaque et sanctitate veritatis, qui de die in diem proficiendo renovatur, transfert amorem a temporalibus ad aeterna, a visibilibus ad intellegibilia, a carnalibus ad spiritalia; atque ab istis cupiditatem frenare atque minuere, illisque se caritate alligare diligenter insistit. Tantum autem facit, quantum divinitus adiuvatur. Dei quippe sententia est: Sine me nihil potestis facere. In quo profectu et accessu tenentem Mediatoris fidem cum dies vitae huius ultimus quemque compererit, perducendus ad Deum quem coluit, et ab eo perficiendus excipietur ab Angelis sanctis, incorruptibile corpus in fine saeculi non ad poenam, sed ad gloriam recepturus.* Translation by A.W. Haddan (with my own minor adjustments), in: P. Schaff (ed.), *A Select Library of Nicene and Post-Nicene Fathers*, series 1, vol. 3, Edinburgh 1887 (reprint 1994), 17–228.

the individual. Not even baptism brings about a complete change in the life of new Christian through its instantaneous remissions of all sins. However, baptism is perceived as a necessary condition in the transformation of the self, marking the beginning of a long process in which change installs itself gradually only through the constant support of the divine grace. The transformation of self is, thus, the result of a process which is envisioned to bring conversion to fulfillment in the life to come.

Conclusions

To attribute to Augustine the main responsibility for creating an ideal of great sinners redeemed from the errors of their past life in the flash of a moment, as some interpreters have argued adopting Nock's paradigmatic view on conversion,[84] is to read Augustine fragmentarily, based only on the conversion narratives presented in Book 8 of the *Confessions*, but ignoring the theological discourse in which these narratives are embedded and, indeed, ignoring the existing links between Book 8 and the rest of the *Confessions* as a whole. Augustine's views on conversion as an instantaneous event represent only one part of the story. Throughout his works, he also describes conversion as a general orientation towards God or, more precisely, a return to God which unfolds over a long period of time. Augustine maintains these seemingly contradictory views on conversion simultaneously. Moreover, his earliest works provide conclusive evidence that right from the beginning Augustine was aware of both models of conversion, and that he does not construct a new model of conversion as a sudden and dramatic event while writing the *Confessions*. Given the protreptic nature of the *Confessions*, Augustine exploits the latter model more than usual because it enables him to achieve his self-confessed aim in writing this work, which is that of stirring up his readers to follow in his footsteps and convert to God. However, despite this emphasis on the immediacy of conversion, the *Confessions* are also rife with the image of conversion as a progressive return to God. As such, conversion is a supernatural process initiated by God long before the voluntary acquiescence of the human being to God's call. While this voluntary assent of the human being to God may be expressed by Augustine in terms that evoke immediacy or abruptness, the change that this commitment implies is a progressive change which when supported by divine grace makes conversion to reach completion only in the life to come.[85]

---

84 See above, note 17.
85 Cf. also Engberg and Bremmer in the present volume for sudden vs. processual conversions.

Luther H. Martin

'The Devil is in the Details'. Hellenistic Mystery Initiation Rites: Bridge-Burning or Bridge-Building?

Abstract: Martin uses theories from the cognitive study of religion to evaluate the change that took place in the initiation rites of the mystery cults. In these, the change occurred in the minds of the individual, it was social rather than (just) religious, and while Christianity emphasised bridge-burning, mystery initiation rituals were highly bridge-building.

– Le bon Dieu est dans le détail[1]

Introduction

Experiences of religious change in the context of the so-called Hellenistic mystery cults were primarily the consequence of their initiatory ceremonies. But did these changes necessitate an exclusivist burning of family or other social bridges, as with some forms of the early Christianities, or did membership in these new cults allow for bridge-building relationships not only to other insiders, but to those outside of the cults as well?

The question of whether initiation into the Hellenistic mystery religions represents bridge-burning or bridge-building rests, of course, on assessments of the evidence that has survived. Evidential details concerning these rites have, however, been distorted by several dated and/or overly-generalised historiographical assumptions. First, is an influence of nineteenth-century historical romanticism, whereby the "mystery cults" became understood as conservers and transmitters of occult knowledge. Second, is a synoptic essentialisation of what are, in fact, diverse rites among and even within these various mystery traditions. Third, is a confusion of first person accounts with third person, historiographical explanations, even descriptions, of these rites. And, finally, a view of initiatory consequences biased by Christian understandings. I should like briefly to address each of these assumptions as they impinge upon the question of whether membership in the Hellenistic mystery religions should be judged to be more inclusive or exclusive.

---

1 Although this phrase is often attributed to Gustave Flaubert, its origin is unknown; it is, however, the basis for the subsequent adage, "The Devil is in the details".

1. Occultation of the mysteries

The idea of a Hellenistic period of history was first proposed from the midst of nineteenth-century German romanticism by Johann Gustav Droysen. In his classic, three-volume *Geschichte des Hellenismus* (1836–1843),[2] Droysen delimited a Hellenistic period as the time from Alexander to Augustus. This criterion was based, of course, on the "great man" theory of history, a view popularised by Thomas Carlyle, the British disciple of German romanticism and contemporary of Droysen.[3] It was in this context of romanticism that an emphasis on the sense of "mystery" (*mysteria*) was recast from its etymological meaning of "initiation" (*initia*)[4] into one of the "conservation and transmission of secret doctrine."[5] This accent on the Hellenistic mysteries as reservoirs of occult knowledge was especially heightened by the influence of Helena Blavatsky (1831–1891) and her theosophical movement upon the understanding and study of religion generally.[6] Thus, at the end of the nineteenth century, Franz Cumont could describe the Greek mystery cults as "secret societies, the esoteric doctrine of which was made known only after a succession of graduated initiations"[7] – an exclusivist understanding of the mysteries still retained by some modern scholars.[8]

However, in light of successive waves of initiates into the Eleusinian mysteries, for example, some 3000 a year at their height,[9] or an estimate of upwards to 40,000 into the Roman cult of Mithras over its 200 year

---

2 J.G. Droysen, *Geschichte des Hellenismus*, 1836–1843; see now the edition by E. Bayer, Munich ²1980.

3 T. Carlyle, *On Heroes, Hero-Worship and the Heroic in History*, London 1841.

4 W. Burkert, *Ancient Mystery Cults*, Cambridge 1987, 7.

5 L.H. Martin, *Secrecy in Hellenistic Religious Communities*, in: H.G. Kippenberg / G.G. Stroumsa (eds.), *Secrecy and Concealment. Studies in the History of Mediterranean and Near Eastern Religions*, Leiden 1995, 101–121 (117–121).

6 J. Borup, *Zen and the Art of Inverting Orientalism. Buddhism, Religious Studies, and Interrelated Networks*, in: P. Antes / A.W. Geertz / R.R. Warne (eds.), *New Approaches to the Study of Religion. Regional, Critical and Historical Approaches*, Berlin 2004, 451–487 (454–457).

7 F. Cumont, *The Mysteries of Mithras*, New York ²1956, 29. Cumont's *Mysteries* reproduces the 'Conclusions" of his earlier *Textes et monuments figures relatifs aux mystères de Mithra* from 1896 (Brussels ²1956, viii).

8 E.g., M. Meyer, *The Ancient Mysteries. A Sourcebook*, San Francisco 1987, 4; D. Ulansey, *The Origins of the Mithraic Mysteries. Cosmology and Salvation in the Ancient World*, New York 1989, 3; and H. Koester, *Introduction to the New Testament*, vol. 1 (*History, Culture and Religion of the Hellenistic Age*), Berlin ²1995, 192.

9 P. Foucart, *Les mystères d'Éleusis*, New York 1914, 351.

history,[10] and given the inebriated revels of the Dionysian devotees, any understanding of the mysteries as "among the best kept secrets of the ancient world"[11] would seem to be an implausible conclusion – especially given the evolutionary and cognitively based penchant for gossip among *Homo sapiens* and its social benefits for them (as argued by, e.g., Robin Dunbar).[12] Rather, most scholars today, largely under of the influence of cognitive anthropology, now recognise the performative character of the Hellenistic mystery cults. In the prescient conclusion of Erwin Rohde, "[i]t was difficult to let out the 'secret', since there was essentially no secret to let out."[13]

The question of inclusion into or exclusion from the Hellenistic mysteries, in other words, does not depend upon possession of some previously concealed knowledge. Rather, secrecy was a social claim that identified group boundaries. "Secret society" is, in other words, a redundant category.[14] As Ramsey MacMullen concludes, while there may have been "tiny circles" of small groups claiming an "oath-bound" exclusivity, as there have been throughout human history, the "so-called [scil. Hellenistic] mysteries were, in general quite open, come-as-you-wish ceremonies, to which as large an audience as possible was attracted" by a number of various cognitively affective practices.[15] In this sense, all religions, indeed, all social groups are ones that "initiate", i.e., that recruit and convert. Were this not the case, the transgenerational viability of these groups would have been compromised. We might then consider some other designation than "mystery" or "secret" for these initiatory groups, perhaps "private" vs. "public".

---

10 This estimate is based on an average number of 25–30 initiates in the over 700 mithraea that have been discovered throughout the expanse of the Roman Empire, i.e., 17,500 to 21,000. Since the actual number of mithraea is estimated to have been, perhaps, twice those discovered, the estimated total number of initiates into the Roman cult of Mithras would have been ca. 35,000 to 42,000 initiates.

11 K. Clinton, *The Mysteries of Demeter and Kore*, in: D. Ogden (ed.), *A Companion to Greek Religion*, Malden 2007, 342–356 (342); G. Mylonas, *Eleusis and the Eleusinian Mysteries,* Princeton 1961, 226; Burkert, 1987, 90; C. Kerényi, *Eleusis. Archetypal Image of Mother and Daughter*, Princeton 1967, xxxvi. 105.

12 R. Dunbar, *Grooming, Gossip and the Evolution of Language*, Cambridge 1996.

13 E. Rohde, *Psyche. The Cult of the Souls and Belief in Immortality among the Greeks* (W.B. Hillis, trans.), London 1925, 222.

14 Martin, 1995.

15 R. MacMullen, *Paganism in the Roman Empire*, New Haven 1981, 23f.

2. Essentialisation of the mysteries

Occultation is an example of the larger issue of essentialising the mysteries. Although cognitive anthropologists have refocused research on the
performative character of the Hellenistic initiation rites, the "presentist"
character of this research has generally resulted in ahistorical typologies
which tend to conflate the historical, i.e., contextualised, data for these
rites into essentialised qualities. George Mylonas, for example, who gives
a detailed account of the historical development of the Eleusinian site,
nevertheless concludes his study with a synoptic account of *"The* Eleusinian Mysteries" enacted there (emphasis added).[16] Similarly, Sharon Heyob
speaks of *"The* Cult of Isis among Women" (emphasis added),[17] and Man-
fred Clauss writes about *"The* Roman Cult of Mithras" (emphasis added)
together with his synoptically-constructed, uniform "sacred narrative"
for this widely-distributed, but decentralised cult.[18] On the other hand,
Giulia Gasparro has emphasised that "[t]here is a need, both legitimate
and methodologically correct, to avoid generic definitions" of the mysteries.[19] And, Walter Burkert has concluded that it is "inappropriate" to use
the term *mystery religions* as a pervasive and exclusive name for a closed
system.[20]

    As an example of the developmental variability of mystery rites (and at
the risk of making my own overgeneralisations), we can review at least three
broad stages in the history of the Eleusinian mysteries. Apart from possibilities of their Mycenaean origins,[21] there was an early, perhaps, prototypical
stage of the mysteries as a local Eleusinian family cult, a subsequent development of the mysteries into a Pan-Hellenic cult, and, finally, a stage in which
the mysteries were opened to all Roman citizens.[22] These developments primarily represented shifting political and demographic contexts within which

---

16 Mylonas, 1961, 224–285.
17 S.K. Heyob, *The Cult of Isis among Women in the Graeco-Roman World*,
    Leiden 1975.
18 M. Clauss, *The Roman Cult of Mithras. The God and His Mysteries* (R. Gor-
    don, trans.), New York 2000, 62–101.
19 G.S. Gasparro, *Mysteries and Oriental Cults. A Problem in the History of
    Religions*, in: J.A. North / S.R.F. Price (eds.), *The Religious History of the Roman
    Empire. Pagans, Jews, and Christians*, Oxford 2011, 276–324 (277).
20 Burkert, 1987, 10.
21 On the continuity of Mycenaean cult activity with the later celebration of the
    Eleusinian mysteries, see M.B. Cosmopoulos, *Mycenaean Religion at Eleusis.
    The Architecture and Stratigraphy of Megaron B*, in: M.B. Cosmopoulos (ed.),
    Greek Mysteries. The Archaeology and Rituals of Ancient Greek Secret Cults,
    London 2003, 1–24; Mylonas, 1961, 16. 29. 33.
22 Mylonas, 1961, 7.

the Eleusinian rites were performed, which surely challenges any essentialist understandings and interpretations of their practices.

The Eleusinian family cult

The "mysteries" initially celebrated at Eleusis were presumably those of the *Eumolpidae* and the *Kērykes*, noble Eleusinian families from which the hierophant of the Eleusinian cult and the "priest of the altar" were respectively chosen throughout its long history.[23] According to the *Homeric hymn to Demeter*, Eumolpus, the fictive ancestor of the Eumolpid family, was among those to whom Demeter had first revealed her mysteries (h.Cer. 473–479). The *Kērykes* were clearly the "second family" of the mysteries, and their claim to this authority is less clear.[24] This family-based cult was undoubtedly opened to citizens of the Eleusinian city state. Organised, like most of the Graeco-Roman mysteries, as fictive kin associations, they admitted new members through initiatory rites that were patterned upon existing juridical processes of adoption.[25]

Initiations into many local, small-scale associations have been identified by Harvey Whitehouse as "imagistic"[26] or, what in this case is similar, as examples of the "special-agent" rituals identified by Robert McCauley and Thomas Lawson.[27] Such "imagistic" or "special agent" rites are characterised as enacted by authorised surrogates of the gods (such as the Eleusinian hierophant), are infrequently performed with respect to the ritual patient (e.g., the Eleusinian initiations were performed once every year, but only once per initiate), and are characterised by a high level of affective pageantry that results in "spontaneous exegetical reflections" by the initiates and in intimate group cohesion among fellow initiates (e.g., shared bonds with the Eumolpids as fictive kin). We might agree that this is a reasonable characterisation of what we know of the early Eleusinian mysteries.

The Pan-Hellenic cult of Eleusis

Following the annexation of Eleusis into the Athenian state in the seventh-century BCE, admission to the Eleusinian mysteries was opened to citizens

---

23 Id., 233.
24 Id., 234.
25 L.H. Martin, *Akin to the Gods or Simply One to Another. Comparison with respect to Religions in Antiquity*, in: H.-J. Klimkeit (ed.), *Vergleichen und Verstehen in der Religionswissenschaft*, Wiesbaden 1997, 147–159 (155).
26 H. Whitehouse, *Modes of Religiosity. A Cognitive Theory of Religious Transmission*, Walnut Creek 2004, 70–75.
27 R.N. McCauley / E.T. Lawson, *Bringing Ritual to Mind. Psychological Foundations of Cultural Forms*, Cambridge 2002, 26–33.

of Athens and, subsequently, to all Greeks, i.e., to all speakers of the Greek language. Although rites of Eleusinian initiation continued to be celebrated annually with a characteristically elevated level of affective pageantry, they no longer resulted in any enduring social cohesion among initiates. Rather, the mysteries had gradually morphed from initiations into an intimate, small-scale association of fictive kin into a large-scale "imagined community" encompassing all Greeks,[28] now under the dynastic jurisdiction of the *Eumolpidae*. These now expansive rites of Eleusinian initiation, in other words, no longer emphasised "spontaneous exegetical reflections" among individual initiates – though such may have continued to have been evoked – but rather an administratively-regulated affirmation of Pan-Hellenic ideology in support of a collective Greek identity. Given the interrelationship of the religious and the political domains in antiquity, whatever transgenerational continuities that may have been conserved in the ritual performances, must surely have been understood in light of these changed political conditions, as they would be under the impending empire of Rome.[29]

The Roman era cult of Eleusis

During the Roman Republic, privileges of initiation into the Eleusinian mysteries were extended from all Greeks to all Roman citizens. Indeed, the Eleusinian sanctuary was expanded during the Roman period under imperial patronage, especially by Hadrian, Antoninus Pius, and Marcus Aurelius. And, at least since Hadrian, celebrations of these mysteries were explicitly linked to his establishment in 131/132 of the "Panhellenion", a philhellenic federation of Greek cities based in Athens.[30] As Christopher P. Jones has pointed out, "[t]wo commemorative arches, copies of the Arch of Hadrian in Athens," which were erected either during the reign of Antonius Pius or, later, during that of Marcus Aurelius, "stood in front of the main

---

28 B. Anderson, *Imagined Communities. Reflections on the Origin and Spread of Nationalism*, London 1991.

29 H. Bowden, *Cults of Demeter Eleusinia and the Transmission of Religious Ideas*, in: I. Malkin / C. Constantakopoulou / K. Panagopoulou (eds.), *Greek and Roman Networks in the Mediterranean*, London 2009, 70–82 (77).

30 C.P. Jones, *The Panhellenion*, in: Chiron 26 (1996), 29–56; A.J. Spanforth / S. Walker, *The World of the Panhellenion*, in: JRS 75 (1985), 78–104 (esp. 100). On network theory, see D.J. Watts, *Everything is Obvious. Once You Know the Answer*, New York 2011; N.A. Christakis / J.H. Fowler, *Connected. How your Friend's Friends' Friends Affect Everything You Feel, Think, and Do*, New York 2011; and A.-L. Barabási, *Linked. How Everything is Connected to Everything Else and What It Means for Business, Science, and Everyday Life*, New York 2003. For the application of network theory to the Mediterranean world, see Malkin / Constantakopoulou / Panagopoulou (eds.), 2009.

entrance of the sanctuary at Eleusis, and each carried the inscription: *To the (two) goddesses and to the emperor, the Panhellenes.*[31] And, as Michael Cosmopoulos has noted, the Eleusinian mysteries, like other cults during the Roman period, were used by their patrons "to generate and secure [scil. political and financial] benefits [...] from Rome."[32]

A new cosmopolitan worldview, represented by Ptolemaic cosmological revolution and politically by Roman imperial rule, eclipsed the Pan-Hellenic Eleusinian practices that nevertheless continued to be represented in locative terms by the traditional three-storied view of the cosmos.[33] The new cosmological worldview of the Roman period, on the other hand, vitiated claims to any local or distinctively ethnic identity as a result of initiation. Rather, the Eleusinian mysteries, like the concurrently developing Roman state religion, seem to have developed into practices identified by Whitehouse's predictions for variables associated with a "doctrinal" mode of religiosity.

According to Whitehouse, the doctrinal mode of religiosity is characterised by a set of beliefs, which remain stable, and which become encoded in semantic memory through repetition as a set of scripts. Of course, neither the Eleusinian mysteries nor official Roman religion was characterised by any "stable set of beliefs". Both, however, were characterised by an orthopraxy, the one characterised by open initiation, the other publically accessible. The performances of both had to be precise, the precision of which was administratively controlled, and which would become encoded in semantic memory not as a set of theological scripts, but as a set of behavioural schemas.[34]

Celebration of the Eleusinian mysteries retained a widespread popular appeal throughout the Roman period (e.g., Cic., Leg. 2.14,36). And various cults of *Demeter Eleusinia*, which may have practiced rites introduced from, modeled upon, or mimicking the Eleusinian, continued to be founded well

---

31 Jones, 1996, 36; Mylonas, 1961, 166f.
32 M.B. Cosmopoulos, *Concluding Remarks*, in: Cosmopoulos (ed.), 2003, 263f. (264).
33 The Eleusinian sanctuary represented this cosmos topographically with its site of initiation, the *Telesterion*, built into a sacred "mountain" and with an entrance to the underworld at its base. On the typology "locative-utopian", see J.Z. Smith, *Map is Not Territory. Studies in the History of Religions*, Leiden 1997, xii. 100. 308f.
34 L.H. Martin, *Imagistic Traditions in the Graeco-Roman World*, in: L.H. Martin / P. Pachis (eds.), *Imagistic Traditions in the Graeco-Roman World. A Cognitive Modeling of History of Religions Research*, Thessaloniki 2009, 237–247 (241f.); P.N. Doukellis, *Hadrian's Panhellenion. A Network of Cities*, in: Malkin / Constantakopoulou / Panagopoulou (eds.), 2009, 285–298 (290f.).

into the second century.[35] Increasingly, however, Eleusis seems to have developed into a fashionable pilgrimage destination – analogous to the Vatican today, where curious tourists, secular as well as sacred, flock – until they were terminated in the final decade of the fourth century by the anti-pagan decrees of Theodosius.

Rather than any exclusivist expectations of bridge-burning, the initiation rites of the Eleusinian mysteries seem to have represented, throughout their history, an escalating scale of religio-political inclusion that employed modalities of ritual practice which differed with expanding inflections of politics and administration. In their final stage of development, the celebration of the Eleusinian mysteries seemed to complement those of Roman state religion in that both appealed to, or sought to appeal to, a diverse but cosmopolitan population. The collapse of traditional social groupings and the anonymity of the new large-scale society afforded the conditions for the appeal and re-emergence of small-scale, special-interest associations, such as numerous *collegia*, and such cults as the Roman mysteries and the early Christianities.[36] However, only the latter consolidated themselves into a exclusivist alternative to the claims of its religious rivals and, consequently, established itself, first, as an alternative to Roman imperial power but, subsequently, as the ally of that power.

Roman mystery cults

A number of the small-scale religious associations that emerged during the second-century Roman Empire expressed themselves through a rhetoric of secrecy. Such rhetoric, however, largely represented a discursive prophylactic against a homogenising identity under the imperial state, an agenda increasingly reinforced by the cult of the emperor.[37] Among these groups were the Hellenistic mystery cults, some of which were apparently modeled upon the example of Eleusis.[38] Whereas Roman state religion conformed to Whitehouse's prediction for a doctrinal tradition of transmission, as did, increasingly, the Eleusinian mysteries, the Hellenistic mysteries generally corresponded to his predictions for an "imagistic" tradition. It must be remembered that the traditional Hellenistic cults, such as those of Dionysos and Isis, did not develop "mystery" practices until the second century CE.[39]

---

35 Bowden, 2009, 76f.
36 L.H. Martin, *The Anti-Individualistic Ideology of Hellenistic Culture*, in: Numen 41 (1994), 117–140 (125).
37 Martin, 1997, 35.
38 Burkert, 1987, 9; Heyob, 1975, 57.
39 However, see Bøgh in this volume (27, n.6) for another contention in regard to the cult of Dionysos.

The Roman cult of Mithras is the most paradigmatic of these new Roman mysteries because of their exclusively Roman provenance and their exponential spread from that century.

Historical puzzles

Essentialism is the view that certain categories – such as "Hellenistic mysteries" – represent an underlying unity and inflexible reality that gives them a distinctive identity.[40] Such views are a developmentally early bias in human cognition,[41] with which historians must continue to contend. To reject an essentialised view of the Hellenistic mysteries is to understand them and their various rites of initiation as a dynamic tangle of historical details. The significance of initiation into the Eleusinian cult, for example, varied depending upon whether initiation was into an early Eleusinian fictive kin association, into the inclusive orthopraxis of ensuing pan-Hellenism, or into that of the even more expansive cosmopolitanism of imperial Rome. Similarly, the early significance of initiation for itinerant Egyptian merchants into ethnic fictive kin associations, the patroness of which was Isis, must have been different from that of Roman citizens who were initiated into her mysteries. Or initiations into the Mithras cults held in early mithraea, such as of the Casa di Diana, two small rooms within an Ostian *insula*, must have been different from those subsequently held in such large mithraea as the Baths of Caracalla in downtown Rome or in the Mithraeum of Santa Prisca on the Aventine.[42] And although there might have been some informal networking among theophorically common cults,[43] there was no centralised, even regional, administration of their empire-wide distribution. Consequently, the significance of initiation into any one of these must certainly have varied from one of their cells to another, both across space and over time.

   What is the relationship of initiation into the various varieties of the mysteries? What is the relationship of initiation into one or more of the mysteries, on the one hand, and devotion to the emperor cult, or to the empire-wide public cults, the organisation of which they mimicked?[44] What is the relationship of

---

40 S. Gelman, *The Essential Child. Origins of Essentialism in Everyday Thought*, New York 2003, 3.

41 Gelman, 2003.

42 We do not know, of course, whether such incremental increases in the size of mithraea corresponded in any way to their increased historical successes.

43 V. Gabrielson, *Brotherhoods of Faith and Provident Planning. The Non-public Associations of the Greek World*, in: Malkin / Constantakopoulou / Panagopoulou (eds.), 2009, 176–203.

44 E.g., Gabrielsen, 2009, 182. 186.

these Graeco-Roman mysteries to the new, contemporaneously-developing, empire-wide Christian practices? Since the practices of a group are correlate with its scale, even the relative size of these different groups and associations is important.[45] Too often, essentialisations, such as the occultation of the mysteries, have distorted or obscured such detailed historical data from these different groups and their practices. Nevertheless, we can conclude that all of these different Hellenistic groups seem to have been characterised by an increasingly egalitarian, ideological/sociological bridge-building character that contrasted with, for example, the earlier, socially-exclusive organisation of the *poleis*, and with the cults associated with them, such as the Eleusinian.[46]

3. Evidential ambiguity

While there is an abundance of evidence from surviving material culture, including epigraphy, documenting the differentiated histories of Hellenistic mystery cults, there is little to no textual evidence. This paucity of texts suggests that these cults, with their emphasis on ritual performance rather than doctrine, simply did not themselves produce many texts, if any at all.[47] Might the assumption about the existence of such mythological or canonical texts, and an anticipation that they might still be discovered, simply represent a Christian bias concerning the narrative nature of religious expression? There are, of course, a number of textual references *about* the mysteries – from Plato (e.g., Lg. 2.14; Phd. 69d; Phdr. 246a) to the polemics of the Christian Church Fathers. And, there are a few texts about which arguments have been advanced that they are, in fact, narratively concealed mystery myths, for example, Reinhold Merkelbach's hypothesis concerning the Hellenistic "novels".[48] The novel for which Merkelbach makes the strongest case as representing something of mystery rites is the *Metamorphoses* of Apuleius, or, as it is better known, *The Golden Ass*.

The Golden Ass, whereby the novelist-philosopher presumably reflects narratively upon his own initiation into the mysteries of Isis, has been seized upon by text-centric historians of religion as a *locus classicus* for an understanding of the Hellenistic mysteries. There is no doubt that texts, such as *The Golden Ass*, provide historians of religion with an invaluable resource

---

45 L.H. Martin, *When Size Matters. Social Formations in the Graeco-Roman World*, in: C.J. Hodge / S.M. Olyan / D. Ullucci / E. Wasserman (eds.), *The One Who Sows Bountifully. Essays in Honor of Stanley K. Stowers*, Providence 2013, 229–241.

46 Gabrielsen, 2009, 182. 186.

47 But see, in this volume, Beck for a Mithraic catethical text and Bilde which mentions books in (at least some of) the mystery cults.

48 R. Merkelbach, *Roman und Mysterium in der Antike*, Munich 1962.

for understanding mystery rites of initiation. However, the problem arises when first-hand subjective *descriptions* of the mystery initiations, even assuming their relative accuracy, are confused with third-person, i.e., historiographical, reports for these same rites.[49] Cognitive-science research has now shown that the accuracy of first person accounts are generally unreliable, whatever the subject of consideration,[50] an explanatory recognition that has been most productively explored by behavioural economists.[51] An understanding of those cognitive processes whereby reflections and expressions are shaped may aid historians to retrieve more accurate readings of their literature sources.

For example, a great deal of attention has been directed to such literary/ anecdotal affirmations among the mystery sources as "rebirth", a metaphor often interpreted with reference to some sort of afterlife. But is such an understanding salient or does it represent a Christian interpretative bias?[52] For Apuleius, for example (Met. 11.14; 16; 21), the metaphor did not refer to an afterlife, but to his rhetorical transformation from an ass, i.e., from a befuddled Roman Everyman, into enlightened humanity in this world under the protections and blessings of the goddess Isis (Met. 11.6). Other interpretations of "rebirth" include, of course, allusions to agrarian cycles, especially with reference to the early Eleusinian mysteries, to expressions of a kind of timeless phenomenology of existence (i.e., existentialist interpretations by, e.g., R. Bultmann). Even Paul spoke of a this-worldly "spiritual life" following initiation (Rom 6:4; Col 2:12; 3:1) – as did the Gnostics who followed him.[53]

4. Initiatory consequences

To return to my initial point, if mystery initiations are not into some reservoir of occult knowledge, then the question of whether mystery cult initiation

---

49 L. Oviedo, *Religious Experience. First-, and Second-, and Third-Person Accounts*, in: Archivio di Filosofia / Archives of Philosophy 74 (2006), 391–401.

50 E. Pronin, *The Introspection Illusion*, in: Advances in Experimental Social Psychology 41 (2009), 1–67; R. E. Nisbett / T. D. Wilson, *Telling More than We can Know. Verbal Reports on Mental Processes*, in: Psychological Review 84/3 (1977), 231–259; A. Berthoz, *Emotion and Reason. The Cognitive Neuroscience of Decision Making*, Oxford 2006.

51 E.g., D. Ariely, *Predictably Irrational. The Hidden Forces that Shape our Decisions*, New York 2008; D. Kahneman, *Thinking, Fast and Slow*, New York 2011.

52 Burkert, 1987, 3.

53 E.g., *Acta Pauli et Thecla* 14; Nag Hammadi Library 1.2 (*Treatise* 1.4: *De Resurrectione* 45.15,39).

resulted in bridge-burning or in bridge-building turns finally on what initiates are initiated into. Lawson and McCauley follow Arnold van Gennep's classic *Les rites de passage* (1960) to argue that such rites "mark a change from one type of socially defined status to another."[54] The question about the constructive or the exclusionary character of ritual then depends upon an understanding of the social differentiations offered by the cult context within which particular rites were performed.

Social transformations

Two contemporaneous initiatory groups offer contrasting examples of social differentiation, the Mithraic cells, on the one hand, and the early Jesus groups, on the other. Whereas the Mithraic cells generally offer an example of bridge-building, some of the early Jesus groups offer rather dramatic examples of bridge-burning.[55]

For those Mithraic cells that served primarily a military demography – those actually situated in military garrisons, for example, the *Castra Praetoria,* the home barracks of the famous Praetorian Guards in Rome (CIMRM 397, 398), or those deployed to military outposts along the *limites,* for example, those along Hadrian's Wall (CIMRM 838–869)[56] – initiations could only have been bridge-building. It is, first of all, inconceivable that any exclusionary subgroup would have been tolerated within a military context, since such social fragmentation would compromise the disciplinary efficiency of military operations. Further, I have previously argued that Mithraic cells along the *limites* may have served as bridge-building instruments of Romanisation as non-Romans were increasingly recruited into the Roman legions.[57]

The Mithraic cells represented highly-cohesive groups, the boundaries of which were clearly delineated and supported by bridge-building, if demanding,

---

54 E.T. Lawson / R.N. McCauley, *Rethinking Religion. Connecting Cognition and Culture,* Cambridge 1990, 50; A. van Gennep, *The Rites of Passage* (M.B. Vizedom / G.L. Caffee, trans.), Chicago 1960. Cf. Edmonds in this volume for the pitfalls of using the van Gennepian tripartite schema to interpret rituals as initiatory.

55 Cf., e.g., in the present volume Cooper / Corke-Webster for familial conflicts in Christian conversions; Bøgh's contribution deals with the social-emotional benefits of Bacchic initiation, cf. however, also Bøgh for the conflicts (and boundaries drawn) between Bacchants and others, according to Livy's story of the Bacchanalian affair.

56 CIMRM = the serial monument entries in M.J. Vermaseren (ed.), *Corpus Inscriptionum et Monumentorum Religionis Mithriacae,* 2 vols., The Hague 1956–1960.

57 L.H. Martin, *Reflections on the Mithraic Tauroctony as Cult Scene,* in: J.R. Hinnells (ed.), *Studies in Mithraism,* Rome 1994, 217–224.

rites of initiation. Like the other mystery cults, the Mithraic were non-exclusive in the sense of an apparently unrestricted welcome of new adherents from the population it served, and their initiates were not prohibited from inductions into other of the mysteries. In addition to social support, however, the constructed boundaries of the Mithraic cells would have provided their mobile military membership a prophylactic against foreign threats, such as banditry and disease, as they were redeployed throughout the dangerous and disease-ridden borderlands and backcountries of Empire. This protection would also have been a characteristic of other of the bounded associations of the Roman world, such as the Isiac, in their pursuit of international trade.[58]

Some of the early Jesus groups, on the other hand, resembled certain modern cult groups in their demands that newly baptised initiates renounce their biological family in exclusive favour of the fictive kin organisation characteristic of these new movements (Matt 10:37 parr.; Matt 12:48–49 parr.).[59] Some of the early Jesus people even represented their reputed leader as saying to a potential follower whose father had just died: "Leave the dead to bury their own dead and follow me" (Matt 8:22 = Luke 9:60). This is an especially radical demand since it required renunciation of the ancestral ethnicity that was the very basis of social and individual identity in the Palestinian context.[60] In contrast to the expanding inclusivity of the Eleusinian mysteries and to the bridge-building strategies of social cohesion by the Hellenistic mysteries (but like the ethnic-based exclusivity of the Hellenistic Judaisms), it would seem that the bridge-burning demands of the early Christian groups represented the first overt development of formal social exclusivism among groups in the Roman world, an exclusivism regulated by their initiatory rites.

Transformation of self

The effects of mystery initiation entailed changes not only in the socially attributed status of the initiate, but also in the self-view of the initiate.

A. *The mind of the initiate*

Aristotle's oft-cited remark that mystery initiation had to do with *pathos*, i.e., with "experience" rather than with *mathēma* or "knowledge", is an

---

58 L.H. Martin, *The Ecology of Threat Detection and Precautionary Response from the Perspectives of Evolutionary Psychology and Historiography. The Case of the Roman Cults of Mithras*, in: Method and Theory in the Study of Religion 25 (2013), 431–450.

59 See Rebillard in this volume, however, on the less radical reality of Christian conversions in Tertullian's Carthage.

60 Cf. Crook's contribution in this book on collectivity in the ancient Mediterranean.

observation compatible with recent research on the performative character of ritual initiation. However, according to the full passage from Aristotle, the initiate, in addition to "experiencing" underwent *diatethenai*, a "change in the state of mind" (Arist., fr. 15),[61] whether that change was conscious or not. This reference to the "mind of the initiate" has been neglected in favour of scholarly emphases on explaining mental states in terms of social context and control. This "mind-blind" research is understandable since there is virtually no historical evidence that might shed light on the "mind of initiates", either before or after they underwent initiation into the mysteries. In recent years, however, this situation has been enhanced with empirical evidence from experimental anthropology and from the cognitive and neuro-cognitive sciences about changes that typically occur in human brains while undergoing rites analogous to those documented from the Graeco-Roman mysteries.[62]

B. Cognitive transformations

Whitehouse has characterised the practices associated with the imagistic mode of initiation as "rites of terror",[63] a characterisation that resonates well with contemporaneous descriptions of the Hellenistic mystery rites. The second-century philosopher Celsus, for example, described the Dionysian rites as inducing "phantoms and terrors" (Or., Cels. 4.10). And, the fourth-century philosopher Themistius described the initiatory rites at Eleusis as a wandering "through the dark," during which, he continues, "come all the terrors before the final initiation, shuddering, trembling, sweating, amazement" (Stobaeus, Ecl. 4.52.49, citing Plutarch (fr. 178) from whom the passage might actually be derived). All of the mystery initiation rites made use of rich sensory displays employing vivid and symbolic colours, esoteric imagery, exotic masks and costumes. The effects of these astonishing displays, exaggerated by the somatic deprivations of ritual preparation, were further heightened by the confusing visual effects of flickering light of torches or that of the of oil lamps at night or in darkened chambers of initiation and by the disorienting aural effects of exotic sounds and unfamiliar rhythms.[64] Such practices employ tractable, neuro-cognitive processes that render initiates

---

61　Burkert, 1987, 89. On this fragment, cf. also Bilde's article in the present volume which argues that some knowledge was indeed transmitted in the mystery cults.

62　E.g., D.L. Smail, *On Deep History and the Brain*, Berkeley 2008; L.H. Martin, *The Deep History of Religious Ritual*, in: L.H. Martin, *Deep History, Secular Theory. Scientific Studies of Religion,* Berlin 2014, 254–271.

63　H. Whitehouse, *Arguments and Icons. Emergent Modes of Religiosity*, Oxford 2000, 21–33.

64　L.H. Martin, *Aspects of 'Religious Experience' among the Hellenistic Mystery Religions*, in: Religion and Theology 12/3–4 (2005), 349–369 (353).

into any social group more or less cognitively disoriented, vulnerable and, consequently, primed to interpret and to understand the experiences induced by shared membership practices in terms of the specific context of their performance, whether that context is catechetical or cosmological.[65]

Historians of religion have long recognised that many features of initiatory rites are cross-culturally similar and recurrent. For example, the historian of religion Raffaele Pettazzoni noted, almost a century ago, structural parallels between the initiation rites of the Greek mystery cults and those of some Australian tribes,[66] and some fifty years later, Maarten Vermaseren suggested that certain features of Roman Mithraism might be found among tribal initiation rites of, what he termed, "the primitive peoples of Australia, Africa, and America."[67] However, phenomenological similarities such as these were somewhat whimsical as they proposed no theoretical basis for their ethnographic analogies.[68] Neuro- and cognitive scientists are now providing a theoretical basis for the kinds of recurring, cross-cultural patterns that historians of religion have long recognised in their data. The effects of these behavioural and cognitive defaults are being confirmed by contemporary cognitive and experimental anthropologists.[69] Such pan-human defaults, a consequence of our common evolutionary history, predispose and channel contextually variable and socially-specific constructions of practices and concepts into the kinds of recurrent patterns discerned by earlier historians of religion.

Conclusion

Many groups during the Hellenistic period, including the primarily social, political, and commercial associations (*collegia*), made cursory claims to the

---

65 L.H. Martin, *Hellenistic Religion. An Introduction*, New York 1987, 65f. 80; Martin, 1995.

66 R. Pettazzoni, *I Misteri. Saggio de una Theoria storico-religiosa*, Bologne 1924 (reprinted in 1997), 21–44.

67 M.J. Vermaseren, *Mithras. The Secret God*, New York 1963, 129.

68 F. Graf, *Initiation. A Concept with a Troubled History*, in: D.B. Dodd / C.A. Faraone (eds.), *Initiation in Ancient Greek Rituals and Narratives*, London 2003, 3–24 (4).

69 E.g., E. Cohen, *The Mind Possessed. The Cognition of Spirit Possession in an Afro-Brazilian Religious Tradition*, Oxford 2007; D. Xygalatas, *Fire-walking and the Brain. The Physiology of High-Arousal Rituals*, in: J. Bulbulia / R. Sosis / E. Harris / R. Genet /C. Genet / K. Wyman (eds.), *Evolution of Religion. Studies, Theories, and Critiques*, Santa Margarita 2008, 189–195; D. Xygalatas, *Can the Study of Religion be Scientific?*, in: D. Wiebe / P. Pachis (eds.), *Chasing Down Religion. In the Sights of History and the Cognitive Sciences. Essays in Honour of Luther H. Martin*, Thessaloniki 2010, 531–549; D. Xygalatas, *Fire-walking in the Balkans. High Arousal Rituals and Memory*, in: I. Czachesz / T. Bíró (eds.), *Changing Minds. Religion and Cognition through the Ages*, Leuven 2011, 193–209.

patronage of a particular deity.[70] Because of these claims, such theophoric, but otherwise ordinary groups are often identified by modern scholars as "religious".[71] This identification problematises the common understanding by cognitivists that "religious" refers to those domains or practices legitimated by claims to the authority of super-human agents, even when those claims are superficially customary or socially inconsequential and beg the perennial question of what is to be considered "religious".

There is now a growing consensus among historians of religion that those Hellenistic theophoric groups generally referred to as "mysteries" were "special-interest associations" that were defined not only by their claims to the authority of one deity or another, but by their cognitively affective sets of initiatory practices characterised by a cursory rhetorics of secrecy. These initiation practices were, however, not clandestine rites that transmitted reservoirs of some kind of occult knowledge, but were conventions that conferred upon initiates a certain identity in the socially remote context of empire.

A cognitive science of religion is increasingly mapping a pan-human mental scaffolding upon which socially contingent initiatory practices, such are those of the Hellenistic mysteries, are constructed. However, a full understanding of any history of religious phenomena, understanding, for example, whether the Hellenistic mystery initiations were bridge-building or bridge-burning, requires attention not only to the gap-filling theoretical models of pan-human behavioural and cognitive proclivitries being mapped by cognitive scientists and to theoretically-grounded ethnographic analogies, but also to the contextual particulars of the historical data. While the contributions of cognitive science to historiography is essential and historians would be foolish to neglect them,[72] the gods of the Hellenistic world and judgements about which practices, justified by claims to their authority, are inclusive or exclusive, are fully understood only in terms of the details of time, place, and demography.[73]

---

70 J.S. Kloppenborg, *Collegia and Thiasoi. Issues in Function, Taxonomy and Membership*, in: J.S. Kloppenborg / S.G. Wilson (eds.), *Voluntary Associations in the Graeco-Roman World*, London 1996, 16–30 (18f.).

71 Gabrielsen, 2009, 177; Martin, 2005, 350. 359.

72 L.H. Martin, *The Future of the Past. The History of Religions and Cognitive Historiography*, in: Religio. Revue pro Religionistiku 20/2 (2012), 155–171 (reprinted in Martin, 2014, 343–358).

73 J. Sørensen, *Past Minds. Present Historiography and Cognitive Science*, in: L.H. Martin / J. Sørensen (eds.), *Past Minds. Studies in Cognitive Historiography*, London 2011, 179–196; and D. Wiebe, *Beneath the Surface of History?*, in: Martin / Sørensen (eds.), 2011, 167–177.

Kate Cooper and James Corke-Webster

Conversion, Conflict, and the Drama of Social Reproduction: Narratives of Filial Resistance in Early Christianity and Modern Britain

Abstract: The authors examine the element of family conflict in conversion experiences. As a way to understand what is often at stake in these conflicts, they compare the *Acts of Paul and Thecla* with a recent novel about the Pakistani community in Britain. Mother-daughter tension is at the core of both narratives, and in both cases it functions to explore the vulnerability of social reproduction in a marginal community.

Some decades ago, the American scholar Dennis MacDonald wrote of a "battle for Paul" in second-century narrative sources,[1] and nowhere is this more true than in thinking about models of Christian conversion. Paul takes centre stage in the public preaching of the canonical book of Acts that preserves a stylised picture of the earliest days of Christian mission. But in non-canonical texts preserving a very different picture of Christian conversions this public performer Paul is replaced by an alluring pseudo-romantic figure, a lure to female adolescent protagonists who follow him into a Christian life, leaving their homes and family life behind. The implication of these latter texts is seemingly that this departure from home is a necessary corollary to rejection of an inherited identity.[2]

Produced predominantly during the second to fourth centuries CE, the *Apocryphal Acts of the Apostles* have proved a lively testing-ground for recent scholarship on cultural hybridity in late antiquity.[3] One of the most

---

1 D.R. MacDonald, *The Legend and the Apostle. The Battle for Paul in Story and Canon*, Philadelphia 1983.

2 For survey and discussion of family discontent in Christian martyr literature, see K. Cooper, *Resistance, Obedience, and Conversion in the Early Christian Household*, in P. Clarke / C. Methuen (eds.), *The Church and the Household. Studies in Church History*, Woodbridge 2014, 5–22, along with K. Bradley, *Sacrificing the Family. Christian Martyrs and their Kin*, in: Ancient Narrative 3 (2003), 150–181. For a valuable response to Bradley's article, with supplements and corrections, see J.N. Bremmer, *The Social and Religious Capital of the Early Christians*, in: Hephaistos 24 (2006), 269–278.

3 V. Burrus / D. Boyarin, *Hybridity as the Subversion of Orthodoxy? Jews and Christians in Late Antiquity*, in: Social Compass 52/4 (2005), 431–441, with V. Burrus, *Mimicking Virgins. Colonial Ambivalence and the Ancient Romance*, in: Arethusa 38 (2005), 49–88.

potentially exciting areas of this work is a re-consideration of the role of householders in maintaining the provincial social order, and how a child, by withdrawing filial piety and obedience toward the head of household, could work to de-stabilise the wider social order. The present essay considers what "conversion" meant to individuals in the Roman provinces of the second and third centuries in light of the relationship between mother and daughter. What did it mean for a parent to hand on a cultural and religious identity to a child in this society? For the most part, in narratives of child or adolescent conversion, ancient Christian readers seem to have been expected to sympathise with the "resisting" child rather than the "controlling" parent. Does the same hold true when the parent is female?

We will focus our attention on two sources. The first is the second-century *Acts of Paul and Thecla*, in which a teen-aged daughter refuses an arranged marriage proposed by her widowed mother. The second is Nadeem Aslam's twenty-first-century novel *Maps for Lost Lovers*,[4] which explores the world of Pakistani immigrant communities struggling to adapt to life in modern Britain. Mother-daughter tension is at the centre of both narratives, and in both cases the difficulty of the mother-daughter relationship captures the vulnerability of social reproduction in a marginal community. In both cases, the daughter's refusal to accept her mother's guidance escalates into a violent confrontation.

Naturally, the social dynamics in modern Bradford differ from those of the world of the *Apocryphal acts*, not least in the power balance between parent and child. In Aslam's narrative the parents are struggling to keep ancestral traditions alive against the tide of assimilation, while in the *Acts of Paul and Thecla* we are led to believe that conformity to inherited tradition generally goes unquestioned, and thus that it is the adolescent, not the parent, who is in the more vulnerable position.

Adolescent withdrawal in the *Apocryphal Acts of the Apostles*

In the canonical *Acts of the Apostles*, which have served as the dominant narrative of the initial spread of Christianity in the first century CE, the narrative focus is on missionary encounters between adult males, often in a public setting. A large part of the text is dedicated to the missionary activity of the apostle Paul (formerly Saul) of Tarsus, as he preaches in the marketplaces and synagogues of Mediterranean towns. In the *Apocryphal acts*, by contrast, missionary encounters often reach into more intimate domestic settings, and the apostle's preaching takes place not only in public, but also in

---

4   Nadeem Aslam, *Maps for Lost Lovers*, London 2005.

the courtyards of private houses.[5] The listeners are frequently young women – married or unmarried – who in converting to Christianity must extract themselves from domestic relationships which the apostle and his Christian teaching have disrupted. The model of conversion here is grounded in the arena of social reproduction, and these narratives draw on the "everyday" tensions within ancient households.[6]

The *Acts of Paul and Thecla* exemplify this perspective on conversion to Christianity. This anonymous Greek text, usually dated to the second century,[7] begins when a young woman, Thecla, sitting at her window, is captivated by the echoing words of the itinerant Paul preaching in the courtyard of the house across the street. Her mother, Theocleia, becoming worried by her daughter's obsessive focus on Paul, calls Thecla's fiancé Thamyris (a leading citizen of the city) for assistance, but they fail to regain her attention. Thamyris has Paul arrested and thrown in prison, but Thecla bribes his guard by night and joins him in prison where she is found by her panicked family the following morning. During Paul's subsequent trial, Thecla refuses to answer the governor's questions about him, at which point in a moment of high drama her mother calls for her daughter to be burnt alive. Thecla is then miraculously saved and leaves Iconium to follow Paul around the Mediterranean. Having endured a similar test in Antioch after a prominent local citizen falls in love with her and has her condemned to the beasts in fury at being rebuffed, Thecla is baptised by Paul. She returns home and visits her mother, attempts a reconciliation and then departs again, living out her life in a cave as an ascetic for the next seventy-two years.

Paul's arrival is the root cause of Thecla's opposition to her marriage, and his preaching sparks Thecla ignoring her mother and fiancé. This preaching concerns the question of the necessity of marriage. When Thecla was rooted to her window, she "listened night and day to the discourse of virginity and prayer and did not look away from the window, but paid earnest heed to the

---

5   See Bremmer in the present volume for a study of the *Apocryphal acts*.

6   For further discussion of domestic models of conversion in the *Apocryphal acts* and related literature, see K. Cooper, *The Household as a Venue for Religious Conversion*, in: B. Rawson (ed.), *A Companion to Families in the Greek and Roman Worlds*, Oxford 2010, 183–197; ead., *Ventriloquism and the Miraculous. Conversion, Preaching, and the Martyr Exemplum in Late Antiquity*, in: K. Cooper / J. Gregory (eds.), *Signs, Wonders, and Miracles. Studies in Church History*, vol. 41, Woodbridge 2005, 22–45, and ead., 2014, 5–22.

7   V. Burrus, *Chastity as Autonomy. Women in the Stories of the Apocryphal Acts*, Lewiston 1987; S. Davis, *The Cult of Saint Thecla. A Tradition of Women's Piety in Late Antiquity*, Oxford 2001, 6–35; S. Johnson, *The Life and Miracles of Thecla. A Literary Study*, Cambridge 2006; J.W. Barrier, *The Acts of Paul and Thecla. A Critical Introduction and Commentary*, Tübingen 2009.

faith, rejoicing exceedingly." The details of this discourse of virginity and prayer are also revealed to us:

> Blessed are the pure in heart, for they shall see God; blessed are they that have kept the flesh chaste, for they shall become a temple of God; blessed are they that control themselves, for God shall speak with them; blessed are they that have kept aloof from this world, for they shall be called upright; blessed are they that have wives as not having them, for they shall receive God for their portion; blessed are they that have the fear of God, for they shall become angels of God; blessed are they that have kept the baptism, for they shall rest beside the Father and the Son; blessed are the merciful, for they shall obtain mercy, and shall not see the bitter day of judgment; blessed are the bodies of the virgins, for they shall be well pleasing to God and shall not lose the reward of their chastity; for the word of the Father shall become to them a work of salvation against the day of His Son, and they shall have rest forever and ever.[8]

Paul's preaching here reveals to Thecla for the first time possibilities for her life beyond marriage. Paul himself provides an alternative to the dependence on a male protective figure that her mother was presenting to her in Thamyris.

In fact, the *Acts of Paul and Thecla* is structured around the question of Thecla's unfulfilled marriage. Tensions over that marriage lie behind the flash points between mother and daughter that form two of the narrative's pivotal moments. Structural narratologists term such key moments in narratives *functional events* and use them as a means to plot narrative progression and structure.[9] William Hendricks has also suggested that plot structure is driven by confrontation, so one can narrow down the pivotal *functional events* by identifying those where two actors or groups of actors confront one another.[10] Thecla's departure from Iconium is sparked by her initial clashes with her mother Theocleia over her refusal to marry. And her eventual decision at the end of the narrative to live in a cave in Seleucia comes after she returns home and attempts the reunion with her mother, again discussing marriage.[11]

---

8 *The Acts of Paul and Thecla* 5–6.
9 Building on the seminal work of Roland Barthes, Mieke Bal defines them as follows: "Functional events open a choice between two possibilities, realise this choice, or reveal the results of such a choice. Once a choice is made, it determines the subsequent course of events in the developments of the fabula." Mieke Bal, *Narratology. Introduction to the Theory of Narrative*, Toronto 1997, 184.
10 W.O. Hendricks, *Methodology of Narrative Structural Analysis*, in: Semiotica 7 (1973), 163–184.
11 Although outside the scope of this essay, Thecla's departure from Antioch (where she travels with Paul in the central part of the story) is also motivated by a violent clash over the question of marriage, but here with the local governor, rather than with a family member.

Thecla's mother Theocleia's concern begins when Thecla starts ignoring her fiancé Thamyris because she is captivated by Paul:

And as she did not stand away from the window, her mother sends to Thamyris; and he comes gladly, as if already receiving her in marriage. And Theocleia said: I have a strange story to tell you, Thamyris; for assuredly for three days and three nights Thecla does not rise from the window, neither to eat nor to drink; but looking earnestly as if upon some pleasant sight, she is so devoted to a foreigner teaching deceitful and artful discourses, that I wonder how a virgin of such modesty is so painfully put about. Thamyris, this man will overturn the city of the Iconians, and your Thecla too besides; for all the women and the young men go in beside him, being taught to fear God and to live in chastity. Moreover, also my daughter, tied to the window like a spider, lays hold of what is said by Paul with a strange eagerness and awful emotion; for the virgin looks eagerly at what is said by him and has been captivated. But go near and speak to her, for she has been betrothed to you.[12]

It is both Thecla's neglect of her planned marriage that concerns Theocleia, as well as a fear that more young people will be similarly corrupted, and indeed Thecla had seen "many women going in beside Paul."[13] This fear over the matter escalating is crucial. Later, after events have escalated and Paul finds himself before the governor, the latter recognises that "they bring no small charges against you."[14] Paul is accused of completely undermining the social fabric. When Theocleia snaps and calls for her daughter's death it is out of fear at the effect of her examples on others:

And having called a council, he [scil. the governor] summoned Thecla and said to her: Why do you not obey Thamyris, according to the law of the Iconians? But she stood looking earnestly at Paul. And when she gave no answer, her mother cried out, saying: Burn the wicked *wretch;* burn in the midst of the theatre her that will not marry, in order that all the women that have been taught by this man may be afraid.[15]

Thecla's crime is not simply her refusal to accept the particular marriage with Thamyris, but her adoption of a position that undermines the whole institution of marriage. Her choice is a break from the *status quo*, a repudiation of the principles of social reproduction and a warning that more might echo her choice and do the same.[16]

In exposing the crisis point to which a conversion to Christianity could bring a small, provincial community in the Roman Empire, the *Acts of Paul*

---

12 *The Acts of Paul and Thecla* 8–9.
13 *The Acts of Paul and Thecla* 7.
14 *The Acts of Paul and Thecla* 16.
15 *The Acts of Paul and Thecla* 20.
16 Cf. Crook in this volume on the problems with individual actions in a collectivistic society.

and Thecla confront the disturbing reality of conversion in the social world of the ancient Mediterranean. It recognises that an individual's conversion to Christianity does not simply impact them, but likely has a much wider impact on their family, friends, and the wider community.

The novel before the novel: Identity crisis and the literature of dislocation

In its dramatic narrative of love and adventure, *The Acts of Paul and Thecla* resemble other non-Christian fictional narratives being written in the eastern part of the Empire at this time, in particular the so-called ancient Greek novels produced between the 1st century BCE and the 3rd century CE (of which five are extant).[17] These five novels all tell similar stories of adolescent Greeks living under the Roman Empire, members of the local elites of urban provincial centres. The plots of the five extant romances are all broadly similar. An unmarried couple are separated from their families and usually, subsequently, from each other – normally violently through shipwreck or kidnapping. They are then propelled into a chain of adventures as they travel around the Mediterranean before being reunited and married.[18] Thecla's story employs a related narrative arc. Thecla leaves both family and home city to follow her beloved (with Paul and his proffered Christianity serving as "love interest"), journeying around the Mediterranean, undergoing dramatic adventures before an eventual return to her home city.[19] Even many of the set tableaux are repeated, including other suitors, trial scenes, near death experiences, etc.[20]

Though traditionally dismissed by scholars as sub-standard romantic literature, more recently there has been an appreciation of the novels'

---

17 *Leucippe and Clitophon, Chaereas and Callirhoe, An Ephesian tale, Daphnis and Chloe,* and *An Ethiopian story.* For translations and comment, see B.P. Reardon, *Collected Ancient Greek Novels,* Berkeley 1989.

18 *Daphnis and Chloe* is arguably different in kind, as the main characters never leave their idyllic pastoral setting, but while the genre of this work is admittedly more complicated (it has many features of ancient pastoral literature as well), many of the standard plot features are retained.

19 The similarities between early Christian literature and the novels have frequently been pointed out. They were categorised into common thematic elements by Rosa Söder in 1932: the element of travel, the aretological element, the teratological, the tendentious element, and the erotic element; taken from R. Söder, *Die apokryphen Apostelgeschichten und die romanhafte Literatur der Antike,* Stuttgart 1932. More recently, see S. Davis, 2001, 10–12.

20 For more detail, see V. Burrus, 1987, 7–30. Burrus traces in detail, for example, the close similarities between Thecla's story and *Chaereas and Callirhoe* 50–58.

sophistication and significance for cultural studies.[21] In particular, post-colonial approaches suggest that these five novels were the textual productions of an elite Greek-speaking literary culture learning to live under the reality of a vast and cosmopolitan Roman Empire.[22] Briefly put, Greek-speaking regional elites were coming to terms with their loss of self-governance in the wake of Roman conquest and the gradual establishment of Roman administration and bureaucracy. The novels reflect this sense of dislocation. The state is symbolised by the family unit (a common ancient parallel), and the wandering central couple represents the urban elites trying to find a place for themselves in a new cultural order.

If the adventures of the couple reflect the effort of a displaced elite to adapt to the hybrid identity situation of life under Rome, then they are also a way of thinking about the question of Roman hegemony.[23] On this reading, the novels' ubiquitous "happy ending" is more than just narrative convention. It represents a reaffirmation of the *status quo* whose validity has been called into question by the dislocation of the couple from their native environment.[24] Marriage is the symbol of social continuity; it represents the couple's re-integration into the hometown they had lost. Marriage, the vehicle for producing children, is the guarantee of the civic order's continuation.

Christian romances like the *Acts of Paul and Thecla* echo the novels not only in form, but in context too. Like the elite writers responsible for the novels, the Christian writers were part of a subordinate polity learning to live under Roman rule. But where the Greek novels affirm the value of the family and the state it represents, many Christian texts reject it and affirm instead the individual's withdrawal from fulfilling expectations imposed by

---

21 There are no longer any significant voices suggesting that the ancient novels cannot be considered relatively sophisticated literary products whose authors had a good grasp of many of the rhetorical principles of the so-called second sophistic movement. In fact, the novels have been shown to be very self-aware, see, for example, the instances of "meta"-literary concerns, detailed in S. Goldhill, *Foucault's Virginity. Ancient Erotic Fiction and the History of Sexuality*, Cambridge 1995.

22 See, e.g., D. Konstan, *Sexual Symmetry. Love in the Ancient Novel and Related Genres*, Princeton 1994; R. Pervo, *Profit with Delight. The Literary Genre of the Acts of the Apostles*, Philadelphia 1987, 97.

23 See, e.g., T. Whitmarsh, *"Greece is the World." Exile and Identity in the Second Sophistic*, in: S. Goldhill (ed.), *Being Greek under Rome. Cultural Identity, the Second Sophistic and the Development of Empire*, Cambridge 2001, 269–305 (273); see also T. Whitmarsh, *Greek Literature and the Roman Empire. The Politics of Imitation*, Oxford 2001, 2.

24 K. Cooper, *The Virgin and the Bride. Idealized Womanhood in Late Antiquity*, Cambridge 1996, 21–44.

the wider community.[25] Hence, the characters in much Christian literature produced in this period do not end up happily married; they die as martyrs instead. At the end of the *Acts of Paul and Thecla*, the heroine attempts the reunion with her mother, which would be expected in the five ancient novels, but instead of marrying she retreats to a cave in a city hundreds of miles from home. She enjoys a long life of asceticism which culminates, in one version of the text, in martyrdom.[26]

Reading the *Acts of Paul and Thecla* as dislocation literature allows us to see its treatment of conversion against a broader landscape of provincial anxieties about social reproduction. It also allows a useful comparison with the modern British novel, *Maps for Lost Lovers*, born of similar circumstances. *Maps for Lost Lovers* treats the similar dislocation faced by a Pakistani immigrant family living in an unidentified British town, referred to by characters simply as "Dasht-e-Tanhaii" (The Wilderness of Loneliness).[27] The novel traces a year in the life of a married couple, the husband Shamas and his wife Kaukab, and their family's attempts to come to terms with the disappearance of Shamas' brother Jugnuand and his lover Chanda, a suspected honour killing. These two were living together out of wedlock because the young woman was waiting for a long-deferred divorce from her husband in Pakistan. Their disappearance occurs before the novel begins, and we learn that her brothers have been arrested for the crime. Shamas and Kaukab have three children, two boys, Charag and Ujala, and a daughter, Mah-Jabin. All three children are grown up, have left home, and are estranged to varying degrees from their parents. As the novel progresses, the strains in Kaukab and Shamas' own marriage are explored, as are those in her daughter's and those of many other minor characters.

The mother Kaukab is the magnetic pole around whom the family revolves. The novel's questions about the place of this Pakistani community in modern Britain are distilled down to this one woman's abortive attempts to remain true to Pakistani and Islamic customs while raising her family in Britain, an environment she neither understands nor likes. Her relationships with her children serve as reminders, to us and to her, of her repeated failures

---

25 See, e.g., Burrus, 1987, 58–60.

26 See, e.g., Cooper, 1996; also ead., *The Voice of the Victim. Gender, Representation and Early Christian Martyrdom*, in: Bulletin of the John Rylands Library 80 (1998), 147–157; J. Perkins, *The Suffering Self. Pain and Narrative Representation in the Early Christian Era*, London 1995, and ead., *Roman Imperial Identities in the early Christian Era*, London 2009.

27 As Aslam himself says, "I don't give the location or name of the town because I wanted the reader to be as confused about his surroundings as my characters – immigrants to this alien place – were." See http://www.threemonkeysonline.com/als/_nadeem_aslam_interview.html, last accessed 23/05/2014.

to convince them to act "correctly" and in line with the values of their family and community. When Kaukab's children return home, Aslam dedicates significant time to discussing their upbringing in the years before the novel is set. Mah-Jabin is the child we encounter most and around whom the ever-present question of social reproduction crystallises. Mah-Jabin left home for an arranged marriage in Pakistan when she was sixteen, a decade before the events of the novel. The marriage lasted only two years, and she is now divorced. In consequence, her confidence in her upbringing and faith has been heavily shaken and she is living an independent life, no longer living up to the religious or social expectations her mother has of her. Mah-Jabin's "apostasy" serves the same narrative function as Thecla's conversion. The change in religious outlook has a profound impact on her familial relationships, and the mother-daughter relationship in particular. Chapter 6 (entitled *The Madonnas*) documents Mah-Jabin's visit home and her interactions with her mother.

Mah-Jabin, twenty-seven and living and working in London, is divorced from the first cousin in Pakistan she had married aged sixteen, for which marriage she blames her mother Kaukab. For her part, Kaukab does not recognise the legitimacy of that divorce, and that wound underpins all their interactions.[28] In *The Madonnas*, the conversation of mother and daughter continually circles this central issue and repeatedly sparks violent altercation between the two: Kaukab slaps her daughter, bangs her head repeatedly against a wall and swings a knife at her (perhaps accidentally). Structurally, too, the narration alternates between this visit home of Mah-Jabin, flashbacks describing the history between mother and daughter and the circumstances in which Mah-Jabin was originally married and left home, and comments upon the marriages of other girls in the neighbourhood.[29] Mah-Jabin's anger at Kaukab arises because her mother encouraged her in an arranged marriage even though her own arranged marriage had made her unhappy. Kaukab on the other hand is upset at her failure to successfully marry her daughter, and her inability to make her daughter see the religious and cultural significance of that marriage.[30] Marriage, and the cultural continuity it represents, is again at the core the narrative and its tensions here.

As we saw in the *Acts of Paul and Thecla*, what is really at stake in these mother-daughter conflicts is social reproduction, represented by the institution of marriage. Thecla and Mah-Jabin are not just rejecting proposed husbands.

---

28 Aslam, *Maps*, 91.
29 E.g., Aslam, *Maps*, 107f., on a visiting neighbour's concerns about a disobedient daughter who will not obey her husband. Bal, 1997, 82, comments that "Playing with sequential ordering is not just a literary convention; it is also a means of drawing attention to certain things, to emphasise [...]."
30 Aslam, *Maps*, 115.

They are repudiating the process of social reproduction their mothers are trying to engineer, and it is that radical rejection which lies behind their mothers'
extreme reactions. In this literature of dislocation the marriage of the child is
the medium by which the younger generation confirms the values of the older
and is tied back into the social fabric. The failure or refusal of marriage, on the
other hand, is representative of the younger generation's rejection of the value
system of the older, and thus of the older generation's failure to engineer social
reproduction. It is this, and not simply the individual marriage rejected, that
prompts the extreme reaction of the two mothers.

It is therefore the existential fragility of the community producing these
narratives, represented in the texts by the family unit, which renders the
question of generational dispute so very important. These narrative inci-
dents where younger generations leave the sphere of family influence represent communities facing, through the protective lens of narrative, the likeli-
hood of their own continued existence in the future. The question of social
reproduction, of the older generation's desire to reproduce itself and so ensure the persistence of its values and ideals, is pronounced precisely because
it emerges in a context where that persistence is threatened.

The question of the marriage of the younger generation is symbolic of
this. The successful marriage at the end of the ancient Greek novels represents a commitment to and strengthening of the *status quo*.[31] The refusal to
accept an arranged marriage, by contrast, is a narratively powerful illustration of the fact that the heroine has crossed a cultural line. Thecla and Mah-
Jabin's arranged marriages acquire new significance. We cannot understand
the twin figures of Kaukab and Theocleia, or their attitudes towards their
daughters, without appreciating the cultural significance of the literary motif
of marriage as a marker of successful social reproduction where the younger
generation accepts the religious and social identity offered by the older, and
thus the significance of its failure.

Sympathy with the devil: Narrative focalisation and the cognitive wound of dissonant empathy

In both *The Acts of Paul and Thecla* and *Maps for Lost Lovers*, the failure
of the two daughters' marriages is the reason for mother-daughter conflict
and lies behind the violent outbursts of both mothers. Once we appreciate
what is really at stake in these literary scenarios, a further fascinating aspect
of the texts becomes apparent. Both narratives treat their maternal figures,
who might easily have served simply as villainous foils, with a surprising
amount of sympathy. In *Maps for Lost Lovers*, the text pays attention to the

---

31 Cooper, 1996, 31.

motivations, emotions, and rationalisations of Kaukab as well as Mah-Jabin. Moreover, towards the end of the chapter in question, Mah-Jabin's marriage is revealed as having been arranged at her own request.[32] Kaukab is no simplistic villain, but a mother tormented by her circumstances and incomprehending in the face of what she perceives to be her child's wilful disobedience and failure to empathise. The complexity of this character and the sympathy she can evoke, prompts us to look again at the sketch of Theocleia in *The Acts of Paul and Thecla*. Here as well, close inspection reveals that the author seems to cultivate sympathy towards the mother as well as the daughter.

One technique by which an author provokes sympathy for a character is by revealing that character's internal emotions and motivations. Narratologists – initially, the French scholar Gérard Genette, but followed by Mieke Bal and others – have made a distinction in what is observed in a text (*focalisation*) between the *perceptible* and the *non-perceptible*. The former constitutes actions and speech visible or audible to all in the sequence of events in a narrative; the latter to dreams, thoughts and feelings that are only visible if explicitly described. We might well expect in this Christian text, where Thecla is the main protagonist and heroine, to be told only of her internal hopes.[33] But in fact *non-perceptible* objects are focalised for both. We actually learn comparatively little about Thecla's internal dynamics, and she speaks very little. By contrast, we see more of her mother Theocleia's worry and concern when she summons Thamyris and explains her concern to him.[34] After Thamyris has tried to talk to his fiancé to no avail, Theocleia appeals to her daughter herself.[35] Their joint failure produces grief throughout the whole household. The author dedicates more narrative time to the traumatic effects of the family disruption on Theocleia than its effects on Thecla.

Sympathy for the mothers is further cultivated by the reader's appreciation of the peculiar vulnerabilities of their position. The focus on female characters in *The Acts of Paul and Thecla* (later in the text, in Antioch, Thecla is taken in by a patroness, Tryphaena, and is supported vocally at moments of crisis by a seemingly ever-present crowd of female supporters) is characteristic of other early Christian literature, but is particularly prominent here.[36] Aslam also favours female protagonists, saying for example that:

---

32 Aslam, *Maps*, 116.
33 For example, her joy at hearing Paul preach in *The Acts of Paul and Thecla* 7.
34 See, e.g., J.A. Landa / S.O. Jaén (eds.), *Narratology. An Introduction*, London 1996, particularly 116–125; and G. Genette, *Narrative Discourse. An Essay on Method*, Ithaca 1980.
35 *The Acts of Paul and Thecla* 10.
36 The prevalence of women in *The Acts of Paul and Thecla* is treated in detail by Davis, 2001, 8–18; the prominence of women in the *Apocryphal acts* is discussed

Sufi poets of Islam have always used women as the rebels within their poetry –
women strive and rebel and try to face opposition. Always, always it was the
vulnerability of women that was used to portray the intolerance and oppression of the times. The women – more than the men – attempted to remake the
world, and failed. But in their attempt they became part of the universal story
of hope.[37]

However, this prominence of women in both narratives also exposes the lack
of male support they receive, and our sympathies for Kaukab and Theocleia
must surely increase when we realise how exposed both are within their
societies. In both narratives, the father figure is underplayed or absent. In
Maps for Lost Lovers, Mah-Jabin's return home revolves entirely around
her interactions with her mother. Shamas – Kaukab's husband and Mah-
Jabin's father – plays no direct part in this chapter. On those occasions when
he is referred to, we glimpse the lack of unity in this family:

Oh, your father will be angry, oh, your father will be upset: Mah-Jabin had
grown up hearing these sentences, Kaukab trying to obtain legitimacy for her
own decisions by invoking his name. She wanted him to be angry, she needed
him to be angry. She had cast him in the role of the head of the household and
he had to act accordingly: there were times when he came in to inform the
young teenagers that something they had asked from their mother earlier – the
permission for an after-hours school disco, for example – was an impossibility,
and it was obvious from the look on his face that he personally had no problem
with what the children wanted.[38]

In *Maps for Lost Lovers*, mother and father do not speak with a unified
voice and fundamentally disagree on the upbringing of their children. Further, elsewhere in the novel, Shamas engages in a prolonged extra-marital
affair, and even a past incident of domestic abuse is revealed.[39] In the *Acts of
Paul and Thecla*, too, male family members are conspicuous in their absence.

---

more generally in S. Davies, *The Revolt of the Widows. The Social World of the
Apocryphal Acts*, Carbondale 1980, and Burrus, 1987. See also Bremmer in this
volume.

37 http://www.threemonkeysonline.com/als_page2/_nadeem_aslam_interview.
html; last accessed 23/05/2014.

38 Aslam, *Maps*, 111.

39 Aslam, *Maps*, 116. This disconnect between the interests of mother and father is expressed explicitly by the couple's youngest son Ujala who says to his
parents towards the end of the novel (324): "There couldn't have been a more
dangerous union than you two: *you* were too busy longing for the world and the
time your grandparents came from, they and their sayings and principles; and *he*
was too busy day-dreaming about the world and the time his grandchildren were
to inherit. What about your responsibilities to the people who were around you
here in the present?"

When she is concerned about her daughter, Theiocleia goes to her daughter's fiancé Thamyris for assistance. There is no mention of any husband, brothers, or uncles. Theocleia is head of her own household.[40] A mother and daughter, both unmarried, would have been vulnerable in the ancient patriarchal, patronage-based society where security relied upon the visibility of support from a prominent man. The visibility of the Roman household meant that to be deficient there was to be deficient publically too.[41] To the ancient reader, the weakness of Theocleia's household, the vulnerability of her position and therefore the reasons for her desire that her virgin daughter marry soon and marry well, would have been strikingly apparent.[42]

This concern is made apparent at the very end of the text. Though Thecla was silent in their early interactions, when she returns home after her travels and attempts a reconciliation, she makes the following appeal to her mother: "If you desire money, the Lord will give it to you through me. Or if you desire your child – look, I am here in front of you."[43] Thecla – more understanding now after her adventures than in her earlier stubborn silence – implies that her mother had been motivated by either maternal loss or by finance. The latter surely refers to the financial security available if Thecla had married Thamyris, explicitly said to be the foremost citizen of the city and extremely rich.[44] The text draws attention to the fact that Theocleia's social security relied upon her daughter's society marriage. Her public denunciation of her daughter can even perhaps be read along these lines as a last ditch attempt to save herself in a rapidly deteriorating situation where she risked being entirely socially isolated.[45]

The *Acts of Paul and Thecla* is therefore not simply a conversion narrative that assumes the simple necessity of the Christian cutting ties with their callous pagan parents. It is a narrative that explores Christian conversion

---

40 See, e.g., K. Cooper, *Band of Angels. The Forgotten World of Early Christian Women*, London 2013, ch. 8.

41 R.P. Saller, *Patriarchy, Property and Death in the Roman Family*, Cambridge 1994, 72.

42 Noted also by MacDonald, 1983, 50f.

43 *The Acts of Paul and Thecla* 43.

44 *The Acts of Paul and Thecla* 7. J.N. Bremmer, *Magic, Martyrdom and Women's Liberation in the Acts of Paul and Thecla*, in: J.N. Bremmer (ed.), *The Apocryphal Acts of Paul and Thecla*, Kampen 1996, 36–59 (41f.), discusses Thamyris' membership of "the highest circle of the town," though he includes Thecla in that circle, too.

45 Compare, for example, K. Cooper on the last gasp public attempts of Perpetua's father to get his daughter to sacrifice to the emperor, in: K. Cooper, *A Father, a Daughter, and a Procurator. Authority and Resistance in the Prison Memoir of Perpetua of Carthage*, in: Gender and History 23/3 (2011), 685–702.

in particularly difficult social circumstances. Further, and extraordinarily, it pays attention to the subjectivities of those left behind and acknowledges the confusion, grief, and fear a conversion to Christianity might engender.

Conclusion

The comparison of the recent novel *Maps for Lost Lovers* is a useful lens through which to view *The Acts of Paul and Thecla*. The rich, multi-layered portrait of the tormented mother Kaukab enables us to tease out similar complexities for Theocleia. In particular, it is the sympathy evoked for these two characters, who could so easily have been dismissed as villains, which emerges most strongly. This sympathy is grounded in the reader's appreciation of the fragility of their positions, two women struggling alone to orchestrate social reproduction and ensure the continuity of their families and ways of life, in alienating circumstances which threaten to overwhelm both them and their communities.

In concluding, we wish to turn again to the concept of dislocation literature. These texts are playing with identity models that readers could use to cope with the difficulties of their environments. Christian literature of martyrdom and asceticism deliberately foils the marriage ideal representative of social reintegration in the ancient Greek novel by constructing identity models which borrow the literary form, but reject its proposed social integration. Instead, it advocates that the Christians focus on personal redemption and the welfare of the Christian community rather than the household and the Roman state it represents. But, in *The Acts of Paul and Thecla* we have found a genuine understanding of the social complexities involved in any proposed conversion, and a surprising sympathy for the parental figure left behind when the child turns to Christianity. This sympathy demands explanation. We offer here a tentative hypothesis only. The anonymous author of *The Acts of Paul and Thecla* presents an identity model in this text that encourages its reader to reject the requirement of social reproduction when they conflict with the requirements of the faith community. But the text does not seem to advocate the simultaneous rejection of the family.[46] It is telling that Thecla never rejects Theocleia, and in fact even returns home to try to convert her. Almost the final words of the text are her plea that the opportunity of getting her daughter back is open to her.[47] Indeed, in one version of the text we cannot be certain that her mother does not in fact convert.[48]

---

46 Bremmer, 1996, 44, makes a similar observation.
47 *The Acts of Paul and Thecla* 43.
48 The manuscript record is unclear on the result of her appeal. *The Acts of Paul and Thecla* is extant in the original Greek and several ancient translations,

Thecla offers her mother an alternative social reality, one that will provide her both with divine support and the company of her daughter. Thecla does not reject her family in favour of the Christian polity. She rejects one model of society and chooses another, into which she then tries to incorporate her family. The distinction is crucial.

including a Coptic papyrus in which the mother's response is unresolved. See further W. Schneemelcher *et al.* (eds.), *New Testament Apocrypha,* vol. 2 (*Writings Relating to the Apostles, Apocalypses and Related Subjects*), translation by R. McL. Wilson, Louisville 1992, 213–270; and K. Haines-Eitzen, *Engendering Palimpsests. Gender, Asceticism, and the Transmission of the Acts of Paul and Thecla,* in: W. Klingshirn / L. Safran (eds.), *The Early Christian Book,* Washington 2005, 177–193 (186).

Radcliffe G. Edmonds III

There and Back Again: Temporary Immortality in the Mithras Liturgy

Abstract: This article argues that many rituals previously categorised as rites of initiation because they fit the tripartite structure in Gennep's rites of passage should be analysed in terms of another model, that of rites of purification or sanctification. In such rituals, the religious focus is upon the shifts in relationship with the god, rather than upon the change of status on earth or any change of lifestyle afterwards.

> This immortalisation takes place three times a year.
> γίγνεται δὲ ὁ ἀπαθανατισμὸς οὗτος τρὶς τοῦ ἐνιαυτοῦ.[1]

To the modern sensibility, to become immortal three times a year seems a paradox.[2] Immortality should be a permanent thing if anything is, so becoming immortal should be a once for all time transformation, a departure from the condition of mortality and passage into the permanent state of immortality. The temporary immortality promised by the ritual instructions for the so-called "Mithras Liturgy" challenges our assumptions about the nature of

---

1 PGM 4.748–49. I make use of the text of the PGM in K. Preisendanz / A. Henrichs (eds.), *Papyri Graecae magicae. Die Griechischen Zauberpapyri*, 2 vols., Stuttgart ²1973–1974, and the translation by Meyer in H.D. Betz et al., *The Greek Magical Papyri in Translation. Including the Demotic Spells*, Chicago 1997, with some modifications, especially from Betz, *The "Mithras Liturgy". Text, Translation, and Commentary*, Tübingen 2003, where noted. I would like to thank Birgitte Bøgh and the other participants of the Conversion and Initiation conference for providing the opportunity to explore the issues in this paper and for their help and critiques, both during the conference and after. All errors remaining are the products of my own ignorance, carelessness, or obstinacy.

2 As S.I. Johnston has noted, immortalisation "has a permanent ring to our ears, trained as we are to think in terms of the dichotomy 'immortal vs. mortal', and yet the Mithras Liturgy specifically mentions 'immortalisation' procedures that last only a day and that can be undertaken up to three times a year (line 747). Clearly, 'becoming immortal' (ἀπαθανατισμός) did not mean that the Liturgist became a god, as Heracles had for example, but rather that for the duration of the ritual he was of a status equal to the gods, or perhaps simply that he was protected from death" (*Rising to the Occasion. Theurgic Ascent in its Cultural Milieu*, in: P. Schäfer / H.G. Kippenberg (eds.), *Envisioning Magic. A Princeton Symposium and Seminar*. Leiden 1997, 165–194 (179)).This paper is an attempt to take Johnston's observation further and contextualise it within the practices of purification that were a necessary part of the interactions of mortal and divine.

immortality in the religions of the ancient Mediterranean world, calling into question as well the modern models of initiation and conversion that have been used to understand the nature of rituals that bring the ritualist into a state of closer contact with the divine. In this paper, I examine the ritual ascent in the spell from the Great Paris Magical Papyrus (PGM 4.475–834), commonly known as the "Mithras Liturgy", as a way to problematise these models and to argue that many rituals previously categorised as rites of initiation should be analysed in terms of another model, that of rites of purification, sanctification, or consecration.

The "Mithras Liturgy" was so named by Albrecht Dieterich, who saw in the text the traces of a genuine ritual of initiation into the cult of Mithras. The text gives detailed instructions for a rite of immortalisation (ἀπαθανατισμός) through a vividly described journey through the heavens to a meeting with the supreme god Helios Mithras. The spell occupies lines 475 to 834 of a 36 page papyrus codex now in the Paris Bibliothèque Nationale, labelled number 4 in Preisendanz's collection of the Greek Magical Papyri, a group of texts dating mostly from the third and fourth centuries CE, probably from the region of Thebes in Egypt. For Dieterich, "a genuine Mithras liturgy of an ascension of the soul and its immortalisation, an ἀπαθανατισμός, has been inserted into a magical ritual for the exploration of the future."[3]

While most scholars now agree with Nock that the "Mithras Liturgy" is neither a liturgy nor, properly speaking, "Mithraic", recent scholars have nevertheless followed in Dieterich's footsteps seeking the original ritual which has been inserted into the magic spell.[4] Reinhold Merkelbach has argued that the text preserves the remnants of an initiatory ceremony for the consecration of priests of the Egyptian Pshai-Aion, adapted for magical use.[5] The most recent editor, Hans Dieter Betz, rejects Merkelbach's hypothesis, but nevertheless presumes that the magic spell has been adapted from a

---

3   A. Dieterich, *Eine Mithrasliturgie,* Leipzig 1903, 85: "In die zur Erforschung der Zukunft ausgestaltete Zauberhandlung eine echte Mithrasliturgie der Himmelfahrt der Seele und ihrer Unsterblichmachung, ein ἀπαθανατισμός, eingelegt ist" (trans. of Betz, 2003, 136).

4   A.D. Nock, *Greek Magical Papyri,* in A.D. Nock / Z. Stewart (eds.), *Essays on Religion and the Ancient World,* Cambridge 1972, 176–194 (192). Originally published in JEA 15 (1929), 219–235.

5   R. Merkelbach / M. Totti, *Abrasax. Ausgewählte Papyri religiösen und magischen,* vol. 3 (*Zwei griechisch-ägyptische Weihezeremonien*), Opladen 1992, 40: "Es wird sich also auch bei der Pariser Unsterblichkeits-Liturgie ursprünglich um die Weihezeremonie für einen Priester hohen Ranges oder sogar einen König handeln, was in Ägypten beinahe dasselbe war. Das Ritual wird dann später so angepaßt worden sein, daß es auch bei Initiationen minderen Ranges Verwendung finden konnte."

ritual that originally provided initiation.[6] For many modern scholars, as for Dieterich, the fact that the ritual provides immortalisation indicates that it could not originally be intended for divination, but rather for the permanent transformation of the status of the ritualist, whether into the formal status of a priest or as an initiate of some kind of mystery cult.[7] In the analysis, the Christian ritual of baptism often provides the model for such a transformation, a permanent rebirth into immortal life as a member of a privileged group. From such a perspective, the question to be asked is what was the *original* religious context of the rite? And what kind of mystery cult or temple *originally* used this ritual to admit members transformed by this process of deification?

I argue that this approach fundamentally misrepresents the nature of the ritual in the "Mithras Liturgy". This text is better understood, not as an initiation ritual that brings the performer to a new status, but rather as a ritual that temporarily purifies him for a brief meeting with a god. Rather than looking to models of initiation into groups or conversion to a new mode of religious life, scholars should look instead to the pattern of rituals

---

6 Betz seems to suggest that the text was devised by an Egyptian priest for the worship of Mithras in Egypt: "Conceivably, Egyptian learned priests such as the author of the Mithras Liturgy became devoted to Mithras, even while they served as priests in the Egyptian temples. The author's intense devotion to Mithras should not be denied its own integrity. [...] Given the syncretistic aura of Hellenistic Egypt, there was plenty of room in the Egyptian temples for Egyptian as well as Greek deities, so why not Mithras? If the priests were charged with developing the liturgies appropriate for worshipping so many other deities, why not for Mithras?" (Betz, 2003, 23). He raises the possibility that it might not have been a strictly Mithraic cult, but he assumes that the ritual comes from the context of an initiation into a mystery cult: "Since he was initiated in a mystery cult, it could indeed have been an Egyptian adaptation of Mithraism, but it could have been just as well some other mystery cult which had appropriated Mithraic elements" (Betz, 2003, 137f.).

7 E.g., M. Smith: "The reviser turned it into a ritual for divination, which had to be repeated as new questions arose, but kept the wording of the earlier text which shows that its original purpose was once-for-all 'immortalisation', i.e., deification" (*Transformation by Burial (1Cor 15:35–49; Rom 6:3–5 and 8:9–11)*, in: S.J.D. Cohen (ed.), *Studies in the Cult of Yahweh*, vol. 1, Leiden 1996, 110–129 (127)). Cf. N. Janowitz: "As a ritual for immortalisation, the *Liturgy* was probably originally meant to effect a one-time transformation" (*Magic in the Roman World. Pagans, Jews, and Christians*, London 2001, 81). Merkelbach / Totti, 1992, 233: "Man wird doch eher vermuten, daß die aufwendige Zeremonie ursprünglich nur zu wenigen, ganz besonderen Anlässen benützt worden ist und erst sekundär zu verschiedenen Zwecken herangezogen wurde." Even Johnston, 1997, 180, suggests that "initiation might magically help the magician resist" the lure of the evil demons encountered in the ascent.

designed to admit worshippers into a temple or other sacred space. Such rituals of purification or sanctification are common in the religions of the Graeco-Roman world, and they range in complexity from simple lustrations to elaborate practices of abstinence and purification. The greater the sanctity and the more significant the contact between mortal worshipper and the divine, the more complex the ritual must be, but scholars have often failed to see some of these most elaborate rituals of sanctification as part of the same spectrum of purification rituals, classifying them instead with initiation rituals. Petersen, however, draws some useful distinctions between initiations and purifications, pointing out that, while both are concerned with changing the state or essence of persons, the change wrought by an initiation is permanent, irreversible without other special ceremonies.[8] By contrast, the change in state of a rite of purification is temporary, a special improvement along the spectrum of profane to pure that quickly wears off as the individual returns to contact with the ordinary world.

The "Mithras Liturgy", then, must be understood as a form of extreme purification rather than the relic of an initiation. Rather than using the text to look back for some imagined original rite of initiation worthy of this process of immortalisation, we should analyse it for a better understanding of the dynamics of mortal and divine interactions in the religions of the ancient Graeco-Roman world. The ritualist goes through a process of temporary immortalisation in order to meet face to face with his god because he needs to be of the status of the immortals to meet with the immortals in their immortal world. The transformation in the "Mithras Liturgy" is not an initiation, a permanent movement from one status to another, but rather a journey there and back again – and again and again, if the magician so chooses.

The Mithras Liturgy à la van Gennep

The model most often employed by recent scholars for understanding rituals of initiation is van Gennep's tripartite *rite de passage*, which handily divides the ritual into three phases of separation, liminality, and reaggregation. The initiand leaves his former state, passes through a liminal phase that involves contact with the divine, and returns to the world but with a new status. The new status may be that of an adult rather than a child, a married person

---

8 A.K. Petersen, *Rituals of Purification, Rituals of Initiation. Phenomenological, Taxonomical and Culturally Evolutionary Reflections*, in: D. Hellholm / T. Vegge / Ø. Norderval / C. Hellholm (eds.), *Ablution, Initiation, and Baptism. Waschungen, Initiation und Taufe*, vol. 1, Berlin 2011, 3–40 (30): "The qualitative changes acquired by the ritual participant through the completion of the ritual are of an irreversible nature, i.e., they cannot be lost unless, and very seldom, a new narratively staged ritual process is initiated."

instead of unmarried, a shaman or priest instead of a layman, an initiate instead of one of the profane mob, but the rite effects the transformation. The "Mithras Liturgy" is easily analysed as a rite of passage according to the schema of van Gennep, with a phase of separation from the mortal world, a liminal phase at the very threshold of the divine world, and a return to the mortal world. This correspondence with the famous tripartite schema has led scholars to see the "Mithras Liturgy" as a rite of initiation, transposed perhaps in the decadent world of the syncretistic magician to a vulgar divinatory ritual, but whose *original* nature is revealed by this tripartite structure to be the initiation into some mystery cult. It is worth considering the "Mithras Liturgy" à la van Gennep.

The spell illustrates, with vivid and graphic images, the phases of a van Gennep rite of passage. The separation phase involves the magician leaving the familiar world of mortals and going to the fantastic world of the divine. The magician must first replace all of the mortal elements of his (or her) body, leaving behind the perishable nature of mortals in the corruptible mortal realm. The magician invokes the *archai*, the primal elements or originary nature, of his being, going through air (*pneuma*), fire, water, and earth:

> First origin of my origin, AEÊIOYÔ, first beginning of my beginning, PPP SSS PHR[] spirit of spirit, the first of the spirit in me, MMM, fire given by god to my mixture of the mixtures in me, the first of the fire in me, EY EIA EE, water of water, the first of the water in me, OOO AAA EEE, earthy substance, the first of the earthy substance in me, YE YOE, my complete body.[9]

Each of these mortal elements must be replaced with immortal elements – immortal water, immortal fire, immortal spirit – so that the magician may "envision the immortal [...], envision with immortal eyes – I, born mortal from mortal womb, but transformed by tremendous power and an incorruptible right hand!"[10]

Once the process of separating himself from his mortal elements and replacing them with immortal ones has taken place, the magician literally separates himself from the world of mortals, rising up through the heavens by breathing in the rays of the divine sun:

---

9 PGM 4.486–495: [Γ]ένεσις πρώτη τῆς ἐμῆς γενέσεως· αεηιουω, ἀρχὴ τῆς ἐμῆς ἀρχῆ<ς> πρώτη πππ σσσ φρ[·], πνεῦμα πνεύματος, τοῦ ἐν ἐμοὶ πνεύματος πρῶτον μμμ, πῦρ, τὸ εἰς ἐμὴν κρᾶσιν τῶν (490) ἐν ἐμοὶ κράσεων θεοδώρητον, τοῦ ἐν ἐμοὶ πυρὸς πρῶτον ηυ ηια εη, ὕδωρ ὕδατος, τοῦ ἐν ἐμοὶ ὕδατος πρῶτον ωωω ααα εεε, οὐσία γεώδης τῆς ἐν ἐμοὶ οὐσίας γεώδους πρώτη υη υωη, σῶμα τέλειον ἐμοῦ.

10 PGM 4.504–505; 517–520: Ἐποπτεύσω τὴν ἀθάνατον ἀρχὴν τῷ ἀθανάτῳ πνεύματι [...] τοῖς ἀθανάτοις ὄμμασι, θνητὸς γεννηθεὶς ἐκ θνητῆς ὑστέρας, βεβελτιωμένος ὑπὸ κράτους μεγαλοδυνάμου καὶ δεξιᾶς χειρὸς ἀφθάρτου.

Draw in breath from the rays, drawing up three times as much as you can, and you will see yourself being lifted up and ascending to the height, so that you seem to be in mid-air. You will hear nothing either of man or of any other living thing, nor in that hour will you see anything of mortal affairs on earth, but rather you will see all immortal things.[11]

Through these preliminary rites, the magician has removed himself from the realm of mortal affairs and has set off on his journey to the divine.

This journey to the center of the universe takes place in the realm betwixt and between the realm of mortals and the fully divine world, and this journey is again easily understood in terms of the liminal phase of van Gennep's schema. While the magician does not pass through seven planetary spheres, he does pass through a celestial realm of the stars and planets, the visible gods, at the center of which lie the doors of the sun.[12] The magician then recites an incantation to open the fiery doors of the sun, at which point he stands upon the very limen, the threshold of the world of the supreme gods:

You will see the doors open and the world of the gods which is within the doors, so that from the pleasure and joy of the sight your spirit runs ahead and ascends. So stand still and at once draw breath from the divine into yourself, while you look intently.[13]

---

11 PGM 4.537–544: Ἕλκε ἀπὸ τῶν ἀκτίνων πνεῦμα γ' ἀνασπῶν, ὃ δύνα[σ]αι, καὶ ὄψῃ σεαυτὸν ἀνακουφιζόμενον [κ]αὶ ὑπερβαίνοντα εἰς ὕψος, ὥστε σε δοκεῖ[ν μ]έσον (540) τοῦ ἀέρος εἶναι· οὐδενὸς δὲ ἀκούσει [ο]ὔτε ἀνθρώπου οὔτε ζῴου ἄλλ<ου>, οὐδὲ ὄψῃ οὐδὲν τῶν ἐπὶ γῆς θνητῶν ἐν ἐκείνῃ τῇ ὥρᾳ, πάντα δὲ ὄψῃ ἀθάνατα.

12 PGM 4.545–585. Dieterich saw a Mithraic passage through the seven spheres, an argument immediately rejected by Cumont and others because of the lack of correspondence with Mithraic monuments. Betz, 2003, 134–141, still divides the passage into seven scenarios, which he thinks do have a resonance with Mithraic imagery, but these seven scenarios do not correspond to planetary spheres. As I have argued elsewhere, however, the cosmology of the Mithras Liturgy is the tripartite division between sublunar material world, ouranian world of the stars and planets, and a hyperouranian realm of the gods; see R. Edmonds, *At the Seizure of the Moon. The Absence of the Moon in the Mithras Liturgy*, in: S.B. Noegel / J.T. Walker / B.M. Wheeler (eds.), *Prayer, Magic and the Stars in the Ancient and Late Antique World*, Pennsylvania 2003, 223–239; and id., *The Faces of the Moon. Cosmology, Genesis, and the Mithras Liturgy*, in: R. Boustan / A.Y. Reed (eds.), *Heavenly Realms and Earthly Realities in Late Antique Religions*, Cambridge 2004, 275–295.

13 PGM 4.624–629: Καὶ ὄψῃ ἀνεῳγυίας τὰς θύρας καὶ τὸν κόσμον τῶν θεῶν, ὅς ἐστιν (625) ἐντὸς τῶν θυρῶν, ὥστε ἀπὸ τῆς τοῦ θεάματος ἡδονῆς καὶ τῆς χαρᾶς τὸ πνεῦμά σου συντρέχειν καὶ ἀναβαίνειν· στὰς οὖν εὐθέως ἕλκε ἀπὸ τοῦ θείου ἀτενίζων εἰς σεαυτὸν τὸ πνεῦμα.

The magician does not enter fully into the world of the gods, but stands at the door to ask the Sun himself for an audience with the supreme ruler of the universe. This liminal experience continues as the advent of the greatest of gods is preceded by a chorus of seven asp-faced maidens and seven bull-faced youths, whom the magician must greet appropriately. Finally comes the epiphany of the supreme god:

> You will see lightning-bolts going down, and lights flashing, and the earth shaking, and a god descending, a god immensely great, having a bright appearance youthful, golden-haired, with a white tunic and a golden crown and trousers, and holding in his right hand a golden shoulder of a young bull: this is the Bear which moves and turns heaven around, moving upward and downward in accordance with the hour. Then you will see lightning-bolts leaping from his eyes and stars from his body.[14]

The Persian trousers and the bull's shoulder mark this deity as Mithras, the higher sun for whom the visible sun is merely the door warden. The magician stands face to face with this supreme god and asks the god directly for favour, and the god responds directly. This direct contact of human and god is the ultimate liminal moment, the point at which the two worlds meet.

The final phase in van Gennep's schema is reaggregation; the ritual must end with the magician's return to the ordinary world. The god departs (728), and the magician stands speechless in awe, but the impact of this meeting is so great that the magician will remember, in future times after the ritual has ended, every detail of the epiphany.[15] Apart from this reference to the future, however, the "Mithras Liturgy" has nothing that corresponds to van

---

14 PGM 4.694–705: Ὄψῃ κατερχομένας ἀστραπὰς καὶ φῶτα (695) μαρμαίροντα καὶ σειομένην τὴν γῆν καὶ κατερχόμενον θεὸν ὑπερμεγέθη, φωτινὴν ἔχοντα τὴν ὄψιν, νεώτερον, χρυσοκόμαν, ἐν χιτῶνι λευκῷ καὶ χρυσῷ στεφάνῳ καὶ ἀναξυρίσι, κατέχοντα τῇ δεξιᾷ χειρὶ μόσχου (700) ὦμον χρύσεον, ὅς ἐστιν Ἄρκτος ἡ κινοῦσα καὶ ἀντιστρέφουσα τὸν οὐρανόν, κατὰ ὥραν ἀναπολεύουσα καὶ καταπολεύουσα· ἔπειτα ὄψῃ αὐτοῦ ἐκ τῶν ὀμμάτων ἀστραπὰς καὶ ἐκ τοῦ σώματος ἀστέρας ἀλλομένους.

15 PGM 4.724–733: "After you have said these things, he will immediately respond with a revelation (725). Now you will grow weak in soul and will not be in yourself, when he answers you. He speaks the oracle to you in verse, and after speaking he will depart. But you remain silent, since you will be able to comprehend all these matters by yourself; for at a later time (730) you will remember infallibly the things spoken by the great god, even if the oracle contained myriads of verses" (Ταῦτά σου εἰπόντος εὐθέως (725) χρησμῳδήσει. ὑπέκλυτος δὲ ἔσει τῇ ψυχῇ καὶ οὐκ ἐν σεαυτῷ ἔσει, ὅταν σοι ἀποκρίνηται· λέγει δέ σοι διὰ στίχων τὸν χρησμὸν καὶ εἰπὼν ἀπελεύσεται, σὺ δὲ στήκεις ἐνεός, ὡς ταῦτα πάντα χωρήσεις αὐτομάτως, καὶ τότε (730) μνημονεύσεις ἀπαραβάτως τὰ ὑπὸ τοῦ μεγάλου θεοῦ ῥηθέντα, κἂν ἦν μυρίων στίχων ὁ χρησμός).

Gennep's phase of reaggregation. The vivid images of the journey up to the heavens are not repeated in a journey back to earth, nor does the magician take an alternate route, shooting down as a star like the souls at the end of Plato's myth of Er.[16] The spell provides no information about the magician's life after this ritual, no explanation of how this epiphany of Helios Mithras has changed his life, no description of the magician's new status in earthly life as a result of his experience.

The mystery of the Mithras Liturgy

This gap in the perfect van Gennepian schema is usually explained with reference to the presumed differences between the *original* ritual, which of course must have been a perfectly formed initiatory ritual, and the later, corrupted version, which merely made use, in magic's parasitical fashion, of the liturgy from a mystery cult. The *original* ritual, various scholars have argued, must have been an initiation that transformed the initiand into divine status. As Smith claims, "The reviser turned it into a ritual for divination which had to be repeated as new questions arose, but kept the wording of the earlier text which shows that its original purpose was once-for-all 'immortalisation' i.e., deification."[17]

However, the wording of the text does not, in fact, suggest that this hypothetical *original* ritual was cut off by the redacting magician just before the reaggregation phase. On the contrary, the text shows throughout that the immortalisation performed in the ritual is a temporary and repeatable experience, rather than a once-for-all deification. The performer of the rite never seeks a permanent change in identity, nor does his performance grant him admission into a group comprised of others who have been similarly deified. The references to mysteries in the text have led scholars to imagine a mystery cult group into which the performer was initiated (in the imagined *original* rite), but a closer examination of these references shows that such speculations depend less upon the text and more upon scholars' assumptions about the evolution of religion from authentic mystery cults to decadent magical syncretisms.

To be sure, the text does show that it is the product of redaction and revision. In the first set of instructions following the description of the ascent

16 Plato, R. 621b: "And after they had fallen asleep and it was the middle of the night, there was a sound of thunder and a quaking of the earth, and they were suddenly wafted thence, one this way, one that, upward to their birth like shooting stars" (ἐπειδὴ δὲ κοιμηθῆναι καὶ μέσας νύκτας γενέσθαι, βροντήν τε καὶ σεισμὸν γενέσθαι, καὶ ἐντεῦθεν ἐξαπίνης ἄλλον ἄλλῃ φέρεσθαι ἄνω εἰς τὴν γένεσιν, ἄττοντας ὥσπερ ἀστέρας).

17 Smith, 1996, 127.

into the heavens, the reader is informed that the ἀπαθανατισμός, the immortalisation, is to be performed three times a year (748). Later in the text, however, the author claims to have received a revelation from the god to change some of the aspects of the ritual. The rite is to be performed once a month, at the full moon (798), rather than three times a year beginning in a new moon (at the seizure of the moon, 754).[18] It is worth noting that no explanation is deemed necessary for multiple immortalisations taking place instead of a once-for-all transformation, but the change from three to twelve in a year needs the explanation of a direct revelation from the god.

Although the references to *mysteria* and a *mystes* have led scholars to assume that the immortalisation rite is a relic of the ritual that initiated someone into membership of a mystery cult, the use of the terms in the text actually suggests an entirely different background. On the hypothesis that the initiate is immortalised or deified by his initiation into the mystery cult, immortality is the end result of initiation – he becomes a *mystes* through this rite of immortalisation.[19] However, the text itself begins with a request to provide immortality to a *mystes*, "Be gracious to me, O Providence and Psyche, as I write these mysteries handed down and for an only child I request immortality, for a *mystes* of this our power."[20] The one to whom the mysteries are being handed down, perhaps the daughter mentioned a few lines later, is already a *mystes*, but she is in need of the ritual to provide immortalisation. This daughter and the fellow initiate (*symmystes*) mentioned later are the only others who appear in the text; there is no group into which the magician – or his daughter – are initiated by means of the spell. The ritual, then, does not make her a *mystes*; it makes a *mystes*

---

18 PGM 4.791–799: "Many times have I used the spell and have wondered greatly. But the god said to me: 'Use the ointment no longer, but, after casting it into the river, consult while wearing the great mystery (795) of the scarab revitalised through the twenty-five living birds, and consult once a month, at full moon, instead of three times a year'." (Πολλάκις δὲ τῇ πραγματείᾳ χρησάμενος ὑπερεθαύμασα· εἶπεν δέ μοι ὁ θεός· μηκέτι χρῶ τῷ συγχρίσματι, ἀλλὰ ῥίψαντα εἰς ποταμὸν <χρὴ> χρᾶσθαι φοροῦντα τὸ μέγα μυστήριον (795) τοῦ κανθάρου τοῦ ἀναζωπυρηθέντος διὰ τῶν κε ζῴων ὀρνέων, χρᾶσθαι ἅπαξ τοῦ μηνός, ἀντὶ τοῦ κατὰ ἔτος γ', κατὰ πανσέληνον).

19 Betz, 2003, 193: "The decisive insight gained from his initiation is that he has come to understand himself as an individual self (ἐγώ εἰμι), identified by his secret name."

20 PGM 4.475–478: Ἰλαθί μοι, Πρόνοια καὶ Ψυχή, τάδε γράφοντι τὰ <ἄ>πρατα, παραδοτὰ μυστήρια, μόνῳ δὲ τέκνῳ ἀθανασίαν ἀξιῶ, μύστῃ τῆς ἡμετέρας δυνάμεως ταύτης. Betz reads ἀθανασίαν instead of ἀθανασίας and μύστῃ instead of μύσται. I here follow Betz's suggestion (Betz, 2003, 92) that πρατα may be a scribal error for παραδοτὰ, rather than a reference to "for profit" or, with an alpha privative supplied "not for profit".

temporarily immortal, just as the *symmystes* brought along to hear the revelation from the god purifies himself to be immortalised along with the performer of the ritual:

> If you also wish to use a fellow initiate, so that he alone may hear with you the things spoken, let him remain pure together with you for 7 days, and abstain from meat and the bath.[21]

To be sure, the ritual is referred to as *mysteria*, both in the exordium and in the rite itself. The author of the text is writing down the *mysteria*, and the magician in the text tells the supreme god that the god himself has founded and created the *mysterion*:

> O Lord, while being born again, I am passing away; while growing and having grown, I am dying; while being born from a life-generating birth, I am passing on, released to death – as you have founded, as you have decreed, and have established the mystery.[22]

However, *mysterion* does not always mean an initiatory rite, and even within the text it is also used to describe the ritual for creating the special ointment needed for the ritual.[23] Indeed, the magician anoints the face of his *symmystes* with the "mystery", that is to say, the ointment, while uttering the words of the invocations under his breath so that the other cannot hear the words for himself (745–747). When the new revelation comes to change the ritual, the god tells the magician to cast the ointment into the river and use instead the *mysterion* of the scarab revitalised through the twenty-five living birds (795). The mysteries involved in the "Mithras Liturgy" are special rituals that bring direct contact with the supreme god, but they are not initiations. Just because the rite can be analysed in terms of van Gennep's tripartite schema does not mean that it is actually an initiation.

The Mithras Liturgy as a rite of extreme purification

These mysteries are in fact better described as consecrations or sanctifications, or even simply purifications. An initiation involves a permanent

---

21 PGM 4.733–735: ἐὰν δὲ θέλῃς καὶ συνμύστῃ χρήσασθαι ὥστε τὰ λεγόμενα ἐκεῖνον μόνον σύν σοι ἀκούειν, συναγνευέτω σοι <ζ'> (735) ἡμέρας καὶ ἀποσχέσθω ἐμψύχων καὶ βαλανείου.

22 PGM 4.719–724: κύριε, παλινγενόμενος ἀπογίγνομαι, αὐξόμενος καὶ αὐξηθείς (720) τελευτῶ, ἀπὸ γενέσεως ζωογόνου γενόμενος, εἰς ἀπογενεσίαν ἀναλυθεὶς πορεύομαι, ὡς σὺ ἔκτισας, ὡς σὺ ἐνομοθέτησας καὶ ἐποίησας μυστήριον.

23 Cf. the remarks of Nock, *Hellenistic Mysteries and Christian Sacraments*, in Nock / Stewart (eds.), 1972, 796–801.

change of status and identity and admission into a group whose members are defined, at least in part, by their performance of the initiation ritual.[24] A ritual of purification involves a change in status, from impure to pure, from unconsecrated to consecrated, from profane to sacred. As the Latinate *profane* indicates, such a transformation of status marks the difference between something that belongs outside of the temple or other sacred space – *pro fanum*, and something that belongs within the sacred space.[25] Purification is a relative process; one can be more or less purified, brought to a level of sanctity appropriate for different circumstances. As Parker notes, there is no real difference in concept between washing one's hands to go in for dinner and purifying oneself before entering a temple to worship a god, only a matter of scale.[26] The appropriate level of purity to meet with a god is far greater than that required to partake of food with one's family. Then again, the level of purity required to dine with the Queen is far greater than with one's children, and the level of purity required to meet face to face with the supreme ruler of the universe is naturally far greater than that required to enter a small shrine set up to a local hero. These rituals of preparation and purification to enter the presence of the deity can be called *mysteria* if they are so special that they are secret from the general populace, especially if, as in the "Mithras Liturgy", they are directly created and founded by the deity himself.[27]

Rather than a liturgy, which etymologically means a communal festival, or even a solitary shamanic initiation, the "Mithras Liturgy" is this kind of

---

24 Cf. Petersen, 2011, 30 (cited in n. 8). He also notes the element of incorporation into a group: "Intransitive/reflexive ritual with an ambivalent final state as in initiations into associations or special cults" (Petersen, 2011, 31). See Beck in this volume for actual Mithraic initiations which involves becoming a member of a group, and Marshall for the importance of the group in theurgic conversions.

25 Ibid., 32: "The idea of the ontological difference characteristic of religions of blessing in particular permeates all rituals of cleansing. There can be no ritual approach towards or even encounter with the god/gods, unless the ritual object has been transformed into a state in which it poses no contaminating danger to the god/gods."

26 R. Parker, *Miasma. Pollution and Purification in Early Greek Religion*, Oxford 1983, 20: "Cleanliness is, in fact, not a special preparation for worship but a requirement for formal, respectful behaviour of any kind; there is no generic difference between the lustrations that precede prayer and those that precede a meal."

27 Cf. the Eleusinian mysteries, given to the people directly by the goddess Demeter. Of course, there must often be an intermediary in the transmission, like Orpheus who was credited with establishing the Eleusinian mysteries, or, as in the "Mithras Liturgy", the double intermediary of the archangel who transmits the mystery from Mithras to the author of the text, who, by writing, hands it down again.

purificatory ritual of sanctification. In the text, the magician indeed describes his own rebirth through the replacement of mortal elements by immortal ones as a *hagiasma*, a process of making holy. These rites of sanctification are not ordinary purifications, but especially holy ones, so the magician may claim to be ἁγίοις ἁγιασθεὶς ἁγιάσμασι sanctified by holy consecrations (522) – Greek embraces the cognates as much as English avoids them.

The "Mithras Liturgy" seems to share the idea, expressed for example in Firmicus Maternus' treatise on astrology, that the mortal man is a microcosm of the cosmos, an image composed of the same elements as the whole.[28] In order to ascend to the higher levels of the cosmos, the magician must replace the material, sublunar elements of his being with the higher elements that belong to the immortal world of the gods (502–508). The magician asks to be given over to immortal rebirth (τῇ ἀθανάτῳ γενέσει) so that he may gaze upon the immortal element with immortal spirit (ἐποπτεύσω τὴν ἀθάνατον ἀρχὴν τῷ ἀθανάτῳ πνεύματι) (501–505). The magician explicitly claims that "it is impossible for me, born mortal, to rise with the golden brightnesses of the immortal brilliance" (529–530); nevertheless, "I, born mortal from mortal womb, but transformed by tremendous power and an incorruptible right hand," [...] "today I am about to behold, with immortal eyes [...] and with immortal spirit, the immortal Aion and master of the fiery diadems." The immortal rebirth is a transformation of his elements from mortal to immortal so that he can behold, as like to like, the immortal world of the gods. This process of assimilation to the divine (ὁμοίωσις θεῷ) is likewise important in the Platonic tradition, from the appearance of the idea in Plato's *Theaetetus* to the late Neoplatonists like Olympiodorus who saw it as the ultimate goal of philosophy.[29] The magician stresses the change from mortal origins to divine in his address to Helios at the doors of the sun:

> I, so and so, whose mother is such and such, who was born from the mortal womb of such and such, and from the fluid of semen, and who, since he has been born again from you today, has become immortal out of so many myriads in this hour according to the wish of god the exceedingly good.[30]

The fleshly womb and semen that produced his mortal nature have been replaced by the immortal elements.

---

28 Firm., Math. 1.90–91 (proemium to book 3); cf. Betz, 2003, 109.
29 Cf. Pl., Tht. 176d. Olympiodorus, In Phd. 1.2, simply defines philosophy as the assimilation to the divine, ὁμοίωσις γὰρ θεῷ ἡ φιλοσοφία.
30 PGM 4.644–650: ἐγὼ ὁ δεῖνα τῆς δεῖνα, γενόμενος ἐκ θνητῆς ὑστέρας τῆς δεῖνα καὶ (645) ἰχῶρος σπερματικοῦ καί, σήμερον τούτου ὑπό σου με<τα>γεννηθέντος, ἐκ τοσούτων μυριάδων ἀπαθανατισθεὶς ἐν ταύτῃ τῇ ὥρᾳ κατὰ δόκησιν θεοῦ, ὑπερβαλλόντως ἀγαθοῦ, προσκυνῆσαί σε ἀξιοῖ.

This transformation, although it may be described in terms of death and rebirth, is not a permanent change. While Betz compares the consecrations to Christian baptism, the ritual does not welcome the magician into a new group of the baptised nor permanently change his status.[31] On the contrary, the change is only for a short time, πρὸς ὀλίγον (523), and the magician will fall once again under the yoke of "present bitter and relentless Necessity" (525) that burdens all those in the realm of mortals. This Necessity (*Anangke*) is not simply death, as Merkelbach suggests, but rather the entire apparatus of fate that rules over the sublunary world.[32] In Stoic and Neoplatonic cosmologies, the highest levels of divinity are beyond the control of Fate or Necessity, and the cosmology of the "Mithras Liturgy" seems to share this notion. While he is in the celestial realm, wandering about with the planets and stars, he is free from Fate, but after his meeting with the supreme god he returns to the mortal world, back to his mortal nature and the oppression of the Necessity that shapes all mortal affairs.

Once again, however, this return is only temporary, for the magician can ascend again, out of the material and mortal world to meet with the god. The freedom from *Anangke* is temporary, just for the duration of the ritual, but the bondage is escapable every time the magician performs the ritual, whether that is thrice a year or even once a month. The magician has attained no new status as a result of his journey there and back again, no permanent transformation of life; the only thing that survives the transition back between worlds is the divine revelation, the hexameter oracles the god speaks that will remain indissolubly in the magician's memory.

Patterns of purification rituals from simple to extreme

This apparently paradoxical form of temporary immortality is not as peculiar as it seems to our modern sensibilities; the ancient world provides a number of illuminating parallels. Perhaps the closest is the report in Porphyry's

---

31 Betz, 2003, 123, and n. 209. Cf. F. Graf, *Baptism and Graeco-Roman Mystery Cults*, in Hellholm / Vegge / Norderval / Hellholm (eds.), 2011, 101–118 (105), who suggests that the absence of discussion of the distinction between one time permanent washing and repeated purifications in the ancient evidence stems from the polytheist argument against Christian originality – baptism was no different from regular lustrations.

32 Merkelbach / Totti, 1992, 237: "Nicht mehr von jener 'Schuld' beschwert, welche man der ἀνάγκη zurückzahlen muß = nicht mehr vom Tode beschwert. Der Initiierte hat seine frühere Existenz hinter sich gelassen." Betz, 2003, 115, cites a variety of parallels for "liberation from the oppression by ἀνάγκη, εἱμαρμένη, τύχη, and χρεία."

Life of Plotinus that his master achieved the supreme union with the One principle of the cosmos four times in his life. "For to him the goal and aim of life was to achieve oneness and to come near to the god over all things. And this aim he achieved perhaps four times while I was with him by his ineffable power."[33] Plotinus' One did not appear in the vivid images of the "Mithras Liturgy" with lightning bolts flashing around the trousered form of Mithras, but abstractly, "that God appeared, the God who has neither shape nor form, but sits enthroned above the Intellectual-Principle and all the Intellectual-Sphere."[34] While the Master attained this height four times, Porphyry tells us that he has achieved this union only once so far.[35] This Neoplatonic union with the supreme divinity of the universe, while not quite as frequent as the once a month "Mithras Liturgy", is nevertheless a temporary and repeatable process that leaves the philosopher back in the same mortal status he had before the union.

The hexameter oracles provided by Mithras at the culmination of the meeting also find a parallel in the Chaldaean oracles so revered by the Neoplatonists. While these verses remain only in scattered fragments quoted by Proclus and other Neoplatonists, many similarities appear between the cosmology of these Oracles and that which appears in the "Mithras Liturgy".[36] The theurgical practices associated with these Oracles bear numerous resemblances to the magical techniques of the "Mithras Liturgy", especially the ascent with the rays of the sun, and there is every reason to believe that the composition of the "Mithras Liturgy" comes out of a religious context familiar with these theurgical practices.

Of course, the "Mithras Liturgy" and the entirety of the Great Paris Magical Papyrus come from an Egyptian religious context, and scholars have speculated about Neoplatonic theurgy in Egypt.[37] Not only does

---

33 Porphyry, Plot. 23.15: Τέλος γὰρ αὐτῷ καὶ σκοπὸς ἦν τὸ ἑνωθῆναι καὶ πελάσαι τῷ ἐπὶ πᾶσι θεῷ· Ἔτυχε δὲ τετράκις που, ὅτε αὐτῷ συνήμην, τοῦ σκοποῦ τούτου ἐνεργείᾳ ἀρρήτῳ.

34 Porphyry, Plot. 23.10–12: ἐφάνη ἐκεῖνος ὁ θεὸς ὁ μήτε μορφὴν μήτε τινὰ ἰδέαν ἔχων, ὑπὲρ δὲ νοῦν καὶ πᾶν τὸ νοητὸν ἱδρυμένος.

35 Porphyry, Plot. 23.12f.: "And indeed I myself, Porphyry, declare that I drew near and became one with him, when I was in my sixty-eighth year" (Ὧι δὴ καὶ ἐγὼ Πορφύριος ἅπαξ λέγω πλησιάσαι καὶ ἑνωθῆναι ἔτος ἄγων ἑξηκοστόν τε καὶ ὄγδοον).

36 Cf. the arguments in Edmonds, 2003 and 2004, Johnston, 1997, and, ultimately, H. Lewy, *Chaldaean Oracles and Theurgy. Mysticism, Magic and Platonism in the Later Roman Empire*, Paris ²1978 (ed. by M. Tardieu), whose reconstruction of the Chaldaean Oracles relies heavily on the Mithras Liturgy.

37 Betz, 2003, 35, sees the cosmology as middle Stoic with no trace of Neoplatonic influence, comparing the ideas of the 1ˢᵗ century CE Stoic and priest of Isis,

Iamblichus put his exposition of the theory of theurgy in the mouth of an Egyptian priest, but the Hermetic writings mingle theurgical ideas with an Egyptian revelatory background. Other scholars, however, have noted the similarities between the prescriptions for purification and ascent in the "Mithras Liturgy" and the rites of entering the presence of a god in an Egyptian sanctuary, arguing that the rite can be simply traced back to Egyptian temple rituals.[38] Such rituals, however, should not be called "initiations" any more than the "Mithras Liturgy", since they too provide a temporary shift of status for the individual to enter the presence of a god rather than a permanent change of status and entry into a group. Likewise, the purity regulations for entering a temple, found in various of the so-called Greek Sacred Laws, show a similar pattern of purification before entering the place of the god.[39] Indeed, such sanctification rituals for approaching a god are neither specifically Greek nor Egyptian, but part of a general pattern of purification rituals in the ancient Mediterranean. As the author of a Hippocratic treatise theorises about the general principle of separating sacred and profane and requiring purification to pass from ordinary space into the place of the gods:

> We mark out the boundaries of the temples and the groves of the gods so that no one may pass them unless he be pure, and when we enter them, we are

---

Chaeremon of Alexandria, but see Edmonds, 2003 and 2004, for a discussion of the similarities with Neoplatonic materials. See G. Fowden, *The Egyptian Hermes. A HistoricalAapproach to the Late Pagan Mind*, Princeton 1993, for a discussion of theurgy and Hermetism.

38 J. Gee, *Review of Betz 2003*, in: Review of Biblical Literature 2 (2005), provides a chart of parallels with a sequence from the *Book of the Dead*, scenes from the Bark Shrine at Karnak, and the *Document of Breathings Made by Isis* that shows the acts of purification before entry into the sanctuary of the god, which is sometimes referred to as a heaven.

39 E.g., IG 2², 1365, 8–11; 18–25 (Attica, 1ˢᵗ century CE): "No one is to enter unpurified. Let him be made pure from garlic and pork. [...], and he is purified from a corpse on the tenth day; from a woman on the seventh; from manslaughter never around this place; from abortion the 40ᵗʰ; from a woman, those having washed from the head down on the same day" (μηθένα ἀκάθαρτον προσάγειν· καθαρισζέστω δὲ ἀπὸ σκόρδων καὶ χοιρέων· [...] Καὶ ἀπὸ νεκροῦ καθαρίσζεσται δεκατ<αί>αν, ἀπὸ γυναικέων ἑβ<δ>ομαία<ν>, ἀνδροφόνον μηδὲ περὶ τὸν τόπον, ἀπὸ δὲ φθορᾶς τετταρακοσταίαν, ἀπὸ δὲ γυναικὸς λουσάμενοι κατακέφαλα αὐθειμερί). Cf. SEG 28, 421, a *lex sacra* from Megalopolis in Arcadia that restricts entry into the sanctuary for sacrifice to those who have been purified, specifying different number of days after various causes of impurity (ranging from eating goat to having sex to giving birth). Purification again seems to consist of waiting and washing (in some cases, from the head down).

sprinkled with holy water, not as being polluted, but as laying aside any other pollution which we formerly had.[40]

Entering a temple to worship a god can easily be analysed à la van Gennep, with the purification separating the person from profane status, the encounter with the statue of the god in the temple as a liminal moment, and a return to profane space upon exiting the temple.

A quick sprinkling of water from one of the *perirrhanteria* located at the entrance to a temple is of course far less elaborate and intense than the entire element by element reconstruction in the "Mithras Liturgy", but the procedure for consulting the oracle of Trophonius at Lebadea provides a more complex parallel. Pausanias recounts the elaborate process of preparation, involving days of abstinence, special baths and anointings, and draughts from the fountains of Lethe and Mnemosyne.[41] The specially prepared one then goes to the oracle to consult with the god, sometimes receiving an audible message from the god, sometimes a vision. As Bonnechere has noted in his study of the evidence pertaining to this shrine, the terminology of mysteries is sometimes used of the rites, but there is no evidence that undergoing the rituals involved in the consultation provided initiation into some group of people especially dedicated to Trophonius.[42] The rite did produce a change of state, in that the one returning from the consultation lost his ability to laugh, but even this change was temporary. Like the magician in the "Mithras Liturgy", the one consulting Trophonius is struck out of his wits, but after he recounts his experience to the priests at the shrine, he begins his return to normal life:

> After his ascent from Trophonius, the inquirer is again taken in hand by the priests, who set him upon a chair called the chair of Memory, which stands not far from the shrine, and they ask of him, when seated there, all he has seen or learned. After gaining this information they then entrust him to his relatives. These lift him, paralysed with terror and unconscious both of himself and of his surroundings, and carry him to the building where he lodged before with Good Fortune and the Good Spirit. Afterwards, however, he will recover all his faculties, and the power to laugh will return to him.[43]

---

40 Hp., Morb. Sacr. 148.55: αὐτοί τε ὅρους τοῖσι θεοῖσι τῶν ἱερῶν καὶ τῶν τεμενέων ἀποδεικνύμενοι, ὡς ἂν μηδεὶς ὑπερβαίνῃ ἢν μὴ ἁγνεύῃ, εἰσιόντες τε ἡμεῖς περιῤῥαινόμεθα οὐχ ὡς μιαινόμενοι, ἀλλ᾽ εἴ τι καὶ πρότερον ἔχομεν μύσος, τοῦτο ἀφαγνιούμενοι.

41 Paus. 9.39,2.

42 P. Bonnechere, *Trophonios de Lébadée. Cultes et mythes d'une cité béotienne au miroir de la mentalité antique*, Leiden 2003, 217, cf. 132.

43 Paus. 9.39,12: τὸν δὲ ἀναβάντα παρὰ τοῦ Τροφωνίου παραλαβόντες αὖθις οἱ ἱερεῖς καθίζουσιν ἐπὶ θρόνον Μνημοσύνης μὲν καλούμενον, κεῖται δὲ οὐ

As Bonnechere has shown, the Trophonius oracle, despite similarities of pattern and even the use of some terminology of mysteries, cannot be considered an initiatory mystery cult. The Trophonius oracle, like the "Mithras Liturgy", fits the tripartite schema of van Gennep, but is likewise an elaborated version of the sanctification process for approaching a god, not an initiation into a group or even into a new status or identity.

Such rituals of purification or sanctification, whether as complex as the descent to Trophonius or the "Mithras Liturgy's" ascent to Mithras or as simple as a quick sprinkling of water before entering a sanctuary, are a part of a long tradition of rituals that enable mortals to make contact with the gods. In such rituals that bring close contact with the divine, the religious focus is upon the shifts in relationship with the god rather than upon the change of status on earth or any change of lifestyle afterwards. A better understanding of this model may aid in the understanding of the religious conflicts and confusions during this period, when ideas of conversion or initiation into a select group are in competition with this longstanding idea of ritual contact with the divine. Paul's transformative experience on the road to Damascus or the ordeals the Roman legionaries underwent to change themselves into Mithraic initiates stand out all the more in contrast to the temporary immortalisation in the magician's journey there and back again in the "Mithras Liturgy".

πόρρω τοῦ ἀδύτου, καθεσθέντα δὲ ἐνταῦθα ἀνερωτῶσιν ὁπόσα εἶδέ τε καὶ ἐπύθετο· μαθόντες δὲ ἐπιτρέπουσιν αὐτὸν ἤδη τοῖς προσήκουσιν· οἱ δὲ ἐς τὸ οἴκημα, ἔνθα καὶ πρότερον διῃτᾶτο παρά τε Τύχῃ καὶ Δαίμονι ἀγαθοῖς, ἐς τοῦτο ἀράμενοι κομίζουσι κάτοχόν τε ἔτι τῷ δείματι καὶ ἀγνῶτα ὁμοίως αὑτοῦ τε καὶ τῶν πέλας· ὕστερον μέντοι τά τε ἄλλα οὐδέν τι φρονήσει μεῖον ἢ πρότερον καὶ γέλως ἐπάνεισίν οἱ· γράφω δὲ οὐκ ἀκοὴν ἀλλὰ ἑτέρους τε ἰδὼν καὶ αὐτὸς τῷ Τροφωνίῳ χρησάμενος.

Anders-Christian Jacobsen

Identity Formation through Catechetical Teaching in Early Christianity

Abstract: With an outset in identity theories and drawing on the catechetical instructions found in the writings of Cyril of Jerusalem and Augustine, the author argues that 4th century Christian catechetical teaching was aimed at and contributed to identity formation and transformation among persons who recently converted to Christianity, even in the strongest sense of the term "identity".

Baptismal catechesis and early Christian identity formation

In Christianity, catechesis played an important role in conversion processes mainly as a way to educate and socialise new converts into the social and moral rules and the belief system of the new group. But to which degree did this educational effort aim at an individual's or group's transformation of identity – and did it in fact?

In this article, I will describe and discuss two examples of how catechetical teaching was conducted in early Christianity, and whether it contributed to identity formation among persons who recently converted to Christianity.[1] With an outset in identity theories, which have only rarely been applied in relation to this subject,[2] and drawing on the catechetical instructions found in the writings of Cyril of Jerusalem (about 315–386) and Augustine from Hippo (ca. 354–430), I will focus on the following topics: 1) The organisation of catechetical instruction in early Christianity; 2) The contribution of early catechetical instruction to the formation of an individual or collective

---

1   The term "early Christianity" covers late antiquity as well. The elaborated catechumenate is not found until the 4th century: There is some evidence from Irenaeus and then two centuries later, from Cyril and Augustine (see below), wherefore a stable and universal education system among Christians before the 4th century is debatable.

2   One of the few examples I have seen of an active use of the concept of identity in studies of baptism and baptismal preparation, is R. Aasgaard, *Ambrose and Augustine. Two Bishops on Baptism and Christian Identity*, in: D. Hellholm / T. Vegge / Ø. Norderval / C. Hellholm (eds.), *Ablution, Initiation, and Baptism. Late Antiquity, Early Judaism, and Early Christianity*, vol. 2, Berlin 2011, 1253–1283. In this article, Aasgaard considers identity to be a *construct* (1257). Aasgaard is thus in line with the main use of the concept of identity in social and cultural studies, but this is a questionable use of the term, as I will argue below.

identity – or both, with a special focus on the transformation of the baptismal candidates' way of life and their beliefs.

Identity – what is that?

Identity theory was developed in developmental psychology in the beginning of the 1950s by E.H. Erikson. Shortly after, the concept of identity was also used in the humanities and cultural studies after which it quickly spread and developed in many different directions. This weakened the use of the term as an analytical tool because it was used in too many and incoherent ways.[3] In the context of Erikson's developmental psychology, "identity" was something which a person should and would obtain if his or her psychological and social development went well. "Identity formation" designated the process from childhood to adulthood in which a person's identity was formed. Thus, a person's identity was the result of influential intertwined and reciprocal internal, *mental* processes and external, *social* processes, but for Erikson, there was an "identity core" in the individual person which under normal circumstances would develop into a full blown "personal identity". According to Erikson, this personal identity was not *constructed*, but *developed*. However, as the concept spread, especially into the social sciences and cultural studies, identity formation was mainly considered a constructive process. No "identity core" existed which could be developed.

Taken in its ordinary and basic meaning, "identity" – from the Latin *idem* – has to do with that "sameness" which makes something recognisable and identifiable. A person's identity makes the person recognisable through time, at different locations, and in different circumstances. Similarly, a group's identity indicates the sameness which makes the individuals of a given group recognisable as a group, and which makes the group recognisable as the same group in different times and circumstances. P. Stachel calls this a "strong" concept of identity (Stachel, 2005, 404f.). The advantage of this conception of identity is that it builds on the basic meaning of the word. However, for many scholars this is also a weakness because it signals an idealistic coherence and sameness that does not fit a reality which is most often complex and blurred. Such scholars have therefore introduced ideas of "multiple identities", "fluent identities", "identity construction", etc., which

---

3 P. Stachel, *Identität. Genese, Inflation und Probleme eines zeitgenössischen Sozial- und Kulturwissenschaften zentralen Begriffs*, in: Archiv für Kulturgeschichte 87 (2005), 395–425. The following short description of the development of and main positions in identity theory builds on this article. Stachel seems to base his article on a very broad reading of especially North American identity theory, for example P. Gleason, *Identifying Identity. A Semantic History*, in: W. Sollors (ed.), *Theories of Ethnicity. A Classical Reader*, New York 1996, 460–487.

P. Stachel calls "weak" concepts of identity because the term "identity" is in fact used contrary to its basic meaning (Stachel, 2005, 404f.). Stachel agrees that the realities of modern human beings and groups are often shifting and blurred, but this is precisely why the author questions the validity of using the concept of identity to describe such situations.

This problem is also well-known from studies in the history of religions including early Christianity. To avoid so-called essentialist claims about how early Christianity and early Christians came into being and "what" they were, many scholars have talked about the fluent and multiple identities of early Christians and early Christianity[4] – some even talk about the many Christianities.[5] This development raises at least two important questions: 1) Does it make sense to claim any kind of "sameness" in descriptions of early Christianity and early Christians, or are these entities so complex that any claims about "sameness" are implausible? 2) If not, does it, then, make sense to use the concept of identity to analyse these different and complex phenomena called Christianity and Christians?[6] In my opinion, yes. There is so much coherence and sameness in early Christianity that it makes sense to talk about Christians as an identifiable group of people and as individuals who share common identity markers. Indeed, the very fact that most of those who designated themselves as Christians had undergone some form of catechising and baptism is a strong marker of sameness. As examples of other identity markers could be mentioned the fact that Christian communities and individuals maintained contact with other groups and individuals whom they recognised as Christians; that Christian groups and individuals understood themselves as being in historical and geographical continuity

---

4   Cf. R. Miles, *Constructing Identities in Late Antiquity*, London 1999, 1–4; S. Harrison, *Autobiographical Identity and Philosophical Past in Augustine's Dialogue* De Libero Arbitrio, in: R. Miles (ed.), *Constructing Identities in Late Antiquity*, London 1999, 133–158; S.A. Harvey / D.G. Hunter, *The Oxford Handbook of Early Christian Studies*, Part 3 (*Identities*), Oxford 2008; V. Burrus, *Late Ancient Christianity*, Part 3 (*Identities and the Boundaries*), Minneapolis 2005.

5   See, e.g., B.D. Ehrman, *Lost Christianities. The Battles for Scripture and the Faiths we never knew*, Oxford 2005, and Martin in this volume (153).

6   P. Stachel, 2005, 418, quotes R. Brubaker and F. Cooper (*Beyond "Identity"*, in: Theory and Society 29 (2000), 1–47 (1)) for the following sentence: "The argument of this article is that the social sciences and humanities have surrendered to the word 'identity'; that this has both intellectual and political costs; and that we can do better. 'Identity', we argue, tends to mean too much (when understood in a strong sense), too little (when understood in a weak sense), or nothing at all (because of its sheer ambiguity)." Brubaker and Cooper make an important point, yet I do believe that the concept of "identity" still has a value when we do not weaken the concept too much.

with other groups and individuals; that there was a strong mobility among
Christians who moved from one Christian community to another; even the
conflicts about theology and the Christian way of life indicate an awareness
of a real or imagined sameness or identity.[7] Accordingly, it is valid and pref-
erable to use a "strong" concept of identity in relation to the study of early
Christians.

Nonetheless, it is also easy to see in the sources that individual Christians
and Christian groups in late antiquity differed much and in many ways. It is
obvious that the textual sources which describe catechetical instruction in
early Christianity are not uninterested descriptions, but texts loaded with
more or less heavy ideological claims about how true Christianity and true
Christians must be. To state it briefly, the texts probably tell us more about
how bishops wanted Christianity and Christians to be than about how they
really were.[8] Hence, it could be claimed that such texts are mere ideology;
and it could be claimed that everything that the bishops demand from recently converted Christians according to such texts shows that reality was
characterised by the opposite: When the bishops demanded that Christians
should live a morally good life abstaining from, for example, sexual promiscuity, it signalled that Christians in fact had a promiscuous sex life; when
bishops demanded that they should only serve one God, it signalled that
most or at least many Christians worshipped more or many gods taking
part in pagan cults and festivals, etc. To a certain degree, such conclusions
are probably correct.[9] Why should the bishops warn against promiscuity if
nobody lived a life in sexual promiscuity? Why would bishops warn against
participating in pagan cults if no Christians did? On the other hand, we
should, in my opinion, not assume that the ideals preached and taught by
the bishops were *mere* ideology. The existence of catechetical texts and of
many other types of Christian texts shows that there were indeed persons
and groups which identified themselves with and claimed to live up to the
bishops' ideals – even if these ideals were only carried through to a certain
or even limited degree. It is simply not possible for us to assess the exact
borderline between ideology and lived life. Moreover, even ideologically

---

7 As a few examples among many can be mentioned: Paul, who travelled and wrote
   to different Christian communities; 1. Clement, which is a letter from the congregation in Rome to the congregation in Corinth; Irenaeus' claim in *Adversus
   haereses* 1.10,1 that the church which was spread all over the world shared the
   same beliefs; Irenaeus' move from Asia Minor (probably Smyrna) to Lyon where
   he served as a bishop; Augustine's and many other theologians' thousands of letters to other Christians and other Christian communities.

8 This problem is also encountered in conversion studies, see Engberg in this
   volume.

9 Cf. Rebillard's contribution in this volume.

coloured claims provide us with important information about early Christian identity formation.

In the following, I will use these observations about identity theory to inspire my analyses and interpretations of how catechetical instruction took place in early Christianity, and how it influenced individual and collective identity formation.

The organisation of catechetical instruction

In early Christianity, education played an important role in conversion processes mainly as a way to socialise new converts into the social and moral rules and the belief system of the new group. The education thus followed after the decision to become a Christian. In the first centuries of the history of Christianity when most converts were adults, this education took place as a preparation for baptism. Thus, the sequence was: conversion, catechesis and baptism. The organisation of catechesis and baptism differed much from place to place in this early phase.[10] Later, education also followed after baptism.

Cyril from Jerusalem composed his catechetical lectures for the preparation of the catechumens in Jerusalem around 351.[11] At that time, Cyril was presbyter or bishop[12] in the Church of the Holy Sepulchre in Jerusalem which was founded by Constantine the Great.[13] The preserved collection of lectures consists of a pro-catechesis (P), eighteen catechetical lectures (C), and five mystagogical lectures (M). All scholars agree that the *Pro-catechesis* and the eighteen catechetical lectures are written[14] by Cyril, while Cyril's authorship of the five mystagogical lectures has been disputed.[15] Cyril gave

---

10 M.E. Johnson, *The Rites of Christian Initiation. Their Evolution and Interpretation*, Collegeville [2]2007, 41–114, analyses the sources for our knowledge of the organisation of baptismal catechesis and baptism in the pre-Nicene period. See Abate and Bilde in this volume for the much less elaborated pagan and Jewish education related to conversion.

11 A.J. Doval, *The Date of Cyril of Jerusalem's Catecheses*, in: JThS 48 (1997), 129–132. In this short essay, Doval presents the history of research on the dating of Cyril's catechetical lectures and reaches his own conclusion on the dating, which is 351. J. Day, *The Catechetical Lectures of Cyril of Jerusalem. A Source for the Baptismal Liturgy of Mid-Fourth Century Jerusalem*, in: Hellholm / Vegge / Norderval / Hellholm (eds.), 2011, 1179–1205 (1179) follows Doval.

12 It is disputed exactly when Cyril was appointed bishop in Jerusalem.

13 Eusebius, *The Life of Constantine* 3.25–40.

14 To be precise, the lectures were not *written* by Cyril; they were written down by stenographers as Cyril spoke.

15 I shall not reproduce the long discussion about the authorship of the catechetical lectures, but refer to A. J. Doval who has written an authoritative book on the

the pro-catechesis to the catechumens who at the beginning of the Lent had inscribed themselves for baptism which would take place on Easter morning. In this lecture, he admonished the catechumens to be serious about the preparation for baptism and for baptism itself. The candidates should make clear to themselves whether they were ready to undergo baptism and change their lives accordingly. If not, they should leave and return for baptism later when they were ready.[16] Cyril thus tried to rouse the catechumen's expectations to what lay in front of them: On the one hand, he threatened them with the consequences of being unserious, on the other, he lured them with promises about what awaited them if they underwent baptism with seriousness. Those of the inscribed catechumens who decided to continue would then be instructed through a number of catechetical lectures during the forty days of Lent, something which Cyril accomplished mainly by going through the creed paragraph by paragraph.[17] Eighteen of these lectures have been preserved which was probably the number which Cyril gave. Thus, there would not be lectures every day during the Lent.

In addition to the catechetical lectures, the preparation consisted of exorcisms, participation in ordinary services, fasts, etc. During this period of preparation, the baptismal candidates were in a transitory stage between being catechumens and being believers (= those who are baptised). Accordingly, Cyril instructs the candidates not to tell the catechumens (= those who have not yet been inscribed for the intensive period of baptismal preparation) what they will learn during the process of preparation (cf. P 12 and C 1.4). This clearly demonstrates that Cyril considered the period of baptismal preparation as a process of identity change and identity formation. After the preparation, the candidates would be baptised on Easter morning. In the week after their baptism, they would listen to the mystagogical lectures in

---

question: *Cyril of Jerusalem, Mystagoge. The Authorship of the Mystagogic Catecheses*, Washington 2001. As the title indicates, Doval reaches the conclusion that Cyril was the author of the mystagogical lectures. J. Day contests Doval's conclusion and claims that Cyril cannot be the author of these lectures, in *The Baptismal Liturgy of Jerusalem. 4th and 5th Century Evidence in Jerusalem, Egypt and Syria*, Aldershot 2007; and J. Day, 2011. Day's arguments are not convincing, among other things, because she does not realise the importance of the *disciplina arcani* which prohibited Cyril from explaining the full ritual of baptism in his catechetical lectures.

16 Cf. Egeria, *Perigrinatio* 45 concerning the inscription for the Lenten catechumenate.

17 Concerning the development of the Lenten catechumenate, see M.E. Johnson, *From Three Weeks to Forty Days. Baptismal Preparation and the Origin of Lent*, in: StLi 20 (1990), 185–200; id., 2007, 201–218. Johnson provides references to relevant literature.

which Cyril would explain the meaning of the sacraments in which the newly baptised Christians had taken part for the first time on Easter morning.[18]

Augustine's text *(On the catechising of the uninstructed)*[19] was probably written in 399[20] as an answer to an experienced catechist by the name Deogratias from Carthage who was bothered by the feeling that his teaching was often uninspired and even boring. He therefore asked Augustine for advice on improving his catechetical teaching. Augustine responded with different suggestions, for example, the advice that different types of catechumens must be taught in different ways according to their education and preknowledge of Christianity. Hence, Augustine's text is not *per se* a catechetical text, but an instruction in *how* to catechise. Nevertheless, it is an important text for our theme. The text thus tells us two important things about how catechetical instruction was conducted in Augustine's congregation in Hippo Regius and probably also in Carthage where Deogratias taught:

Firstly, we learn from the text that the catechetical instruction was inaugurated by one single meeting between the person who wanted to become a Christian, and a representative (bishop, presbyter, or deacon) from the congregation. It is clear that this first meeting could take the form of a lecture or a dialogue or a combination of these, and it could be either an individual or a collective instruction: Hence, when Augustine speaks of people coming to him asking to be instructed (something which he frequently mentions), he says that the instruction should be adapted to the individual person. This demonstrates that the first catechetical instruction could be individualised. However, he also talks about a group of catechumens so large that they could not all be seated, thus hinting at a collective instruction of the catechumens. The relevant text, *Catechising of the uninstructed*, belongs in the context of the inaugural meeting mentioned above (cf. Harmless, 1995, 150f.). In Hippo Regius, this first instruction of the person who wanted to convert to Christianity ended with both an examination of the candidate's attitude towards the things he had heard, and a decision about whether or not the candidate should be included in the catechumenate (cf. *Catechising of the uninstructed* 26; Harmless, 1995, 150f.).

---

18 For the organisation of the Lenten catechesis, see E. Yarnold, *Cyril of Jerusalem*, London 2000, 33–39.

19 See W. Harmless, *Augustine and the Catechumenate*, Collegeville 1995, 107–155, for an interesting reading of *Catechising of the uninstructed* from a rhetorical perspective.

20 The dating of *De catechizandis rudubus* has also been disputed. L.J. van der Lof has collected the evidence and discussed it together with previous research in: L.J. van der Lof, *The Date of Catechising of the Uninstructed*, in VigChr 16 (1962), 198–204. Van der Lof reaches the conclusion that *De catechizandibus rudibus* was written in 399 and not in 405 as claimed by earlier researchers.

Secondly, the text reveals the basic structure and content of the first cat-echising in Augustine's congregation: The catechumens were told a story about God and the world, beginning with the creation (Genesis 1), mentioning the role of Augustine's own congregation in this story, and pointing to the future fulfilment where the good and bad people will receive their deserved reward or punishment. The catechumens were thus included in a new narrative which aimed at defining their future identity. Below, I will return to the implications of this in regard to the identity formation of the catechumens. But here it will suffice to note that this way of introducing the catechumens to Christian life and beliefs is very different from explaining the creed paragraph by paragraph as we saw it in the case of Cyril.

On the background of *Catechising of the uninstructed,* it is difficult to determine how the catechumenate itself was organised in Hippo Regius. Unfortunately, Augustine did not provide a manual for the organisation and content of the catechumenate which followed the first session of in-struction. A good reason for this may be that such a tightly organised cat-echumenate did not exist in Hippo Regius or in the rest of North Africa. Nevertheless, scattered remarks about the teaching of catechumens can be found in many of Augustine's other writings, e.g., in his sermons given during the Lent and Easter. From such remarks, it can be concluded that there was a forty day Lenten catechumenate before the main date of bap-tism on Easter morning. During this period, the catechumens, who now were called *competentes,*[21] fasted, were exorcised, listened to the readings and the sermons in the ordinary services, and participated in the ceremony of *traditio* and *redditio symboli* which designates the ceremony where the creed was read and commented on for the *competentes* in order to be learned by heart by them. After a week, the *competentes* should be able to recite the creed in public giving it back to the bishop and the congregation (cf. *Sermo* 212–216). It is difficult to assess whether there were additional special sessions of teaching. I leave the question open here because the organisation of the catechumenate is not the main interest of this article. However, I found it valuable to mention its basic outline in order to under-stand the context of the catechesis.[22]

---

21 For this term, see *Sermo* 216.1; Harmless, 1995, 156. The numbers of Augus-tine's sermons follow J.-P. Migne, *Patrologia Latina* 38, Paris 1841.
22 Concerning the organisation of the catechumenate in Hippo Regius, see the de-scriptions in Harmless, 1995, 156–193, and E. Ferguson, *Baptism in the Early Church. History, Theology, and Liturgy in the First Five Centuries,* Grand Rap-ids 2009, 778–784.

Identity formation through catechetical instruction

Below, I will demonstrate that the bishops and deacons, who instructed the catechumens about to be baptised, clearly wanted to bring about a transformation of the identity of the individual catechumens and thereby to integrate them in the collective identity of the local and universal Christian community.

Tutoring Deogratias on how to instruct the catechumens at the first meeting and what to tell them, Augustine says that Deogratias should teach the catechumens the whole story from Gen 1 to the present time of the church. In telling this story, Deogratias should concentrate on its cardinal points. Augustine then continues:

> In this way, not only are the points which we desire most to emphasise brought into greater prominence by keeping the others in the background, but also he whose interest we are anxious to stimulate by the narration does not reach them with a mind already exhausted, and we avoid confusing the memory of him whom we ought to instruct by our teaching.[23]

The quote clearly shows that Augustine wants Deogratias to focus on the outcome of the instruction. Thus, the instruction should stimulate the person about to convert in order to keep his interest for Christianity. The aim is to transform the identity of the listener or listeners.

Cyril's text differs from Augustine's in that Cyril speaks directly to the catechumens. Therefore, his calls to identity transformation are more explicit than what we see in *Catechising of the uninstructed*. Cyril opens his introductory lecture to the baptismal candidates by describing their present situation as being between two different identities, or as being about to leave one identity and enter into a new identity. I quote:

> Already, my dear candidates for Enlightenment, scents of paradise are wafted towards you; already you are culling mystic blossoms for the weaving of heavenly garlands; already the fragrance of the Holy Spirit has blown about you. Already you have arrived at the outer court of the palace: may the King lead you in! Now the blossom has appeared on the trees; God grant the fruit be duly harvested! Now you have enlisted; you have been called to the Colours. You have walked in procession with the tapers of brides in your hands and the desire of heavenly citizenship in your hearts; with a holy resolve also, and

---

23 *Ita et illa quae maxime commendari volumus, aliorum submissione magis eminent; nec ad ea fatigatus pervenit, quem narrando volumus excitare; nec illius memoria confunditur, quem docendo debemus instruere* (*Catechising of the uninstructed* 3.5). The text is quoted after *Aurelius Augustinus. The First Catechetical Instruction*, translated and annotated by J.P. Christopher, *Ancient Christian Writers*, vol. 2, Westminster 1946.

the confident hope which that brings in its train. For He is no liar who said: 'For those who love Him, God makes all things conspire to good.' Yes, God is generous and kind; nevertheless He requires in every man a resolve that is true. That is why the Apostle adds: 'For those who are called in accordance with a resolve.' It is the sincerity of your resolution that makes you "called". It is of no use your body being here if your thoughts and heart are elsewhere.[24]

Rhetorically, the passage repeatedly uses the word "already". The baptismal candidates, to whom he speaks, *already* have a scent of blessings around them; they are *already* gathering spiritual flowers; they are *already* waiting outside the Kings palace, etc. Thus, they are at the border of something new, but they are not yet there. Much good is waiting for them in this new condition, but they have not yet reached it. God is willing to let them in, but they have to make the final decision themselves. It is not enough that the baptismal candidates attend the teaching physically, they must also make a mental decision about changing their identity. Cyril thus describes his audience as being ot the edge of a new identity. Even if Cyril describes how the Holy Spirit and God himself brings about the new condition, he makes it clear that the baptismal candidates themselves must take the final step into the new reality provided by God through the church. This was probably an efficient way to put the baptismal candidates under pressure: They must be active in the spiritual and moral transformation which is about to take place.

This involving strategy is made even clearer later on in the lectures where Cyril either threatens his audience to be wholehearted and do as they are told, or makes promises to them if they follow his advice. For example, he warns against taking part in the baptismal preparations out of curiosity

---

24 Ἤδη μακαριότητος ὀσμὴ πρὸς ὑμᾶς, ὦ ΦΩΤΙΖΟΜΕΝΟΙ, ἤδη τὰ νοητὰ ἄνθη συλλέγετε πρὸς πλοκὴν ἐπουρανίων στεφάνων· ἤδη τοῦ Πνεύματος τοῦ ἁγίου ἔπνευσεν ἡ εὐωδία. Ἤδη περὶ τὸ προαύλιον τῶν βασιλείων γεγόνατε· γένοιτο δὲ καὶ ὑπὸ τοῦ βασιλέως εἰσαχθῆτε. Ἄνθη γὰρ νῦν ἐφάνη τῶν δένδρων· γένοιτο δὲ ἵνα καὶ ὁ καρπὸς τέλειος ᾖ. Ὀνοματογραφία τέως ὑμῖν γέγονε, καὶ στρατείας κλῆσις· καὶ νυμφαγωγίας λαμπάδες, καὶ οὐρανίου πολιτείας ἐπιθυμία, καὶ πρόθεσις ἀγαθὴ, καὶ ἐλπὶς ἐπακολουθοῦσα· ἀψευδὴς γὰρ ὁ εἰπὼν, ὅτι τοῖς ἀγαπῶσι τὸν Θεὸν πάντα συνεργεῖ εἰς τὸ ἀγαθόν. Ὁ μὲν γὰρ Θεὸς δαψιλής ἐστιν εἰς εὐεργεσίαν· περιμένει δὲ ἑκάστου τὴν γνησίαν προαίρεσιν. Διὰ τοῦτο ἐπήγαγεν ὁ Ἀπόστολος λέγων, τοῖς κατὰ πρόθεσιν κλητοῖς οὖσιν· ἡ πρόθεσις γνησία οὖσα, κλητόν σε ποιεῖ· κἂν γὰρ τὸ σῶμα ὧδε ἔχῃς, τὴν δὲ διάνοιαν μὴ ἔχῃς, οὐδὲν ὠφελῇ (P 1). The English texts, here and below, are quoted from *The Works of St Cyril from Jerusalem*, vol. 1–2 (translated by L.P. McCauley / A.A. Stephenson), Washington 1969. The Greek text of the *Catechetical lectures* is quoted from W.C. Reischl / J. Rupp, *Cyrilli Hierosolymorum archiepiscopi opera quae supersunt omnia*, 2 vols., Munich 1848/1860. The text just cited is from vol. 1, 1–26.

without having made a proper decision about full involvement (P 2). After this warning against taking part in the catechetical training without having made an earnest decision, Cyril refers to the New Testament story about the man who took part in a wedding party without having prepared himself by dressing properly (Matt 22:1–14). This man had a poor destiny outside in the darkness. According to Cyril, the same will happen to those who take part in the baptismal preparation without having made an earnest decision about transforming his life (P 3).

Even if the baptismal candidates are earnest and serious about their participation in the preparation for baptism, there are still threats against them. The Devil is always on his watch to lead them astray:

> But a dragon lies in ambush for the traveller; take care he does not bite you and inject his poison of unbelief. Seeing this numerous company winning salvation, he selects and stalks his prey. In your journey to the Father of souls, your way lies past that dragon. How shall you pass him? You must have 'your feet stoutly shod with the gospel of peace,' so that, even if he does bite you, he may not hurt you. With Hope invincible for your sandals and with Faith the guest of your heart, you may pass through the enemy's lines and enter into the house of the Lord.[25]

Cyril thus warns his audience that their new Christian identity does not come easy. Even if they are close to the goal – baptism, they must be on the watch against themselves and against evil powers who want to disturb the process. If they succeed, they will get a new identity through baptism, an identity which Cyril characterises with many positive words. If they do not succeed, they will miss the goal; nothing will change and they will get no reward. Cyril even warns his audience that their struggle will not end with baptism, for even when they have been transformed through baptism, they can still fall away from the goal. This will be even worse than if they choose not to be baptised. They can only receive baptism once, and if they fall away from God and the church after baptism, things cannot be set right again (P 7). If they are not sure that they are able to go through the transformation of identity in baptism, it is better not to begin the preparation, but wait until later.

---

25 Ἀλλὰ δϱάκων παϱὰ τὴν ὁδὸν τηϱεῖ τοὺς πεϱιπατοῦντας. βλέπε μὴ δάκῃ τῇ ἀπιστίᾳ. Βλέπει τοσούτους σῳζομένους, καὶ ζητεῖ τίνα καταπίῃ. Πϱὸς Πατέϱα πνευμάτων εἰσέϱχῃ, ἀλλὰ δι' ἐκείνου τοῦ δϱάκοντος διέϱχῃ· πῶς οὖν αὐτὸν διέλθῃς; Ὑπόδησαι τοὺς πόδας ἐν ἑτοιμασίᾳ τοῦ εὐαγγελίου τῆς εἰϱήνης· ἵνα κἂν δάκῃ, μὴ βλάπτῃ· πίστιν ἔνοικον ἔχε, κϱαταιὰν ἐλπίδα, κϱηπίδα ἰσχυϱάν, ἵνα διέλθῃς τὸν ἐχθϱὸν, καὶ εἰσέλθῃς πϱὸς τὸν δεσπότην (P 16).

Moral and doctrinal identity formation

The preparation for baptism focused on these two areas of identity, morality and doctrines. To be baptised, the baptismal candidates had to know about Christian morality and live accordingly; and they had to know what the right beliefs were and think accordingly:

> True religion consists of these two elements: pious doctrines and virtuous actions. Neither does God accept doctrines apart from good works, nor are works, when divorced from godly doctrine, accepted by God. What does it profit a man to be an expert theologian if he is a shameless fornicator; or to be nobly temperate, but an impious blasphemer?[26]

As will be made clear below, Augustine (in *Catechising of the uninstructed* and in some of his sermons related to preparation for baptism) also insists that there must be a clear connection between doctrinal and moral instruction of the catechumens and *competentes*. The clearest statements about this are, however, found in his text entitled *Faith and works* in which he responds to the suggestions of some laymen who had questioned the moral instructions of catechumens and *competentes*. They had claimed that moral instructions should wait until after baptism in order to avoid that a too strong focus on the moral identity of the catechumens would keep people away from baptism. Augustine's answer to this was that moral instructions had to be part of the baptismal instruction because the *competentes* must put off the old man before they can put on the new:

> If this is not the time to teach them morals that are worthy of a Christian and of this great sacrament which they are so desirous of receiving, then when is it? This is what our opponents would like. In that case, they would allow them to receive baptism without first demanding that they change their evil way of life, without demanding that they first put off the old man and then put on the new. Instead, they would advise just the opposite: first put on the new man, and after you have put on the new man, then put off the old. But that is not what the Apostle says. He says: 'Put off the old man and put on the new' (Col 3:9–10). And the Lord says: 'No man sews a new piece to an old garment and no man puts new wine into old wineskins' (Matt 9:16–17). Moreover, for what other reason do we call them catechumens and put them into this category for a certain time, except that

---

26 Ὁ γὰρ τῆς θεοσεβείας τρόπος ἐκ δύο τούτων συνέστηκε, δογμάτων εὐσεβῶν, καὶ πράξεων ἀγαθῶν. Καὶ οὔτε τὰ δόγματα, χωρὶς ἔργων ἀγαθῶν εὐπρόσδεκτα τῷ Θεῷ· οὔτε τὰ μὴ μετ' εὐσεβῶν δογμάτων ἔργα τελούμενα, προσδέχεται ὁ Θεός. Τί γὰρ ὄφελος, εἰδέναι μὲν τὰ περὶ Θεοῦ δόγματα καλῶς, καὶ πορνεύειν αἰσχρῶς; τί δ' αὖ πάλιν ὄφελος σωφρονεῖν μὲν καλῶς, καὶ βλασφημεῖν ἀσεβῶς (C 4.2). The Greek text is quoted from Reischl / Rupp, 1848/1860, vol. 1, 28–320; vol. 2, 2–342.

they might learn what the faith is and what kind of life is demanded of a Christian?[27]

Augustine and Cyril thus agreed that doctrine and morals had to be taught together to those who were about to be baptised.

Doctrinal identity formation

I will begin this section by jumping backwards in time to Irenaeus of Lyon (2nd century). In his conflict with the Valentinian Gnostics, Irenaeus claimed that there is only one church which is disseminated all over the world, in Spain, Gaul, Germany, Egypt, Libya, etc. This one church with its many branches shares the same beliefs which Irenaeus finds expressed in the *regula veritatis*. This church is one "as if it lived in one house and had one soul, one heart, and one mouth" (haer. 1.10.1–2). It is almost certain that Irenaeus borrowed his version of the *regula veritatis* from a catechetical setting, probably his own congregation in Lyon. Irenaeus thus reveals an ideology in which people who join the Christian community via baptism and prepare through catechetical instruction enter a worldwide community or group with a strong doctrinal identity or "sameness". Members of this community can be identified through the creed which they have learned by heart as part of their catechetical training. Further, they can use this creed to identify themselves or others in cases where their own or other people's relations to the group are blurred or doubtful.[28] It is obvious that Irenaeus' claims are highly ideological. There was no such total doctrinal "sameness" by the end of the second century – Irenaeus' struggle with the Valentinians is a clear indication of this. Irenaeus was, however, undoubtedly convinced that many Christian communities around the world shared the same basic

---

27 *Si tunc tempus non est discendi, quae vita congruat tanto, quod accipere desider-ant, sacramento; quando erit? An vero cum acceperint, in tantis criminibus per-manentes etiam post baptismum, non novi homines, sed rei veteres? ut videlicet perversitate mirabili prius eis dicatur, Induite hominem novum; et cum induti fuerint, postea dicatur, exuite veterem: cum apostolus sanum ordinem tenens dicat, exuite veterem, et induite novum* (Col 3:9–10); *et ipse Dominus clamet, nemo assuit pannum novum vestimento veteri, et nemo mittit vinum novum in utres veteres* (Matt 9:16–17). *Quid autem aliud agit totum tempus, quo catechu-menorum locum et nomen tenent, nisi ut audiant quae fides et qualis vita debeat esse christiani (Faith and Works* 6.9). The English text is quoted after *St. Augus-tine on Faith and Works*, translated and annotated by G.J. Lombardo, *Ancient Christian Writers* 48, New York 1988. See also W. Harmless, 1995, 245–250. The Latin text is quoted from J.-P. Migne, *Patrologia Latina* 40, Turnhout ²1956, col. 202.

28 Cf. Rebillard in this volume on other Christian identity markers.

beliefs as those expressed in his *regula veritatis*. His own voyages around the Mediterranean from Asia Minor to Lyon and his communication with other Christian communities, e.g., about the conflict on the time of Easter celebration, have probably convinced him about this. The people and communities who did not share these beliefs were, in his opinion, not Christians at all. According to Irenaeus, catechetical education thus aims at establishing doctrinal identity among Christians in the individual communities and among the Christian communities.

This early ideal about doctrinal coherence was developed by later theologians such as Cyril and Augustine who also claimed that baptismal catechesis aimed at creating doctrinal identity among Christians. These later catechists focused their doctrinal teaching on central elements in the Christian belief systems.

Already in the *Pro-catechesis* (10–11), Cyril introduces the doctrinal aspect of his catechetical instruction. First, he advises those inscribed for baptism not to be tired and to lack attention even if the bishop will speak too long. The candidates will need the doctrinal teaching, with which they will be provided, because it is their weapon against Greeks, heretics, Jews, and Samaritans who will attack their faith when they are baptised (P 10, cf. also C 4.2). One minor issue is the ordinary sermons; if a catechumen misses one of these, he can pick up later on the points he has missed. The catechetical lectures are different. They are given once and if the candidates miss any of them, the result is like when trees are planted in a wrong season or in a wrong way. The result will be bad, and it cannot be changed. The catechetical lectures are provided in a certain sequence and none of them can be missed – hence, the catechetical instruction is like building a house. The individual stones (= doctrinal elements) must be placed in the building in the correct order, and the corners must be even.[29] Every part of the building must be in its place and be fitted properly with other elements (P 11). Cyril thus explains to the candidates that Christian doctrine is a coherent system where all elements are necessary.

Cyril spends the first three catechetical lectures on introductory matters, such as describing the transitory process which the inscribed catechumens now have begun (C 1); the necessity of repentance from the old way of life (C 2); and a first introduction to what baptism is – still without revealing the ritual and the deeper theological meaning of baptism. This must be hidden from the candidates until after their baptism (C 3). In lecture four, Cyril then opens the doctrinal teaching which will occupy the rest of the catechetical lectures (4–18). In the fourth lecture, he presents a summary of the Christian

---

29 See the contribution by Abate in this volume for the Jews' relative lack of concern with the precise conversion process.

doctrines which the candidates must learn during the Lent. According to Cyril, it is appropriate for the candidates to get such an overview of the doctrines before he begins teaching them in details, since this will make it easier to understand and remember the doctrinal details with which they will be presented during the forty days of Lent. The heading of the lecture claims that ten points of doctrine will be presented in the summary. It is, to be sure, difficult to see from the texts exactly what these ten items are, and how they are counted, but this makes no difference for our purpose. In the summary, Cyril mentions the following themes: God who is one, creator, and the father of Christ; Christ who is the only Son of God the Father, born by a virgin, who died on the cross, was buried, rose from the dead and ascended to heaven, and who will be the future judge of mankind; the Holy Spirit who is also one and part of the Trinity. After these main themes of doctrine, Cyril goes on to explain what the candidates should believe about human beings (namely that they are created by God with body and soul); how Christians should think about consumption of meat; about dressing; about the resurrection of human beings; and finally about what the candidates should believe about the Bible. This fourth lecture is long and quite concentrated, so it must have been one of the days where the catechumens probably have strived not to be tired and unconcentrated.

In the next lecture (5), Cyril speaks about faith. This lecture ends by the *traditio symboli* where Cyril would pass on the creed to the candidates by quoting it line by line. But before doing so, Cyril instructs the candidates about the nature of Christian faith. He obviously follows Paul in pointing to Abraham as the father of faith, but he also gives other examples, such as Mary's faith which was so strong that it could raise Lazarus from the dead (cf. John 11:14–44). After this, Cyril explains that faith has two aspects: one is the faith in Christian doctrines, i.e., that they are true; the other aspect is the faith which is given by Christ to the Christians and which enables them to do and experience things which are above normal human abilities. Having explained faith in this way, Cyril quotes the creed and thereby hands it over to the catechumens. This would have been the first time that the candidates heard the creed in its entirety. Finally, Cyril instructs his audience to learn it by heart and not to write it down. In the following lectures (6–18), Cyril explain the elements of the creed in detail giving one lecture on the God the Father, another on Christ, etc. Having undergone this doctrinal instruction, the baptismal candidates were ready for baptism on Easter morning.

In his *Catechising of the uninstructed*, Augustine focuses his teaching on the narration of the biblical history of salvation from the creation from the beginning to the end of history – including the history of the church until his own time and with a strong emphasis on the eschatological fulfilment. This does not mean that all details of the Bible should be presented, but focus should be on the most important aspects of the history of salvation (cf. *Catechising of the uninstructed* 3–4). Within this framework, Augustine explains the most central elements in Christian dogma. In chapter 3–4, he summarises the whole story by saying that the entire history before the birth of Christ points to his birth and to the church which follows after Christ as his body (3), and that the reason for Christ's birth and for the existence of the church is that God may show us his love (4). Having spent much space on instructing Deogratias how to teach different types of catechumens and other pedagogical matters, Augustine begins, in chapter 18, to give an example of how the history of salvation could be explained to a person asking to be accepted as catechumen. He begins by telling of the almighty God and his creation of the world and human beings; how sin came into the world by the first people's use of their free will; how sin and righteousness will exist together in this world and in the church until the end of the history where God will separate good and evil; how the Israelites were held captive in Egypt and were liberated by Moses and walked through the Red Sea and the desert, how they were later held captive in Babylon and were liberated from there, and how these events should be understood as prefiguring the people's bondage in sin and liberation by Christ (*Catechising of the uninstructed* 18–21). Further, he explains how the history of the world can be divided into six ages (22) and what the mission of the Holy Spirit is (23). Finally, he explains that discipline must be kept because the church is a mixed community consisting of believers and of heretics (24), urging the listeners to be steady in the faith described, not least in the belief in resurrection (25).

Augustine thus suggests to Deogratias that he should retell the biblical story of creation and salvation and thereby include the listeners in the world and the truth of this story. In this way, the identity of the listeners should be changed, and they should be moved from the group of unbelievers to the group of believers – it almost seems as if Augustine had studied modern narrative theories. But is it to be imagined that such story-telling could change the identity of people? Augustine realised that catechumens had many different motives for asking for education and baptism – some good, others bad. If somebody had been scared by the threats of God's future punishments, he was well-prepared for conversion and teaching because he fears what will happen if he does not adhere to the teaching of the church (*Catechising of the uninstructed* 6–7). If somebody, on the other hand, just wanted to please somebody else, this person would probably not be so stable in his belief even if he might change when listening to the teaching (7). Further, not everybody who participates in the catechetical teaching and becomes baptised will believe and live as Christians, according to Augustine. Many catechumens and baptised people would still take part in pagan cults and feasts. Some of them would, at some point in time, repent and abstain from pagan or heretic practices, but others would not. The former would be saved, but the latter would be judged to eternal damnation even if they were baptised. Accordingly, the church is a community with a blurred identity consisting of people who in some cases have multiple religious identities.

The *Catechising of the uninstructed* deals with the initial instruction of persons who wanted to become catechumens. I also briefly described the little we know about the procedures for catechising catechumens and the so-called *competentes*. It is, however, clear from some of Augustine's Lenten-sermons that the congregation in Hippo Regius also practiced the *traditio* and *redditio symboli* which means that during the Lent, the bishop gave the creed to the *competentes* by quoting the elements of the creed and commenting on each of them. After a week, the *competentes* should give the creed back to the bishop, meaning that the *competentes* should have learned it by heart and be able to quote it in front of the bishop and the congregation. An example of this can be found in Augustine's sermon 212 where he presents a summary of the creed and comments on it. He ends the sermon by saying that after baptism, the candidates will begin to love what they believe, and that this will make faith work in the baptised so they please God. This means that the elements of the creed which the *competentes* learn by heart before they are baptised will be active in love after their baptism. Hence, the instruction is the beginning of an identity change which will continue after baptism. The sermons (205–211) which Augustine gave at the beginning of Lent show that the works of love ignited by the creed and the baptism will not be perfect. In these sermons, he thus urges his audience to take the period of Lent as an opportunity to grow in love towards their neighbour.

In sermon 213 (which is also connected to the *traditio symboli*), Augustine again summarises and comments on all elements in the creed, but now he focuses specifically on the concept of the church. He claims that his audience constitutes the church – not alone, but together with all Christians all over the world who belong to the Catholic Church. This means that the *competentes* – whom Augustine focuses on in this context – are told that they will be transferred into a worldwide community of Christians who all confess the same belief when they have received baptism. Further, the members of this church are members of Christ, they are his body. Hence, the *competentes* are on the verge of receiving a new identity (*Sermo* 213.7). It is thus clear that even if there was no fixed system of dogmatic teaching of the catechumens in Augustine's congregation, they were instructed through participation in the services – most concretely in the praxis of *traditio* and *redditio symboli*.[30]

---

30 Cf. W. Harmless, 1995, 274–286. Just as all genuine Christians, according to
    Augustine, shared a common belief expressed in the creed, so they also shared a

Moral identity formation

In his *Pro-catechesis*, Cyril introduces the moral as well as the doctrinal aspects of his catechesis. Regarding the moral aspect, he writes:

> From today, cease from every evil deed; let not your tongue speak unholy words, nor your eye commit evil or rove after vanities. Let your feet take you swiftly to the catechetical instructions. Submit to the exorcisms devoutly. Whether you are breathed upon or exorcised, the act spells salvation. Imagine virgin gold alloyed with various foreign substances: copper, tin, iron, lead. What we are after is the gold alone; and gold cannot be purified of its dross without fire. Similarly, the soul cannot be purified without exorcisms, exorcisms which, since they are culled from the divine Scriptures, possess divine power.[31]

It is clear that preparation for baptism includes a moral purification according to Cyril. This purification takes the form of institutionalised exorcisms which is part of the preparation for baptism, but Cyril also speaks more generally about conversion as a necessary precondition for baptism. In this connection, he thinks of conversion as a conversion from the old way of life and not so much as conversion from pagan or heretical doctrines. In *Pro-catechesis* 4, he rhetorically asks the inscribed candidates whether anyone had prohibited their inscription because of their (bad) morals. The answer is no because the candidates were accepted for preparation even if their moral condition were problematic. Thus, after the inscription the candidates have forty days to convert from their former lifestyle and thus improving their moral standards.

After these introductory remarks, Cyril spends the second catechetical lecture on the themes *confession of sin* and *conversion to a new life*. Cyril often describes sin by mentioning a few concrete acts like adultery, fornication, and murder. These examples are key-words including all kinds of immoral acts. According to Cyril, sin is thus, basically, immoral acts. Further, sin is

---

common prayer, the Lord's Prayer, which invested them with a common language that they should use when they approached God. Learning the Lord's Prayer was also part of the curriculum for *competentes* in Augustine's congregation, cf. *Sermo* 56–59 and Harmless, 1995, 286–293.

31 Ἀργησον ἀπὸ τῆς σήμερον ἀπὸ παντὸς φαύλου πράγματος· μή σου λαλησάτω ἡ γλῶσσα ἄσεμνα ῥήματα· μή σου τὸ βλέμμα ἁμαρτανέτω, μηδὲ ῥεμβέσθω τὰ μὴ χρήσιμα. Οἱ δὲ πόδες σου εἰς τὰς κατηχήσεις σπευδέτωσαν. Τοὺς ἐπορκισμοὺς δέχου μετὰ σπουδῆς· κἂν ἐμφυσηθῇς, κἂν ἐπορκισθῇς, σωτηρία σοι τὸ πρᾶγμα. Νόμισον εἶναι ἀργὸν χρυσὸν, καὶ δεδολωμένον, ποικίλαις ὕλαις ἀναμεμιγμένον, χαλκῷ, καὶ κασσιτέρῳ, καὶ σιδήρῳ, καὶ μολύβδῳ· ζητοῦμεν τὸν χρυσὸν μόνον ἔχειν· χρυσὸς μὴ δύναται ἄνευ πυρὸς καθαρθῆναι τὰ ἀνοίκεια·οὕτως ἄνευ ἐπορκισμῶν οὐ δύναται καθαρθῆναι ψυχή· εἰσὶ δὲ θεῖοι, ἐκ θείων γραφῶν συνειλεγμένοι (P 8–9).

something which people choose themselves. People are endowed with a free will and can therefore choose to sin or not to sin. Cyril admits that it often is the Devil – a fallen created being – who implants ideas of sin into people's souls. But the Devil cannot make people do anything that they do not accept with their free will. Nobody can be forced to sin. People are therefore responsible for their own sins, and they will be punished for their sins at the final judgment. This threat about eternal punishment is a main theme in Cyril's moral teaching; it is considered by him to be the main reason why people chose to be baptised. However, when sin is a consequence of people's freely chosen immoral acts, it is also possible for people to repent and stop sinning. The baptismal candidates must undergo such a moral conversion during the forty days of preparation. Having done so, God in his mercy will forgive previous sinners through baptism, but afterwards the baptised Christian must avoid sinning. Cyril lists a number of examples of the huge sins that God has forgiven. If God can forgive Adam, Noah, and others, he can and will also forgive the baptismal candidates who are marked by trivial sins like fornication or theft. And further, if mighty, proud, and powerful people like, for example, King David were not too proud to repent in public, then nor should Cyril's audience be too proud to confess their sins and repent. Conversion, confessions of sins, and exorcisms were thus an important part of the preparation for baptism, also in the last intense period of forty days in the Lent.

In *Catechising of the uninstructed*, Augustine does not spend much time on moral education. He mainly writes about doctrinal matters. However, a few times he indicates that the catechetical instruction should also include moral matters. In chapter 7, he simply says, in passing, that the precepts of a Christian life should briefly be presented to the catechumens – although with the necessary details in order to avoid that the catechumens will be led astray by immoral people in the church, such as drunkards, adulterers, fornicators, participators in public spectacles, etc. The newcomers to the church should know enough about a Christian moral life to avoid the conclusion that being a Christian can be combined with these immoralities. For since the church, according to Augustine, was filled with people practicing these amoralities and even claiming that such a manner of life could be combined with being a Christian, the new members of the Christian communities risked coming to the same conclusion if they were not warned. Augustine continues the moral exhortations in chapter 16 where such instructions are included in the advice which he presents to Deogratias. He warns against the troubles deriving from wealth mentioning the brevity of this and other pleasures such as honour, theatrical shows, races, etc. Such things might lead to short-termed worldly pleasures, but they also result in a bad conscience. It is therefore better to avoid such pleasures and, in turn, have a good conscience. Being a

Christian gives no temporal advantages, but eternal salvation. In the treatise called *Faith and works* (6.9; 7.11; 27.49), Augustine also maintains that the instruction of the catechumens must include teaching on both moral and dogmatic aspects of Christianity (cf. above and Ferguson, 2009, 781f.). The correct belief must result in love toward one's neighbour. Moral themes are also very often prominent in Augustine's sermons to which both catechumens and *competentes* have listened.

Conclusions

The reading above of Cyril's and Augustine's treatises, lectures, and sermons has shown that according to these two theologians, the catechetical instruction of people before their baptism aimed at bringing about a transformation of their identity – in the strong meaning of the concept. They should change their way of life as well as their beliefs. Does this mean that the catechists should assist the baptismal candidates in constructing a new identity? Yes, from one point of view, the candidates should abandon their old identity and create a new. They should put off the old man and put on a new man. However, seen from another point of view, the new identity could and should not be a totally new construct. It must always build on a basic kernel – the createdness of all human beings. The idea of God as creator and people as created beings is to both Cyril and Augustine an important part of Christian doctrine. This is what constitutes humanity, according to these two and many other early Christian theologians. To put off the old man means to remove everything that disturbs the humanity of people. To put on the new man means to (re-)build the humanity of people. Thus, according to Cyril and Augustine, catechetical identity formation is not pure construction, but reconstruction and development of the created humanity in people.

It is also clear from what we have seen above that the pre-baptismal instruction of catechumens aimed at introducing and socialising them into a group or community with a certain and quite well-defined moral and dogmatic identity. There might be many differences between different local Christian communities and between Christian communities in different periods of time. But it is quite clear that both Augustine and Cyril considered themselves and their congregations to be part of a worldwide Christian community which shared certain beliefs and moral standards. This can be seen, for instance, in the creedal formulations they use in their teaching, in their many references to biblical texts as the basis for their teaching, in their shared moral values, etc.

Naturally, it can be discussed how successful Cyril, Augustine, and their fellow Christian teachers were in this endeavour. It is clear from the warnings, which they so often formulate against being loose and neglecting in doctrinal and moral matters, that the identity formation was not always successful. Many of the baptised Christians were apparently stuck in their old habits and beliefs. This, however, does not mean that the baptismal candidates were stuck in their old identity, whatever it might have been, or that they only got one more additional identity to their collection of multiple identities when they became Christians. Being instructed and baptised inferred a new identity on the baptised Christians. When the baptised Christians fell back in their old habits this was not considered as a transient switch to another parallel identity, but as falling away from their new identity as Christians. Their new identity as Christians was still their identity against which their lives were measured by themselves and by their fellow Christians. Baptismal catechesis is thus all about identity formation.

Per Bilde

The Role of Religious Education in six of the Pagan Religions of the Hellenistic-Roman Period[1]

Abstract: Bilde examines the sources from Orphism, the mysteries in Eleusis, the cult of Bacchus, Cybele (and Atargatis), Isis, and Mithras which illustrate the existence of pagan education. Although nothing identical to the elaborated Christian catechumenate has been preserved in the remaining sources, Bilde demonstrates that religious education was not unique to Christianity.

1. Purpose, background, focus, issue, and sources

The purpose of this essay is to carry out an examination of the possible existence of some sort of religious education in six of the pagan religions in the Hellenistic-Roman period – Orphism, the mysteries in Eleusis and of Bacchus, Cybele (and Atargatis), Isis, and Mithras.

The immediate background of this project is the obvious existence in early Christianity of the institution of the catechumenate that was established during the first 300 years of Christian history.[2] In the present essay, however,

---

1 Unfortunately, I was unable to take part in the conference where the essays in the present volume originally were presented, but before the conference, I sent the first version of my essay to all the participants. After the conference, some of the participants have been so kind to send me their critical remarks and suggested supplements to the first version, and here I wish to thank Luther H. Martin and Tobias Georges for their proposals. I would also like warmly to thank the anonymous peer reviewer for his/her fruitful suggestions. In particular, however, I want to thank the editor of the present volume, Birgitte Bøgh, who has invested a lot of time and energy in order to help me extend the religio-historical material underlying my paper. Finally, I wish to express my gratitude to prof. Tom Tregenza, University of Exeter, who has helped me to correct my English. The original version of this essay also included studies of religious education in early Judaism and Christianity. When the revised version of this text proved to be much too long, I had to cut out these two religions.

2 Cf. T.M. Finn, *Early Christian Baptism and the Catechumenate*, Collegeville 1992, esp. 3–7; J. Daniélou, *La catéchese dans la tradition patristique*, in: E. Ferguson (ed.), *Conversion, Catechumenate, and Baptism in the Early Church*, New York 1993, 279–292; L.D. Folkemer, *A Study of the Catechumenate*, in:

I intend to focus on the six pagan religions mentioned above: Did conversion and initiation into these religions include some sort of religious education which can be compared with the Christian catechumenate?

The general context of my project is the old discussion about the relationship between early Christianity and the contemporary pagan religions, in particular the so-called mystery religions.[3] The core of this problem seems to me to be the issue of the originality of Christianity: Did this religion present anything absolutely new?[4] How much Judaism did it include, and what are, more precisely, the similarities and differences between early Christianity and the pagan Hellenistic-Roman religions? This broader issue can, for example, be examined in relation to studies of the Christian sacraments,[5] of the problem of conversion to Christianity,[6] of the question of the Christian community and organisation,[7] and so forth. It is in this presupposed context that I turn my eyes towards the question of religious education in relation to conversion and initiation.

As far as I know, this subject has never been studied thoroughly, at least not in the form of dissertations or other scholarly in-depth studies focusing on this problem.[8] Among recent scholars who have actually discussed this

---

Ferguson (ed.), 1993, 244–265; A. Tuck, *Aux origins du chatéchuménat*, in: Ferguson (ed.), 1993, 266–277; E.J. Yarnold, *The Awe-Inspiring Rites of Initiation*, Collegeville 1994. Cf. in particular Jacobsen in this volume.

3 Cf., e.g., the discussions in A.D. Nock, *Early Gentile Christianity and Its Hellenistic Background*, New York 1964, 109–145; M.P. Nilsson, *Geschichte der griechischen Religion*, vol. 2 (*Die hellenistische und römische Zeit*), Munich1961, 679–701; W. Burkert, *Ancient Mystery Cults*, Cambridge 1987, esp. 3. 28f. 43-53. 66–88. 101; L.H. Martin, *Hellenistic Religions*, New York 1987, 118–126; J.Z. Smith, *Drudgery Divine*, London 1990; R. Beck, *The Religion of the Mithras Cult in the Roman Empire*, Oxford 2006, 41–64; L.T. Johnson, *Among the Gentiles. Greco-Roman Religion and Christianity*, New Haven 2009, esp. 1–14; H. Bowden, *Mystery Cults in the Ancient World*, London 2010, 24. 209f. 213. Unfortunately, this subject, which was eagerly discussed in the so-called Religio-Historical School, has been neglected in recent research, cf., e.g., R. von Haeling (ed.), *Griechische Mythologie und Christentum*, Darmstadt 2005; R. Stark, *The Triumph of Christianity*, New York 2011.

4 Cf. P. Bilde, *The Originality of Jesus. A Critical Discussion and a Comparative Attempt*, Göttingen 2013.

5 Cf. Nock, 1964.

6 Cf. A.D. Nock, *Conversion*, London 1933.

7 Cf., e.g., Ph. Harland, *Associations, Synagogues and Congregations*, Minneapolis 2003.

8 In most textbooks on and general presentations of the Hellenistic-Roman religions, including or excluding Christianity and Judaism, this subject is regrettably neglected, cf., e.g., J. Ferguson, *The Religions of the Roman Empire*, London ²1982; R. Turcan, *The Cults of the Roman Empire*, Oxford 1996; M.B.

problem, Hugh Bowden, among others, has argued in favour of the hypothesis that religious education did not exist in the pagan religions.[9]

The surviving sources that may possibly illustrate the problem are rather few and very poor.[10] We are not so fortunate that examples of religious educational programmes in the pagan religions have been preserved.[11] Nonetheless, some sources (see section 5) indicate that this type of religious education did in fact exist.

2. Definitions and procedure

The description above of the purpose of the present essay requires some preliminary considerations and definitions of the key terms, namely "education", "conversion", and "initiation".

First, the concept of "education": I use this term in a sense that is related to the Christian term "catechism", however, not in the technical sense that this word gradually obtained as referring to instruction in Christian dogma

---

Cosmopoulos, *Greek Mysteries*, London 2004. B. Ego / H. Merkel (eds.), *Religiöses Lernen in der biblischen, frühjüdischen und frühchristlichen Überlieferung*, Tübingen 2005, is on religious teaching in a broader sense, and it does not include the pagan Hellenistic-Roman religions. I have found some discussions of this problem only in a few works, such as Nilsson, 1961; Burkert, 1987; Martin, 1987; C. Riedweg, *Mysterienterminologie bei Platon, Philon und Klemens von Alexandrien*, Berlin 1987; Beck, 2006; A. Henrichs, *"Hieroi Logoi" and "Hierai Bibloi"*, in: CP 101 (2003), 207–266; and Bowden, 2010, 140–147.

9 Cf. Bowden, 2010, 6–25. 40–48. 212–221. Bowden argues that pagan initiations primarily conveyed an emotional experience, and that the "initiates were not given any explanation of what they had experienced" (2010, 206), cf. several other scholars such as, e.g., R. Stark, *Cities of God*, San Francisco 2006, 103–107; cf. n. 16 below. More cautious is Beck 2006, 41–64, who presents a useful discussion of the problem of doctrine and doctrinal teaching in the Mithras mysteries, and who argues that the initiation to Mithras did not primarily convey doctrinal instruction, but rather an emotional experience. At the same time, Beck admits that some religious teaching did in fact take place, cf. Beck's contribution in the present volume.

10 Cf., e.g., Burkert, 1987, 66.

11 Regarding Christianity, such programmes are hinted at in Luke 1:4 and referred to by later church fathers such as Hippolytus of Portus, Cyril of Jerusalem, Ambrose of Milan, John Chrysostomus of Antioch, Theodore of Mopsuestia and Augustine, but not by earlier Christian authors, and not at all by Jewish and pagan writers from this period, perhaps apart from the so-called Mithraic catechism from Egypt, cf. W.M. Brashear, *A Mithraic Catechism from Egypt <P.Berol. 21196>*, Vienna 1992 (cf. section 5.6). In his comprehensive *Histoire de l'Éducation dans l'antiquité*, Paris 1965, H-I. Marou has no general section on religious education. The same is true about Ego / Merkel (eds.), 2005.

and ethics by the means of questions and answers, but in a broader sense of instructions relevant to the future (possible) initiation of a person, who had been converted, that is, that he/she was provided with supplementary information about the relevant myth(s) and their interpretations together with the ritual requirements and the moral behaviour related to the conversion and the future initiation.

Second, I do not accept Nock's definition of the concept of "conversion",[12] primarily because Nock approaches the Hellenistic-Roman religions with a modern, pietistic definition of conversion based on the long Christian tradition from Augustine over Martin Luther to August Francke (1663–1727) and William James (1842–1910). On this background, I suggest that we extend the meaning of the term "conversion" to include all other mystery religions in the Hellenistic-Roman period which exerted an attraction on an individual and could be followed by the same individual's decision to apply for an initiation into one of the mystery religions. Thus, by "conversion" I understand the change of mind of an individual who had been attracted to a certain religion, an attraction that had been followed by the same individual's decision to apply for initiation into the godhead in question.[13]

Thirdly, the concept of "initiation": This term is less disputed than the term "conversion", and I use it in the generally accepted sense of referring to the transitory rites leading from one ritual status with less religious purity and knowledge to a higher ritual status in which the individual in question possesses a surplus of religious purity and knowledge.[14] This implies that I consider the Jewish circumcision and the Jewish proselyte baptism as well as the Christian baptism and the initiations into the other Hellenistic-Roman mystery religions as similar initiatory rituals.

The point of departure for my studies of the possible existence of religious education in the pagan religions in the Hellenistic-Roman period has been the institution of the Christian catechumenate, that is, the organised religious instruction of Christian converts given before and preparing their approaching baptism (cf. the references in notes 2 and 11). I have chosen as my specific point of departure the *Apostolic Tradition* of Hippolytus of Portus from the beginning of the third century, one of the earliest extant sources

---

12 Cf. Nock, 1933, 7. 14f. 138.

13 With this definition, I am closer to the definitions presented by M.B. McGuire, *Religion. The Social Context*, Belmont 1992, 71, and Bøgh in the present volume (40). Cf. also Marshall's article in this volume on a form of pagan conversion.

14 Cf. V. Turner, *The Ritual Process*, New York 1969; J.P. Schjødt, *Initiation between two Worlds. Structure and Symbolism in Pre-Christian Scandinavian Religion*, Odense 2008, 11–84.

providing details on this institution.[15] Here, as in many other sources, the content of the pre-baptismal catechesis consists of at least the following three elements: 1) doctrinal education (cf., e.g., Luke 1:4), 2) ethical instructions (cf., e.g., Did. 1–6), and 3) what may be called ritual requirements such as ritual purity, obtained by washing or bathing, fasting, sexual abstinence, etc.

I begin my essay (section 3) by presenting a brief summary of the view of Bowden (2010) and his associates against whom I turn my arguments in sections 4–5. I build up my critique of this position by some preliminary general considerations concerning conversion and initiation. This will be continued by calling attention to some texts speaking generally about the use of books and referring generally to (religious) teaching in the mystery religions (section 4). These preliminary considerations are followed by the central part of my essay consisting of an investigation of a selection of relevant sources on the six pagan religions mentioned above. Here, I will be looking for references, hints, or allusions to religious education (sections 5.1–6). This examination is concluded by a brief suming up of my results (section 6).

3. The position of my opponents

Bowden and others do not accept the idea that religious instruction also took place in the pagan Hellenistic-Roman religions.[16] This view is often based on the following texts: First, Aristotle (fr. 15), quoted by Synesius of Cyrene: "Aristotle claims that those who are being initiated into the mysteries are to be expected not to learn (*mathein*) anything, but to suffer some change, to be put into a certain condition, i.e., to be fitted to some purpose."[17] Bowden does not consider the possibility that the initiates mentioned in Aristotle's text could have been instructed before their initiation. Bowden and his associates claim that this text of Aristotle finds support in another fragment of a lost work by Plutarch,[18] quoted by Stobaeus (Ecl. 4.52,49):

---

15 Cf. D. Botte, *La tradition apostolique de Saint Hippolyte. Essai de reconstitution*, Munich 1963; G.J. Cuming, *Hippolytus. A Text for Students*, Bramcote Notts 1976. In the present context it is not important that the authorship of Hippolytus is disputed.

16 Cf. n. 9. Other scholars, e.g., G.E. Mylonas, *Eleusis and the Eleusinian Mysteries*, Princeton 1961, 239–285; Burkert, 1987, 29. 43. 46. 66–88; Beck, 2006, 5. 41–43, agree with Bowden at least to a certain extent. See also Martin in this volume (162. 165).

17 Dio 10.48a. The translation is borrowed from D. Ross, *The Works of Aristotle*, vol. 12 (*The Fragments*), Oxford 1952, 87. This text is also quoted and interpreted in, e.g., Mylonas, 1961, 262; Burkert, 1987, 69. 89.

18 Fr. 178, not 169 as indicated in Burkert 1987, 162, n. 11; Bowden 2010, 230, n. 35.

> It [scil. the soul] has an experience like that of the men who are undergoing initiation into great mysteries; and so the verbs *teleutan* (to die) and *teleisthai* (to be initiated), and the actions they denote, have a similarity. In the beginning, there is straying and wandering, the weariness of running this way and that, and nervous journeys through darkness that reach no goal, and then immediately before the consummation every possible terror, shivering and trembling and sweating and amazement. But after this, a marvellous light meets the wanderer, and open country and meadow lands welcome him.[19]

It is the main argument of these scholars that the "greater mysteries" in the Telesterion in Eleusis were not a pedagogical experience of learning, but a soul shaking and shocking emotional experience.[20]

4. General considerations

In the following description and analysis, I intend to demonstrate in details that Bowden's position is contradicted by a series of information in the six cults examined in section 5. First, however, I will discuss some texts which can be interpreted as referring generally to the existence of religious education in the mystery religions.

First, a text by Clement of Alexandria's *Stromateis* (5.70,7–71,1). Here, Clement describes the "Greek mysteries," and among other things he writes: "Then follow the smaller mysteries, the aim of which surely is to prepare the coming events by the means of teaching (*didaskalia*)." It appears obvious that Clement is here referring to the mysteries in Eleusis, and in the text quoted, he seems to claim that during the lesser mysteries in Athens some sort of teaching about the greater mysteries and the initiation in Eleusis took place. On the background of this text, it is possible to interpret Aristotle and Plutarch as referring exclusively to the greater mysteries in Eleusis. In other words, on the background of Clement's text it is possible to maintain that the initiates learnt what they had to learn during the lesser mysteries, or before them, or on their way from Athens to Eleusis.[21]

---

19 I read Plutarch according to the Greek text and the English translation by F.H. Sandbach, *Plutarch's Moralia in sixteen volumes*, vol. 15 (*Fragments*), London 1969.

20 Sometimes, this group of scholars also refers to Dio Chrysostomus who in his Olympian Oration on the origin of the idea of divinity describes an initiation scene and here also emphasises the emotional experience of the initiates (12.33).

21 Cf. Burkert, 1987, 69 ("Learning is not denied in the mysteries, but rather is presupposed."). The same view can be found in H.-J. Klauck, *Die religiöse Umwelt des Urchristentums*, vol. 1 (*Stadt- und Hausreligion, Mysterienkulte*), Stuttgart 1995, 81: "Zwar liegen den einzelnen Kulten längere mytische Göttererzählungen

In Demosthenes' oration *De corona* (18.259), the author criticises his political enemy, Aischines, and here he describes how Aischines as a young man used to help his mother when she practised her initiations:

> On reaching manhood, you attended your mother's initiation sessions and read the texts (*tas biblous*) for her, and helped to conduct the rest of the ceremony: wrapping the initiates in fawn-skins, and mixing the wine, purifying them, plastering them with clay and bran and scraping it off, raising them up from their lustration, and bidding them say 'I have escaped the evil, I have found the better.'[22]

The "texts" mentioned by Demosthenes are called "books" in Greek, and they could be technical handbooks advising Aischines' mother how to proceed, but they could also contain religious instructions for the initiates.[23] If the words of Aristotle and Plutarch, quoted in section 3, are interpreted in connection with these texts from Clement and Demosthenes, then, consequently, the texts by Aristotle and Plutarch do not necessarily exclude religious instruction in the pagan mystery religions. In my opinion, this interpretation is supported by the following a priori considerations: All sorts of participation in a cult, including all applications to be accepted as a candidate for initiation into a mystery religion, seem to me to presuppose some sort of general as well as some sort of specific knowledge. Firstly, interested candidates ought at least to be familiar with the relevant myths. Secondly, they must have had some ideas about the advantages and profits that could be obtained by being initiated, and thirdly, they must have been instructed to know something about the ritual and moral requirements that were attached to these initiations.

With these considerations, I point to the simple fact that participation in specific initiations seems to be unthinkable without a good deal of knowledge, and this knowledge could be acquired either at home, or at school, or by some other specific instructions including those organised by professionals related to the temples of the mystery religions, as we know it from Apuleius on Isis (cf. section 5.4).

---

zugrunde, aber diese wurden entweder schon bei der Vorbereitung vermittelt [...] oder man konnte sie aus dem allgemeinen Mythenvorrat als bekannt voraussetzen."

22 The Greek text and the English translation can be found in S. Usher (ed. and trans.), *Greek Orators*, vol. 5 (*Demosthenes. On the Crown*), Warminster 1993, 140f.

23 In Plato's *Republic* 364bc, we also find a reference to a "heap of books by Musaios and Orpheus," and the royal decree by Ptolemy IV Philopator from 215–214 BCE refers to "holy books" in the cult of Dionysos (BGU 6.12,1), cf. Burkert, 1987, 70.

5.1 Orphism[24]

One of the famous Orphic gold tablets was found in Hipponion in South Italy and dates from ca. 400 BCE.[25] It reads as follows:

> This is the work of Mnemosyne. When he [scil. the person to be buried] is on the point of dying toward the well-built abode of Hades, on the right side there is a fountain and near it, erect, a white cypress tree. There the souls, when they go down, refresh themselves. Don't come anywhere near this fountain! But further on you will find, from the lake of Mnemosyne, water freshly flowing. On its banks, there are guardians. They will ask you, with sagacious discernment, why you are investigating the darkness of gloomy Hades. Say: 'I am the son of Earth and starry Heaven; I am dry with thirst and dying. Give me, then, right away, fresh water to drink from the lake of Mnemosyne.' And to be sure, they will consult with the subterranean Queen, and they will give you water to drink from the lake of Mnemosyne. So that, once you have drunk, you too will go along the sacred way by which the other *mystai* and *Bacchoi* advance glorious.[26]

These gold tablets are neither meant to convey religious education with the purpose of preparing a convert for his/her coming initiation, nor should they, however, be interpreted as the so-called Egyptian "death books",[27] given to the deceased and meant as a sort of guidance for their journey through the underworld. I suggest that we consider whether these gold plates could be interpreted as a sort of dogmatic memory help. The entire text focuses on the correct memory of the dead person, whose memory of her/his true origin is supposed to be absent in the present situation, but her/his drinking of the

24 On Orphism generally, see, e.g., W.K.C. Guthrie, *Orpheus and Greek Religion. A Study of the Orphic Movement*, Princeton ²1993; L.J. Alderink, *Creation and Salvation in Ancient Orphism*, Chicago 1981; H.D. Betz, 'Der Erde Kind bin ich und des gestirnten Himmels', in: F. Graf (ed.), *Ansichten Griechischer Rituale*, Stuttgart 1998, 399–419; F. Graf / S.I. Johnston, *Ritual Texts for the Afterlife*, London 2007; A. Bernabé / J. San Cristóbal, *Instructions for the Netherworld*, Leiden 2008; Bowden, 2010, 148–155. In contrast to several other scholars, Bowden maintains that there never existed "a whole religious movement [...] which they called 'Orphism'" (2010, 139). In the present context, however, this discussion is not indispensable.
25 Cf. Guthrie, ²1993, 148–193, in particular 171–187; Betz, 1998; Bernabé / San Cristóbal, 2008, 9–59.
26 I have borrowed the English translation from Bernabé / San Cristóbal, 2008, 9f. The text is also quoted and discussed in Bowden, 2010, 148–150. The expression *Mystai* and *Bacchoi* is probably a *hendiadys*, see J. San Cristóbal, *The Meaning of* βάκχος *and* βακχεύειν *in Orphism*, in: G. Casadio / P.A. Johnston (eds.), *Mystic Cults in Magna Graecia*, Austin 2009, 46– 61 (53).
27 Cf. R. Merkelbach, *Isis Regina – Zeus Serapis. Die griechisch-ägyptische Religion nach den Quellen dargestellt*, Stuttgart 1995, 23–36; Henrichs, 2003, 225–227.

water from Mnemosyne seems to be the necessary presupposition to revive the memory of this true origin. The central position of Mnemosyne and the phrase: "you should recall," that appears in several of the gold tablets, support this suggestion. Then we have to consider the possible roots of this person's true memory, and I suggest that this memory presupposes a preceding instruction to the deceased before death concerning his/her descent, i.e., from the heavenly world to the earth. In other words, this "memory" may refer to a complete "anthropology" and "eschatology" as presupposed in these texts.[28] Finally, I point to the two last lines of the text quoted above where the two words *mystai* and *bacchoi* appear. They seem to refer to the final eschatological goal that appears to be dependent of the remembrance mentioned above. In addition, these two words point directly to a ritual of initiation (cf. n. 26).

If this interpretation can be accepted, these gold plates should not be categorised as a sort of Greek "death books", but as texts presupposing a ritual of initiation and some religious education, an instruction which again presupposes some sort of conversion, namely to Orphism. Accordingly, these gold tablets presuppose partly a whole dogmatic system concentrated on man's anthropology, i.e., his or her origins in the heavenly world, and his or her eschatological salvation after death (cf. note 28), partly a ritual encompassing his or her conversion, religious education, and initiation. Thus, I understand our text as presupposing both some sort of conversion and a sort of religious education before the conversion and initiation.[29]

All this supports my interpretation of the Orphic gold tablets as referring to a sort of dogmatic memory of the Orphic theology taught to the Orphic converts in connection with their conversion and initiation. According to the text, however, this true memory was later forgotten, and the gold plate buried with the dead person is meant to help him or her to overcome this oblivion.

5.2 Eleusis[30]

People's participation in the lesser and greater mysteries in Athens and Eleusis also seems to presuppose a thorough knowledge of the myths about

---

28 Cf. Alderink, 1981; Betz, 1998; Graf / Johnston, 2007, 94–136.
29 W.K.C. Guthrie, an expert on Orphism, also argues that the idea of conversion was present in Orphism in a form that can be compared with the same idea in Christianity ([2]1993, 207).
30 On the Eleusinian mysteries generally: Nilsson, 1961, 90–95. 345–358; Mylonas, 1961; G.S. Gasparro, *Misteri e culti mistici di Demetra*, Rome 1986, 27–134; M.W. Meyer, *The Ancient Mysteries. A Sourcebook*, San Francisco 1987, 15–45; Bowden, 2010, 26–48; J.N. Bremmer, *Initiation into the Eleusinian Mysteries. A Thin Description*, in: C.H. Bull *et al.* (eds.), *Mystery and Secrecy in the Nag Hammadi Collection and other Ancient Literature*, Leiden 2011, 375–397.

Demeter, Persephone (Kore), Hades, and other relevant figures.[31] Without
such knowledge, the rituals, the initiations in Athens and Eleusis, and the
visual demonstrations (*ta deiknymena, ta drômena* and *ta epopteia*) in the
Telesterion in Eleusis would not have any meaning.

I assume that the final initiation in Eleusis presupposes a conversion as
understood above (section 2) as well as some religious education that could
have taken place both before the conversion and/or in the period between
the lesser mysteries in Athens and the greater mysteries and the final initiation in Eleusis. Even though we have only weak traces of a proper religious
education, the myths and rituals behind the Eleusinian mysteries presuppose
that such a phenomenon must have existed.[32] Regarding the content of this
religious education, I refer primarily to the Hymn of Demeter and several
other texts and inscriptions which all presuppose or refer to this doctrine or
myth (cf., e.g., Merkelbach, 1995, 23–36).

Moreover, we know that in the Telesterion not only awful, dramatic
events took place (*ta deiknymena, ta drômena* and *ta epopteia*). Also words
were pronounced (*ta legomena*).[33] Therefore, it cannot be excluded that during the greater mysteries in the Telesterion both dramatic events, appealing
to the feelings of the participants, and some sort of oral religious teaching took place. In his work *De Legibus*, Cicero praises the Athenians for
their establishment of the mysteries in Eleusis which have contributed to
teaching barbarian human beings to be civilised. According to Cicero, it
was through these initiations "that we have learned the basic principles of
living" (*ita revera principia vitae cognovimus*).[34] In his *Tusculan Disputations*
Cicero returns to the teaching of the religious initiations, again, probably, the

---

31 Cf. Gasparro, 1986, 29–87.

32 Also Riedweg writes that in the Eleusinian mysteries the "teaching" and "learning" belonged to the preparation during the lesser mysteries (1987, 9). I suggest
that we distinguish between three types of Eleusinian education or teaching: 1)
knowledge of the fundamental myth about Persephone, Demeter and Eleusis,
2) the necessary information about the rituals of the upcoming two initiations
(given by a mystagogue), and 3) some interpretations of the meaning and significance of both given to the initiate.

33 Mylonas guesses that "the *legomena* were perhaps nothing more nor less than
brief ritualistic and liturgical formulae which supplemented and made clear to the
initiate the performance he was witnessing" (1961, 273). In his drama *The Frogs*
(311–459), Aristophanes refers to the Eleusinian mysteries, and here he appears
to presuppose hymns as well as moral teaching (cf. Meyer, 1987, 32–38).

34 Leg. 2.36. A.R. Dyck, *A Commentary on Cicero's* De Legibus, Ann Arbor 2004,
352, quotes B.S. Spaeth, *The Roman Goddess Ceres*, Austin 1996, 17: "this transition [scil. from barbarism to civilisation] does not have merely a historical or
societal significance, but also a personal mimetic meaning. By becoming initiated
into the mysteries of the goddess, the individual is tamed and cultivated."

Eleusinian mysteries: "Examine the sepulchres of those which are shown in Greece; recollect, for you have been initiated, what lessons are taught in the mysteries; then you will perceive how extensive this doctrine is."[35]

Accordingly, I propose that we interpret Aristotle's statement, quoted above (section 3), that they "are not supposed to learn anything" to mean "anything *new*" because everybody was supposed to have learned and thus to know the myths about Persephone and Demeter already before the greater mysteries. I conclude, therefore, that some sort of religious education must also have existed in the Eleusinian mysteries either before the initiates' conversion, during the lesser mysteries in Athens, during their march from Athens to Eleusis, or during the final initiation in Eleusis.

5.3. The cult of Bacchus[36]

In the present context, my main source is Livy's report on the intervention of the consul S.P. Albinus and the Roman senate in order to crush what they thought to be a political conspiracy against the Roman state.[37] The whole story in Livy is presented and interpreted as an account of a political conjuration prepared by a dubious group of morally unscrupulous human beings – the initiates of Bacchus (Dionysos). The author has no interest whatsoever in the religious side of the Bacchus cult in Italy, and we learn only a few details about the cult, in particular on the preparation for the initiation.

According to Livy's report (Liv. 39.9,1–4), Publius Aebutius' mother, Duronia, had promised during an illness of her son that, if and when he recovered, he would be initiated into the Bacchanalia, the rites of Bacchus. Livy writes that before his initiation, Aebutius was required to abstain from sexual intercourse for ten days; on the 10th day he should first eat a meal, then purify himself ritually, and after these purifying rituals his mother would introduce him *in sacrarium* (39.9,4). Here, too, however, it is my interpretation that the initiation to Bacchus must have presupposed some knowledge of the relevant myths on Bacchus, the maenads, the rituals, and the purpose and character of the initiation to Bacchus. Accordingly, the story in Livy presupposes, first, some sort of conversion, and second, some sort of preparatory religious education, partly knowledge of the relevant myths, partly the specific instructions concerning the preparation for the initiation which followed as a conclusion.

---

35 Tusc. 1.13. I have borrowed the translation from C.D. Yonge (ed. and trans.), *Cicero's Tusculan Disputations*, New York 1891.

36 On the Bacchus cult generally: Nilsson, 1961, 358–372; Meyer, 1987, 61–109; Turcan, 1996, 291–327; Bowden, 2010, 105–136.

37 I read Livy according to the Latin text in and the English translation by E.T. Sage, *Livy with an English Translation in fourteen Volumes*, vol. 11 (*Books 38–39*), Cambridge 1936, 240–275.

Of these elements, it is especially the ritual requirements before the initiation that is mentioned in Livy. On the other hand, the importance of this single element is confirmed by a Greek inscription from 2nd – 1st century BCE which says that the initiates should "know" (ginôskeis) the holy purification and "learn" the rites (mathein ta orgia).[38] Perhaps, there is also an allusion to the other elements, the relevant myths and other religious education, in Livy 39.18,3: "Those who had merely been initiated and had made their prayers in accordance with a ritual formulae, the priest dictating the words."[39] This "ritual formula", carmen sacrum, proves that there existed in the Italian Bacchus cult a written ritual, and I suggest that this ritual in one way or another was related to the Bacchic myths and dogma. Finally, I suggest that such myths and dogma were taught to the initiates by the priests of Bacchus.

General considerations on the character of the initiation to Bacchus as well as these two specific elements in the text thus indicate that some sort of religious instruction also appears to have taken place in the Roman initiations to Bacchus.

5.4 The cult of Isis[40]

In the present context, I restrict myself primarily to Apuleius' Metamorphoses, Book 11.[41] According to 11.5–6, Isis revealed herself to Lucius in a dream in which she told him to do what she commanded him. On the following day, when the opening of the sailing season in Corinth is described to have been marked by a great Isiac ceremony, and when a procession

---

38 SEG 28, 841: [K]αὶ μορφὰν Βρομίου τὰς [τελετάς τε θεοῦ,] ὄφρα σὺ γινώσκῃς ἱεροῦ λουτ[ροῖο μετασχών] πάντα λόγον μύστην παντὸς ἐόντα βίου, καὶ σιγᾶν ὅ τι κρυπτὸν ἐπιστάμενος καὶ ἀϋτεῖν ὅσσα θέμις, στείχῃς ὄργια ταῦτα μαθών.

39 Qui tantum initiate errant et ex carmine sacro, praeunte verba sacerdote, praecationes fecerant (Sage, 1983, 268–271).

40 On the Isis cult generally, I refer to Nilsson, 1961, 622–639; R.E. Witt, Isis in the Ancient World, Baltimore [2]1997; J.G. Griffiths, Plutarch's de Iside et Osiride, Cambridge 1970; id., The Isis-Book (Metamorphoses, Book XI), Leiden 1975; Meyer, 1987, 157–196; Merkelbach, 1995; Turcan, 1996, 75–129; E.A. Aslan et al. (eds.), Iside. Il mito, il mistero, la magica, Milano 1997; F. Dunand, Isis. Mère des dieux, Paris 2000; Bowden, 2010, 156–180.

41 I read the text according to J.A. Hanson (ed. and trans.), Apuleius, Metamorphoses, Books VII–XI, Cambridge 2001. Despite the fact that Apuleius' work is a piece of literary fiction, many scholars accept that it comes close to the historical reality, e.g., U. Egelhaaf-Gaiser, Kulträume im römischen Alltag, Stuttgart 2000. The main reason for this assessment is the many agreements between Apuleius and the other sources on Isis. I accept this assessment.

honouring Isis would take place, Lucius (who was still in his asinine figure) was told to approach a particular priest of Isis who on his *sistrum* was wearing a bunch of roses. Isis ordered Lucius to take one of these roses and eat it. This act, she said, would bring about Lucius' metamorphosis back to his human shape. This metamorphosis can be interpreted as the first stage in Lucius' conversion and salvation. Furthermore, Isis is reported (11.6) to have commanded Lucius, that, after his *metamorphosis*, he should dedicate the rest of his life to Isis:

> You will clearly remember and keep forever sealed deep in your heart the fact that the rest of your life's course is pledged to me until the very limit of your last breath. Nor is it unjust that you should owe all the time you have to live to her by whose benefit you return to the world of men. Moreover you will live in happiness, you will live in glory, under my guardianship (Hanson, 2001, 303).

I interpret this revelation as the first part of a religious education which also indicates that from now on, Lucius should live in close connection to his divine liberator, Isis. In his novel, Apuleius describes that supplementary religious instruction by Isis' priests would follow, in particular by her high priest Mithras. Isis as well as Mithras are reported to have given commandments and instructions to Lucius concerning his practical life and concerning his preparation for his approaching initiation(s). These instructions also contain dogmatic teaching, in particular, that the coming initiation would have consequences for Lucius' destiny after death (11.6).

This interpretation finds support in Apuleius' mention of a book (*de libro litteris*) in the context of the Isis cult (11.17). In 11.22, Apuleius describes these books in greater detail: "he brought out from the secret part of the sanctuary some books inscribed with unknown characters" (*profert quosdam libros literis ignorabilibus praenotatos*).[42] Accordingly, holy books existed in the Isis cult as well as in several other pagan religions (cf. section 4). Apuleius may also refer to such books in 11.19, where he describes how Lucius had obtained knowledge about the rules and demands concerning his future initiation to Isis:

> With repeated commands she [scil. Isis] urged me[43] now at least to be initiated, since I had long been destined for her rites. But although I was eagerly willing, I was held back by a conscientious fear; for I had learned through thorough

---

42 In his commentary, Griffiths does not comment on these "books" (1975, 266f. and 284f.). If these books were written in hieroglyphs, Mithras would certainly be able to translate their contents into Greek.

43 This "me" is one of several indications of an identification between Apuleius and Lucius, that is, that this work contains autobiographical traits, cf. Griffiths, 1975, 1–7.

investigation (*quod enim sedulo percontaveram*) that the obligations of her cult
were difficult.

Probably, the expression "thorough investigation" refers to instruction, either in writing or orally. Accordingly, these hints indicate that converted
candidates hoping to be initiated to Isis received religious instruction.

Summing up, I interpret Isis' revelations to Lucius as having caused a di-
vinely inspired conversion. Lucius had "sinned" because of his curiosity
(11.15), and he had now been saved in the sense that the terrible curse of
his transformation into a donkey had been lifted. After Lucius' conversion
and partial salvation, Apuleius writes that Lucius was commanded to remain
obedient to Isis and to be the "slave of the goddess" (11.15). Accordingly, I
interpret this part of Apuleius' novel as follows: In the period between his conversion and the first part of his salvation, and the second part of his salvation,
his "rebirth", i.e., his (first) initiation (11.14; 16; 24), Lucius received religious
education and preparatory instructions concerning his approaching initiation.
This means that in this case, too, the conversion and the initiation of Lucius
presuppose instruction in the relevant myths and rituals related to Isis.

This interpretation of Apuleius' text on Isis receives some support from
three other sources: Statius, Plutarch, and an inscription from Ostia. Statius
(ca. 45–95 CE) writes about a Roman commander on his way to Alexandria:
"Under your (scil. Isis') protection, let him learn whence comes the fertile
licence of marshy Nile, why common animals are on par with the great
gods [...],"[44] clearly testifying to the need and custom of teaching about
fundamental truths in the cult of Isis. Another piece of evidence supporting my hypothesis about the existence of religious education in the cult of
Isis is an inscription from Ostia, found on an altar in a temple dedicated
to Serapis, and dated to around 200 CE.[45] This inscription mentions a certain "Publius Calpurnius Princeps" who is called *educator*. The publisher,
Laurent Bricault, suggests that "l'*educator* serait ici le prêtre qui fut chargé
d'enseigner, a son jeune élève, les préceptes de la doctrine isiaque" (2005,
591). Finally, Plutarch's extensive work on Isis and Osiris is obviously a

---

44 *Te praeside noscatunde paludosi fecunda licentia Nili*, etc. (Silv. 3.2,107f.), cf.
    D.R.S. Bailey (ed. and trans.), *Statius. Silvae,* Cambridge 2003, 196f. In *Contra
    Celsum* 3.19, Origen writes that "the Egyptians show many mysteries (probably
    those of Isis) [...] and obscure explanations." Accordingly, this text, too, appears
    to attest that explanations were presented during the mysteries of Isis. Other
    sources are even more clear that only initiates knew the meaning of the Egyptian
    rites and "facts", such as a fragment by Callimachus (561) and Heliodorus, Ae-
    thiop. 9.9.
45 Published in L. Bricault, *Recueil des inscriptions concernant les cultes isiaques*,
    Paris 2005, no. 503/1131.

secondary, allegorical, Platonising interpretation of the Egyptians myths and the rites of initiation to Isis. I think, however, that this type of literature is a very clear piece of evidence of the fact that the old myths had to be explained and interpreted, and I suggest that the same is true about the initiates to Isis: Of course, they studied the myths, and of course they tried to understand, explain, and interpret these myths in relation to their upcoming personal initiation. Hippolytus of Portus confirms this information in *Refutations of all Heresies* (5.7,22f.) by writing that the rites in the mysteries of Isis were only "understandable" to the initiates, but "unintelligible" to those who have not been initiated. This means that Hippolytus presupposes that the initiated had received some religious education.[46]

5.5 Cybele and Atargatis[47]

We have very little evidence on religious education in the cults of Cybele and Atargatis.[48] On the other hand, I am convinced that also initiations to these two goddesses presupposed teaching material of the same sort as those examined above. In Lucian's work on the Syrian Goddess, there is no explicit information on initiation, conversion, and religious education.[49] But in Emperor Julian's *Hymn to the Mother of the Gods* we do find material testifying to the existence of religious education in the cult of Cybele. Right in the beginning of the hymn, Julian poses a number of rhetorical questions indicating that Julian is going to explain the meaning of Cybele and Attis/Gallus:

---

46 The existence of the so-called Isis-aretalogies is yet another piece of evidence of the existence of an elaborated Isis theology. The aretalogies testify to the existence of a religious interest in an actual and relevant understanding and interpretation of Isis, in other words, of the existence of religious education in the myths and in the ritual and moral requirements to the initiates.

47 On Cybele and Atargatis generally, I refer to P. Bilde, *Atargatis/Dea Syria. Hellenization of her Cult in the Hellenistic-Roman Period*, in: P. Bilde *et al.* (eds.), *Religion and Religious Practice in the Seleucid Kingdom*, Aarhus 1990, 151–187; L. Roller, *In Search of God the Mother. The Cult of Anatolian Cybele*, Berkeley 1999; Turcan, 1996, 28–74; B. Bøgh, *Mother of the Gods* (PhD diss.), Aarhus University 2009; Bowden, 2010, 83–104.

48 Cf. the presentation in Bowden, 2010, 83–104.

49 I read Lucian's work on the Syrian Goddess according to A.M. Harmon (ed. and trans.), *Lucian in Eight Volumes*, vol. 4, Cambridge 1969, 337–411. Perhaps, it is possible to interpret the rite of castration performed by the *galli*, described in paragraphs 6; 15f.; 20; 26f. and 50–52, as a rite of initiation. In that case, Lucian presents the basic, underlying myth about Adonis/Attis (§§ 6–8) and Combabus (§§ 19–27), and perhaps these myths could be interpreted as a sort of religious education related to conversion and initiation. Something similar may be assumed about castration in relation to initiations to Cybele.

Ought I to say something on this subject also? And shall I write about things not to be spoken of and divulge what ought not to be divulged? Shall I utter the unutterable? Who is Attis or Gallus, who is the Mother of the Gods, and what is the manner of their ritual of purification?[50]

Julian answers these questions later in his hymn (from paragraph 161c and so forth) by giving the ancient myths and traditions of Cybele a Neoplatonic interpretation of the same type as those given by Plutarch in his work on Isis and Osiris, and by Porphyry and other ancient authors in their works on Mithras (cf. below). These works, as well as his initial comments, prove that the ancient myths behind the mystery cults were not only told and read, but also interpreted, discussed, and "revealed".

We do not have to get lost in the details of Julian's interpretation. In the present context, it is enough to note and conclude that the myths of Cybele and Attis were interpreted and discussed in antiquity, and certainly not only in a Neoplatonic manner. When it seems to be a fact that these myths were interpreted and discussed by philosophers and others, I think that we are justified in assuming that there must have been an even greater need to teach, to interpret, and to discuss these myths and rituals for would-be converts and initiates.

5.6 The Roman cult of Mithras[51]

In the context of discussing possible traces of religious education in the Roman cult of Mithras, it is worth considering combining the numerous small reliefs, found as a figurative band, almost as a strip, around many major representations of Mithras killing the bull, which can be assumed to

---

50 Or. 159a. I read Julian's hymn according to W.C. Wright (ed. and trans.), *The Works of Emperor Julian*, vol. 1, Cambridge 1980, 411–503.

51 On the Roman Mithras cult: Nilsson, 1961, 667–679; M.J. Vermaseren / E.E. van Essen, *The Excavations in the Mithraeum of the Church of Santa Prisca in Rome*, Leiden 1965; H.D. Betz, *The Mithras Inscriptions of Santa Prisca and the New Testament*, in: NT 10 (1968), 62–80; R. Turcan, *Mithras Platonicus. Recherches sur l'hellénisation philosophiques de Mithra*, Leiden 1975; R. Gordon, *The Sacred Geography of a Mithraeum. The Example of Sette Sfere*, in: Journal of Mithraic Studies 1 (1976), 119–165; Id., *Mystery, Metaphor and Doctrine in the Mysteries of Mithras*, in: J.R. Hinnels (ed.), *Studies in Mithraism*, Rome 1994, 103–124; Merkelbach, *Mithras*, Hain 1984; Meyer, 1987, 199–221; P. Bilde, *The Meaning of Roman Mithraism*, in: J.P. Sørensen (ed.), *Rethinking Religion. Studies in the Hellenistic Process*, Copenhagen 1989, 31–47; R.D. Ulansey, *The Origin of the Mithraic Mysteries*, Oxford 1989; W.M. Brashear, *A Mithraic Catechism from Egypt*, Wien 1992; Turcan, 1996, 195–247; M. Clauss, *The Roman Cult of Mithras. The God and the Mysteries*, New York 2000; Beck, 2006; Bowden, 2010, 181–197.

be interpreted as illustrating the salvatory life of Mithras,[52] with the Latin verses found on one of the walls of the mithraeum found under the Church of Santa Prisca in Rome (from ca. 200 CE).[53]

In this mithraeum, a number of Latin inscriptions have been revealed. They seem to be fragments of Mithraic hymns otherwise unknown. According to Betz, these hymns represent traditional Mithraic cultic material (1990, 72f.). In the present context, I have to ask whether these inscriptions might be understood as fragments of teaching material (cf. Beck in his contribution to the present volume).

The most relevant of these verses run as follows: No. 3: "This young bull which he carried on his golden shoulders according to his ways." No. 6: "Him (or: that) who (or: which) is piously reborn and created by sweet tings." No. 7: "You must conduct the rite through clouded times together." And no. 9: "And you have saved us after having shed the eternal blood."[54] Probably these verses combine the Mithraic ritual service with the Mithras myth as it is known from the reliefs mentioned above.[55] Accordingly, it cannot be excluded that these two groups of sources attest to the existence of religious teaching material in the Roman cult of Mithras.

The so-called Mithraic Catechism from Egypt (cf. Brashear, 1992, 18f.) is so brief (one page!) and fragmentary that it is difficult to reconstruct a coherent text. On the other hand, the fragment clearly indicates some questions regarding the interpretation of the figures and ideas in the Mithraic religion, e.g., "Who is the father?" and didactic responses as, e.g., "The one who

---

52 Examples can be found in, e.g., Burkert, 1987, 73f. and fig. 11 (with commentary); Turcan, 1996, 212. 222; Clauss, 2000, 53–57. 62–101; Bowden, 2010, 186 (fig. 126). 188 (fig. 128). Cf. Beck on "The reconstruction of Mithraic doctrine from iconography" (2006, 16–25. 57f.). Beck continues by describing his own interpretation of Mithraic doctrine (2006, 59–62) in a way that is not far from my own interpretation (but cf. n. 55 below).

53 Cf. Vermaseren / van Essen, 1965; Betz, 1990.

54 I have borrowed these translations from Meyer, 1987, 207. Many scholars suspect that no. 7 should rather be regarded as the invention of M. Vermaseren. Burkert, 1987, 111f., however, accepts the text reproduced above; this problem need not be discussed here.

55 On the Mithras myth, see, e.g., Clauss, 2000, 62–101. My hypothesis of a Mithras myth implies that by religious education in this cult, I postulate something much more comprehensive than what Beck defines as "some fundamental principles of the Mithraic mysteries" or as "axioms" or as "the overarching truths of a religion" (2006, 5f.). My proposal is closer to the last three of the four *modes* in which, according to Beck, "singly or concurrently, the symbol system of the Mithraic mysteries could be apprehended by its initiates," in particular no. 3, "the giving and receiving of words (logia, explications, teaching, esoteric epigraphic phrases, etc." (Beck, 2006, 7).

(begets) everything" (cf. Brashear 1992, 19), and this form clearly reminds us of Christian and Gnostic catechesis. This hypothesis finds support in the well-known text by Porphyry, *De antro nympharum* 6.1: "The Persians call the place a cave where they introduce an initiate to the mysteries (*mystagogountes*), revealing to him (*telousin ton mystên*) the path by which souls descend and go back again."[56] Here, we probably find a secondary, Platonic reinterpretation of an older Persian myth (cf. Turcan, 1975). I assume, however, that "teaching" was involved in both cases.[57] Porphyry's text continues by quoting a certain Euboulus, and in the writing *De abstinentia*, mentioned above, Porphyry refers to a book on Mithras by a certain Pallas. In *Contra Celsum* (1.12) Origen confirms that the Mithraists interpreted and explained their myths: "Among them [scil. the Persians], there are mysteries which are explained rationally by the learned among them."[58]

Accordingly, I agree with Roger Beck who interprets these texts as testimonies to Mithraic religious instruction: "In this weak sense of *ad hoc* teaching, it is likely that there was indeed a 'doctrine' of the descent and departure of souls in the Mithraic mysteries" (2006, 43, cf. 59–64). Even Bowden is convinced that some teaching went on in the mithraea: "Possibly, too, some kind of teaching took place" (2010, 189). At the same time, however, Bowden rejects that this teaching contained any elements of Mithraic dogma: "Mithraic 'doctrine' was probably not taught" (2010, 189). In contrast to Bowden, I find it difficult here to separate myth and doctrine.

If we presuppose a sort of conversion of the person who had decided to ask to be initiated to Mithras, I think that we are allowed to consider interpreting the relief and the Latin verses from Santa Prisca as traces of the Mithraic myth and dogma without which neither a conversion nor an initiation to Mithras would be meaningful. Accordingly, I claim that in the Roman cult of Mithras as well we have sufficient evidence to justify the assumption that some sort of conversion in the sense mentioned above (section 2) took place, and that some sort of religious education in the relevant myths and rituals of Mithras was given in this religion, probably in connection with the upcoming initiation.

---

56 Quoted from Beck, 2006, 41. In Porphyry, Abst. 4.16, we also find the idea of a Mithraic dogma on the transmigration of souls, and Origen writes in *Contra Celsum* about the "teaching of the Persians" and "the Persian theology," as described by Celsus (6.22).

57 Cf. Brashear, 1992, and Gordon, 1994, who also discuss the relations between an original mythic story and possible secondary (allegorical and Platonic) interpretations of this myth.

58 I read Origen according to P. Koetschau, *Origenes Werke*, vol. 1 (*Die Schrift vom Martyrium Buch 1–IV gegen Celsus*), Leipzig 1899; H. Chadwick (ed. and trans.), *Origen Contra Celsum*, Cambridge ²1980.

5.7 Conclusion

I believe that I have now made it clear that in the six pagan cults examined above, conversion and participation in the rites of initiations presupposed a certain amount of knowledge of the relevant myths and rituals as well as the ritual and moral requirements demanded from the converted candidates for initiation. In addition, I have presented so much empirical evidence from these six religions that I am justified in claiming that some religious education did in fact take place. Finally, I think that we are now entitled to assume that various sorts and levels of such education could take place either before the conversion (vague and general knowledge), or between the conversion and the initiation (more specific and concentrated education), or during the very initiation.

6. Results

The most important discovery obtained in my examination of the material in section 5 is the insight that despite all the other differences between Christianity and the six pagan Hellenistic-Roman religions, there seems to have existed an element of religious education in all of them.[59] The considerable differences in the amounts of surviving sources are mainly due to the fact that Christianity won the religious contest in antiquity, and after its victory Christianity did very little to preserve the sources of its enemies. This religious education seems to have been related to the conversion of the individual in question, and, particularly, to the ritual of initiation. In section 5, I have also found that this element of religious education in the six pagan religions seems to vary a great deal, and that it appears to have taken place at different moments in what we may call the process of conversion and initiation. It could begin some time before the conversion; it could be more concentrated up to the conversion; it could take place between conversion and initiation, and it could also continue during and after the initiation. Thus, it may be fruitful to speak about a common structure in these seven religions consisting of conversion, religious education, and initiation, a structure that seems to belong to and to be an expression of the growing Hellenistic-Roman individual culture with its changing identities.

When first seen and discovered, this structure seems to be obvious and logical. Logically, an initiation presupposes a personal attraction, a personal choice and a personal decision, in other words, what I call a conversion (cf. section 2), and both this conversion and the following initiation likewise

---

59 Nilsson, too, emphasises that religious education took place in the mystery religions: "Es gab Erklärungen und Belehrungen in den Mysterien" (1961, 693).

presuppose knowledge, and knowledge presupposes instruction or education. You have to know something about the deities, the cult, and the religion you wish to approach and take part in, and this insight of course holds
true even more when you want to be initiated. This means that you cannot
avoid getting to know the myths, the ritual requirements, and the ethics of
the cult in question, and this is true for Christianity as well as for the six
pagan Hellenistic-Roman religions I have examined.

Accordingly, the main conclusion of the examinations carried out in this
essay is that in the Hellenistic-Roman period, religious education[60] did not
only exist in Christianity. It existed also in Judaism in the relatively few
cases that proselytising and conversion actually took place.[61] Furthermore,
I have presented sufficient evidence in section 5 to claim that we also have
to accept that, despite the relatively modest evidence, it has also been practised in the six pagan Hellenistic-Roman religions examined there. An individual person's attraction to a religion, and his/her decision to approach
this religion with the intention to apply for initiation logically presuppose
some acquaintance with the myths and rituals of the religion in question.
Otherwise, such an approach would be meaningless. However, I claim that
my examinations in section 5 of the six pagan religions has confirmed this
apriori consideration because of the sheer number of references to and hints
at such education presented there.

Moreover, I have argued that this religious education appears to have consisted of the following five types: 1) general reading and learning of the relevant myths of the religion in question, 2) more concentrated studies of the
religion to which an individual might have decided to convert, 3) religious
education organised by teachers belonging to the cult in question aiming
at the approaching initiation, 4) possible (secret) education during the very
initiation, and 5) possible continued studies after the initiation. However, it
should also be emphasised that all these five types did not seem to have been
practiced in all the six religions analysed in this essay.[62]

Finally, this investigations and these results call for an explanation of the
growing role of this sort of religious education that obviously took place in

---

60 I repeat that religious education should not be understood as a purely intellectual
   enterprise because it consisted of at least the three elements, mentioned in section 2:
   doctrinal instruction (myths), moral injunctions, and ritual requirements.
61 Before the year 100 CE, I have only found three texts indicating conversion,
   religious education, and initiation: 1 QS 1.16–3.12; Josephus, Ant. 20.34, and
   the tract *Joseph and Aseneth* 16.14. See Abate in this volume for texts relating to
   education and conversion after this period.
62 This result is also relevant for the topic of conversion as a process, not a sudden
   event (see in this volume Cvetković, Engberg, and Bremmer for this debate).

Christianity. My preliminary guess will be to point, first, to the general influence of the role of education in Hellenistic-Roman society, particularly in philosophy, secondly, to Judaim's unique character as an exclusive religion based on a holy scripture claimed to contain exclusive revelation from the Jewish god Jahve to his chosen people, and, thirdly, to the apologetic needs of Christianity in order to explain, first, its complex relationship to Judaism and, secondly, its opposition to all other Hellenistic-Roman religions as a consequence of Christianity's claim to possess the exclusive religious truth.

Roger Beck

Educating a Mithraist

Abstract: Mithraic initiation was in itself an educational experience, but the initiands must also have received some kind of formal instruction. Beck explores how this might have been done by looking at different Mithraic sources whose function was, at least partly, educational; they instructed both the initiand and the immediate Mithraic community, by reminding it of functions, relationships, and authority within the group.

Although initiation into the mysteries was itself the supreme educational experience, it should not be assumed that initiands and initiates of the Mithras cult never received any kind of formal instruction. The initiand was a pupil who moved, prompted by the initiator, to a new level of understanding, though little or nothing of the lesson may have been put into words.[1] With one probable and another *im*probable exception, there is of course no extant Mithraic creed and no text which could have been taught, learned, and transmitted esoterically; nor should we expect to find one, since Mithraism, broadly speaking, was an "imagistic" rather than a "doctrinal" religion.[2] Nevertheless, the mysteries were surely too complicated and too coherent to have been transmitted solely by rites of initiation and ad hoc Q&A sessions with a Father or other senior member. Somehow, the cult myth must have been taught, the tauroctony (i.e., the image of Mithras killing the bull) explicated, and the mithraeum as "cave" and "cosmic model" explained.[3] In this chapter, I shall explore how this might have been done, beginning with the so-called "Mithraic Catechism from Egypt" and the so-called "Mithras Liturgy", and then moving on to other verbal material such as the graffiti in the Dura and Santa Prisca Mithraea.

---

1   See also Bilde's contribution in the present volume for education in the Mithraic and other mystery cults.
2   For the distinction, see Harvey Whitehouse, *Arguments and Icons. Divergent Modes of Religiosity*, Oxford 2000; id., *Modes of Religiosity. A Cognitive Theory of Religious Transmission*, Walnut Creek 2004. Cf. Martin's contribution in this volume for the cognitive approach in relation to the mystery cults.
3   That the mithraeum represents a "cave" and as such serves as an "image of the universe" is reported by Porphyry in his essay "On the cave of the Nymphs" (*De antro Nympharum*, esp. 6) and has been confirmed archaeologically: see my *Religion of the Mithras Cult in the Roman Empire*, Oxford 2006, 16f. 41f. 102–118. In regard to the complicated Mithraistic learning, contrast with the lack of intellectual demands in Bacchism (Bøgh in this volume). Cf. also Jacobsen for the extended Christian doctrinal education in Christianity.

The "improbable" exception to my generalisation about the absence of Mithraic sacred texts is the so-called Mithras Liturgy, and it is improbable precisely because few, if any, now think it is either a liturgy or Mithraic, although it is generally recognised that it drew eclectically on bits and pieces of genuine Mithraic material.[4] Rather, it is a prescription, of a familiar kind, for a celestial ascent by a Graeco-Egyptian adept. Among other celestial powers, the adept encounters Mithras. There is indeed an educational component, in that the adept is allowed to bring along a junior partner. But of course what is being taught to both the adept and his colleague is not Mithraism in any systematic or "confessional" sense.

This leaves my "probable" exception, the so-called – and I think appropriately so-called – "Mithraic Catechism from Egypt." The document in question is a fourth-century papyrus fragment from Hermupolis in Egypt (P.Berol. 21196).[5] It was published by William Brashear in 1992.[5] It contains Mithraic terms, or more precisely terms which *would* be Mithraic in the proper context: "lion-place" (*leonteion*), lion, father. The form is self-evidently initiatory and catechetical. Two parties are to be engaged in a dialogue: one party is instructed how to answer (imperative *lege* = "say") the questions of the other party (*erei* = "he will say"). This is sufficient to warrant the hypothesis that the document was indeed an actual Mithraic catechism, preparatory to initiation into the Lion grade, or else that it was appropriated, for whatever purposes, from such an original. If so, it is a precious example of the *legomena* (things spoken) which accompanied Mithraic *drômena* (things performed). The Lions constituted the pivotal central grade of the Mithraic hierarchy, with three grades below them and three above. They were the first of the "participants" (*metechontes*); up to that point initiates had been "servitors" (*hypêretountes*).[6] The Fathers, of course, constituted the senior grade, with the authority of Mithras himself in the cult and its community.

Other than this catechism, esoteric Mithraic words and sentences are known to us from two types of provenance: first, quotations in extant literary sources, predominantly Christian, thus hostile and willfully uncomprehending; second, graffiti and dipinti in excavated mithraea. I shall start with an example of the former, a quotation in Firmicus Maternus' *On the error of profane religions* (Err. 5.2):

> Those who worship the gentleman who drives off cattle transfer his rites to the power of fire, just as their prophet has handed down to us the saying:

---

4   H.D. Betz, *The "Mithras Liturgy"*, Tübingen 2003. On the text's purpose, see the study by R.G. Edmonds III in the present volume.

5   Brashear, *A Mithraic Catechism from Egypt*, Vienna 1992.

6   Porph., Abst. 4.16,3.

Initiate of the cattle-theft, right-hand clasper of the glorious Father.
Him they call Mithras, and they transmit his rites in secluded caves, and so, plunged in the obscure squalor of darkness, they ever avoid the grace of splendid and serene light.[7]

Firmicus' polemical point is obvious, the immediate context of his argument less so. His general target here is the worship of the physical elements, and in due course he comes to the element of fire. As was common knowledge, Mithras is a sun god. Therefore, to worship Mithras is to worship fire. Fire gives off light, and the world's great illuminator is the sun. Is it not strange, then, that these Mithraists worship the sun in the darkness of caves? To appreciate the argument, one must realise that mithraea were known esoterically as "caves," and that several of them were indeed situated in natural caves. On that point Firmicus is historically right.

But there is worse. Mithras is an admitted cattle-rustler, an *abactorem bovum*, and the Mithraists are actually initiated into and celebrate this "cattle-theft". Firmicus can prove the point with one of their very own sayings. So the goings-on in a mithraeum are more than just strange; they are deeply sinister, for they celebrate a crime in that typically criminal venue, the bandits' cave. Their very language shows the mysteries of Mithras to be an initiation into a criminal conspiracy.

Let us now switch from a Christian's easy polemical exploitation of this apparently self-incriminating Mithraic saying to the saying's original use within the mysteries, and to the question of whether it might have served an educational function there.

First, is it genuine? Or has Firmicus or his source made it up in order to "frame" the Mithraists as persons of evil intent? Since the discovery of similarly dense hexameter sayings in the dipinti in the Santa Prisca Mithraeum (see below), where they are obviously genuine, scepticism about the phrase Firmicus has found out about seems unwarranted. And the fact that the saying is in Greek is likewise unproblematic. So of course are the Dura graffiti (on which, also, see below). Moreover, since Firmicus does not tell us that he was drawing on a particular community somewhere in the Empire, there is no point in objecting that most Mithraists spoke Latin, not Greek.

Next, the form of the saying. It is a greeting in two vocative phrases. The addressee is an "initiate" (*mysta*), and as such he is entitled to grasp the

---

7　*Virum vero abactorem bovum colentes sacra eius ad ignis transferunt potestatem, sicut propheta eius tradidit nobis dicens:*
Μύστα βοοκλοπίης, συνδέξιε πατρὸς ἀγαυοῦ.
Hunc Mithram dicunt, sacra vero eius in speluncis abditis tradunt ut semper obscuro tenebrarum squalore demersi gratiam splendidi ac sereni luminis vitent.

right hand of the "Father" (*syndexie patros*). The Father is the Father (or *a* Father) of the particular Mithraic community into which the *mystes* is being or has been initiated.

We can identify at least three parties to this exchange: the speaker, the *mystes* addressed, and the Father whose right hand the *mystes* may now grasp. A fourth party is the composer. The saying is in the form of a dactylic hexameter, and the speaker, obviously, is not improvising. Fifth, there is an audience: a complete hexameter is not used for a one-on-one greeting. Sixth and last, we must add Mithras, who is the instigator of the cattle-theft and the cattle-rustler-in-chief. That identity is confirmed for us by Porphyry who at *De antro Nympharum* 18 speaks of Mithras as *bouklopos theos* ("the cattle-thieving god"). The cult title corresponds precisely to the activity. To call someone an "initiate of the cattle-theft" is effectively to call him an initiate of Mithras.

The relationship between two of these parties, the Father and Mithras, needs to be appreciated. In the economy of the cult, a Father is a surrogate of Mithras (as a Sun-Runner is a surrogate of the Sun and a Persian a surrogate of the Moon). In the cult's political economy, he administers the business of Mithras, just as, say, a procurator in a Roman province takes care of the Emperor's business on his behalf – hence the term: *pro-curator*. Now, let us bring in the third party, the initiate. Note in particular that grasping the community *Father's* right hand *ipso facto* makes him an initiate of *Mithras'* cattle stealing. The language of the saying may be Greek, but the concept of relationship expressed (initiate to Father to Mithras) is Roman.

Almost certainly, the saying's intended context is a ceremony of initiation. The new initiate is greeted. The same seems to be the case with another formula quoted by Firmicus Maternus (Err. 19.1): "Behold Nymphos! Hail Nymphos! Hail New Light!" (ἰδέ Νύμφε, χαῖρε Νύμφε, χαῖρε νέον φῶς).[8]

A Nymphos is an initiate of the second grade. The name of the grade is itself strange: a masculine ending on a stem denoting a female person, a bride (*nymphê*). That aspect of the grade, whatever it is, does not concern us now. Here the Nymphos is hailed as the "new light", presumably as someone who brings "new light" to the community. Here too, though less directly, another party is intimated: the planet Venus, the patron of the grade (as Mercury is the patron of the first and lowest grade, the Ravens, and Mars the patron of the third grade, the Soldiers). Venus is of course both the Morning and the Evening Star. Qua the former, she is Phôsphoros/Lucifer, the "light-bringer".

---

8 Translated by R. Gordon, *Reality, Evocation and Boundary in the Mysteries of Mithras*, in: Journal of Mithraic Studies 3 (1980), 19–99 (50). This article, in my opinion, is still the best study of the Mithraic grades.

Now while the *context* for these and other such sayings is probably cult rites of initiation, their *function* is, at least in part, educational. The point is not simply that the sayings have to be taught and learnt – though obviously they do – but that they convey information: they *instruct*. Whom do they instruct? First and foremost, the initiand or new initiate; secondly, the immediate Mithraic community, by reminding it of functions, relationships, and, in our first example, authority within the group.

How do these sayings instruct? Cognitive studies of memory and transmission in religion have established that what is most memorable, and consequently what is most readily and accurately transmitted, is that which is minimally counter-intuitive.[9] In religions and in stories alike, we tend to remember and transmit what violates the natural order in some regard, but not in all regards. Let us take as an example the Mithraic rock-birth. That Mithras was born not from a gynaikomorphic mother, but from a rock is memorable. And this memorable "fact" is transmitted both by sculptured and painted representations and by phrases recorded epigraphically.[10] In a striking phrase, the rock is "the rock that gave birth" (*petra genetrix*). Note the single violation of the natural order: a rock gives birth to an anthropomorphic god. It does not do so while, say, uttering prophecies about its son's future or flying through the air. In all respects except parturition, it is a regular, silent, immobile rock.

In each of the two Mithraic sayings preserved by Firmicus Maternus there is an element of the counter-intuitive which makes them memorable. In the first, it is the transgressiveness. If the initiate thought that he was being inducted into an *entirely* respectable community, he was not *entirely* correct: he was joining a gang of "cattle-rustlers". But he need not worry: he will not be asked to go out and steal cattle "in real life", for he is only a "cattle-rustler" in quotes. In the second saying, the memorable oddity does not lie in calling the initiate the "New Light". That is just an analogy, and a rather trite one at that. No, the memorable oddity is the repeated grade name, Νύμφε ... Νύμφε. As Richard Gordon has pointed out, "the Mithraic word Νύμφος/Nymphus occupies a deliberately impossible semantic space," where "it mediates between the two mutually exclusive terms of the binary opposition bride vs. groom."[11]

---

9 See, for example, Whitehouse, *Modes*, 2004, 30–33. Cf. also the contribution by Martin in this book which goes into more details with the cognitivist approach to the ancient mystery cults.

10 For illustrated examples and explication, see M. Clauss, *The Roman Cult of Mithras. The God and His Mysteries* (R. Gordon, trans.), Edinburgh 2000, 62–68; E. Lissi-Caronna, *Il mitreo dei Castra Peregrinorum (S. Stefano Rotondo)*, Leiden 1986, 29. 31, and pls. 30, 31.

11 Gordon, 1980, 48f.

Third and last, *what* do these sayings teach? In fact, we have already answered that question. They teach precisely those esoteric truths which I have had to discuss in a plodding, exoteric fashion in order to demonstrate *how* they instruct.

We may now turn to texts preserved in mithraea, principally graffiti and dipinti, i.e., scratched and painted texts. First, though, let us glance at the labeling of images. Explicitly calling the scene of the rock-birth *petra genetrix* ("the birth-giving rock") is not unique. We also find the scene of Mithras abducting the bull, hauling it off with its hind legs over his shoulder, called *transitus dei*, the "transit" or "crossing".[12] But why? Guessing an answer is perhaps less important than appreciating the term's oddity and hence its educative value as a piece of memorable *esoterica*. Returning to the rock-birth, we also find the scene called *natura dei*, the "god's *nature*".[13] Now one's *natura* can and does mean one's nature or character *by* birth. But the nature or character *of* one's birth? Surely an etymological stretch – which is precisely the point!

Dipinti and graffiti abound, respectively, in the Santa Prisca Mithraeum on the Aventine Hill in Rome and the Dura Europos Mithraeum on the empire's eastern frontier. Many of the Santa Prisca dipinti are executed in hexameter verse, an obvious mnemonic device.[14] Their immediate context is important. On both sides of the aisle, they accompany scenes of procession in which members of the Lion grade predominate, some identified by their personal names. On the right side (as one enters), the procession leads towards an enthroned Father next to the cult-niche. Painted acclamations take the form of (for example): *Nama Militibus tutela Martis* ("Hail to the Soldiers under the protection of Mars").[15]

Only the Father is distinguished with the more fulsome phrase: "Hail to the Fathers, from orient to occident, under the protection of Saturn" (*Nama Patribus ab oriente ad occidentem tutela Saturni*).[16] For an initiate, then, the lessons of these dipinti and what they illustrate are as follows:

---

12 For examples, see the Epigraphical Index to M.J. Vermaseren, *Corpus Inscriptionum et Monumentorum Religionis Mithriacae* (henceforth CIMRM), 2 vols., The Hague 1956–1960, s.v. *transitus*.

13 For examples, see the Epigraphical Index to CIMRM, s.v. *natura, nascor*.

14 For the verse dipinti, see H.D. Betz, *The Mithras Inscriptions of Santa Prisca and the New Testament*, in: NT 10 (1968), 62–80. For the best illustrations of the frescos and dipinti, see U. Bianchi (ed.), *Mysteria Mithrae*, Leiden 1979, 885–929, pls. 1–25. On the mithraeum in general, see M.J. Vermaseren / C.C. van Essen, *The Excavations in the Mithraeum of the Church of Santa Prisca in Rome*, Leiden 1965.

15 CIMRM 480.5.

16 CIMRM 480.1.

1. The esoteric word of acclamation of fellow initiates is the Persian *Nama*.
2. There are seven grades in a hierarchy leading from Ravens (most junior) to Fathers (most senior).
3. Each grade is under the protection of one of the seven planets. Thus, it is Mars qua planet which takes care of Mithraic Soldiers, not simply Mars the warrior god.
4. Fathers are everywhere supreme.

On the opposite side of the aisle, an analogous procession is composed entirely of Lions. They are depicted moving towards the feasting Mithras and Sol. An important lesson of the scenes and grade phrases on *both* sides is the special relationship between Mithras and the Father and between Sol and the Sun-Runner. In the cult context, it is the Father and the Sun-Runner together who replicate the feast of the two gods. Reinforcing the lesson is the representation of the server in the banquet scene: he is painted with a raven's head which indicates that if this were an actual cult feast, he would be an initiate of the Raven grade.

But like the best sort of esoteric lessons, these scenes and grade phrases, as they offer answers at one level, pose new questions at another. The Father is the surrogate of Mithras at the banquet, while the Sun-Runner is the Sun's. But Mithras himself is DEUS *SOL* INVICTUS MITHRAS. However, to ease cognitive dissonance, the texts offer the insight that while the seven grades cannot match the seven planets one for one if the structure must accommodate two "Suns," an *aporia* is circumvented by putting the cult Father "under *Saturn's* protection".

Before turning to the verse texts on the left-hand wall at Santa Prisca, let us look briefly at the graffiti in the Dura Mithraeum,[17] since most of them concern grades and individual grade-holders. As at Santa Prisca they are mostly greetings and acclamations, *Nama*-phrases predominating. But in contrast to the Santa Prisca dipinti, keyed to the sequences of fresco depictions, the Dura graffiti are haphazard, ad hoc scrawls. Thus, although they tell us much about grade names and variants and about the cultists as individuals, obviously they did not and could not serve a coherent educational purpose. Only two of the graffiti have what one might call teachable content. One is what I think of as the fireman's nightmare: the expression *eisodos/exodos* ("entry/exit") scratched on a column near which there was no actual, physical "way in" or "way out" – or ever had been![18] Elsewhere I have argued that the phrase marks the mid point of the aisle where *symbolically*

---

17 E.D. Francis, *Mithraic Graffiti from Dura-Europos*, in: J.R. Hinnells (ed.), *Mithraic Studies*, vol.1, Manchester 1975, 424–445.
18 CIMRM 66.

the gates of genesis and apogenesis through which souls enter and leave the world of mortality are located.[19]

The second resembles in form and content the Santa Prisca dipinti which we are about to review:

> Fiery breath, which is for the Magi too the baptism/lustration of holy (men)
> (πυρωπὸν ἄσθμα τὸ καὶ μάγοις ἢ νίπτρον ὁσίων).[20]

This graffito is eminently compact and paradoxical, thus both memorable and teachable: breath which is fiery, but also liquid, used for holy people and thus for Magi, too. As should be clear by now, it is not my intention to explicate the saying, to say what it "means".

The remaining dipinti on the left-hand wall in the Santa Prisca Mithraeum are very much of this sort. Unlike the grade acclamations, they are not generally keyed to the scenes below. Nor do they form a progression: one text does not lead to the next. Each is self-contained. I shall take a single example, one which happens to complement the Dura graffito above, as Richard Gordon appreciated.[21] Both have to do with fire. Here is the Santa Prisca text:

> Father, receive those who burn incense, Holy one, receive the Lions, through whom we offer incense, through/by whom we are ourselves are consumed.[22]

First, the text takes the form an elegiac couplet. In Latin poetry, the couplet can be repeated indefinitely to form quite a long composition. Alternatively, a single couplet can stand by itself as an epigram, which I think is the case here. The saying is self-contained; it raises no expectation of something still to come. It might have to be explicated, but it does not have to be completed.

Next, it has a speaker and a context, like the saying preserved by Firmicus Maternus with which we started ("Initiate of the cattle-theft," etc.). The speaker is participating in a rite in which he is asking a "Holy Father" to receive the "incense-bearing Lions".

The addressee is explicit. He is a Father (or one of the Fathers) of the Mithraic community. But is he *just* a Father? Surely not. *In* the Father – or *behind* the Father, or *above* the Father, whatever preposition one chooses – is not Mithras, whose surrogate the cult Father is, also intended? Is not he the one who is properly asked to receive the incense-burning Lions? After all, one burns incense for a god, not for his human counterpart.

---

19 Beck, 2006, 111.
20 Translated by Gordon, 1980, 36.
21 Gordon, 1980, 36.
22 *Accipe thuricremos, Pater, accipe, Sancte, Leones, per quos thuradamus, per quos consumimur ipsi* (lines 16–17 in H.D. Betz, 1968, 78; translated by Gordon, 1980, 36).

The second line introduces another party, the communal "we". The Lions *burn* the incense (*thuricremos*), but they do so on *our* behalf: it is *we* who *offer* the incense (*thuradamus*), and, paradoxically and alarmingly, "are through" the Lions "ourselves consumed" (*per quos thuradamus, per quos consumimur ipsi*).

All along, we have been concerned not so much with the precise esoteric meanings of the preserved sayings as with *how* those meanings, whatever they might have been, were conveyed to initiates within the mysteries of Mithras. The last example illustrates well how language is crafted for educational ends to convey dense, but memorable messages through the shock of the paradoxical and the counter-intuitive.

Elisabetta Abate

Observations on Late Antique Rabbinic Sources on Instruction of Would-Be Converts[1]

Abstract: Abate investigates which kind of education rabbinic Judaism envisioned in connection with conversion. The sources reveal the requirements for valid conversion, and they also imply that an on-going process of acculturation will continue to unfold after formal conversion, but they display no attempt at exerting control over the further stages in this process.

Introduction

According to late antique rabbinic views, with a certain degree of variation throughout the sources, the requirements for a valid conversion to Judaism include acceptance of the Torah, proper intention, circumcision, immersion, and sacrifice.[2] Scant attention is devoted to the instruction of would-be converts, namely in two parallel texts describing how a non-Jew or a non-Jewess could join Israel (as will be seen below, Yevamot 47ab in the Babylonian

---

1   I wish to thank the members of the "Velux Group", and particularly Dr. Birgitte Bøgh, for kindly inviting me to contribute to this volume, as well as the participants of the conference at Ebeltoft for their remarks. I am also grateful to Prof. Günter Stemberger (University of Vienna) for commenting on the reflections I shared on that occasion. I also thank Pete Walton for his consultation on the English language usage in the paper. This revised version thereof has been prepared within the framework of the Courant Research Centre "Education and Religion" (University of Göttingen), funded by the German Initiative of Excellence.

2   L.H. Schiffman regards acceptance of the Torah "in its widest sense" (i.e., as full identification with Israel and the halakhic way of life) as a fundamental component of the conversion procedure and ceremony described in the sources examined below in this contribution, alongside circumcision, immersion, and sacrifice (L.H. Schiffman, *Who Was a Jew? Rabbinic and Halakhic Perspectives on the Jewish-Christian Schism*, Hoboken 1985, 19–32 (21)). Acceptance of the Torah is also emphasised by S.J.D. Cohen, *The Beginnings of Jewishness. Boundaries, Varieties, Uncertaintie*s, Berkeley 1999, 218f. On proper intention, see Cohen, 1999, 218f. 226–228. 231–234; G.G. Porton, *The Stranger within Your Gates. Converts and Conversion in Rabbinic Literature,* Chicago 1994, 151f. For scholars who indicated circumcision, immersion, and sacrifice as the rabbinic requirements of conversion (based on Sifre Numbers Shelaḥ 108), see Porton, 1994, 132–134. 152–154, who conversely stresses the flexibility and lack of unanimity of the sources. On sacrifice, inapplicable after the destruction of the Temple in 70, see Porton, 1994, 134–139.

Talmud, and Gerim 1:1; 4). The aim of this contribution is to illustrate aspects of both sources relating to the question of which kind of education rabbinic Judaism envisioned in connection with conversion and also to touch upon a complementary phenomenon: a relative lack of concern about defining the process that would lead converts to become competent members in the new group and new religion. A thorough investigation of these topics lies far beyond the present limits. However, I hope that the reflections proposed here might serve as an introduction and lead to future developments.

The sources

Yevamot 47ab (henceforth Yev. 47ab) is a *baraita* (i.e., a tradition attributed to Palestinian sages of the Mishnaic period, but not preserved in the Mishnah) within an extended *sugya* or literary unit in the Babylonian Talmud (Yevamot 46a–48b).[3] On the basis of form analysis, this *sugya* has been identified as a "tractate within a tractate" dealing with the conversion procedure and consisting of a later Babylonian reweaving of six *baraitot* and of the corresponding discussions (*gemara*).[4] Overall, the later reworking displays a tendency towards the institutionalisation of the conversion procedure and an increasing stringency in the acceptance of converts that would reflect Babylonian developments (ca. 5th or 6th century, or beyond) of earlier Palestinian (ca. 2nd century) and Babylonian (ca. 3rd and 4th centuries) concerns.[5] Towards the end of this contribution, I will consider whether this tendency can be detected in connection with the question of instruction for would-be converts. The second main source is the unique parallel of this *baraita* (Gerim 1:1; 4), found in the tractate Gerim, "Proselytes". Gerim, like the other so-called minor tractates of the Babylonian Talmud, appears to have been redacted in Palestine during the second half of the first millennium, primarily on the basis of earlier materials.[6]

---

3 For an overview of the late antique rabbinic period and its literary offspring, see particularly G. Stemberger, *Einleitung in Talmud und Midrasch. Neunte, vollständig neubearbeitete Auflage*, Munich 2011 (71–115 on the rabbis; 211–247 on the Babylonian Talmud; 219f. on the *baraitot* within the latter). For scholarship on the *sugya*, see references in M. Lavee, *The 'Tractate of Conversion' – BT YEB. 46–48 and the Evolution of Conversion Procedure*, in: EJJS 4/2 (2011), 169–213 (173, n. 9).
4 See Lavee, 2011, 171f. and *passim*.
5 Thus Lavee, 2011, 169f. and *passim*.
6 R. Brody, *The Geonim of Babylonia and the Shaping of Medieval Jewish Culture*, New Haven 1998, 109f. See also M.B. Lerner, *The External Tractates,* in: S. Safrai (ed.), *The Literature of the Sages. First Part. Oral Torah, Halakha, Mishna, Tosefta, Talmud, External Tractates*, Assen 1987, 367–403. The thorough

In the following, I will introduce the procedure as envisioned in both sources, suggesting that one should rather speak of two procedures for they diverge in at least two main areas (circumcision, and instruction for women). Then, I will turn to their content with regard to instruction for converts.[7] Yev. 47ab states:

> [Yev. 47a] Our Rabbis taught: A (potential) convert who approaches to be converted, they say to him: 'Why have you decided to approach (us) to be converted? Do you not know that Israel(ites) at this time are pained, oppressed, harassed, and torn, and that afflictions come upon them?' If he says, 'I know and am unworthy,' they accept him immediately. And they make known to him a few of the light commandments and a few of the severe commandments. And they make known to him the sin of (the violation of the laws of) gleanings, the forgotten sheaf, the corner of the field, and the poor tithe. And they make known to him the punishment for (violation of) the commandments. They say to him: 'Make sure you realise that, before you arrived at this measure, if you had eaten forbidden fat you would not have been liable to punishment by *karet*;[8] if you had profaned the Sabbath you would not have been liable to punishment by stoning. But now, were you to eat forbidden fat you would be liable to punishment by *karet*; were you to profane the Sabbath you would be liable to punishment by stoning.' And just as they make known to him the punishment for (violation of) the commandments, they make known to him their reward (for their fulfilment). They say to him: 'Make sure you realise that the world to come was made only for the righteous, and that Israelites at this time are not able to receive [Yev. 47b] either the larger part of the good (that is due to them) or the larger part of the chastisement (that is due to them).' But they do not (speak) too much to him, nor are they too detailed with him. If he accepts, they circumcise him immediately. If shreds remain on him that impede the circumcision, they circumcise him a second time. When he has healed, they immerse him immediately, and two disciples of the sages stand over him and make known to him a few of the light commandments and a few of the severe commandments. When he has immersed and risen (from the water), behold, he is like (an) Israel(ite) in all respects. (In the case of) a woman, women make her sit in water up to her neck, and two disciples of the sages stand near her outside (the place of the

---

investigation of method and purpose of Gerim is a desideratum (Cohen, 1999, 215), as well as a critical edition entailing a systematic comparison of the tractate and all its parallel sources in rabbinic literature (Lavee, 2011, 179 and n. 18). Therefore, among other aspects not yet ascertained, its relationship to the Yevamot text remains unclear.

7   For a detailed analysis of these sources, see Cohen, 1999, 198–238 (revised version of S.J.D. Cohen, *The Rabbinic Conversion Ceremony*, in: JJS 41 (1990), 177–203).

8   Premature or sudden death, as opposed to death by execution (e.g., stoning).

immersion), and make known to her a few of the light commandments and a few of the severe commandments.[9]

Gerim 1:1; 4 reads as follows:

[1:1] Whoever desires to be converted, they do not accept him immediately, but they say to him: 'Why do you wish to be converted? Behold, you see that this nation is downtrodden and tortured more than all (other) nations, and that many diseases and afflictions come upon them, and that they bury their children and grandchildren, and they are killed because of (their observance of) circumcision and immersion and the remainder of the commandments, and they do not practice their customs publicly like all the other nations?' If he says, 'I am unworthy to put my neck in the yoke of Him who spoke and the world came to be, blessed is He,' they accept him immediately. But if he does not (answer thus), he is dismissed and wanders off. If he accepts upon himself they bring him down to the immersion house and they cover him with water until the place of his nakedness. They say to him a few of the details of the commandments, on condition that he contribute gleanings, the forgotten sheaf, the corner of the field, and the tithe. Just as they say to a man (a few of the details of the commandments), thus do they say (them) to a woman, on condition that she be careful (in her observance of) menstruation, bread-dough offering, and the lighting of the (Sabbath) lamp. When he has immersed and risen from water, they speak to him kind words, words of comfort, 'To whom have you attached yourself? Happy are you (for you have attached yourself) to Him who spoke and the world came to be, blessed is He. The world was created only for the sake of Israel, and only Israel were called children of God, and only Israel are dear before God. And all those (other) words that we said to you, we said them only to increase your reward.' [...] [1:4] A man immerses a man [but does not immerse a woman]; a woman immerses a woman but (does) not (immerse) a man.[10]

Instruction for converts in the making

According to Yev. 47ab, the initiative of conversion is taken by the somewhat liminal figure of "the convert who approaches to be converted" (רייגתהל אבש רג), perhaps a sympathiser already familiar with some aspects of Jewishness without being a Jew by birth.[11] The very first precondition of his acceptance as a

---

9   Translation as in Cohen, 1999, 199–202, which is based on A. Liss (ed.), *Tractate Yevamot*, vol. 2, Jerusalem 1986, 193–199.
10 Translation as in Cohen, 1999, 200f., based on M. Higger (ed.), *Seven Minor Tractates*, New York 1930, 68f.
11 On this possibility, see the heuristic model through which S.J.D. Cohen accounts for the process of becoming "less a gentile and more a Jew," and particularly the fourth category, touching on practice of Jewish rituals and daily life, in Cohen, 1999, 140–174 (149f.) (originally published as Cohen, *Crossing the Boundaries and Becoming a Jew*, in: HThR 82 (1989), 13–33). But see also the objection

candidate for conversion[12] is that, upon examination, he expresses his awareness of the sufferings the People of Israel are enduring, and of his being unworthy of belonging to it. This instead makes him worthy of belonging, for it reveals his willingness to share Israel's lot.[13] It also indicates his internalising the historical memory and self-representation of the group he wishes to join (an aspect that merges with *pathos* in Gerim). Thus, after having been accepted on this basis, he is imparted four pieces of information. First of all, he hears about some of the light and some of the severe commandments (a well-attested distinction in rabbinic literature, whose force in this context is unclear).[14] Then he learns that avoiding making contributions to the poor from one's harvest is a sin[15] or, possibly, that the unjustifiable collection of poor men's tithes is sinful and amounts to an abuse of the new status as a Jew.[16] He is taught that transgression of food laws (provided that the reference to forbidden fat functions as a *pars pro toto* indication) and of Sabbath's observance will result in death; such a warning, at least ideally, concerns the irreversibility of his adherence to the new religion and group and about separation from gentiles.[17] Lastly, he is told that one's getting a share in the world to come depends on his merit in this world (i.e., it is not automatically attached to a change of status, but requires active practice).

After introducing these four aspects, the anonymous voice in the text recommends moderation when elaborating the details of Jewish practice.[18] This

---

that interethnic friendships in the Mediterranean and Near Eastern worlds, such as amity between Jews and gentiles, were not "primarily engines of 'assimilation' and acculturation," in S. Schwartz, *Conversion to Judaism in the Second Temple Period. A Functionalist Approach*, in: S.J.D. Cohen / J.J. Schwartz (eds.), *Studies in Josephus and the Varieties of Ancient Judaism. Louis H. Feldman Jubilee Volume*, Leiden 2007, 223–236 (226).

12 Thus Cohen, 1999, 203, explains the turn of phrase "He is accepted immediately."

13 On the expectation that the convert takes upon himself the past, present, and future of Israel, see Schiffman, 1985, 21; cf. Crook in this volume on the collectivistic culture of the Jews.

14 Cohen, 1999, 205.

15 Schiffman, 1985, 22, understands the text as specifically singling out "[L]aws regarding charity for the poor [...] as the only essential subject of discussion." However, the text speaks only about contribution from one's harvest and is therefore relevant only for converts who own land in *Eretz Israel*.

16 This is the interpretation provided by Cohen, 1999, 205f. and nn. 12f.

17 On dietary habits and the Sabbath as the most evident among Jewish identity markers, see, e.g., Porton, 1994, 150 and n. 107. Cf. Rebillard in this volume for Christian identity markers, and Jacobsen for the way the creed functioned to mark out a Christian identity.

18 Porton, 1994, 149f. and n. 104.

point implies that further familiarity with the halakhic way of life, that is, proper life conduct ensuring and consisting of compliance with the Torah, is left for future developments. The latter are, however, not specified, which I shall touch on later. The first series of teachings is now completed, and if the convert in the making accepts them, he is in turn accepted again, as was the case for his accepting Israel's lot. Acceptance of the Torah is in fact, as hinted at in the introduction, a prerequisite of conversion, and one of the purposes of instruction of would-be converts. In illustrating this point, L.H. Schiffman construed Yev. 47ab in light of Tosefta Demai 2:5, a rabbinic tradition that rules as follows:

> [A convert who took (or takes) upon himself all the precepts of the Torah except one, they do not accept him.] Rabbi Yose in the name of Rabbi Yehudah says: 'Even a small thing from the subtleties of the scribes.'[19]

Whereas the views in this Tosefta passage champion a *crescendo* of stringency in rabbinic opinions about the would-be convert's willingness to take upon himself the Torah, they do not expand on the circumstances under which he is supposed to learn the precepts.[20] In other words, they are not about instruction. This remark prompts a distinction to be drawn between the requirement of acceptance of the Torah as a *sine qua non* of valid conversion and familiarity with the rabbinic *halakhah*. This distinction seems in fact to be implied in the nature of the instruction envisioned in the conversion procedure, as the candidate is provided only scant information of what is expected of him. Regarding the procedure's informative purpose and especially the extension of the information itself, S.J.D. Cohen refers to the above tradition (Tosefta Demai 2:5) as the passage taking the maximalist approach in rabbinic literature, and to the midrash on Ruth 1:16–17 as a text expressing a more moderate position about the scope of instruction for converts. The fullest version of this Midrash is that preserved in Yev. 47b, specifically in the *Gemara* on the recommendation to restrain information to the candidate. It entails Ruth's acceptance of Naomi's prohibition

---

19 See Schiffman, 1985, 22, based on S. Lieberman, *Tosefta According to Codex Vienna with Variants from Codex Erfurt, Genizah Mss. and Editio Princeps (Venice 1521), Together with References to Parallel Passages in Talmudic Literature and a Brief Commentary. Seder Zera'im*, New York 1955, 69; id., *Tosefta ki-fshuṭah, Order Zera'im, Part 1*, New York 1955, 212. The translation is mine. For the parallels in which this tradition is preserved, see Babylonian Talmud (tractate Bekhorot 30a), Sifra (Qedoshim pereq 8:3 (ed. Weiss 91a)), Sifre Numbers 112 (ed. Horovitz 121). For further discussion of the topic and of this tradition, see Cohen, 1999, 228–234 (229–231).

20 With this regard, Schiffman assumes that only the laws he knows of are meant (Schiffman, 1985, 22).

of exceeding the Sabbath limits and of non-marital intimacy, the 613 commandments, the denial of idolatry, the four modes of execution inflicted by the court, and the two kinds of court-supervised burial. Cohen writes: "These midrashim are based on the exegesis of Scripture, not actual practice. They demonstrate, however, that the instruction of converts did not have to treat all the commandments in detail and could consist of a rather cursory summary of large issues."[21] Again, it appears that the relevant sources do not rule on the acquisition of halakhic competence. Their main concern is rather about the would-be convert's awareness of his responsibility.

Once accepted for the second time, the would-be convert is circumcised – twice if necessary.[22] After healing, he is immersed in water in the presence of two of the sages' disciples who instruct him a second time, but only in "a few of the light commandments and a few of the severe commandments." I shall return to this expression below and explore possible reasons for the duplication of instruction. For now, I shall conclude this concise interpretation of the procedure's account by noting that upon emerging from water, the "convert who approaches to be converted" is deemed an Israelite in all respects: the language of status change seals the conversion that he himself initiated.[23] At this point, the text abruptly shifts to the conversion of women by outlining a similar procedure to that for male would-be converts: immersion, witnessed by women,[24] with basic instruction in "a few of the light commandments and a few of the severe commandments" from two of the sages' disciples. The presence of women as witnesses and the safe distance that male instructors are kept at are not "the only differences in the procedure for males and females."[25] The gender unevenness that characterises the unfolding of the procedure for women and the content of instruction reveals a lack of insistence and emphasis on female acceptance of the Torah, proper intention, and awareness of future obligations.

I will now return to the duplication of instruction in the procedure for men. As seen above, the latter entails a first set of teachings before circumcision, and a second set during immersion. Both share core basic information about "a few of the light commandments and a few of the severe commandments," but

---

21 For this interpretation, see Cohen, 1999, 229f. and n. 80, quoting Ruth Rabbah on 1:16–17 as edited in M.B. Lerner (ed.), *Midrash Ruth Rabbah According to Ms. Oxford 164* (PhD diss.), Jerusalem 1971, 76–78.
22 On the requirement of a second operation to avoid the dissimulation of circumcision, see Cohen, 1999, 225 and further literature in n. 66.
23 On the occurrence of the language of status change in Yev. 47ab (but not in Gerim), see Lavee, 2011, 179f. and n. 20.
24 See Gerim 1:4.
25 Thus Cohen, 1999, 208.

the first expands on the content by referring to the agricultural laws in support of the poor, and to the punishment and reward correlated respectively to the transgression and the observance of the commandments. A possible account of this phenomenon underlines that both the instruction that immediately precedes circumcision and its repetition during immersion are aimed at ensuring that appropriate motivation inspires these acts and, ultimately, conversion.[26]

I would like to pursue this argument further by suggesting that close attention be paid to part of the procedure that might help reveal a further dimension of the narrative, namely the mention of healing. Healing is important through being an implicit indicator of the passing of time between circumcision and immersion or, in other words, of a suspension of the ceremony for the time needed to recover. In fact, if one wishes to read this *baraita* as evidence of an actual practice, at least to some extent, and not as a textual concoction without basis in historical fact, then one should consider the temporal dimension that is constrained in a linear descriptive sequence. If so, one could imagine that while healing there is a risk that the convert in the making would forget the information received before circumcision. Repeating the information when the procedure is resumed would thus amount to renewed instruction. That would underlie a strategy to reinforce the would-be convert's awareness of the message he had been transmitted before circumcision, and to further foster his intention of accepting the commandments. Still in this line of reasoning, another option would be to regard the renewed instruction after the ceremony's suspension as a very last test of the would-be convert's intention before completing the procedure. However, this would also require the clause "If he accepts" before immersion, which is missing. A third option is to see the second set of information not as a renewed learning situation, for which it would be too brief, but rather as a ritual comparable to the instruction of the catechumens during baptism.[27]

I shall now turn to the procedure of conversion as envisioned in Gerim 1:1; 4, and principally to the parts relevant to instruction.[28] As seen above, this source opens by specifying that "Whoever desires to be converted" is not to be accepted immediately, but rather to be examined and warned as to the persecution and sufferings of Israel, and only if he expresses his unworthiness is he then accepted immediately, and otherwise dismissed. "If he accepts (Israel's lot) upon himself," he is immersed in water and instructed in "a few of the details of the commandments, on condition that he contribute gleanings, the forgotten sheaf, the corner of the field, and the tithe." The

---

26 Cohen, 1999, 226. 228.
27 I thank Prof. Stemberger for pointing that out to me.
28 For a full discussion of the procedure as envisioned there, see Cohen, 1999, 211–217.

mention of agricultural charity laws is obviously reminiscent of the parallel text, but the wording "on condition that" in Gerim 1:1 underlines the would-be convert's future halakhic responsibility and tests his awareness and proper intention. These requirements were already noted in Yev. 47a.[29]

In contrast to the instruction for women in the Yevamot text, the instruction envisioned here displays a remarkable gender symmetry,[30] in that it expands on women's duties by stressing that a female would-be convert is to be instructed in "a few of the details of the commandments, on condition that she be careful" in keeping the commandments on menstrual purity, dough offering, and the kindling of the Sabbath lamp. Since negligence or transgression of these three precepts is traditionally presented as the cause of death in childbirth,[31] their mention somewhat corresponds to death by *karet* or stoning – the punishment for a male would-be convert for transgressing the commandments in the first set of instruction in Yev. 47a. Gender symmetry in the instruction is not the only trait that differentiates the procedure as envisioned in Yev. 47ab from that conceived of in Gerim 1:1; 4, to the extent that it would be appropriate to speak of two procedures: their structure, although similar, differs also in the lack of circumcision in the minor tractate, which has its focal point in immersion.[32]

After immersion, the (male) would-be convert is addressed with welcoming words of comfort. It has been noted that, in comparison to Yev. 47ab, Gerim 1:1 puts emphasis more on the people of Israel than the commandments, in that it expands on the sufferings of Israel in the opening speech as well as on the uniqueness of Israel in the closing speech while reducing the section on the precepts.[33] I would like to highlight the intensive emotional

---

29 In Cohen's words, "[U]nless we are to believe that for Gerim the agricultural tithes for the poor are the absolute essentials of Judaism, the phrase (scil., 'on condition that') would seem to have the force of 'for example' or 'specifically'." (Cohen, 1999, 216). However, the conjunction ‑ש על מנת ל‎ ("on condition that") "underlines the interest or intention of the subject" (M. Pérez Fernández, *An Introductory Grammar of Rabbinic Hebrew*, Leiden 1997, 234); hence my slightly different interpretation. I acknowledge that the tithes are mentioned as an example of biblical laws, as in the continuation for women. Here, too, essential laws regarding *kashrut* are not mentioned.

30 A sort of symmetry, although imperfect, also characterises Gerim 1:4 on witnessed immersion: "A man immerses a man; a woman immerses a woman, but not a man."

31 Mishnah Shabbat 2:6 and numerous parallels in later works.

32 Although Gerim knows of circumcision (Gerim 1:1–2; 2:1–2; 2:4), it does not locate it in the core of the conversion procedure. See the discussion in Cohen, 1999, 214–216.

33 Thus Cohen, 1999, 212.

charge in which this phenomenon results, with its accent on worry and pain in the initial words, and the release generated by the consolation in the conclusion. In this light, Gerim insists on the individual's internalisation of the group's collective narrative and self-representation, exposing a function of the instruction of would-be converts that borders on identity construction.[34] Only to a minor extent was that observable in the initial warning about Israel's sufferings formulated in Yevamot.[35]

As far as the content of instruction is concerned, both sources provide little halakhic information for would-be converts. Schiffman remarked that proselytes could not be expected to learn all about *halakhah* before experiencing it; hence the sampling of the commandments during the ceremony meant mostly a means to foster their sense of responsibility.[36] Also Cohen stressed that instruction in a few representative commandments would serve this purpose, and that the rest would be acquired by means of future learning.[37] However, to the best of my knowledge, the future learning of the new members of the Jewish fold is neither ruled upon, nor extensively described in other sources. One could recall a famous sequence of three stories in the Babylonian Talmud (tractate Shabbat 31a) in which the gentle Hillel, in contrast to the harsh Shammai, welcomes three gentiles as proselytes even though their motivations were not considered correct by the rabbis.

The first gentile insists on being accepted as a convert on condition that he be taught only the Written Torah (i.e., the Hebrew Bible), but the following day acknowledges the need to rely on his teacher's authority and on the Oral Torah (i.e., rabbinic tradition) as well. The second demands to be accepted on condition that he be taught the whole Torah while standing on one leg, whereby he is told: "What is hateful to you, do not to your neighbour: that is the whole Torah, while the rest is the commentary thereof; go and learn it."[38] The third wishes to convert in order to be appointed a high

---

34 Cohen notes that the monitory words of the opening section "serve to heighten the drama of the ceremony" (Cohen, 1999, 232 and n. 87), but does not relate this to the construction of the identity of the would-be convert.

35 This observation modifies, to my mind, Cohen's statement that "[I]n this ritual, by which a gentile becomes a member of the Jewish people, the Jewish community is conspicuously absent" (Cohen, 1999, 235).

36 Schiffman, 1985, 21, with reference to our *baraita* in Yevamot. For further reading, see his study *Sectarian Law in the Dead Sea Scrolls. Courts, Testimony, and the Penal Code*, Chico 1983, 156–159, where he observes "[a] similar phenomenon regarding the instruction of new members of the Qumran sect" (ibid., 84, n. 23).

37 Cohen, 1999, 230f., and n. 82 for further references.

38 H. Freedman, *Shabbath*, in: I. Epstein (ed.), *The Babylonian Talmud. Translated into English with Notes, Glossary and Indices. Seder Mo'ed. In Two Volumes*, vol. 2, London 1938, 139f.

priest after hearing Ex 28:4 and its depiction of priestly attire; however, he later comprehends the falsehood of his ambitions through his own (!) midrashic interpretation of the verse.

These stories chiefly illustrate the difference between conversion and commitment,[39] but also suggest that a limited amount of knowledge was admitted as a prerequisite for conversion, for the essential would be learnt afterwards.[40] However, they do not spell out how the new Jews were supposed to concretely engage in further learning. No other sources deal extensively with the converts' learning process, not only *during*, but also *after* the conversion ceremony. No devices or strategies are foreseen for the proselytes to put their newly acquired Jewish identity into practice in ways fitting rabbinic standards. This is remarkable because Jewish identity, as conceived of in rabbinic sources, is not "an abstraction, such as a logical, theoretical contrast between self and other," but a "concrete reality which is articulated in a social environment and in a physical *milieu.*"[41]

If the Torah is deemed to distinguish Israel from other nations as a bodily and dynamic constituent of Jewish personal identity – fitting examples are Sabbath observance, the festivals, and the calendar[42] – it follows that new converts would require a great deal of training in order to be able to distinguish themselves from non-Jews. In point of fact, some sources question the proselytes' capability of properly observing the commandments, and especially their obligations to participate in holidays and sacred rituals, due to not having been raised in a Jewish environment.[43] Participation in the full life of the community would ensure the proselytes' acquisition of traditions, customs, and practices.[44] Nevertheless, the sources focus on the interruption of their old social bonds without touching on the ways they could establish new networks (with the exception of their relationship with the rabbis themselves). This would have enhanced not only their commitment to the new group,[45] but also their further cultural socialisation.

A possible explanation for the scant information imparted during the conversion ceremony is the prohibition of teaching Torah to a gentile.[46]

---

39 Porton, 1994, 196–200 (199).

40 Cohen, 1999, 230, n. 82.

41 S. Stern, *Jewish Identity in Early Rabbinic Writings,* Leiden 1994, 51.

42 Stern, 1994, 51–81 (71. 74. 76–78).

43 Thus Porton, 1994, 183. 213. 357, n. 112 (for the example of the prohibition of forming a separate association for the Passover sacrifice enjoined upon converts found in the Palestinian Talmud, tractate Pesaḥim 8:7, Venice 36a, and in the Babylonian Talmud, tractate Pesaḥim 91b).

44 Porton,1994, 199.

45 Porton, 1994, 207–211 (208).

46 Cohen, 1999, 231 and n. 84, with reference to Stern, 1994, 214, n. 116.

However, this reason is in itself not sufficient to explain the lack of concern in regulating the details of the proselytes' future acquisition of Jewish identity and practice once they are accepted as Israelites. This could be interpreted as conversion being a relatively infrequent occurrence. Thus, rabbinic discussions on it might be aimed at refining aspects of rabbinic law rather than defining the details of the real situations of conversion.[47]

Lastly, it is time to consider the question, raised in the introduction, of whether the later Babylonian tendency towards higher stringency in accepting converts, identified by M. Lavee in the *sugya* of which Yev. 47ab is a component, can also be detected with regard to instruction. An important premise for this is that the comparative method employed by Lavee to analyse the *sugya* is not applicable to our specific *baraita* as it lacks parallels besides Gerim 1:1; 4 itself. Therefore, the answer to the present question is rather speculative. However, two comments are in order: on the one hand, some degree of institutionalisation can be seen in the very inclusion of instruction in the procedure for valid conversion. On the other, the halakhic information imparted to the would-be converts is only slight and shows no attempt to rule extensively and precisely about present or future acquisition of halakhic competence although this would ensure the distinctiveness of the convert as a Jew, and not as a gentile any longer; moreover, instruction is not entrusted to institutional bodies: the only figures endowed with educational tasks are the anonymous instructors who impart the male would-be convert his first set of teachings, and the two disciples of the sages responsible for instruction of both men and women during immersion. This can be contrasted with a characteristic of the later Babylonian reworking of earlier materials in the *sugya*, namely the introduction of a court for conversion devised in the *baraita* immediately preceding Yev. 47ab in the *sugya*, which appears to be a Babylonian construct and absent from other Palestinian sources.[48] One is inclined to conclude that the "Babylonian efforts to further reinforce the boundaries of Jewish identity",[49] observable throughout the *sugya*, did not entail an articulated plan for the education of converts and, in the general reweaving of earlier layers of tradition found in the *sugya*, were not transferred to this specific *baraita*.

---

47 Thus Porton who attempts to explain "the inconsistency concerning the ritual requirements for conversion" (Porton 1994, 152–154. 333, n. 136). *Contra* Porton's depiction of the uncertainty of the ritual requirements, see, however, Cohen, 1999, 221, n. 52.
48 On the introduction of the court, see Lavee, 2011, 178f. 182. 186–188.
49 Formulation borrowed from Lavee, 2011, 169.

Conclusion

In the vast corpus of late antique rabbinic literature only two passages are devoted to the instruction of converts in the making, Yev. 47ab and Gerim 1:1; 4. In both, however, instruction undoubtedly features among the prerequisites for valid conversion to Judaism, for it serves functions such as verifying the would-be convert's intention of adhering to the new group's lot, historical memory, and self-representation; ensuring his readiness to take upon himself the Torah even without being fully competent in the halakhic ways moulded by the rabbis; and informing him of his future responsibilities. Considerably more attention is paid to the process involving male would-be converts whereas women are mentioned marginally, especially in Yevamot. Conversely in Gerim, the instruction undergone by women is given more prominence, in that it counterparts the instruction for men in an even manner.

Both texts envision instruction as taking place *during* the formal procedure of conversion and not as a preparation for it, but also not as further learning afterwards. Unless they are in effect content with the specific pieces of information they impart about the commandments, our sources imply that an ongoing process of acculturation and acquisition of halakhic competence will continue to unfold after formal conversion. Interestingly, however, they display no attempt at exerting strict control over the further stages in this process, for example by better determining some of the representative pieces of information or by appointing figures endowed with formal educational tasks. A possible explanation is that the rabbinic circles of late antiquity enjoyed a limited control over the process, or at least over its developments in the broader non-rabbinic Jewish society, but this should not eclipse the continuous attention paid to proselytism by rabbinic sources throughout the whole rabbinic period.[50] Most instruction of converts remained informal, through socialisation in a Jewish community, therefore "one who converts all by himself is not regarded as a proselyte" (Yev 47a). To insist too much on formal instruction of the would-be convert would have limited conversion to literate people and would have excluded the illiterate majority.

---

50 See L. Miralles Maciá, *Conversion and Midrash. On Proselytes and Sympathisers with Judaism in Leviticus Rabbah,* in: JSJ 42 (2011), 58–82 (59f.), with reference to A. Linder, *The Jews in Roman Imperial Legislation,* Detroit 1987, 78–86.

Tobias Georges

The Role of Philosophy and Education in Apologists' Conversion to Christianity: The Case of Justin and Tatian

Abstract: Georges investigates the role of philosophy in the conversions of Justin and Tatian. He explores the two apologists' relationship to each other and to Greek philosophy after their conversion and compares the close connection between philosophy, education, and conversion in Justin's and Tatian's situation to other contemporary conversions.

> In the same book [scil. the Dialogue with Trypho], [scil. Justin is] calling attention to his conversion from Greek philosophy to the true religion, [scil. telling] that it had taken place not irrationally, but with deliberation on his part.[1]

According to this judgment by Eusebius, Justin Martyr performed a well-considered conversion, μεταβολή, from Greek philosophy to the true θεοσέβεια translated here as true religion – that is, Christianity. Reading the passage in Justin's dialogue, which Eusebius is referring to, one might ask whether Eusebius is distorting things somewhat by describing Greek philosophy as the item Justin is converting from in his move towards Christianity. Still, when looking at this passage, philosophy seems to play a major role in Justin's conversion.

It is precisely this role of philosophy in connection with conversion to Christianity I wish to focus on in my paper. For many of Justin's contemporaries, philosophy represented in a certain way the apex of παιδεία (*paideia*) of ancient education[2] and, therefore, in highlighting the role of philosophy, I am stressing the role of an essential part of education in connection with conversion. The group of converts I want to shed light on are Christians dealing with philosophy in the second half of the second

---

1 Ἐν ταὐτῷ δὲ καὶ τὴν ἀπὸ τῆς Ἑλληνικῆς φιλοσοφίας ἐπὶ τὴν θεοσέβειαν μεταβολὴν αὐτοῦ, ὅτι μὴ ἀλόγως, μετὰ κρίσεως δὲ αὐτῷ γεγόνει, δηλῶν, ταῦτα γράφει. Eus., h.e. 4.8,5 (ed. E. Schwartz, Leipzig 1922, 132). Translation: R. Deferrari, Washington ³1981, 220.

2 See K. Rosen, *Von der Torheit für die Heiden zur wahren Philosophie. Soziale und geistige Voraussetzungen der christlichen Apologetik des 2. Jahrhunderts*, in: R. von Haehling (ed.), *Rom und das himmlische Jerusalem. Die frühen Christen zwischen Anpassung und Ablehnung*, Darmstadt 2000, 124–151 (131–137) and, e.g., Gr. Thaum., pan. or. 6.73–80.

century; they could be called "intellectuals"[3] and are to be found among
the group of authors traditionally referred to as early Christian apologists.[4]
Justin is counted as a major figure among them. In my analysis, I will focus
on Justin and also concentrate on Tatian, the Syrian. Both have described
their conversion in elaborate accounts, which my analysis can use as a
starting point: Justin in dial. 2.1–8.2, Tatian in orat. 29–30. And as we
will see, both attribute an important role to philosophy within the context
of their conversion. Focusing on Justin together with Tatian, on the one
hand, makes it possible to compare their accounts and see the nuances
between the two descriptions which were written at around the same time
(155–177, possibly 160–165).[5] On the other hand, focusing on Justin and
Tatian is quite promising because Tatian was probably Justin's pupil and,
therefore, philosophical education might have played a crucial role in their
relationship – and perhaps Justin's education even contributed to Tatian's
conversion.

In a first paragraph, I will address questions of historical context and
method (1): I will describe the role that this kind of conversion plays within
the wider phenomenon of people becoming Christians during the early centuries; I will ask what sources we have and in what way they serve to tell us
something about the connection of philosophy, education and conversion.
On that basis, I will focus on the role of philosophy and education in connection with conversion according to Justin's and Tatian's accounts (2). I
will ask what role philosophy plays on their path to conversion, what the
specific feature is of the Christian faith in the very context that makes them
convert, and what their relation is towards the philosophy recognisable as
"non-Christian" following their conversion. Finally, I will reflect on the concrete context of conversions as depicted by Justin und Tatian – the assumed
relation between Justin and Tatian will allow some rather speculative conclusions – and I will ask in what way their cases can be seen as typical in
early Christianity (3).

---

3   Concerning this term, see A. Fürst, *Christentum als Intellektuellen-Religion. Die
    Anfänge des Christentums in Alexandria*, Stuttgart 2007, 9–11.
4   On the question of how to define this term, fundamental reflection has been done
    in Aarhus. On this, see A.-C. Jacobsen, *Apologetics and Apologies. Some Defini-
    tions*, in: J. Ulrich / A.-C. Jacobsen / M. Kahlos (eds.), *Continuity and Disconti-
    nuity in Early Christian Apologetics*, Frankfurt 2009, 5–21; A.K. Petersen, *The
    diversity of Apologetics. From Genre to a Mode of Thinking*, in: A.-C. Jacobsen
    / J. Ulrich / D. Brakke (eds.), *Critique and Apologetics. Jews, Christians and Pa-
    gans in Antiquity*, Frankfurt 2009, 15–41. Cf. Engberg in this volume.
5   On those dates, see below, 275 and 280.

1. Historical context and method

Certainly, the "intellectual" kind of conversion we find in Justin's and Tatian's case with its emphasis on philosophy and education does not represent the standard of becoming a Christian. As many sources from the second century point to Christians coming from all social strata, and especially from the unlearned classes,[6] it becomes clear that for many people, higher levels of education – we need not even talk of philosophy – played a negligible role in their conversion process. It must be noted, though, that education as such was crucial in the process of becoming a Christian: For being socialised in the Christian community, converts – who, in the early centuries, were mainly adults – had to learn the basic contents of the Christian faith and its moral and social rules. From the second century on, the so-called catechumenate developed as an instrument of Christian education that took place before baptism – a kind of education which certainly differs from the one I will focus on here.[7] Unfortunately, prior to the 4th century, we know little about the details of the catechumenate.[8] What the sources from the time before – i.e., besides the *Traditio apostolica*, mostly scattered hints in the writings of the "intellectual Christians" mentioned above (the illiterate majority did not write) – tell us is that from the 2nd century on there was a kind of Christian education prior to baptism which tended to become increasingly regulated, but that there still were many different ways of conceiving this step.

So, while many people seem to have received their Christian education mainly within the context of the so-called catechumenate, and while the sources do not give us a detailed picture of that education, there is a – presumably small – Christian elite of "intellectuals" talking about their conversion whose accounts have been preserved.[9] And in those accounts, the catechumenate does not play a role.[10] Instead, we find the connection between philosophy and conversion I wish to focus on. This opposite evidence means that we should not overestimate what we find in Justin and Tatian, and take it as a model for Christian conversion in general. I will return to

---

6   See, e.g., Just., 1 apol. 60.11; 2 apol. 10.8. Cf. Also Bremmer in this volume.

7   On the catechumentate, see P. Gavrilyuk, *Histoire du catéchuménat dans l'Église ancienne*, Paris 2007; M. Metzger / W. Drews / H. Brakmann, *Katechumenat*, in: RAC 20 (2004), 497–574.

8   See Metzger / Drews / Brakmann, 2004, 517f.

9   Concerning those accounts, see also J. Engberg in this volume and id., *"From Among You are We. Made, not Born are Christians." Apologists' Accounts of Conversion before 310 AD*, in: Ulrich / Jacobsen / Kahlos (eds.), 2009, 49–77.

10 This does not exclude the possibility that their kind of conversion was in some way connected to the catechumenate; they simply make no mention of the catechumenate in their accounts, but, instead, of philosophy.

this point later. For the moment, let me just state that, still, it is that kind of conversion that is related in the sources and, besides other ways of conversion, this kind seems to be crucial because it offered a way for the intellectual elites to approach Christianity – an important precondition for the spread of Christianity in the society of the Roman Empire.

Of course, we must ask in what way Justin's and Tatian's accounts tell us what role philosophy or education actually played in their conversion. Certainly, their accounts are literary depictions. They are written from a perspective after conversion – how much would we like to have documents they had written beforehand? We do not know the degree to which their conversions happened the way they tell us. This is true especially in the case of Justin's account: We do not know if the dialogue between Justin and Trypho, the Jew, – into which Justin's account is embedded – took place, nor do we know if the dialogue between Justin and the old man, which is interwoven into this dialogue and crucial for Justin's conversion, is based in reality, if the old man is referring to an actual person. There was a major discussion on that item in research, but in the end no definitive answer could be found.[11] Still, even if the depictions of those conversions were fictitious, those accounts show how their authors conceived their own conversion, and which motifs and factors they regarded as relevant. Certainly, the accounts also show how their authors wanted their conversion to be understood by a pagan audience – and against this background, it is no surprise that the accounts are shaped according to pagan philosophers' conversions.[12] However, it seems to me that this intention can hardly be separated from the Christian writers' own perception of conversion. And so, I think that those depictions, while they are certainly biased, remain our best evidence if we want to bring out the aspects that, according to the authors, were crucial in the context of conversion. What I will do in order to confirm the information taken from those accounts is look for parallel data to be found in Justin's and Tatian's work, both in their writings individually and when compared.

Philosophy was, according to the two authors, at least one aspect within the context of their conversion, and I am going to elaborate on its role. Thus, I shall concentrate on conversion rather than initiation. Of course, "philosophy" is a wide, ambiguous term. To grasp it, I will start from what

---

11 See S. Heid, *Iustinus Martyr I*, in: RAC 19 (2001), 801–844 (804); P. Bobichon (ed.), *Justin Martyr. Dialogue avec Tryphon*, 2 vols., Fribourg 2003, 129–166. Cf. also the contribution by Cvetković on this problem in relation to Augustine.
12 For pagan philosophers' accounts of conversion, see J. Hahn, *Der Philosoph und die Gesellschaft. Selbstverständnis, öffentliches Auftreten und populäre Erwartungen in der hohen Kaiserzeit*, Stuttgart 1989, 59f.

our Christian authors call philosophy, and by highlighting their references, the meaning of "philosophy" will become clearer.

2. The role of philosophy and education in connection with conversion according to Justin's and Tatian's accounts

So let us turn to the role of philosophy and education in connection with conversion to Christianity and focus on Justin first. The account he gives is quite famous. As I have already stated, it is to be found in the prologue of his *Dialogue with Trypho, the Jew*, a work he composed, most probably, in Rome, in the years between 155 and 160.[13] In the prologue, Justin tells us: He met Trypho and his "friends" (9.2: ἑταῖροί) in the Ξυστός and he was recognised as a "philosopher" by him (1.1) – the "friends" have been interpreted as Trypho's pupils,[14] the Ξυστός as the colonnade of a γυμνασιόν where philosophers used to hold discussions.[15] Justin and Trypho started a debate on the use of philosophy for the search of God, in the course of which Trypho asked Justin: "Explain to us just what is your opinion of these matters, and what is your idea of God and what is your philosophy."[16] Starting from this request, Justin relates his conversion, his path to Christianity. So, as the frame for this account already insinuates, philosophy is quite important in this context.

Justin begins his account by stating in dial. 2.1: "Philosophy is indeed one's greatest possession and is most precious in the sight of God, to whom it alone leads us and to whom it unites us."[17]

Following this statement, Justin depicts his journey to God – which he will finally find in Christianity – as a way through philosophy. Of course, at the end of this journey, philosophy and Christianity merge together, because Christianity is, for Justin, the way to God. But at the beginning, Justin has no idea of Christianity. Philosophy, in his account, is represented by the traditional ancient schools of philosophy, and Justin searches for God by getting to know those very schools one after the other (dial. 2.3–6): Justin

---

13 See Heid, 2001, 804; W. Kinzig, *Justin*, in: ⁴RGG 4 (2001), 719f. (719).

14 See, e.g., A. Harnack, *Judentum und Christentum in Justins Dialog mit Trypho, nebst einer Collation der Pariser Handschrift nr 450*, in: Texte und Untersuchungen zur Geschichte der altchristlichen Literatur 39/1 (1913), 47–98 (53. 59).

15 See, e.g., Bobichon (ed.), 2003, 569f.

16 Καὶ ὅς ἀστεῖον ὑπομειδιάσας · Σὺ δὲ πῶς, ἔφη, περὶ τούτων φρονεῖς καὶ τίνα γνώμην περὶ θεοῦ ἔχεις καὶ τίς ἡ σὴ φιλοσοφία, εἰπὲ ἡμῖν. Just., dial. 1.6 (Bobichon (ed.), 2003, 186). Translation: T. Falls, Washington ³1977, 149.

17 Ἔστι γὰρ τῷ ὄωτι φιλοσοφία μέγιστον κτῆμα καὶ τιμιώτατον θεῷ, ᾧ τε προσάγει καὶ συνίστησιν ἡμᾶς μόνη. Just., dial. 2.1 (Bobichon (ed.), 2003, 186). Translation: Falls, ³1977, 149.

goes to a Stoic, then to a Peripatetic, and to a Pythagorean teacher. But none can give him what he is looking for. So he goes to a teacher of the Platonists, whom he holds in much higher esteem than the teachers before: The "perception of incorporeal things [...] overwhelms" him and the "Platonic theory of ideas adds wings" to his mind.[18] This fondness for Platonic philosophy is echoed in 2 apol. 12.1, where Justin, looking back at his time before conversion, states: "For when I myself took delight in the teachings of Plato."[19] And his familiarity with ancient philosophy is, in general, largely reflected in the two apologies.[20]

However, according to the account in the *Dialogue*, Justin finally meets the mysterious figure of an old man[21] who involves him in a dialogue about philosophy. In this dialogue, the old man points to the deficiencies and impassability in the philosophy Justin pleads for until that moment, that is, first of all, in Platonic philosophy (3.1–6.2): He shows that Justin is not able, as he desires, to perceive God "by the mind alone" (3.7). In the end, when Justin, having become baffled, asks the old man for the doctrines he can follow, the man reveals his identity as a Christian and exposes his faith (7.1–2). Persuaded by the old man's reasoning, Justin turns to Christianity (8.1).

Before focusing on the turning point of Justin's conversion, I would first like to look back at the journey leading up to it and call attention to the role that ancient philosophy played along the way. It is conspicuous that Justin highlights his journey through the philosophers' schools, and especially his pleading for Platonic thought that much. Why does he not reject pagan philosophy straightaway in order to show the superiority of the Christian faith? It seems that, for Justin, his own way to Christianity was not conceivable without exploring the philosophers' schools: Even if Justin was disillusioned by reality, he was convinced that in principle, the philosophers were the ones whose aim was the search for God (2.1) and the "investigation of the truth" (2.2).[22] And for finding the true God, Justin needed those philosophers. As Justin says in dial. 3.3: "Man cannot have prudence without philosophy and straight thinking. Thus, every man

---

18 Καί με ἦρει σφόδρα ἡ τῶν ἀσωμάτων νόησις, καὶ ἡ θεωρία τῶν ἰδεῶν ἀνεπτέρου μοι τὴν φρόνησιν. Just., dial. 2.6 (Bobichon (ed.), 2003, 190). Translation: Falls, [3]1977, 150f.
19 Καὶ γὰρ αὐτὸς ἐγώ, τοῖς Πλάτωνος χαίρων διδάγμασι. Just., 2 apol. 12.1 (text and translation: D. Minns / P. Parvis (eds. and trans.), *Justin, Philosopher and Martyr. Apologies*, Oxford 2009, 316f.).
20 See P. Lampe, *Die stadtrömischen Christen in den ersten beiden Jahrhunderten. Untersuchungen zur Sozialgeschichte*, Tübingen [2]1989, 353–361.
21 On the interpretation of this figure, see Bobichon (ed.), 2003, 580f.
22 Cf. Just., dial. 3.4: "Philosophy is the knowledge of that what exists, and a clear understanding of the truth." Translation: Falls, [3]1977, 152.

should be devoted to philosophy and should consider it the greatest and most noble pursuit."[23]

Certainly, in the account, those are Justin's words on philosophy prior to his conversion. However, we will see that, in principle, he did not change his mind after it: In Justin's eyes, philosophy teaches man how to think, and thereby indicates the way to the truth and to God. It is interesting to consider, in this context, the observation that the dialogue between the old man and Justin undermining Platonic philosophy largely resembles Platonic dialogues in terms of style.[24] One could interpret this phenomenon as follows: Guided by the old man, Justin rejects, bit by bit, his former type of philosophy. But still, it is the kind of thinking and arguing he has learnt through this philosophy that persuades him to abandon it and follow a new way.

Having seen how important philosophy was on the way to conversion, we must ask: What is it that makes Justin convert to Christianity in the end? In order to answer that question, we must look at the words the old man uses in order to reveal his Christian faith, in dial. 7. Let me quote the decisive passages:

> A long time ago [...] there lived blessed men who were just and loved by God, men who spoke through the inspiration of the Holy Spirit and predicted events that would take place in the future, which events are now taking place. We call these men Prophets. They alone knew the truth and communicated it to men [...], they reiterated only what they heard and saw when inspired by the Holy Spirit. Their writings are still extant. [...] Above all, beseech God to open to you the gates of light, for no one can perceive or understand these truths unless he has been enlightened by God and His Christ.[25]

According to Justin's account, it is these words that made him turn to Christianity: Once the old man has left, Justin states: "But my spirit was

---

23 Ἄνευ δὲ φιλοσοφίας καὶ ὀρθοῦ λόγου οὐκ ἄν τῳ παρείη φρόνησις. Διὸ χρὴ πάντα ἄνθρωπον φιλοσοφεῖν καὶ τοῦτο μέγιστον καὶ τιμιώτατον ἔργον ἡγεῖσθαι. Just., dial. 3.3, (Bobichon (ed.), 2003, 190–192). Translation: Falls, ³1977, 152.

24 On this, see Heid, 2001, 804.

25 Ἐγένοντό τινες πρὸ πολλοῦ χρόνου πάντων τούτων τῶν νομιζομένων φιλοσόφων παλαιότεροι, μακάριοι καὶ δίκαιοι καὶ θεοφιλεῖς, θείῳ πνεύματι λαλήσαντες καὶ τὰ μέλλοντα θεσπίσαντες, ἃ δὴ νῦν γίνεται· προφήτας δὲ αὐτοὺς καλοῦσιν. Οὗτοι μόνοι τὸ ἀληθὲς καὶ εἶδον καὶ ἐξεῖπον ἀνθρώποις, μήτ' εὐλαβηθέντες μήτε δυσωπηθέντες τινά, μὴ ἡττημένοι δόξης, ἀλλὰ μόνα ταῦτα εἰπόντες ἃ ἤκουσαω καὶ ἃ εἶδον ἁγίῳ πληπωθέντες πνεύματι. Συγγράμματα δὲ αὐτῶν ἔτι καὶ νῦν διαμένει [...]. Εὔχου δέ σοι πάντων φωτὸς ἀνοιχθῆναι πύλας· οὐ γὰρ συνοπτὰ οὐδὲ συννοητὰ πᾶσιν ἐστιν, εἰ μὴ τῳ θεὸς δῷ συνιέναι ὁ Χριστὸς αὐτοῦ. Just., dial. 7.1–3 (Bobichon (ed.), 2003, 202–204). Translation: Falls, ³1977, 159f.

immediately set on fire, and an affection for the prophets, and for those who are the friends of Christ, took hold of me."[26]

Taking the words of the old man and Justin together, we can guess that it is the prophets' words that persuaded Justin, the prophets' predictions as interpreted by the "friends of Christ", the Christians. While Justin gave many details on his path through pagan philosophy, when it comes to the contents of Christian faith, he says only little. From this account alone, it would be difficult to say what he is converting to. But thanks to what he reveals in the rest of the *Dialogue* and in his two *Apologies* – those are all his writings that remain – we know that Justin alludes to the Christian faith and the Christian interpretation of the scripture, which is, in Justin's time, the Septuagint: The prophets have annunciated Christ, the son of God, and in Jesus Christ, those annunciations have been fulfilled. Saying that "Their writings are still extant," Justin seems to show that the scripture was crucial in this conversion. And we can imagine that Justin, with his philosophical education, did not just acknowledge what an old man had told him, namely that the prophecies came true in Christ, but that he read the scripture in order to convince himself of what the Christians had said. While the account does not tell us about that, Justin's arguments towards Trypho and his reasoning in the second part of his *1ˢᵗ apology* largely reflect how he read the scripture and based his theology on it.

If it is the prophets' words transmitted through scripture that are crucial in Justin's conversion, how does this relate to the eminent role of philosophy in this context? For Justin, the prophets "alone knew the truth and communicated it to men." So, scripture contains precisely the goal he is striving for on his journey through philosophy: truth. But here, we come to the point where Justin sets a limit on ancient philosophy: Whereas before he wanted to perceive God and the truth "by the mind alone" (3.7), the old man teaches him that he would not be able to. However, the prophets attested to by the scripture know and communicate the truth "through the inspiration of the Holy Spirit," as the old man underlines twice. And as they only teach what they were inspired to by God's spirit, man cannot perceive the truth "unless he has been enlightened by God and His Christ." So, what Justin opposes to the perception of the truth by the mind alone, which he learned to look for at the pagan philosophers' schools, is of of the truth by God, mediated by scripture.

This critique in ancient philosophy does not mean that Justin, once he has become a Christian, generally rejects philosophy. On the contrary, he ends

---

26 Ἐμοὶ δὲ παραχρῆμα πῦρ ἐν τῇ ψυχῇ ἀνήφθη, καὶ ἔρως ἔχεί με τῶν προφητῶν καὶ τῶν ἀνδρῶν ἐκείνων, οἵ εἰσι Χριστοῦ φίλοι. Just., dial. 8.1 (Bobichon (ed.), 2003, 204). Translation: Falls, ³1977, 160.

his account of his conversion by saying: "while pondering on his [scil. the old man's] words, I discovered that this was the only sure and useful philosophy. Thus it is that I am now a philosopher."[27]

Following those words, Christian faith becomes "the only sure and useful philosophy" in which Justin finds what he was looking for. The term Justin was familiar with is maintained, but now Christian faith claims to be the true content of this term. Having transformed the term this way, Justin can declare his move to Christianity as a conversion to philosophy, to Christian philosophy, in the same way as contemporary pagan philosophers depicted the fundamental change they underwent as a conversion to philosophy.[28] In this sense, the final statement of his account has to be interpreted: Instead of saying: "This is how I became a Christian", Justin states "Thus it is that I am now a philosopher."

When Justin describes his conversion to Christianity as a conversion to philosophy which only takes place after a long exploration of the traditional philosophers' schools of antiquity, we must ask: How does he judge those schools, how does he judge pagan philosophy after conversion? When Christian faith is "the only sure and useful philosophy," it is clear that those types of philosophy cannot be "philosophy" in the full sense. That superior place is occupied by Christian thinking. From that perspective, Justin's critique against Stoic, Peripatetic, Pythagorean, and even against Platonic philosophy gets its foundation.

Still, he chooses the name "philosophy" stemming from that very tradition as a means of labeling Christian thinking. And even if for the reader it is clear that there must be a difference between pagan philosophy and Justin's Christian philosophy, nowhere does Justin draw a terminological line between "our" and "your philosophy". Furthermore, the term "philosophy", in itself, has a clear positive meaning for Justin:[29] There is no passage in his apologies in which he openly criticises someone called a "philosopher" although he often mentions Platonists and Stoics and though he harshly criticises pagan ways of thinking and living. In Justin's eyes, if someone is not behaving as a philosopher should, he has no right to be called a

---

27 Διαλογιζόμενός τε πρὸς ἐμαυτὸν τοὺς λόγους αὐτοῦ ταύτην μόνην εὕρισκον
    φιλοσοφίαν ἀσφαλῆ τε καὶ σύμφορον. Οὕτως δὴ καὶ διὰ ταῦτα φιλόσοφος
    ἐγώ. Just., dial. 8.1f. (Bobichon (ed.), 2003, 204). Translation: Falls, ³1977, 160.
28 See Hahn, 1989, 59f.; Heid, 2001, 807.
29 On this, see T. Georges, *Die christlichen Apologeten des 2. Jahrhunderts und
    ihr Verhältnis zur antiken Philosophie. Justin und Tertullian als Exponenten un-
    terschiedlicher Grundorientierungen?*, in: Early Christianity 3 (2012), 321–348
    (335f.).

"philosopher" (1 apol. 4.8; 7.3; 26.6).[30] So, it becomes obvious that Justin
has the intention not to overemphasise the dividing line; instead, he tends to
stress the common tradition: It is the ancient love of wisdom he refers to for
his Christian philosophy; it is this philosophy he had become familiar with
and which shaped his education.[31]

Looking at the outline of the role of philosophy in connection with Justin's account of his conversion, one could still say: But this is only what
Justin tells us. Certainly, we have no proof as to what degree Justin's report refers to what actually happened. But important features of what he
tells us are confirmed if we compare it to another account which shows,
besides differences that also have to be considered, striking similarities. So
let us turn to Tatian's account, which he gives in the *Oratio ad Graecos*
– his only work that remains entirely and in its original form.[32] *Oratio
ad Graecos* seems to have been composed between 165 and 172 (or even
177), probably also in Rome.[33] What Tatian tells us about his conversion
is much shorter. It is not an entire story, as in Justin, dial. 2–8; it is rather
a summary. We find it in chapters 29–30, and there is an additional reference in chapter 35.

The very frame of this account is interesting: In the earlier chapters (21–
28), Tatian heavily criticises Greek culture and, from chapter 25 onwards,
especially Greek philosophy.[34] Right after talking about the conversion in
orat. 31.1, Tatian goes on to say: "Now I think it is appropriate that I should
prove that our philosophy is older than Greek practices."[35] So, it is obvious
that the account of his conversion is set into a context where philosophy is

---

30 The teachers Justin met in dial. 2 are called "those reputed philosophers" in
    dial. 7.1 (transl. Falls, ³1977, 159), so the critique against them is not a critique
    against real philosophers!
31 Of course, within this perspective on philosophy, Justin cannot hold back the
    crucial aspect of Christian revelation caused by God himself. In 2 apol. 13, it
    becomes pretty clear how Justin integrates Christian and ancient philosophy – by
    pointing to the divine Logos.
32 For the *Diatessaron*, see W. Petersen, *Tatian's* Diatessaro. *It's Creation, Dissemi-
    nation, Significance, and History in Scholarship*, Leiden 1994.
33 See J. Trelenberg (ed.), *Tatianos. Oratio ad Graecos. Rede an die Griechen*,
    Tübingen 2012, 8–15; M. Fiedrowicz, *Apologie im frühen Christentum. Die
    Kontroverse um den christlichen Wahrheitsanspruch in den ersten Jahrhun-
    derten*, Paderborn 2000, 53.
34 Only in the chapter 28 which is very short, Tatian is focusing another topic, that
    is, legislation.
35 Νῦν δὲ προσήκειν μοι νομίζω παραστῆσαι πρεσβυτέραν τὴν ἡμετέραν
    φιλοσοφίαν τῶν παρ' Ἕλλησιν ἐπιτηδευμάτων. Tat., orat. 31.1 (M. Whit-
    taker (ed.), *Oratio ad Graecos and Fragments*, Oxford 1982, 54–56). Transla-
    tion: Ead., 1982, 55–57.

a major topic. In this context, after polemicising against Greek philosophy and legislation, Tatian relates in orat. 29.1f.:

> Therefore, when I had seen these things and had also taken part in mysteries and had scrutinised the rituals conducted everywhere [...], when I was by myself I began to seek by what means I could discover the truth. While I was engaged in serious thought I happened to read some barbarian writings, older by comparison with the doctrines of the Greeks, more divine by comparison with their errors. The outcome was that I was persuaded by these because of the lack of arrogance in the wording, the artlessness of the speakers, the easily intelligible account of creation of the world, the foreknowledge of the future, the remarkable quality of the precepts and of the doctrine of a single ruler of the universe. My soul was taught by God.[36]

When Tatian says that he "had seen these things", he is certainly referring to his observations in Greek philosophy he had earlier criticised, and this allows the conclusion that Tatian, like Justin, explored pagan philosophy as an integral step on his way to Christianity. However, it needs to be remarked that, compared to Justin's experience with this philosophy, Tatian's seems to be rather superficial: There is no place where he mentions having visited a teacher representing one of the ancient schools of philosophy, and the critique he is alluding to with "these things" is not only a critique against Greek philosophy, but a broader critique in many aspects of Greek culture surpassing philosophy. This coincides with his reference to the fact that he "had also taken part in mysteries and had scrutinised the rituals conducted everywhere" – by the way, here is one instance where we find the terminology of initiation in the context of conversion.

Considering Tatian's allusions, it seems that his exploration of Greek philosophy on the path to Christianity was, more than in Justin's case, part of a comprehensive exploration of Greek culture, including its mythology and rituals. Still, with this exploration, Tatian emphasised, like his assumed teacher, philosophy's ultimate goal, the search for truth: He tells us that he "began to seek, by what means he could discover the truth." And, like for Justin, in the

---

36 Ταῦτ' οὖν ἰδών, ἔτι δὲ καὶ μυστηρίων μεταλαβὼν καὶ τὰς παρὰ πᾶσι θρησκείας δοκιμάσας [...], κατ' ἐμαυτὸν γενόμενος ἐζήτουν ὅτῳ τρόπῳ τἀληθὲς ἐξευρεῖν δύνωμαι. Περινοοῦντι δέ μοι τὰ σπουδαῖα συνέβη γραφαῖς τισιν ἐντυχεῖν βαρβαρικαῖς, πρεσβυτέραις μὲν ὡς πρὸς τὰ Ἑλλήνων δόγματα, θειοτέραις δὲ ὡς πρὸς τὴν ἐκείνων πλάνην· καί μοι πεισθῆναι ταύταις συνέβη διά τε τῶν λέξεων τὸ ἄτυφον καὶ τῶν εἰπόντων τὸ ἀνεπιτήδευτον καὶ τῆς τοῦ παντὸς ποιήσεως τὸ εὐκατάληπτον καὶ τῶν μελλόντων τὸ προγνωστικὸν καὶ τῶν παραγγελμάτων τὸ ἐξαίσιον καὶ τῶν ὅλων τὸ μοναρχικόν. Θεοδιδάκτου δέ μου γενομένης τῆς ψυχῆς. Tat., orat. 29.1f. (Whittaker (ed.), 1982, 52–54). Translation: Ead., 1982, 53–55.

end it seems to be his encounter with the Christian scripture, that is, the Septuagint, that makes him convert to Christian faith and convinces him while he is searching for the truth: As he says, he was "persuaded by some barbarian scriptures." Beyond the fulfillment of the prophecies ("the foreknowledge of the future"), which Justin also mentions, Tatian enumerates additional features of these scriptures that convinced him: First of all, their antiquity, as well as their soundness, their plainness, their teachings of one God, creator, and their precepts. However, as in Justin's case, it is through those very writings that God reveals his truth to him: "My soul was taught by God."

The factors leading to Tatian's conversion according to this account are confirmed in his reference in orat. 35.1 – apart from the scripture whose crucial role is reflected in some instances in the *Oratio ad Graecos* that are quite scattered, but noticeable (orat. 5.1; 13.3; 15.1; 15.4; 30.2):

> All this I set down not from second-hand knowledge, but after much travel. I followed your studies and came across many devices and many notions, and finally I spent time in the city of the Romans and got to know the varieties of statues which they brought home with them from you. For I do not try [...] to strengthen my case with other men's opinions; I want to compose an account of everything that I personally came to know. So having taken my leave of Roman arrogance and Athenian cold cleverness – incoherent bases of doctrine – I sought out the philosophy which you consider barbarous.[37]

Again, we find Tatian's extensive studies of Graeco-Roman culture and his ambitions of knowing, which culminate in his conversion to "barbarous philosophy". This term for Christian thinking resembles what we have seen in Justin: Although Tatian's conversion marks a difference between his thinking and Greek philosophy, he calls it by the very name "philosophy", so that the common roots can be grasped. However, there is a difference between Tatian and Justin: While the latter does not stress the difference, Tatian emphasises it with the ironic label "barbarous". The term "barbarous philosophy" is crucial for Tatian, as can be seen at the very end of orat., in 42.1, where he repeats it when he says:

---

37 Ταῦτα μὲν οὖν οὐ παρ' ἄλλου μαθὼν ἐξεθέμεν, πολλὴν δὲ ἐπιφοιτήσας γῆν καὶ τοῦτο μὲν σοφιστεύσας τὰ ὑμέτερα, τοῦτο δὲ τέχναις καὶ ἐπινοίαις ἐγκυρήσας πολλαῖς, ἔσχατον δὲ τῇ Ῥωμαίων ἐνδιατρίψας πόλει καὶ τὰς ἀφ' ὑμῶν ὡς αὐτούς ἀνακομισθείσας ἀνδριάντων ποικιλίας καταμαθών. Οὐ γάρ [...] ἀλλοτρίαις δόξαις τἀμαυτοῦ κρατύνειν πειρῶμαι, πάντων δὲ ὧν <ἂν> αὐτὸς ποιήσωμαι τὴν κατάληψιν, τούτων καὶ τὴν ἀναγραφὴν συντάσσειν βούλομαι. Διόπερ χαίρειν εἰπὼν καὶ τῇ Ῥωμαιων μεγαλαυχίᾳ καὶ τῇ Ἀθηναίων ψυχρολογίᾳ δόγμασιν ἀσυναρτήτοις, τῆς καθ' ὑμᾶς βαρβάρου φιλοσοφίας ἀντεποιησάμην. Tat., orat. 35.1 (Whittaker (ed.), 1982, 64–66). Translation: Ead., 1982, 65–67.

All this, men of Greece, I have compiled for you – I Tatian, a philosopher among the barbarians, born in the land of the Assyrians, and educated first in your learning and secondly in what I profess to preach.[38]

In this final passage condensing Tatian's conversion, beyond the self-nomination as "barbarous philosopher", there is another interesting feature: Tatian says that "he was educated," παιδευθείς. This leads us to the observation that in Tatian, besides the term "philosophy", the term παιδεία, "education", plays a major role in connection with his conversion: *Paideia* is *the* term for ancient, Greek education. It is this term that names the many aspects of Greek culture, including but also surpassing philosophy that Tatian has explored on his way to Christian faith. And, like the term "philosophy", Tatian claims that very term for the Christians: In two instances, in orat. 12.5 and 35.2, he is speaking of ἡμετέρα παιδεία [our, that is, Christian *paideia*] as opposed to the Greek culture of his audience. In the same manner, he is opposing ἡμετέρα φιλοσοφία [our, that is, Christian philosophy] (orat. 35.1) and οἱ παρ᾽ ὑμῖν φιλόσοφοι [your, that is, Greek philosophers] (orat. 19.1; 25.1). So we can see, on the one hand, how philosophy and *paideia* are converging in Tatian's conversion: While Justin is emphasising only philosophy, for Tatian, the whole of *paideia* seems to have played a major role, while it still culminated, also for him, in philosophy. On the other hand, it can be stated that Tatian, after his conversion, is stressing the differences between pagan and Christian philosophy and education much more than Justin, thereby certainly also showing how important pagan learning was on his path to Christianity.

3. Final questions

At the end, I want to ask two questions. First of all: How can we imagine the concrete context for a conversion like in Justin's and Tatian's case? What Justin tells us about this setting is quite legendary, and Tatian is not interested in the setting. So we cannot but speculate. But let me put forward a theory that, in my opinion, makes sense, at least in Tatian's case: Tatian, in *Oratio*, refers to Justin twice, in a way from which it can be concluded that he was his pupil in Rome.[39] Moreover, this is confirmed by Irenaeus who was, only

---

38 Ταῦθ᾽ ὑμῖν, ὦ ἄνδρες Ἕλληνες, ὁ κατά βαρβάρους φιλοσοφῶν Τατιανὸς συνέταξα, γεννηθεὶς μὲν ἐν τῇ τῶν Ἀσσυρίων γῇ, παιδευθεὶς δὲ πρῶτον μὲν τὰ ὑμέτερα, δεύτερον δὲ ἅτινα νῦν κηρύττειν ἐπαγγέλλομαι. Tat., orat. 42.1 (Whittaker (ed.), 1982, 76). Translation: Ead., 1982, 77.

39 In orat. 18.6, Tatian is referring to the "admirable Justin" (ὁ θαυμασιώτατος Ἰουστῖνος; translation by Whittaker (ed.), 1982, 36f.); in orat. 19.2, he tells that Crescens, the Cynic, had "set about involving Justin – as he did me too –

some three decades later, bishop in Lyon (haer. 1.28,1). And Tatian does not seem to have been Justin's only pupil: In the account of the martyrdom of Justin and his companions in Rome combined with Justin's own writings, we have quite good evidence that Justin had his own "school" in Rome – that means, a small circle comprising a teacher and his pupils who were looking for intellectual discourse, open to Christians and Non-Christians, very similar to contemporary pagan philosophers' schools.[40] Justin's school in Rome would have been the ideal context for Tatian's conversion: There, Tatian could have pursued his exploration of ancient *paideia* and philosophy, and he could have encountered the scripture of the Christians. And, with Justin, he would have had a teacher explaining the Christian understanding of that scripture to him. Tatian, in his conversion's account, does not talk of a teaching figure, but Justin does: The mysterious old man in the *Dialogue*, no matter how the deeper meaning of this figure is interpreted, in the text is identified, step by step, as a Christian teacher. And it is likely that Justin as well as Tatian acceded to the scripture's message aided by a teacher.

My second and last question is: What light does Justin's and Tatian's case shed on the role of philosophy and education in connection with conversion in second-century Christianity? I already said at the beginning that their cases, most probably, do not represent the standard for becoming a Christian.[41] However, for the group of authors they are traditionally counted among, the apologists, their cases could be quite typical. The other apologists, in general, referring to their conversion, do not go into as much detail as Justin and Tatian. But in their writings, first of all, they also argue using the education they grew up with, and especially the philosophy stemming from that background. This fact makes it easy to assume that this education, with philosophy as its apex, played an eminent role within their conversion. Secondly, their writings also attest that the encounter with the scripture of the Christians and the revelation mediated by it was crucial for their conversion. And thirdly, they are also labeling Christian thinking as "philosophy" – as the better philosophy. Certainly, like between Justin and Tatian, there are considerable differences among the apologists in stressing continuity or

---

in the death penalty" (ὡς καὶ Ἰουστῖνον καθάπερ καὶ ἐμὲ [...] τῷ θανάτῳ περιβαλεῖν πραγματεύσασθαι; translation by Whittaker (ed.), 1982, 38f.). Justin himself informs us about the dispute with Crescens in 2 apol. 3. Tatian is not mentioned there, but his own references to his relation with Justin prove his discipleship.

40 See T. Georges, *Justin's School in Rome. Reflections on Early Christian "Schools,"* in: Zeitschrift für Antikes Christentum 16 (2012), 75–87.

41 Cf. Bøgh in the present volume who argues on the basis of modern conversion theories that we should work with different types of conversion in antiquity.

difference between pagan and Christian philosophy. But they all claim the traditional term "philosophy" for their own thinking. Even Tertullian, who is notorious for his harsh polemic against pagan philosophy,[42] calls the Christian faith the "better philosophy" at the end of his writing *De pallio*, when felicitating the philosopher's cloak he's wearing himself (pall. 6.2): "Rejoice, pallium, and exult! A better philosophy has deigned you worthy, from the moment that it is the Christian whom you started to dress."[43]

So, like Justin and Tatian, these Christian intellectuals all seem to attest to at least a conversion to Christian philosophy, even if not, as Eusebius says, to a "conversion from Greek philosophy to Christianity."

---

42 See Georges, *Die christlichen Apologeten*, 2012, 323–328.
43 *Gaude pallium et exsulta: Melior iam te philosophia dignata est ex quo Christianum vestire coepisti.* Tert., pall. 6.2 (M. Turcan (ed.), *De pallio*, Paris 2007, 224). Translation: V. Hunink, Amsterdam 2005, 63.

General Index

Index Locorum

Biblical books and apocryphal literature

Early Christianity in the Context of Antiquity

Edited by David Brakke, Anders-Christian Jacobsen, and Jörg Ulrich

The series ECCA (Early Christianity in the Context of Antiquity) seeks to publish monographs and edited volumes that take as their theme early Christianity and its connections with the religion(s) and culture(s) of antiquity and late antiquity. Special attention is given to the interactions between religion and culture, as well as to the influences that diverse religions and cults had on one another. Works published in ECCA extend chronologically from the second century B.C.E. to the fifth century C.E. and geographically across the expanse of the Roman empire and its immediate neighbors.

Die Reihe ECCA (Early Christianity in the Context of Antiquity) zielt auf die Publikation von Monographien und Sammelbänden, die sich thematisch mit dem frühen Christentum und seinen Beziehungen zu Religion(en) und Kultur(en) der Antike und Spätantike befassen. Dabei gilt das besondere Augenmerk den Wechselwirkungen, die Religion und Kultur aufeinander ausüben, sowie den Einflüssen, die die verschiedenen Religionen und Kulte aufeinander hatten. Zeitlich erstrecken sich die in ECCA publizierten Arbeiten auf das 2. Jh. v. Chr. bis zum 5. Jh. n.Chr., geographisch auf den Raum des Imperium Romanum und seiner unmittelbaren Nachbarn.

Vol. 16   Birgitte Secher Bøgh (ed.): Conversion and Initiation in Antiquity. Shifting Identities – Creating Change. 2014.

www.peterlang.com